# Quantum Deterrence

# Quantum Deterrence

## Encryption, Decryption, and the Arms Race of Math

*By*

*Kenan Durveil*

Vij Books

New Delhi (India)

*Published by*

**Vij Books**
(Publishers, Distributors & Importers)
4836/24, 3rd Floor, Ansari Road
Delhi – 110 002
Phone: 91-11-43596460
Mobile: 98110 94883
e-mail: contact@vijpublishing.com
www.vijbooks.in



ISBN: 978-93-7794-557-2 (HB)

ISBN: 978-93-7794-044-7 (PB)

ISBN: 978-93-7794-486-5 (eBook)



This book was developed using advanced writing tools to support the drafting and ideation process. All content has been thoughtfully curated, refined, and reviewed to ensure quality and relevance.

# Contents

# Introduction

In June 2015, in Washington, D.C., officials were still piecing together the full extent of the breach at the United States Office of Personnel Management when one fact began to settle with a chill all its own: the stolen files were not merely usernames and passwords, but security-clearance forms, fingerprints, background investigations, and the slow, intimate paperwork of state trust. The numbers would later grow to roughly 21.5 million people, according to the agency's own accounting in 2015. The fluorescent hum of federal offices, the dry feel of paper dossiers translated into databases, the bureaucratic ordinariness of the records themselves—these details mattered. They revealed something unsettling. The most valuable secrets are often the least dramatic at the moment they are taken.

The hinge was time itself.

A stolen personnel file does not behave like a looted safe. It matures. A list of contacts becomes a map of influence; an old address becomes a pattern; a disclosed vulnerability, once trivial, can become decisive when joined to later data. Encryption is usually presented as the great antidote to this vulnerability: a mathematical shelter against the exposed wire, the intercepted packet, the curious official, the criminal broker. Yet encryption has always depended on an awkward wager. It does not promise secrecy in the abstract. It promises secrecy under assumptions about machines, costs, institutions, implementation, and the length of time a secret must remain secret. That wager is becoming harder to ignore.

The popular version of the story is too tidy. Quantum computing arrives, old encryption breaks, new encryption replaces it, and the world moves on after a suitably technical interval. Reality is less cinematic and far more political. Stronger computation does not simply threaten ciphers in the manner of a bolt from the blue; it changes behaviour before the breakthrough, if the possibility of future decryption is credible enough. It alters what states collect, what firms retain, what standards bodies rush or delay, what chief information officers can justify to boards, and what counts as prudent negligence. A threat that is not yet operational can still be strategically active. That is the paradox at the heart of the present moment. Data can be worth stealing now because its value may survive the delay. Defending it, by contrast, often requires expenditure, redesign, migration, and institutional discipline years before the danger becomes visible to everyone.

This is where the subject ceases to be merely technical. Cryptography is often described in the language of elegant proof, algorithmic hardness, and trusted primitives. Those things matter. But they live inside an untidy human arrangement of procurement offices, software libraries, certificate authorities, cloud contracts, hardware supply chains, regulators, military planners, and exhausted administrators rotating keys on a Friday evening because a vendor advisory left no graceful choice. Trust is not floating above the world in a cloud of number theory. It is delegated, renewed, audited, cached, forgotten, and occasionally betrayed. When people say that a system is secure, they often mean that several institutions have agreed, for the moment, to behave as though its assumptions are bearable.

That agreement has always been more fragile than the public story admits. Consider DigiNotar, the Dutch certificate authority whose compromise came to light in 2011. From one angle, this was a narrow incident in the specialised domain of public key infrastructure. From another, it was a lesson in how the machinery of trust can fail at scale. Fraudulent certificates, including for Google, were reportedly used to enable interception of users in Iran; browser vendors moved to revoke trust in DigiNotar; the company collapsed. Show the scene and the abstraction resolves into something concrete: a certificate authority is not only a technical service but a political bottleneck. Name the concept, and the problem becomes legible. Trust chains are not neutral plumbing. Explain the mechanism, and the strategic point sharpens. If digital identity is anchored in institutions that can be compromised, coerced, or simply mismanaged, then authenticity is no less historical than confidentiality. The implication is severe. A broken signature or a poisoned trust anchor can reach backwards into archives and forwards into software updates, contracts, and state communications.

It is tempting to hear all this as a counsel of despair, as though the sensible response were to declare the whole field compromised by complexity. That would be lazy. Modern cryptography has worked astonishingly well. Ordinary people send messages, move money, install software updates, authenticate bank sessions, and store data in ways that would have seemed nearly miraculous in earlier decades. Symmetric encryption remains a case in point. Even with quantum computing in view, the most widely discussed quantum advantage against symmetric schemes is generally a quadratic speed-up rather than a magical collapse, which is one reason larger key sizes remain meaningful. There is a limitation here that any serious account must acknowledge: not every secret has a long shelf life, and not every cryptographic primitive is equally vulnerable to future advances. Some communications expire by breakfast. Some systems are threatened less by algebra than by the unlocked laptop in the wrong hotel room. Still, that concession does not rescue complacency. It refines the problem. The issue is not that all secrecy is doomed. It is that long-lived secrets, brittle trust mechanisms, and slow-moving institutions create a particularly dangerous combination.

That combination becomes clearer when one stops imagining encryption as a sealed box and begins to see it as a timetable. A payment authorisation must survive seconds or minutes. A corporate acquisition may require confidentiality for months. A covert source, a weapons design archive, or a trove of biometric identifiers may demand protection for decades. These are different temporal objects, even when they use related tools. Yet organisations habitually flatten them into one compliance category: encrypted, therefore handled. The visible behaviour that follows is familiar. Procurement teams buy what meets today's audit language. Engineers inherit cryptographic libraries as defaults. Legal departments retain data because deletion feels riskier than storage. Security teams model the generic internet attacker because the well-resourced collector over ten years is harder to price, harder to brief, and harder to convert into quarterly action. Risk, in practice, is often whatever can fit into a spreadsheet and survive a committee meeting.

The trouble with this habit is that stronger computation changes incentives even before it changes capabilities. If an intelligence service or a criminal enterprise believes there is a non-trivial chance that certain encrypted material may become readable later, collection itself becomes an investment. Storage is cheap. Patience can be strategic. The phrase "harvest now, decrypt later" has entered public discussion precisely because it captures this logic without requiring melodrama. Diplomatic cables, engineering plans, genomic records, legal archives, and identity databases do not lose their force simply because they sit behind mathematics for the moment. The promise of confidentiality, under those conditions, is no longer a yes-or-no property. It becomes a question about duration, adversary intent, and the credibility of migration.

In August 2024, the US National Institute of Standards and Technology released its first final post-quantum cryptography standards in Gaithersburg, Maryland, after years of public competition and review. The significance of that moment did not lie in a trumpet blast announcing the immediate death of classical public key cryptography. It lay in a quieter admission: the world's most relied-upon institutions were now spending political and engineering capital on the assumption that some of their foundational tools should not be treated as permanent. The room, in a sense, changed temperature. Standards are where mathematics acquires a passport. Once an algorithm becomes a federal profile, a procurement requirement, a vendor roadmap, a checkbox in a certification regime, it stops being merely an idea and starts becoming infrastructure. That transformation is slow, expensive, and unequal. It favours some firms, burdens others, and exposes a truth that technical discussion often hides: cryptography is also power over timing. Whoever can compel a migration, delay it, verify it, or absorb its costs holds an advantage that is not reducible to equations.

This is why key management matters so much, and why it is so often treated like drudgery when it is in fact a measure of institutional seriousness. Algorithms draw the intellectual glamour; keys determine who can act. Where are they generated? Who can export them? Who can authorise recovery? What happens after a merger, when identities overlap and old administrators retain silent powers? The answers rarely appear in public speeches about digital sovereignty, but they decide whether supposedly secure systems can survive contact with real organisations. Hardware security modules, certificate lifecycles, backup policies, insider access, escrow arrangements—these are not peripheral operational details. They are the statecraft of secrecy in miniature. A nation, a bank, or a cloud provider that cannot govern its keys is like a ministry that keeps perfect locks and hands copies to whoever asks nicely.

There is another reason the subject resists simplification. Encryption protects content, but not necessarily context. Secure transport can still leak timing. End-to-end systems can still be undone by backups, compromised endpoints, or recovery features designed for convenience. Metadata—the when, where, with whom, how often—often survives the strongest content protection and can be enough to infer command structures, intimate relationships, political networks, or commercial intentions. The difference between a protected message and a protected pattern is not academic. It marks the distance between secrecy as a technical property and secrecy as a lived condition. A journalist whose messages are encrypted but whose travel and call records trace a source network is not protected in any meaningful human sense. A military unit using encrypted links that still reveal movement rhythms has not vanished from view. Secrecy has edges; adversaries study those edges with devotion.

Legacy systems make those edges jagged. Across hospitals, industrial plants, transport fleets, and satellite or radio environments with intermittent connectivity, old protocols survive because replacing them risks downtime, regulatory friction, or physical intervention at impossible scale. The world is full of long-lived devices that cannot gracefully swap out their cryptographic assumptions. Some were built before the present anxieties were fashionable. Some still function too well to justify the expense of retirement. All of them turn yesterday's design choices into tomorrow's vulnerabilities. Here the hinge appears again: between the neat confidence of a design document and the stubborn life of systems in the field. An outdated root certificate, a forgotten appliance using embedded cryptography, a backup archive replicated across jurisdictions—these are the forms in which strategic exposure often actually exists.

None of this makes deterrence an absurd concept, but it does force a revision of what deterrence can mean in an informational contest. There is little point pretending that quiet collection can be banished by slogans. Much of it cannot. Yet some behaviours can be shaped. Broad interception becomes less attractive when trust anchors can be rotated quickly and misuse is more likely to be detected. Tampering becomes costlier when signatures, inventories, and update channels are governed with discipline. Coercive use of stolen data loses force when retention is limited, segmentation is real, and migration is visible enough to signal resolve without advertising fragility. The most credible signal in cryptography is often not a boast about secret capability but a public demonstration of administrative competence. Readiness deters not by making attack impossible, but by shortening the useful life of what an attacker can gain.

That claim needs modesty. And yet, the history of secure systems suggests that capability without governance curdles into theatre. Open algorithms, independent review, and certification can improve confidence, but they cannot redeem rotten incentives or neglected implementation. Closed hardware may reduce one class of risk while deepening dependence on opaque supply chains. Public reassurance may calm markets while teaching adversaries very little; secrecy may preserve advantage while corroding trust. Every serious institution in this domain lives inside such trade-offs. The fantasy of perfect assurance is itself a security risk, because it encourages brittle promises and punishes honest admission of limits.

The larger question, then, is not whether mathematics matters. It is which kinds of mathematical power become politically meaningful under conditions of uncertainty. A future decryption capability, even if unevenly distributed and imperfectly scalable, would not arrive into a vacuum. It would arrive into a world already shaped by standards battles, archived data, brittle certificate hierarchies, vendor dependencies, and organisations that confuse possession of cryptographic tools with command of cryptographic change. The decisive divide may not be between those who have quantum machines and those who do not. It may lie between those who can migrate trust under pressure and those who discover, too late, that their security was a pile of assumptions held together by habit.

That is the decision point hiding inside the technical vocabulary. When an institution says it is preparing for the next era of computation, is it choosing new algorithms, or is it learning how to inventory what it depends on, rotate what it trusts, delete what it need not keep, test what it claims to have secured, and communicate residual risk without either panic or complacency? The distinction sounds procedural. It is not. It separates security as ornament from security as capacity. The coming contest over encryption and decryption will be fought partly in laboratories and standards forums, certainly, but just as surely in procurement language, migration deadlines, certificate stores, key ceremonies, retention schedules, and crisis playbooks drafted long before any dramatic announcement settles the matter.

At that hinge, secrets become a test of character as much as design. Not personal character in the sentimental sense, but institutional character: the willingness to face delayed consequences, absorb near-term costs, and treat trust as something that must be maintained under changing assumptions rather than inherited as a birthright. The societies, firms, and agencies that understand this will not abolish uncertainty. They will do something more difficult. They will learn how to act under it, while the door is still closed and before the handle turns.

# Chapter 1

# Computation and Secrecy Over Time

What does it mean to call something secure if the answer depends on a machine that does not yet exist in usable form? The question sounds technical until its consequences are made plain. A payment authorisation may need to survive only long enough to clear. A source's identity may need to remain hidden for a lifetime. The word *secure* covers both, yet the burden it carries in each case is radically different.

That gap is where much confusion begins. Encryption is often spoken of as though it were a sealed door: either locked or unlocked, either sound or broken. Real systems do not behave so neatly. They endure pressure over time, under changing conditions, against adversaries with unequal resources and very different levels of patience. A door that holds through the night may fail under a year's worth of tools, access, and observation. Security belongs to a clock as much as to a formula.

A key left on a desk tells the story. The lock may be excellent; the result is still failure. Cryptography attracts prestige because it is mathematical, and mathematics appears to promise clean boundaries. Yet the practical meaning of secrecy depends on more than hidden content. It depends on whether a message can be trusted to remain unchanged, whether the sender is who the system claims they are, whether recovery and rotation are possible when something goes wrong, and whether an institution can keep these promises under strain. Precision matters here because vague confidence is often the first weakness. Terms such as confidentiality, integrity, and authenticity sound settled until they collide with different missions, different time scales, and different tolerances for loss.

Computation complicates this picture in a way that is easy to understate. Stronger machines do not merely threaten to solve hard problems faster. They alter the value of waiting, collecting, and investing. An actor does not need immediate decryption to gain from interception if the information being stored will remain useful years later. A defender does not need certainty about a coming breakthrough to face pressure now, because migration, procurement, redesign, and trust repair all consume time long before any public turning point arrives. The strategic difficulty lies in this asymmetry: collecting can be cheap and quiet, while adaptation is visible, costly, and institutionally awkward.

That asymmetry exposes another habit, one less flattering than most organisations like to admit. Institutions tend to choose threat models that fit their routines. They prepare for the attacker who appears in procurement language, in familiar audits, in vendor presentations, and in compliance forms. They are less comfortable preparing for the patient collector, the adversary who stores rather than spends, the actor whose horizon exceeds a budget cycle or a leadership term. This is not usually stupidity. It is a pattern produced by incentives. Short planning windows reward visible fixes. Long risks are easier to postpone because their harm arrives later and their prevention demands coordination across teams that do not share the same vocabulary, priorities, or authority.

The stakes extend beyond technical competence. They reach into the logic of deterrence itself. In military language, deterrence is often imagined through weapons and retaliation, through visible capabilities designed to raise the cost of attack. Information competition works differently. Much of the most important activity remains hidden, deniable, or ambiguous. Success is often silent. Failure may stay undiscovered for years. Under those conditions, deterrence cannot rest only on the threat of punishment. It also rests on whether a target can reduce the value of what is taken, recover trust after compromise, rotate critical assets without chaos, and demonstrate enough readiness that opportunistic advantage begins to look fleeting rather than durable.

That is why the subject asks for a broader lens than the familiar contest between codemakers and codebreakers. The deeper contest concerns time, institutions, and the ability to govern technical change before crisis makes the choices uglier. A cryptographic system is never just an algorithm. It is an arrangement of defaults, keys, identities, updates, responsibilities, and assumptions about who will act when those assumptions no longer hold. Some of those assumptions are hidden in software. Some are hidden in organisations. The dangerous ones are hidden in both.

The path ahead moves from the promise that encryption appears to make, to the ways stronger computation changes bargaining power before any dramatic event settles the matter, then to the comfortable threat models organisations prefer because they are easier to budget and easier to explain. From there the argument turns outward, asking what deterrence can mean when resilience, migration, and the containment of damage matter as much as secrecy itself. The sequence matters because each problem sharpens the next. Loose language clouds judgement; clouded judgement distorts planning; distorted planning invites precisely the kind of strategic surprise institutions insist they are designed to avoid.

Everything begins, then, with a deceptively simple test. When a system is called secure, what exactly is being promised, for whom, against whom, and for how long? Until those questions are answered without euphemism, the rest is theatre.

## What encryption promises

In August 2013, journalists reported that Lavabit, an encrypted e-mail service based in the United States, had shut down rather than comply with demands that would have compromised its users' privacy. Its founder, Ladar Levison, wrote that he had been forced to choose: become complicit in actions against the American people or walk away from nearly 10 years of work. The concrete outcome was stark. A service built around secure communication ceased operating because the promise it had offered users could no longer be honoured under the conditions imposed on it. The lock was still on the door. Control of the building was the real issue.

That distinction matters more than the rhetoric around encryption usually allows. People often speak as though encryption simply means secrecy, a veil drawn over content so that outsiders cannot read it. Sometimes that is true enough for casual conversation. It is not true enough for serious judgement. A message can remain unreadable while the sender is misidentified. A file can stay confidential while its contents are quietly altered. A system can correctly encrypt data and still fail because the keys are mishandled, the device is compromised, or the institution operating it cannot recover trust after a breach. Five words expose the problem: secrecy is not the whole.

What encryption promises, then, depends on which promise is actually being made. Confidentiality concerns who can read. Integrity concerns whether what arrives is what was sent. Authenticity concerns whether the claimed source is genuine. These are usually introduced as tidy technical categories, but operational life makes them messier, more expensive, and more entangled with human decisions. The categories matter precisely because they prevent one kind of success from being mistaken for another.

A bank transfer and a clandestine relationship may both involve encrypted communication, yet the promise that matters most in each case differs. Confuse those promises, and security turns theatrical.

Consider a card payment authorised in a shop. The visible scene is ordinary: a terminal beeps, a receipt prints, the customer leaves. Behind that ordinary moment sits a narrow timing requirement. The system must protect account details and transaction data from interception long enough to authorise payment, detect tampering, and bind the transaction to a legitimate participant. Confidentiality matters, but for a brief window. Integrity and authenticity matter just as much, perhaps more. If an attacker can alter the amount, substitute an account, replay a transaction, or impersonate a legitimate endpoint, secrecy alone offers little comfort. The name for this is not simply encryption; it is a controlled exchange in which multiple assurances have to hold at once. The implication is practical. When people praise "strong encryption" in payment systems, what they usually need is a package of properties: message secrecy during transmission, accurate identification of the parties, and enough resilience in the surrounding system to settle disputes and reject fraud.

Now place beside it a different case: an informant whose identity must remain concealed for decades. The scene changes immediately. A short-lived transaction becomes a long-lived exposure. Here confidentiality dominates in a more severe way, because disclosure years later may still destroy a life, compromise a network, or permit coercion long after the original exchange. But even here confidentiality does not stand alone. If records can be forged, if attribution can be manipulated, if archives can be correlated with later leaks, then integrity and authenticity return by another route. An intelligence file that remains unreadable but can be silently altered is not safe. A source report that can be plausibly reassigned to the wrong person carries its own danger. Time stretches the meaning of the promise. What counted as secure enough for a payment at noon may be grotesquely inadequate for a human identity that must survive hostile scrutiny twenty years later.

The difference is not philosophical. It is operational. One promise expires quickly; the other matures under pressure. That is why confidentiality cannot be treated as a blanket good measured only by whether the underlying mathematics still resists attack. Confidentiality in practice depends on key handling, storage duration, endpoint security, access controls, backup discipline, and the likelihood that old encrypted material will remain worth reading in the future. A message protected during transit but stored indefinitely in poorly governed archives does not enjoy the same kind of secrecy as a message designed to disappear after use. The visible behaviour is the clue. Does an institution delete sensitive records when their purpose ends, or does it keep them because storage is cheap and accountability feels safer when everything is retained? That choice often decides more than the cipher.

Integrity is often the neglected sibling because it lacks the drama of hidden text. Yet many of the gravest digital harms arise not from reading secrets but from altering records, commands, or software in ways that remain undetected. The 2017 NotPetya attack, first observed in Ukraine and then spreading across organisations worldwide, is a useful reminder, even though it was not principally about breaking encryption. The malware spread in part through a compromised software update mechanism linked to M.E.Doc, a Ukrainian accounting package. The visible event was a vast-scale disruption. The named concept is integrity failure. The explanation is simple enough: when a trusted update channel delivers malicious code, the problem is not that outsiders have read confidential files first. It is that a system accepts something false as authentic and intact. The implication travels well beyond malware. Any environment that relies on signed updates, authenticated commands, or trusted records lives or dies by its ability to detect unauthorised change.

Authenticity, meanwhile, is often mistaken for a more glamorous idea than it really is. At root, authenticity answers a plain question: who is this, and why should the system believe it? In human terms, it resembles the act of checking the person at the door. But digital systems do not see faces. They compare credentials, certificates, signatures, cryptographic proofs, and behavioural patterns. Those checks can be rigorous, but they are never free of institutional assumptions. Someone issues the certificate. Someone secures the signing key. Someone writes the validation rules. Someone decides whether an expired credential is tolerated for compatibility. The machine may verify; the institution still governs. This is why a message can be confidential and still dangerous. If the recipient cannot know who truly sent it, secrecy may shield a forgery.

The DigiNotar compromise in 2011 made that point painfully clear. DigiNotar, a Dutch certificate authority, was found to have issued fraudulent certificates, including certificates reportedly used in attacks on users in Iran. Browsers ultimately revoked trust in the company, and DigiNotar entered bankruptcy. The scene looked technical: certificates, trust stores, browser updates. The real lesson was more unsettling. Authenticity at internet scale depends on delegated trust, and delegated trust creates chokepoints. When a certificate authority fails, the damage does not stop at a single unread message or a single forged login page. It cuts into the shared machinery by which strangers, banks, journalists, ministries, and software packages decide what is genuine. Authenticity, then, is not a decorative extra appended to secrecy. It is one of the conditions under which secrecy can matter at all.

Still, the neat separation between confidentiality, integrity, and authenticity can mislead if treated too literally. Real systems rarely fail in only one dimension. A compromised phone may expose messages despite elegant transport encryption. A stolen signing key may permit malicious updates while preserving the outward appearance of authenticity. A perfectly encrypted archive may become newly vulnerable if future computing reduces the cost of decryption or if the archive's key management was weak from the start. The categories clarify thought; they do not keep the world in separate boxes. One reason institutions make poor decisions is that they hear a term such as confidentiality and imagine the rest will follow automatically. They do not.

A credible limitation deserves attention here. Some systems truly do need less than the full bundle of assurances. Broadcast data intended for public consumption may require integrity and authenticity while confidentiality is irrelevant. Certain sensor readings may tolerate exposure but not manipulation. A public software mirror may prioritise assurance that code is unaltered over secrecy about the code itself. This is not a defect in the framework. It is precisely why the distinctions matter. Security becomes clearer when the required promise is named narrowly rather than praised vaguely. The problem begins when institutions demand every assurance rhetorically, fund only some of them operationally, and then claim success because an encryption feature exists somewhere in the stack.

That mismatch often hides inside the word trust. Trust sounds abstract, almost moral. In practice it means concrete acts of acceptance. A browser accepts a certificate and opens the page without warning. A payments network clears a transaction because the terminal and issuer appear genuine. A civil servant stores a classified report in an archive because the system marks it as protected. A citizen installs an update because the device presents it as verified. Each action is a small surrender to prior judgement. That is why cryptographic language must stay tied to behaviour. Trust is not a feeling. It is permission granted by a process.

The lock returns here. People tend to picture encryption as the lock itself: elegant, visible, reassuring. Yet the stronger image is the keyring and the doorframe. Who cut the keys? Who keeps copies? Who notices splintered wood around the latch? Who decides when the whole lock must be replaced? Confidentiality without authenticity can hide deception. Authenticity without integrity can certify corruption. Integrity without resilience can fail at the first serious disruption. System resilience belongs in the same conversation because promises do not matter only when conditions are normal. They matter when credentials must be revoked, when keys must be rotated, when services degrade, when old devices do not update cleanly, when human operators improvise under pressure. A secure design that collapses into unsafe workarounds during crisis has made a promise it cannot keep.

This is why stronger computation unsettles more than one property at once. Public discussion often narrows the coming challenge to whether future machines may weaken familiar forms of public key cryptography. That concern is real enough, but its deeper force lies in what it reveals about the fragility of promises over time. If authenticity depends on signatures that may not remain trustworthy for the lifespan of a legal archive, the issue is not merely technical replacement. It is evidential continuity. If confidentiality for long-lived records depends on assumptions that may age badly, the issue is not only secrecy in the present. It is whether today's storage decisions are creating tomorrow's coercive opportunities. Computation changes the lifespan of assurances. It changes what prudence requires.

The temptation, especially in bureaucratic settings, is to compress all this into a compliance phrase. Data encrypted at rest. Communications encrypted in transit. Access authenticated. Audit passed. Those labels are not meaningless, but they invite a false calm when detached from context. A payment approved today and an informant protected for decades do not ask the same thing of a system, even if both involve encryption. The former may tolerate short horizons, rapid rotation, and some reliance on fraud recovery. The latter may demand long secrecy, severe compartmentation, minimised retention, and protections against future reidentification that no receipt terminal will ever need. To say both are encrypted is true, but scarcely useful.

The harder and more honest question is narrower. When an institution claims to protect information, which promise is it actually prepared to keep once time, storage, identity, and institutional failure are brought back into view? Until that is answered in operational terms, encryption remains a word doing too much work.

## Stronger computers as strategic change

In October 2019, Google announced that its team had carried out a quantum computation on a processor called Sycamore that, in its telling, would take a classical supercomputer far longer to reproduce. The claim, published in *Nature*, triggered an immediate argument about what had actually been shown and how meaningful the comparison was. The scene mattered anyway. In Santa Barbara, California, the result did not break the internet, empty bank accounts, or dissolve diplomatic secrecy overnight. It changed something subtler first: the plausibility conditions. A possibility that had lived for years in specialist discussion moved closer to executive briefing rooms, procurement calendars, and standards committees. The horizon shifted.

That is how strategic change often begins. Not with a clean technical verdict, but with an alteration in what serious institutions must now treat as conceivable. A capability need not arrive in finished, industrial form to reshape behaviour around it. It only needs to become credible enough that waiting looks less prudent than preparation, and credible enough that collectors begin to value what they can store even if they cannot yet exploit it fully. Computation works on time twice over: it changes what can be solved, and it changes when it becomes rational to act.

A stronger machine is never just a faster calculator. In strategic terms, it alters bargaining power by changing the cost of patience. When computation grows cheaper or more concentrated, actors with storage, capital, and organisational discipline gain options before anyone can point to a dramatic breach. The visible behaviour is mundane. More encrypted traffic is retained. Archives once treated as inert become candidate assets. Security teams reopen old assumptions. Procurement language acquires new clauses about upgradeability and algorithm support. The concept sitting beneath these choices is simple enough to name: capability uncertainty. The explanation is harder, because uncertainty sounds passive when it is often active. It pressures decisions precisely because nobody can specify the date of arrival with confidence. The implication follows. Ambiguity does not freeze strategy; it accelerates it.

This becomes easier to see when one moves away from the fantasy of a single breakthrough day. Computing power has always changed contests before it settled them. During the Second World War, Bletchley Park did not turn codebreaking into a fairy tale of instant omniscience. It turned it into an industrial and organisational problem. Machines, analysts, traffic volume, intercept discipline, and operational choices all had to align. The famous achievement was not that mathematics floated above institutions and won by purity. It was that institutions learned to convert computational advantage into repeated, disciplined exploitation. The lesson survives in altered form. Better computation matters, but its strategic value depends on collection priorities, staffing, storage, throughput, and the ability to decide where precious effort should go first. Capability without organisation remains a laboratory event.

That distinction is especially important in cryptography, where public discussion often treats computational progress as though it were a universal solvent. It is not. Even a major advance affects different promises differently. A short-lived transaction can remain safe enough under conditions that would be intolerable for a long-lived archive. Some systems rely more heavily on symmetric primitives that degrade differently under stronger computational assumptions than familiar public key methods do. Endpoints can still be compromised by means that require no cryptanalytic elegance at all. Yet none of this softens the strategic point. Uneven change still changes the game. An adversary does not need a master key for everything. It may be enough to crack selected archives, impersonate selected identities, or invalidate selected signatures whose evidential life extends far into the future.

The right image is not a cliff edge but a moving window. Once that window appears, institutions must ask a harder question than "Is the cipher broken?" They must ask how long each class of secret must remain protected relative to the plausible lifetime of the computational assumptions protecting it. That is the real force of cryptographic time horizons. A design team building a consumer payment flow can tolerate different risks from a defence ministry archiving source identities or a pharmaceutical firm storing research dossiers. The names of the systems differ; the underlying calculation is the same. How long must confidentiality last? How long must signatures remain trustworthy? How long can a stored key remain a safe anchor? Time stops being background scenery and becomes a strategic variable.

A useful example came into view not through a breach but through a standards process. In August 2024, the US National Institute of Standards and Technology published its first final post-quantum cryptography standards. That decision in Gaithersburg, Maryland, did not certify that conventional public key systems had suddenly become unusable. It did something more consequential for long planning cycles: it signalled that leading public institutions no longer regarded the issue as a distant intellectual exercise. Show the scene and the meaning sharpens. Standards bodies, vendors, and procurement offices rarely reorganise themselves around pure speculation. Name the concept, and the event becomes legible as strategic adaptation under uncertainty. Explain the mechanism, and one sees why. Once a standard exists, the debate moves from whether a problem deserves attention to how quickly organisations can absorb the cost of change. The implication is practical and political. Those that can shape standards, products, and compliance language can pull the timetable of others.

Here bargaining power enters plainly. Computation does not merely threaten defenders; it redistributes advantage among them. Large states, major cloud providers, and dominant platform vendors can spread migration costs across vast infrastructures. They can influence software libraries, hardware support, and certification expectations. Smaller institutions inherit those choices, often with less room to test, negotiate, or delay. This is why stronger computation should not be imagined only as a duel between attacker and target. It also reorganises dependence. A university, hospital, regional utility, or mid-sized manufacturer may understand the risk perfectly well and still remain hostage to vendor roadmaps, procurement rules, and legacy devices that cannot absorb abrupt cryptographic change. The mathematics may be universal. The capacity to respond never is.

The same logic explains why future capability affects present collection. If an intelligence service believes that some encrypted stores may become readable within the useful lifetime of the intelligence they contain, retention acquires a new logic. The visible acts can be dull enough to escape attention: intercept now, store cheaply, index carefully, wait. The concept often attached to this behaviour is "harvest now, decrypt later", but the phrase only matters because it captures a deeper asymmetry. Collection can be modular and opportunistic. Defence is cumulative. The defender must inventory systems, classify data by lifespan, rotate keys, replace brittle dependencies, test interoperability, and persuade leadership to spend money on a threat that has not yet announced itself through catastrophe. One side buys options. The other buys preparedness. Options are usually easier to justify.

This is why uncertainty can strengthen the collector even before it yields a technical breakthrough. The mere chance that future decryption may become cheaper widens the set of data worth taking now, especially where storage costs are modest and the information retains value over long periods. Diplomatic correspondence, design archives, legal records, biometric data, source identities, merger documents, and strategic planning papers do not all age at the same rate. Some decay quickly. Some ripen. Stronger computation makes that distinction commercially and politically significant. A file once too expensive to attack may become a deferred opportunity. A record once harmless because unreadable may become dangerous simply because someone was disciplined enough to keep it.

Still, the picture needs restraint. Capability projections in this domain are famously contested. The history of computing contains no shortage of inflated timelines, misunderstood demonstrations, and announcements crafted as much for investors, bureaucrats, or national prestige as for sober planning. The 2019 Google result drew precisely that sort of response, with critics disputing what the classical comparison really proved. That criticism was not pedantry. It was a reminder that laboratory milestones and operational capability are different species of fact. A machine can perform a striking demonstration under tightly controlled conditions and remain far from breaking widely deployed cryptographic systems at scale. This limitation matters because overreaction carries its own costs: wasted procurement, brittle migration, fashionable fear masquerading as strategy.

Yet caution should not be mistaken for comfort. Uncertain timelines do not erase the organisational lag built into defence. They heighten its significance. Replacing cryptographic foundations across a large institution usually means touching software dependencies, certificates, interfaces, hardware modules, mobile fleets, archived records, vendor contracts, and training materials. Some systems will fail in testing. Some suppliers will arrive late. Some devices will never update cleanly. Some managers will treat the entire matter as technical clutter until a regulator, a customer, or a crisis deprives them of that luxury. Under those conditions, exact prediction becomes less important than the ability to change direction without panic. The problem is not only whether stronger computers arrive. The problem is whether institutions have left themselves any room to move when they do.

That is why defence in this area is organisational before it is triumphant. Mathematics defines what is possible; organisations decide what is survivable. The phrase may sound less glamorous than discussions of quantum algorithms, but it points to the real site of advantage. A disciplined organisation knows where cryptography lives in its estate, which secrets must outlast which threats, who controls keys and certificates, what depends on ageing libraries, and how quickly critical systems can shift without disabling service. Those are visible capacities. They appear in inventories, contracts, test results, incident procedures, and retention schedules. They can be compared, funded, neglected, or faked. The strongest algorithm offers little comfort to an institution that cannot find where it is using the old one.

The moving window appears again here. One organisation treats computational uncertainty as a cue to map its dependencies, classify information by lifespan, and demand migration paths from suppliers. Another keeps the same assurances, the same defaults, and the same retention habits because no breach has yet forced embarrassment. Both may use identical cryptographic tools today. They do not occupy the same strategic position. One is buying time. The other is spending it without accounting.

The deeper significance of stronger computation, then, lies not in a spectacular future headline but in the quiet change it imposes on present judgement. It widens the value of collection, raises the premium on migration capacity, exposes the fiction that security can be reduced to current compliance, and turns time itself into an asset that can be managed well or squandered badly. The technical question remains real and difficult. The strategic question is harsher: when the window starts moving, who notices soon enough to act before their own systems become a record of assumptions they can no longer afford?

## Threat models that organisations avoid

In March 2021, Microsoft disclosed that attackers had exploited previously unknown vulnerabilities in on-premises Exchange Server deployments, and within days organisations across the world were scrambling to assess whether intruders had not only entered their systems but left behind means to return. The visible scene was ugly and familiar: administrators checking logs late into the night, emergency patches applied under pressure, outside responders called in, and leaders asking the same blunt question - are we secure now? In London, Washington, Brussels, and countless server rooms far less noticed, the answer turned out to depend on something many institutions prefer not to face. The initial breach was only part of the story. Persistence mattered more.

The question on the whiteboard was wrong.

Most organisations are comfortable imagining the attacker who wants to get in, do damage, and leave a trace dramatic enough to justify the incident report. They are less comfortable imagining the adversary who enters quietly, studies retention habits, maps dependencies, steals encrypted material for later use, and waits. That difference sounds like a matter of style. It is actually a matter of time horizon, budget logic, and institutional psychology. A threat model is not merely an intellectual exercise. It is a decision about which dangers deserve calendar time, procurement money, logging capacity, contractual pressure on vendors, and executive attention. What institutions choose to imagine determines what they are willing to pay for.

The convenient threat model usually has a recognisable shape. It features a generic internet attacker, often external, opportunistic, and immediate. The attacker scans exposed services, sends phishing messages, hunts for weak passwords, exploits an unpatched system, perhaps deploys ransomware, and tries to monetise or disrupt within a time frame that fits a quarter, a news cycle, or an insurer's reporting template. This model is not fantasy. It describes a great deal of real harm. It also flatters institutions because it fits existing controls. Firewalls, endpoint software, routine patching, penetration tests, awareness training, and annual audits all have a place inside it. The model feels manageable because its outline matches the tools already purchased to answer it.

Show the alternative and the mood changes. A well-resourced collector over ten years does not need speed, visibility, or immediate monetisation. It values persistence, storage, correlation, selective access, and the patient accumulation of data that may grow more useful as context changes or capabilities improve. The name for the gap between these two pictures is threat model compression. Institutions compress long, uneven, politically awkward risk into a shorter, simpler adversary because short adversaries produce cleaner governance. Explain the mechanism and the result looks less like stupidity than bureaucracy behaving as bureaucracy does. Budget cycles reward visible problems. Audit regimes reward evidence that controls exist. Procurement rewards products that promise rapid coverage of named risks. Long-horizon collection, by contrast, resists neat demonstration. Its harms may arrive years later, under new leadership, through consequences that feel indirect rather than spectacular. The implication is severe. Organisations often underprepare for the threats most likely to exploit their patience, not merely their perimeter.

A procurement meeting offers the clearest window into this habit. The security lead asks whether a product supports encryption, multi-factor authentication, standard logging, and policy controls. The vendor says yes, produces a glossy assurance pack, and points to certifications. The purchasing team hears reduced exposure and accelerated approval. Nobody at the table asks a different class of question: which cryptographic components can be replaced without rebuilding the service, how long logs and encrypted archives will persist, whether keys can be rotated under stress, whether identity data can be minimised rather than merely protected, or how the product behaves if a trust anchor must be replaced quickly. The omission is not dramatic. It is procedural. That is precisely why it matters. Risk enters through what feels too awkward, too long-term, or too unfashionably specific to ask while the contract is still moving.

Audit culture intensifies the problem. A checklist is a useful servant and a terrible strategist. It can verify that controls exist, that policies are documented, that data is encrypted at rest, that access reviews occur, that backup procedures are tested. These are not trivial achievements. But a checklist tends to ask whether a control is present, not whether its underlying assumptions remain aligned to the life of the data or the patience of the adversary. When a report records that sensitive archives are encrypted, the sentence sounds reassuring. It may conceal the harder questions. Encrypted with what? Managed by whom? Retained for how long? Recoverable under whose authority? Tied to which vendor's update schedule? The institution receives a passing mark and quietly mistakes administrative legibility for strategic sufficiency.

The SolarWinds compromise revealed how costly that mistake can become. In December 2020, public reporting made clear that malicious code had been inserted into Orion software updates distributed by SolarWinds, a company based in Austin, Texas, allowing sophisticated intrusion into a range of organisations, including United States government departments. The visible failure involved software supply chains and trusted updates. The deeper lesson concerned threat imagination. Many organisations had built their security posture around blocking hostile outsiders at the network edge while granting broad trust to signed, routine software updates from approved vendors. That decision made operational sense under a narrow threat model. Under a patient collector model, it looked different. A trusted pathway became the pathway. The concept here is inherited trust. Explain it plainly and its danger becomes obvious: institutions often outsource part of their threat model to vendors, assuming that approved suppliers carry not only functionality but a large share of the burden of disbelief. The implication is grimly practical. A dependency can function as a blindfold.

Vendor dependence deserves more respect than it usually receives. Not because dependence is always avoidable, but because it quietly shapes what risks an institution can even afford to acknowledge. A hospital relying on specialised imaging equipment, an industrial operator tied to long-service control systems, a ministry running a patchwork of legacy applications, or a university with limited procurement power cannot simply declare cryptographic agility into existence. If a supplier supports one algorithm suite, one identity model, one update cadence, and one retention architecture, the customer inherits those assumptions unless it is willing to absorb extraordinary migration costs. This is the visible behaviour attached to the abstraction of dependence: contracts renewed despite discomfort, old systems retained because replacement threatens downtime, exceptions granted because the business function cannot pause. Institutions do not only choose threat models; they inherit them through what they have already bought.

That inheritance explains why the phrase "internet attacker" can be so misleading. It describes a style of access but not a programme of intent. A generic external attacker may seek broad opportunity, low cost, and rapid yield. A well-resourced collector over ten years acts differently. It prizes continuity over speed. It tolerates low immediate return. It stores encrypted material because storage is cheap and future value may rise. It studies organisational charts, update channels, contractor access, backups, and certificate management because these reveal where trust can be bent without being broken publicly. The first model encourages perimeter hardening and rapid patching. The second demands retention discipline, dependency mapping, key governance, and a far less romantic understanding of what "secure" means once information can be held in reserve against a later moment.

The distinction matters especially in cryptographic settings because encryption can seduce decision-makers into false closure. Once data is labelled encrypted, a procurement board may regard the problem as technically solved. Under the short-horizon attacker model, that may even be partly defensible. The immediate interceptor is denied easy access.

Under the long-horizon collector model, the label proves much thinner. Encrypted archives become target assets if their contents will remain useful for years. Identity records, negotiation files, proprietary designs, source material, and legal communications do not expire on the timetable of a credit-card transaction. Here the threat model changes the meaning of the same technical control. Encryption stops being a finish line and becomes a wager about duration.

A second example shows how institutional incentives help bury that fact. In June 2015, the United States Office of Personnel Management disclosed a breach that exposed highly sensitive personnel and security-clearance data. The attack was not primarily remembered as a tale of failed day-to-day confidentiality in transit. It became a lesson in the strategic value of records whose importance endures. Background investigation files, fingerprints, family links, foreign contacts, debts, and vulnerabilities form a resource for long-term assessment, coercion, and correlation. The scene appears bureaucratic. The implications are not. A short-horizon threat model might treat such stores as merely another class of protected administrative data. A patient collector sees a library. Name the concept and the contrast sharpens: latent intelligence value. Explain it and one understands why the harm from certain breaches unfolds slowly, through future access decisions, susceptibility mapping, and relationship analysis rather than immediate public spectacle. The implication returns to time. Institutions that classify data only by current sensitivity often miss the greater danger posed by future usability.

Still, any serious account needs a limitation. Not every organisation can optimise for decade-long strategic collectors without crippling itself. Resources are finite. Security teams face constant pressure from immediate threats that cause measurable damage now. A hospital struggling against ransomware, a local authority running ageing systems, or a manufacturer dependent on brittle operational technology cannot responsibly ignore short-horizon attackers while meditating on distant cryptanalytic futures. This is a real constraint, not an excuse. It would be foolish to sneer at institutions for prioritising dangers that can shut down services this week.

Yet that concession does not rescue the convenient threat model. It refines the criticism. The problem is not that organisations focus on urgent threats. The problem is that they often build governance structures in which urgent threats crowd out the possibility of holding two time scales in view at once. Immediate operational defence and long-horizon resilience are treated as rival agendas rather than linked obligations. The result is a kind of administrative myopia. Logging is funded, but retention minimisation is postponed. Patching is measured, but dependency inventories remain partial. Encryption is mandated, but archive lifespans go unexamined. Supplier attestations are collected, but migration rights are not negotiated. The whiteboard fills with this quarter's fires while the deeper fuel load stays in place.

Threat models are also social artefacts. They tell stories about competence, blame, and plausible embarrassment. An institution may prefer the generic internet attacker because that adversary feels impersonal and technically bounded. It allows leaders to say that everyone faces these threats and that sensible controls are in place. The well-resourced long-term collector introduces more awkward questions. Which datasets remain valuable for too long? Which suppliers hold too much quiet power? Which exceptions have become permanent? Which executives accepted retention because deletion felt dangerous to their accountability? Which teams know where old keys, old certificates, and old backups still live? Those questions do not flatter anyone. They cut across departments. They expose governance, not only technology.

For that reason the most avoided threat models are often the ones that demand institutional self-knowledge. A team can commission a penetration test without revisiting why it stores certain records indefinitely. It can buy another monitoring tool without asking whether archived encrypted material should have been deleted years earlier. It can adopt standard cryptography and still lack a map of where that cryptography sits, who controls the keys, or how a forced migration would work across mixed suppliers and legacy devices. This is why defence in such settings cannot be reduced to better mathematics. Organisational memory, procurement language, retention habits, and responsibility lines shape exposure just as surely as any algorithm.

The quiet motif here is the filing cabinet. The old picture of security imagined a cabinet that must be locked against prying hands. The modern institution has digitised the cabinet, duplicated it, backed it up, shared it with vendors, indexed it for convenience, and forgotten half the drawers. Then it asks whether the lock is strong. That question is not wrong. It is merely late. A short-horizon threat model peers at the front of the cabinet, looking for forced entry. A long-horizon collector studies the records schedule, the duplicate keys, the off-site storage, and the maintenance contract for the room itself.

Seen this way, the issue is not blame but pattern recognition. Institutions drift towards the threat models their procedures can digest, their suppliers can satisfy, and their auditors can record. They avoid the models that demand longer memory, messier coordination, and harder arguments about what should never have been retained or trusted so casually in the first place. The pressing question is no longer whether an organisation can describe an attacker in plausible terms. It is whether it is willing to picture the adversary whose patience exceeds its own planning cycle - and then discover what that picture makes impossible to ignore.

## Deterrence beyond weapons systems

In May 2017, as the WannaCry ransomware outbreak raced across networks from the United Kingdom to Asia, one of the most striking images came from the National Health Service: hospitals cancelling appointments, staff reverting to paper, screens frozen by a demand note rather than a mysterious military threat. The immediate cause was not the collapse of encryption as such. It was a failure of preparedness around systems, patching, dependencies, and the ability to contain damage once a malicious capability began to spread. In London and elsewhere, the visible outcome was disruption. The strategic lesson was broader. A society can possess advanced technical knowledge and still discover, under pressure, that deterrence is not only about punishing attack. It is also about reducing the value of attack and narrowing the room in which it can succeed.

The old imagery of deterrence remains powerful because it is simple. One side displays force, the other calculates cost, and restraint follows from fear of consequence. That model fits some military settings well enough. It fits information competition only partially. Here the decisive contests often unfold in silence. Intrusions may remain undiscovered. Collection may continue without obvious effect. The most valuable success may be the one nobody notices because nothing explodes, nothing goes dark, and nothing announces itself except a quiet increase in the attacker's knowledge. That changes the grammar of deterrence. The central question is no longer only whether an attacker fears retaliation. It is whether the attacker expects useful gains to persist.

That expectation matters most.

In an information contest, costs, capabilities, and resolve do not disappear; they become harder to display cleanly. A missile test is public by design. A cryptanalytic capability often derives value from secrecy. A well-run migration from one trust anchor to another may matter strategically, yet it produces no dramatic spectacle beyond the absence of catastrophe. The problem is not that deterrence ceases to exist. It is that deterrence must operate through different signals. Systems must show that tampering will be detected, that stolen access will expire, that compromised credentials can be revoked without paralysing operations, that sensitive archives will not remain valuable forever, and that institutions can continue functioning after a breach without surrendering trust entirely. The visible behaviours attached to those claims are plain enough: patch windows shortened, certificates rotated, key material replaced, retention reduced, fallback procedures tested, software dependencies audited, vendor obligations tightened. Deterrence begins to look less like theatre and more like administration under discipline.

That sounds almost indecently mundane, which is one reason people overlook it. Yet the mundane is where credibility lives. A state, bank, cloud provider, or hospital does not deter opportunistic exploitation by issuing lyrical statements about cyber resilience. It deters by making exploitation less profitable. Name the concept and the matter sharpens: denial by resilience. Explain it, and one sees why it belongs inside deterrence rather than outside it. If a target can restore systems rapidly, invalidate stolen credentials, segment critical functions, and prevent compromised data from yielding durable advantage, then some classes of attack begin to promise less reward. The implication is not utopian. Quiet collection may still occur. Some damage will still be done. But the attacker's expected return shrinks, and strategy follows expected return more reliably than slogans do.

A useful case is the 2011 compromise of DigiNotar in the Netherlands. The immediate facts are familiar to specialists: a certificate authority was breached, fraudulent certificates were issued, and browsers eventually revoked trust in the company. For many users the visible event was confusion, warnings, service disruption, and then disappearance. For deterrence, the deeper lesson lay elsewhere. Trust infrastructures do not merely protect communication; they also shape what an adversary can expect to gain by subverting authenticity at scale. Once browser vendors and relying parties proved willing to withdraw trust and reconfigure the practical meaning of a compromised authority, the attacker learned that success could trigger rapid devaluation. This did not erase the harm already done. It did show that the value of a compromise depends on how long it remains exploitable. Deterrence in such cases rests partly on a simple clock. The shorter the useful life of a stolen credential or poisoned trust anchor, the lower the strategic return from obtaining it.

This is why migration capacity matters so much. Not migration as a ceremonial future plan, but as a lived institutional ability to change cryptographic dependencies under stress. A system that cannot rotate keys, replace certificates, update algorithms, or retire brittle components without weeks of chaos effectively advertises something about itself. It signals that any successful compromise may enjoy a long afterlife. A system that can change quickly sends a different message even if it never reveals its private defensive techniques. Here resolve becomes administrative rather than theatrical. It appears in budget decisions, testing discipline, supplier contracts, staffing, inventories, and the unpleasant willingness to rehearse unattractive scenarios before anyone is forced to. The signal is not "we are invulnerable". That would be nonsense. The signal is "your access will decay faster than you think".

The distinction between visible readiness and hidden capability matters because secrecy cuts both ways. A defender may possess significant means of detection or recovery and choose not to disclose them fully. An attacker may possess significant means of collection or decryption and choose the same. Traditional deterrence theory always wrestled with this problem, but cryptographic competition intensifies it. Reveal too much, and one teaches the adversary where to route around the obstacle. Reveal too little, and no one updates their expectations. The result is a delicate economy of proof. Credible signals often come not from boasting about secret powers but from demonstrating public competence in things that can be observed without disclosing sensitive details: the speed of revocation, the clarity of incident handling, the ability to preserve service while replacing compromised components, the discipline to reduce retention, the refusal to let emergency procedures become permanent vulnerabilities.

Think of the spare key.

Every institution keeps one somewhere, literally or metaphorically. Emergency accounts, backup certificates, old compatibility modes, archived credentials, manual override paths, forgotten contractor access: each exists for a reason, usually a good one. Each also tells an adversary something about how the institution behaves under strain. Deterrence in cryptographic settings depends heavily on what happens to the spare key when the building is under pressure. Is it controlled, logged, rotated, and governed by a procedure that assumes abuse is possible? Or is it taped, figuratively speaking, under the flowerpot because continuity feels more urgent than discipline? Many attackers do not need to break the front door if they can predict where the spare key will be found. The strategic implication is brutal in its banality. Governance choices become signals.

The 2020 SolarWinds compromise offers a second anchor. When public reporting showed that malicious code had entered trusted software updates, the episode was widely framed as a supply-chain failure. Correctly so. Yet its deterrence lesson has not been fully absorbed. A software update channel is attractive to an attacker because it promises scale, stealth, and inherited trust. The question for deterrence is not simply how to threaten retaliation after such an intrusion becomes public. It is how to make the pathway less rewarding before the fact and less durable after it. Organisations that can isolate update infrastructure, verify provenance carefully, monitor anomalous behaviour, and cut over to clean states faster change the attacker's calculation. Those that cannot offer a more pleasant prospect. The point is not that resilience makes attacks disappear. It is that resilience can alter which attacks are worth attempting, which is the beginning of deterrence even when attribution remains murky.

Attribution, of course, is a stubborn limitation. Information competition rarely offers the exquisite clarity that retaliation fantasies require. Actors route operations through proxies, shared tools, third-party infrastructure, or overlapping tradecraft. By the time a technical breach becomes politically legible, the opportunity for elegant deterrent signalling may already have passed. This limitation is real. It is one reason analysts sometimes dismiss deterrence language in cyber and cryptographic settings as borrowed prestige from a cleaner strategic age. The criticism bites because some public discussion really does indulge in hand-waving. It mistakes stern rhetoric for causal effect.

Still, the limitation does not kill the concept. It forces refinement. Deterrence in this domain cannot depend solely on the promise of precise punishment after certain attribution. Much of the time it must rely on expectation management before attribution is settled: reducing the attacker's confidence that access will remain hidden, useful, or scalable; reducing the expected shelf life of stolen data; reducing the chance that one compromise yields broad strategic gain. That means denial, degradation, and recovery deserve equal status alongside retaliation. A collector who fears rapid credential invalidation, segmentation, public exposure, and low-value archives may still attack, but the campaign begins under worse assumptions. That matters.

The argument becomes sharper when one distinguishes between deterring behaviours and deterring actors. Some behaviours are more plausibly shaped than others. Broad interception, tampering with software supply chains, coercive use of stolen data, and repeated exploitation of stale credentials all depend on opportunities that institutions can narrow through visible preparation. Quiet collection against a high-value target may remain attractive despite excellent governance. Here deterrence has edges. It would be childish to deny them. Yet strategic life is full of partial successes. An institution does not need to make itself uninteresting to all adversaries. It needs to change enough calculations that attack becomes costlier, less reliable, less durable, or less scalable for the adversaries that matter most.

This is where the earlier discussion of time horizons returns with full force. Cryptographic deterrence is not chiefly about persuading an opponent that attack will be impossible. It is about persuading the opponent that any gains from attack may expire before they can be converted into enduring advantage. If encrypted archives are minimised, then a future decryption capability yields less. If signatures can be replaced and trust anchors migrated, then a stolen credential yields less. If identity systems segment power carefully, then a compromised administrator account yields less. If crisis procedures preserve verification rather than disable it, then disruption yields less. The operative phrase is not absolute security. It is *shrinking payoff duration*. That phrase lacks glamour, but strategy tends to honour what glamour neglects.

Visible readiness therefore matters as a signal of resolve. Resolve in information competition is rarely announced by grand doctrine alone. It appears when institutions absorb near-term pain to preserve future trust. They retire old protocols before the last possible moment. They test revocation procedures that may never be used in public. They demand from suppliers the contractual right to migrate cryptographic components rather than accept static assurances. They shorten retention not because storage is expensive, but because indefinitely readable history is strategically dangerous. These acts are legible, especially to sophisticated adversaries. They communicate that the defender is not treating encryption as decorative compliance. The spare key is being managed, not admired.

A sceptic may object that such signals are too subtle to deter anyone serious. Sophisticated attackers, the objection runs, expect defences to improve and proceed regardless. That is often true at the highest levels of competition. But even there, subtle signals matter because campaigns are built on choice among targets, routes, timings, and levels of investment. Deterrence does not require an adversary to abandon all hostile intent. It requires the adversary to compare options and dislike some of them more than others. The defender who cannot credibly signal readiness to migrate and contain damage becomes easier to rank, easier to prioritise, and easier to revisit. The defender who can do so may still be attacked, but not under the same assumptions of easy persistence.

That leaves a harder problem. What can be signalled without teaching too much? A public commitment to rapid algorithm updates may reassure allies and unsettle opportunists. Detailed disclosure of every dependency and contingency plan would do the opposite. The line between useful transparency and operational self-harm is thin. It must be drawn repeatedly, not solved once. Institutions therefore need a language of proof that does not depend on maximal disclosure: independent assurance, visible exercises, documented migration governance, measured revocation times, trusted review processes, credible public reporting after incidents. None of these eliminates secrecy. They give secrecy a frame that others can evaluate. Without such framing, claims of readiness remain pious fog.

The strategic test is harsher than the public slogan. When an adversary looks at an institution's encrypted systems, does it see a locked room or a building whose owners can swiftly change the locks, isolate the damaged wing, and make anything stolen age badly? The answer will not determine every contest. It will determine more of them than institutions usually admit, and it is the answer their habits are signalling long before any incident forces them to speak aloud.

# Chapter 2

# Modern Cryptography in Institutions

What does it mean for a system to be secure if nobody in the organisation can say, with confidence, where the keys are, who can replace them, or what will happen when a trusted component fails? The question sounds technical until it lands on a recognisable scene: an encrypted service running smoothly, a compliance box ticked, a supplier contract renewed, and a crisis beginning somewhere just outside the frame. The mathematics may be sound. The institution may still be brittle.

That tension sits at the centre of modern cryptography in practice. Most people meet cryptography as a promise made by software: the padlock in a browser, the secure message, the protected database, the signed update. What they are not shown is the chain of custody beneath the promise. Keys must be generated, stored, rotated, and recovered. Certificates must be issued and checked. Libraries must be maintained. Defaults must be inherited from somebody. Validation rules must be written somewhere by someone with authority. The user sees a smooth surface. Underneath sits an administrative machine.

That machine matters because cryptography rarely fails in the way popular imagination prefers. It is comforting to picture a dramatic mathematical collapse, a single brilliant attack that proves the lock was never real. More often the lock holds while the hinges come away. Sensitive files remain encrypted while the key sits in the wrong memory space, the wrong backup, or the wrong administrator's hands. A signed update remains formally authentic while the signing process itself has been compromised. A trusted certificate remains accepted because the surrounding institution has not found a practical way to withdraw trust without breaking too much else. Security, in other words, is often weakest where it appears most routine.

The central trade-off is not between theory and practice in any simple sense. It is between elegant cryptographic assurances and the messy institutional arrangements required to make those assurances durable.

Symmetric systems may resist attack admirably while endpoints leak everything that matters. Public key systems may scale trust across vast networks while concentrating power into naming systems, certificate authorities, and validation choices that few users ever see. Hashes and signatures may appear almost timeless until one asks how long a contract, an archive, or a software supply chain expects them to remain credible. Standards may embody careful review and accumulated expertise while also slowing change precisely when change grows urgent. The more widely a mechanism succeeds, the more expensive it becomes to alter.

That is why modern cryptography should be understood less as a collection of tools than as a distribution of dependence. Institutions depend on code they did not write, hardware they did not fabricate, root stores they do not control directly, update channels they only partly inspect, and procurement frameworks that reward visible assurance more readily than hidden adaptability. Convenience plays a large role here. So does habit. A protocol becomes common not only because it is sound, but because it is built into products, understood by vendors, accepted by auditors, and tolerated by ageing infrastructure. Once that happens, a technical choice hardens into a governance fact.

The stakes run beyond engineering hygiene. When cryptographic trust is delegated through institutions, the question of who governs those institutions becomes strategic. A default selected in a widely used library can shape millions of systems without any one organisation feeling that it has made a grand decision. A certificate rule embedded in software can determine what counts as authentic across borders and sectors. A signing key can become a single point of authority for software that reaches hospitals, ministries, banks, and households. These are not exotic edge cases. They are ordinary features of digital life. Their ordinariness is the danger. People tend to reserve strategic language for obvious drama and miss the quieter forms of power that travel through standards, defaults, and administrative trust.

The next movement follows that power at ground level. It begins with the seeming solidity of symmetric encryption and the operational frictions that gather around it, then passes into the delegated trust of public key systems where names, certificates, and validation rules become choke points rather than neutral plumbing. From there the focus tightens on integrity, signatures, and the stubborn afterlife of broken assurances, before widening to the standards and libraries that quietly decide most organisations' practical posture. The line then reaches the place where cryptography stops looking like pure engineering and starts looking like governance: contracts, compliance, accountability, and the diffusion of responsibility across people who do not share the same threat model.

A spare key in a drawer can clarify the whole subject. It is not the lock that causes anxiety. It is who knows the drawer, who can open it without notice, who records its use, and who has authority to move it when the building changes hands. Modern cryptography in institutions lives in that drawer more often than people admit. The hard question is not whether the organisation uses strong cryptography somewhere in its estate. The harder question is whether anyone can trace how trust actually moves through the place once the drawer is opened.

## Symmetric encryption and its operational limits

In December 2014, Sony Pictures Entertainment was still dealing with the aftermath of a destructive intrusion that exposed internal e-mails, unreleased material, personnel data, and the private machinery of an international media company. Public discussion often focused on embarrassment, attribution, and the theatrical ugliness of the leaked correspondence. A quieter lesson sat underneath. The problem was not that modern symmetric encryption had suddenly failed in mathematical disgrace. The problem was that once attackers reached the right systems, the surrounding controls that should have limited access, protected keys, and contained damage did not hold with enough discipline. The safe door may be excellent. The room still matters.

That is the awkward truth about symmetric encryption in institutional life. It is frequently the strongest part of the arrangement and still not the deciding part. Modern symmetric algorithms, when properly implemented and used with suitable key sizes and modes, have earned their reputation for strength through years of scrutiny. They are fast, efficient, and deeply embedded in storage systems, network protocols, databases, mobile devices, and cloud services. Much of the digital world depends on them without ceremony. Yet that very success encourages a bad habit. Institutions begin to talk as though "using strong encryption" settles the matter, when in practice the hardest questions begin one step earlier and end one step later: where the key is created, where it is stored, how it moves, who can reach it, what the endpoint can reveal, and what happens when ordinary operations make secrecy less important than convenience.

The phrase *encrypted storage* offers a good example of this slippage. It sounds conclusive. A laptop is encrypted. A backup volume is encrypted.

A cloud bucket is encrypted. The phrase gives reassurance because it points to a technical state. But storage encryption is only as meaningful as the conditions under which the decryption key can be invoked. Show the scene and the problem becomes embarrassingly concrete. A server stores sensitive data on an encrypted disk, but the application server that needs the data also stores the decryption key in a configuration file readable to too many administrators. Or the key sits inside a memory space that malware can scrape once the machine is running. Or the same privileged service account can read both the data and the secret needed to unlock it. Name the concept and the failure becomes clearer: co-location of asset and access. Explain it, and one sees why the encryption itself may remain perfectly sound while the overall result is weak. If the burglar finds the key taped inside the cabinet, the cabinet is not meaningfully secured.

This is why symmetric encryption should be understood less as a wall than as a controlled relationship between data, key, and environment. The mathematics protects against certain classes of attack with extraordinary effectiveness. The environment decides whether those protections survive contact with real operations. A key must live somewhere. It may live in application memory, a hardware module, an operating system keystore, a backup system, a container secret store, a mobile device enclave, or a password-derived form that depends on human habits. Each location changes the exposure. Each movement changes it again. When an institution says its data is encrypted, the serious listener should immediately ask a less glamorous question: encrypted for whom, and under what path of access? The answer usually lies not in the algorithm name but in a diagram of workflows, permissions, and failure modes.

The attraction of symmetric cryptography has always been partly practical. It gives institutions a rare thing in security: high performance without ruinous overhead. Bulk data can be protected quickly. Storage volumes can be sealed without paralysing systems. Network sessions can carry large amounts of information with modest computational cost once keys are agreed. This operational efficiency is one reason symmetric encryption remains foundational even in systems that rely on public key methods for exchange and identity. The secret, once established, does the hard labour. But efficiency has a political side inside organisations. Fast, integrated, low-friction protection becomes easy to mandate and easy to misunderstand. Executives hear that encryption is enabled by default. Auditors record that data at rest is encrypted. Procurement teams accept the control as present. Meanwhile the labour of key governance, endpoint hardening, access separation, recovery procedure, and logging discipline remains underfunded because it feels secondary to the elegant success of the cryptography itself.

A common institutional fiction follows. Good crypto equals good security. It does not. Good crypto can coexist with dreadful security outcomes if the surrounding system makes key access too easy, key rotation too rare, or endpoint compromise too rewarding. Consider the routine pattern of a laptop protected by full-disk encryption. If the machine is powered off and the adversary steals only the storage device, the protection may work exactly as intended. If the same machine is seized while logged in, infected while in use, or accessed through a poorly managed administrative tool, the disk encryption contributes very little to the immediate defence. The distinction is neither subtle nor trivial. It reveals what the control was designed to do. Symmetric encryption can protect data against theft of media, offline analysis, unauthorised interception, and some forms of exposure. It cannot rescue a live, compromised endpoint from itself.

That endpoint problem deserves more honesty than it usually receives. Institutions like infrastructure controls because they scale and because they can be purchased in quantities suitable for governance. Endpoints are stubbornly human and operational. They are where users reuse passwords, install unvetted software, click links, grant permissions, ignore prompts, carry devices across borders, connect to unmanaged networks, and leave sessions open at the worst possible moment. They are also where malware can scrape memory, hijack authorised processes, exfiltrate plaintext, and exploit trusted applications after decryption has already happened. The endpoint is where the safe is opened because the business must continue. Once that fact is accepted, a large amount of empty rhetoric about encryption dissolves. Data does not remain encrypted in any meaningful sense when a trusted system must read it to perform its function. The question shifts from whether the cipher is strong to whether the circumstances of use are controlled tightly enough to keep the moment of reading from becoming the moment of loss.

A second example helps sharpen the issue. In 2013, after the disclosure of classified material by Edward Snowden, public reporting drew attention to the ways data could be protected in transit or at rest while still being exposed through insider access, administrative privileges, and the practical arrangement of systems. One need not reduce that episode to a cryptographic case study to see the institutional point. Vast stores of sensitive information may be formally protected by strong technical controls, yet the decisive risk may lie with who can query systems, export records, or combine permissions across domains. The named concept here is privilege concentration. Explain it plainly and its force becomes obvious. If a trusted insider or a compromised administrator can reach the plaintext or the live keys through ordinary workflows, the strength of the underlying symmetric encryption is largely irrelevant to that pathway. The implication is not that encryption was wasted. It is that encryption belongs inside a broader discipline of segregation, monitoring, and access restraint rather than standing in for it.

Keys sit at the heart of this discipline, and they cause more trouble than institutional language usually admits. A symmetric system depends on a shared secret, which means that each additional location where the secret must exist increases the attack surface. Developers want convenience in deployment. Applications want unattended access. Backup tools want recoverability. Operations teams want resilience. Compliance officers want retention. Every one of those wants tends to multiply copies, paths, and exceptions. Soon, the same key may appear in a hardware module, an orchestration layer, a disaster recovery mechanism, a staging environment, and a human-maintained record designed for emergencies. Each copy has a rationale. Taken together, they may turn one secret into an administrative sprawl. The organisation does not lose because the algorithm is weak. It loses because key distribution quietly outruns key governance.

The brief example of encrypted storage with weak key handling captures this perfectly because it is so ordinary. A company encrypts its file store to meet internal policy and external expectations. The data volumes are indeed encrypted with strong symmetric algorithms. Yet the master keys are managed through a process that grants broad administrative access, stores recovery material with insufficient separation, and allows service accounts to retrieve secrets without tight contextual checks. The result looks compliant on paper. Under pressure, it behaves differently. A malicious insider with routine privileges, a compromised orchestration tool, or a successful intrusion into the management plane may gain access to both the encrypted data and the means to unlock it. Here, the visible decision is not mathematical but organisational: who is allowed to touch the key management layer, under what audit trail, and with what separation from the systems that hold the data? Bad answers turn a strong technical control into a decorative one.

Still, any serious account needs a limitation. Symmetric encryption does not deserve to be diminished simply because institutions misuse it. Many bad outcomes would be far worse without it. Lost devices, stolen drives, intercepted traffic, misdirected storage media, and offline forensic attempts can all be blunted decisively by properly deployed symmetric protection. Full-disk encryption on a laptop genuinely changes the consequences of theft if the machine is not already open. Encrypted backups can reduce exposure when physical media goes astray. Strong transport encryption can prevent easy interception on hostile networks. These are not marginal gains. They are substantial and often essential. The mistake lies not in trusting symmetric cryptography to do what it can do, but in asking it to answer threats it was never designed to solve.

That limitation, properly understood, strengthens rather than weakens the larger argument. It forces precision. One can praise the durability of symmetric algorithms while also insisting that deployment realities determine much of their practical value. The safe door really can be excellent. But the room must still be guarded, the key must still be governed, and the person entering the room must still be treated as part of the security problem rather than as a magical exception to it. This is not a romantic insight. It is institutional housekeeping of a very serious kind.

Another source of confusion lies in the word *shared*. In abstract form, a shared secret sounds efficient and elegant. In institutional form, it creates questions about scale and trust. How many services depend on the same secret? Which teams can rotate it? What breaks when rotation happens? Can one environment be cleanly separated from another, or do shortcuts allow development systems to resemble production too closely? Each answer produces a different level of risk. If too many systems depend on the same keying material, compromise spreads sideways. If rotation is painful, the key lives too long. If recovery is informal, emergency access becomes a permanent loophole. These are not exotic edge cases. They are exactly the kinds of daily compromises by which institutions quietly decide how much security they are willing to trade for continuity.

Memory adds another complication that receives too little plain speaking. Symmetric encryption protects stored or transmitted data only until a legitimate process needs the plaintext. At that point secrets may exist briefly in memory, caches, temporary files, logs, or debugging traces. A mature attacker knows this and adjusts accordingly. Why battle the mathematics when the running process is more generous? Show the scene and the problem becomes uncomfortably modern: an attacker lands on a server not to crack the database offline but to watch the application handle it live; a malicious tool waits for a user to unlock a device; a diagnostic dump captures material that was meant to be transient. Name the concept and the mechanism becomes clear: plaintext exposure during use. Explain it and the implication follows. Operational security depends not only on protecting data while sealed, but on limiting what happens when the seal is inevitably broken for legitimate work.

This is one reason hardware-backed key storage attracts institutions despite its own trade-offs. It promises to narrow some of the ugly pathways by making raw key extraction harder and by separating cryptographic operations from general-purpose computing environments. That promise is real, but it does not abolish the problem. A live endpoint can still ask the hardware to perform authorised operations. Poorly designed privilege models can still allow misuse. Recovery and lifecycle procedures can still create new exposures. The hardware may strengthen the safe door; it does not automatically make the room wise. Sensible institutions understand this. Less sensible ones buy secure hardware and then congratulate themselves as if procurement were a substitute for governance.

The broader point is almost irritating in its simplicity. Symmetric cryptography works. Institutions often do not. More precisely, institutions often treat the working mathematics as permission to neglect the messy conditions under which the mathematics must be used. They encrypt the store but spread the secrets. They protect the media but trust the endpoint too broadly. They celebrate efficiency while hiding the cost in silent privilege concentration and awkward recovery paths. Then, after a breach, they speak as though the failure came from nowhere.

The real test is harsher and more useful. When a system claims to protect sensitive data with strong symmetric encryption, can the organisation show where the keys live, how they move, who can reach them, how often they change, what the endpoint can reveal, and what remains protected after a trusted machine is compromised? If those answers are vague, the algorithm may still be excellent. The security promise is not.

## Public key cryptography and trust chains

In August 2011, browser makers began revoking trust in DigiNotar, a Dutch certificate authority, after fraudulent certificates had been issued and used in attacks that reportedly affected users in Iran. The visible outcome was both technical and humiliating. Browsers rejected certificates that had once passed without remark; users saw warnings where trust had previously been silent; a company that had occupied a critical place in the machinery of internet assurance collapsed into bankruptcy. Nothing about the mathematics of public key cryptography had suddenly become absurd. The failure ran through trust, not theory. A passport was forged. The border post mattered.

That is the central fact about asymmetric cryptography in institutions. Its genius lies in allowing strangers to establish secure relationships at scale without first sharing a secret by some secure prior channel. One key can be made public, another kept private, and from that split flows a remarkable range of practical effects: confidential exchange, digital signatures, software verification, device enrolment, secure browsing, remote administration, and much else besides. It solved a very large coordination problem. It did not abolish trust. It reorganised it. Where symmetric systems force attention onto the handling of a shared secret, public key systems force attention onto naming, issuance, validation, and the institutions that decide what a public key is *for* and *whom* it represents.

That shift is easy to miss because asymmetric cryptography often presents itself as pure elegance. The story sounds almost frictionless: publish a key, keep another secret, let mathematics do the rest. But mathematics alone cannot answer a stubborn practical question. When a browser sees a public key offered by a server, how does it know whether that key truly belongs to the entity named on the screen? When a phone receives a software update signed with a particular key, how does it know the signer is the one it should obey? When a ministry, bank, or hospital accepts a digital signature on a document, what binds that mathematical proof to a legal or institutional identity it is prepared to recognise? The answer, again and again, lies in a chain of delegated judgements. Someone issues a certificate. Someone defines a naming rule. Someone writes the code that decides which roots of trust are accepted. Someone chooses how strictly to validate, what to ignore, and how to respond when the chain looks wrong.

A certificate is not merely a cryptographic object. It is a statement backed by an institution. Show the scene and the point becomes less abstract. A browser receives a certificate saying that a public key corresponds to a named website. The certificate bears the signature of an authority already trusted by the browser. The browser checks the signature, checks dates, checks whether the name matches, and then, usually without ceremony, displays a reassuring padlock. Name the concept and one sees it clearly: delegated authentication. Explain it, and the comfort drains slightly from the story. The browser is not discovering trust from first principles. It is inheriting trust through a preloaded set of authorities, rules, and assumptions that users rarely inspect. The implication is strategic. Whoever governs those authorities and rules sits at a chokepoint where global digital confidence is translated into operational acceptance.

This is why naming matters so much. Public key cryptography can prove possession of a private key with exquisite precision. It cannot by itself tell a user whether the holder of that key is genuinely the bank, the government portal, the supplier, or the colleague the interface claims it to be. That apparently modest gap creates an enormous amount of institutional work. Domain names must be registered and controlled. Certificates must bind keys to those names. Validation software must decide what counts as a match, what counts as an error, and when users may proceed anyway. Every layer introduces discretion, and discretion introduces politics. Naming systems are not neutral labels floating above power. They are governed resources, allocated through procedures, disputes, contracts, and technical defaults. A forged identity online does not require breaking the algebra if one can bend the naming process or compromise the institutions that vouch for it.

The attraction of public key infrastructure, or PKI, lies precisely in its ability to make this apparatus scale. One does not need a bespoke trusted courier for every secure session between strangers. Instead, systems rely on chains: a root authority trusted in advance; subordinate authorities permitted to issue certificates; relying parties configured to validate according to specific rules. This arrangement is both ingenious and slightly unnerving. It allows billions of secure interactions that would otherwise be unmanageable. It also concentrates trust in institutions most users have never heard of until something goes wrong. The passport returns here. Travellers rarely think about the document-issuing authority when crossing a border smoothly. They think about it a great deal when the passport turns out to be forged, expired, or suddenly no longer recognised.

The DigiNotar case remains instructive because it exposed the chain in the moment of failure. Fraudulent certificates could impersonate trusted services because browsers, users, and systems relied on a common authority to vouch for identity. Once that authority proved compromised, the value of the certificates depended on how quickly major software vendors could revoke trust and distribute that decision across their products. Show the sequence and the strategic lesson emerges. A single institutional failure propagated through validation rules embedded in countless machines. Name the concept: trust concentration. Explain it, and the discomfort becomes earned. Public key systems distribute secure exchange widely while concentrating decisive authority in comparatively few trust anchors.

The implication is not that PKI is foolish. It is that scale has a political price. Large systems often purchase convenience by creating a few places where failure matters everywhere.

A second example shows the same point from another angle. In 2017, Google and other browser makers pressed for the distrust of Symantec's certificate authority business after longstanding concerns about certificate issuance practices. The eventual result was not a dramatic public collapse of web encryption. It was something more institutional: an orchestrated loss of trust, staged across browser releases, which forced website operators to replace certificates and adapt to a revised trust landscape. The mathematics of signatures remained intact. The strategic event lay in the governance of recognition. A certificate that had worked yesterday could become unacceptable tomorrow because the institutions controlling validation had judged the issuing chain no longer fit for confidence. That is asymmetric cryptography in practice. Trust is not merely computed; it is administered, contested, and withdrawn.

This should also temper romantic talk about decentralisation. Public key cryptography often sounds like a liberation from central control because any individual can generate a key pair. That is true at the level of arithmetic. It is much less true at the level of social acceptance. A self-generated key becomes useful only when others have reason to bind it to an identity, a role, or a service they already care about. Small communities can sometimes do this through direct exchange, manual verification, or tightly controlled internal systems. At internet scale, however, some structure of delegated trust almost always reappears. Someone has to be believed about names. Someone has to ship the software defaults. Someone has to decide which failures are tolerable and which are disqualifying. The dream of trustless operation turns out, in most institutions, to mean trust relocated out of sight.

That relocation has operational consequences. Validation rules sound dry until one sees how much depends on them. Should a system accept a certificate signed with an older algorithm for compatibility? Should it allow a mismatch in one field because legacy devices still depend on it? Should it fail closed, denying access when validation cannot be completed, or fail open to preserve continuity? Each answer produces a different security posture. More importantly, each answer reflects an institutional preference disguised as a technical setting. A finance platform may tolerate less ambiguity than a public information service. A national security system may prefer breakage to silent acceptance. A commercial platform under pressure to reduce user friction may make different trade-offs. Public key cryptography creates the grammar in which these decisions are made. The institution still chooses the sentence.

This is why certificates and naming systems become strategic chokepoints. They control entry into trusted relationships. If a hostile actor compromises a certificate authority, coerces an issuing process, exploits a naming dispute, or takes advantage of lax validation, the result can be broad impersonation without the noisy labour of breaking every endpoint individually. If a defender controls major browsers, operating systems, mobile platforms, or corporate trust stores, that defender can also shape who remains legible as trustworthy. The chokepoint cuts both ways. It can enable scale and discipline; it can also magnify mistakes, power imbalances, and political pressure. Public key systems therefore live in an uncomfortable zone between technical necessity and institutional vulnerability.

Still, any serious account needs a limitation. Not every use of public key cryptography depends on the sprawling public web PKI model. Internal enterprise systems can pin specific certificates, manage private trust hierarchies, or bind keys to devices and identities under tighter governance. Some specialised environments accept reduced flexibility precisely to avoid broad dependence on public certificate authorities. Peer-to-peer tools may rely on manual key verification or narrower trust communities. These arrangements can reduce some of the risks associated with large, shared trust chains. They deserve that credit.

Yet the limitation does not weaken the larger point. It refines it. Even in more controlled settings, trust remains delegated through institutions, procedures, and software choices rather than conjured directly from mathematics. A pinned certificate still depends on who pinned it, how updates occur, and what happens when the key must change. A private corporate PKI still depends on issuance discipline, revocation procedures, hardware protection, identity proofing, and the authority structures governing administrators. Manual key verification still depends on how humans compare information and whether they can detect interference. The form of delegation changes. Delegation itself does not disappear.

One reason institutions underestimate this is that asymmetric systems are so good at making complexity disappear from the user's view. The browser padlock, the signed document, the secure update, the enrolled device - all give the impression that identity has been settled by a neat, invisible mechanism. Users are not asked to see the root stores, certificate policies, intermediate authorities, validation exceptions, or naming dependencies beneath the surface. That invisibility is a feature of usability. It is also a hazard of governance. What cannot be seen is easily mistaken for what does not need governing. Then a failure occurs, and an organisation discovers that its confidence rested on software defaults, vendor decisions, and trust chains it never fully mapped.

The deeper strategic issue is not simply that trust can fail, but that trust can be made to travel farther than responsibility. A certificate authority may issue for systems far removed from the communities affected by its mistake. A browser vendor may change trust decisions for millions of users who have no practical alternative. A cloud platform may define identity relationships that reshape what enterprises consider acceptable authentication. Asymmetric cryptography enables this scale because it is efficient and elegant. Institutional life then turns that efficiency into dependence. A choice made in one layer of the chain becomes law-like in another.

That dependence matters even more when one remembers that trust chains must change over time. Certificates expire. Authorities are distrusted. Algorithms age. Private keys are lost, stolen, rotated, or replaced. Mergers scramble identity boundaries. Legacy devices keep old assumptions alive long after prudence has moved on. Public key cryptography therefore does more than create secure exchange at scale. It creates a continuing obligation to maintain the legitimacy of the exchange. Every certificate issued is also a promise about future revocation, future recognition, and future migration. A chain that authenticates beautifully on a quiet day may become brittle the moment the institution behind it has to change anything substantial.

The passport image returns one last time because it remains stubbornly useful. A passport works not because paper and ink are magical, but because a traveller, an issuing authority, a border official, and a larger system of recognition all cooperate under shared rules. Public key cryptography brings that same structure into digital life, only faster, more invisible, and often more centralised than people realise. The pressing question is not whether the mathematics can support trust. It plainly can. The harder question is whether the institutions within the chain are disciplined enough, transparent enough, and replaceable enough to keep that trust from becoming the single, narrow bridge on which too much of the modern world now stands.

## Hashing, signatures, and permanence

In June 2017, the researchers Marc Stevens, Pierre Karpman, and Thomas Peyrin demonstrated a practical collision attack against SHA-1 in work publicly branded SHAttered, using two distinct PDF files that produced the same hash. Google and CWI Amsterdam announced the result after years of warning that SHA-1 was nearing the end of its safe life. The immediate world did not collapse. Browsers did not melt. Contracts did not vanish. Yet something important became harder to ignore. A fingerprint long treated as reliable had acquired a visible crack.

That crack matters because hashing and signatures govern a different kind of security promise from short-lived confidentiality. A secret message may need protection only until its usefulness decays. A signature on a software update, a legal record, a medical archive, or a government directive may need to remain credible for years, sometimes decades. The clock runs differently here. When integrity and non-repudiation fail, the damage does not consist merely in someone reading what they should not. It consists in the possibility that what was accepted as authentic can no longer be trusted to mean what it once meant. The seal breaks later.

Hash functions sit near the heart of this arrangement because they compress data into a short digest that acts as a practical fingerprint. Change the file, and the digest should change unpredictably. Sign that digest with a private key, and one obtains a compact way to attest that a holder approved a particular document, package, or message of that key. This machinery is wonderfully efficient. It allows software distributors to sign updates and archives to record evidence, devices to verify firmware, and institutions to move trust at speed without manually inspecting every bit. But efficiency has its own price. The more widely a single hash or signature scheme is used, the more attractive it becomes as a target and the more consequential its ageing becomes. One cracked seal can imperil an entire room of records.

The distinction between confidentiality and integrity is often blurred by people who assume all cryptography protects content in roughly the same way. It does not. A confidential message can lose value after a meeting ends, a payment clears, or a negotiation closes. Integrity claims often age far more slowly. If a document was signed ten years ago, the question of whether that signature remains credible may still shape a court case, an audit, a procurement dispute, a treaty archive, or a software supply chain. That is why hashing and signatures are peculiarly exposed to retroactive consequences. A future attack on a signature scheme can travel backwards into the evidential status of old material. The problem is not merely whether an attacker can forge something *today*. It is whether doubt about past authenticity can be made plausible enough to corrode trust *tomorrow*.

A software update offers the clearest illustration because it converts abstract assurance into a machine's decision to obey. A vendor builds a package, computes its hash, signs that digest, and ships the update. The receiving device checks the signature and, if all appears valid, installs the code with elevated trust. Show the scene and the significance becomes almost embarrassingly direct. The signature is not a decorative flourish. It is the gatekeeper between code and execution. Name the concept and the danger becomes legible: delegated integrity. Explain it, and one sees why update signing can become a single point of trust. If the signing key is stolen, if the validation rules are weak, or if the underlying signature scheme later becomes forgeable in practical conditions, the attacker does not need to compromise every endpoint individually. The trust decision has already been centralised for them.

The 2020 SolarWinds compromise remains a harsh reminder of this logic, even though the incident was not caused by a public mathematical break in the signature scheme itself. Malicious code entered software updates distributed through a trusted channel, and organisations that had reason to trust signed packages received poisoned software under the appearance of normality. The relevant lesson here is not that signatures failed to matter. It is that signatures matter so much that their surrounding governance becomes strategically decisive. A valid signature can certify a betrayal if the build process, signing environment, or issuance control is compromised. That is the first uncomfortable truth. A broken signature scheme is disastrous, but a perfectly sound scheme wrapped around a corrupted process can be disastrous too. The seal on the envelope may be genuine even when the wrong letter was placed inside.

This is where hashing enters more subtly. Hash functions help make digital integrity practical because they allow systems to compare concise digests rather than entire documents. They also underpin structures far beyond signatures: file verification, certificate mechanisms, transparency logs, content-addressed storage, password protection systems, and archival workflows. Their main security property, in this context, is collision resistance: the difficulty of finding two different inputs that produce the same output. When that property weakens enough, confidence erodes in stages. The earliest stage may not permit catastrophic forgeries at scale, but it introduces doubt, migration pressure, and awkward edge cases. SHA-

1's long retreat showed this pattern. Long before the 2017 demonstration, serious institutions had already started to move away because the prospect of future collisions was no longer an academic curiosity. The implication was plain. When a fingerprint no longer uniquely names the file, old assumptions about evidence and authorship begin to fray even before disaster becomes routine.

The legal and archival consequences are particularly severe because they depend on long continuity rather than one-off success. A signed contract, a timestamped filing, an archived intelligence report, or a set of medical records may need not just confidentiality but durable evidential weight. Non-repudiation, the claim that a signer cannot plausibly deny having signed, sounds crisp in theory. In practice it rests on a stack of conditions: the private key was under the signer's control, the signature algorithm remained trustworthy, the certificate chain remained meaningful, the timestamping process was reliable, the surrounding records were preserved, and no later technical change made forgery or ambiguity realistic enough to upset judgement. Remove any one of those supports and the legal or institutional force of the signature may weaken. Remove several and the historical record becomes negotiable in precisely the way a serious archive is meant to resist.

This helps explain why future attacks on public key methods disturb signature systems so deeply. A short-lived confidential session can sometimes be protected by reducing exposure time, limiting retention, or switching protocols. A signature on a document or archive has a more awkward burden. It may need to remain verifiable by third parties long after the original infrastructure has aged, the issuing organisations have changed, and the algorithms have fallen out of fashion. The signature becomes a promise aimed at the future. If the cryptographic assumptions under it decay faster than the institutional life of the record, then today's perfectly valid attestation may become tomorrow's dubious relic. That is not science fiction. It is a structural mismatch between the lifespan of evidence and the lifespan of technical trust.

A credible limitation belongs here. Not every weakening of a hash or signature scheme instantly invalidates all prior signed material. Institutions can and often do mitigate ageing through timestamping, countersigning, archival renewal, layered verification, and migration to stronger algorithms before complete collapse. A system may preserve confidence in older signatures if it can show that they were created at a time when the scheme remained trustworthy and were then re-anchored under stronger protections. This matters. Otherwise the subject invites melodrama, and melodrama is a poor analyst. Digital trust seldom dies in one theatrical moment. More often it decays through a period of contested adequacy, partial migration, and uneven institutional adaptation.

Yet that concession should not soften the central point. It sharpens it. The need for archival renewal and layered verification proves that permanence is not a natural property of digital signatures. It is a maintained condition. Somebody must monitor algorithm ageing, re-sign critical records, preserve timestamps, manage certificate chains, and decide which artefacts deserve this extra labour. These are governance decisions disguised as technical housekeeping. A ministry, court, university, software vendor, or bank that ignores them is not, by default, preserving non-repudiation. It is borrowing confidence from the past and hoping the bill arrives after the responsible staff have retired.

The phrase *single point of trust* deserves careful treatment because it is often used lazily. Every complex institution contains concentrations of authority; the question is whether they are visible, controlled, and replaceable. Update signing infrastructure is a particularly vivid example because it collapses many judgements into a single machine-validated act. Was the code built from the right source? Was the release process clean? Was the key protected? Is the certificate chain still accepted? Did the endpoint validate properly? If the signature checks out, the system usually proceeds. That is efficiency of a high order, and it is also a concentration of risk. Attackers notice such things with predatory patience. They do not need to subvert every device when they can study the machinery that authorises many devices at once.

The same pattern appears in contracts and records, though less dramatically than in software. A signed board resolution, a procurement authorisation, or a chain of custody document may look settled because the signature verifies under current tools. But verification is not the whole story. The institution must also preserve the context that makes verification meaningful. Which certificate authority vouched for the signer's identity? What was the status of that certificate at the relevant time? Was the key held securely? Was the timestamp reliable? Could later weaknesses in the hash function create plausible ambiguity about the underlying document? Each question attaches a visible operational burden to the abstraction of trust. Good institutions preserve those answers. Weak ones assume the signature will keep speaking for itself forever, which is a curious superstition dressed in technical language.

Hashing introduces another, quieter problem: the habit of treating digests as timeless identifiers without attention to their future fragility. Repositories, archives, and forensic workflows often use hashes as shorthand for identity because they are compact and machine-friendly. A file matched to a known digest feels settled. But a digest is only as authoritative as the continued soundness of the hash function and the care with which the mapping was maintained. Once a function weakens, its old fingerprints do not instantly become useless, but they stop being effortlessly unquestionable. The sealed envelope has not opened; it has become easier to doubt who sealed it and whether another envelope might now wear the same wax mark. That shift from certainty to contestability is often the real strategic damage.

The contrast with short-lived confidentiality now becomes starker. If a private conversation from this afternoon leaks next month, the harm may still be serious, but its relevance is bounded by context and time. If an update-signing scheme, archival signature process, or document hash used across years becomes suspect, entire classes of prior assurance may need re-examination. The scale is different. So is the political character of the damage. Broken secrecy embarrasses and exposes. Broken integrity destabilises authority. It forces organisations to revisit what was accepted, installed, certified, authorised, or preserved under assumptions no longer beyond dispute. That is why signature infrastructure often deserves more strategic attention than it receives in public debate, which remains oddly enchanted by the drama of confidentiality breaches while neglecting the slower corrosion of authenticity and evidence.

None of this means that institutions should treat all old signatures as doomed or all hash ageing as catastrophic. It means they should stop pretending that cryptographic permanence is self-sustaining. The more a system depends on signatures to prove origin, preserve archives, distribute software, or bind legal acts to responsible parties, the more it depends on a chain of maintenance that stretches far beyond the moment of signing. Algorithms must age well enough. Keys must remain governable. Records must remain interpretable. Migration paths must exist before panic does. The trust conveyed by a signature is never only mathematical. It is historical.

The sealed envelope returns here for one last reason. People assume the danger lies in someone steaming it open. Sometimes it does. But an older and nastier danger lies in a future where nobody can agree whether the seal was genuine in the first place. That is the test hashing and signatures impose on institutions: not simply whether they can certify a document or an update today, but whether they can keep that certification intelligible and credible across the years in which incentives, algorithms, and adversaries all continue to change. The uneasy question is not whether a signature verifies at this moment. It is whether the institution has any real plan for the day verification alone stops being enough.

## Standards, libraries, and default security

In April 2014, administrators across the world were still discovering how deeply the Heartbleed vulnerability had cut through their systems. The flaw sat in OpenSSL, a widely used cryptographic library that had become so ordinary, so infrastructural, that many institutions depended on it without much noticing until the trouble arrived. The visible outcome was not merely a bug report. It was a scramble: certificates replaced, passwords reset, servers patched, dependency maps built in haste because too few organisations knew exactly where the library lived in their estates. One line of code had not undone cryptography itself. It had revealed something more awkward. The lock was common property.

That is often how default security works. Most institutions do not design their cryptographic posture from first principles, selecting algorithms and validation rules with the cold deliberation of a research lab. They inherit it through software libraries, operating system settings, protocol defaults, cloud services, hardware accelerators, developer frameworks, vendor appliances, and compliance templates. The result is not necessarily poor. Often it is the only reason security works at scale at all. But it means that what counts as normal security is usually not chosen afresh by the organisation using it. It arrives preassembled, carrying other people's assumptions about performance, compatibility, trust, and risk.

This matters because the word *standard* contains two different promises, and they do not always sit comfortably together. A standard suggests public scrutiny, collective testing, interoperability, and a shared language through which systems can communicate without bespoke negotiation. It also suggests inertia. Once a protocol, library, or suite of defaults becomes widespread, changing it grows expensive. Legacy systems object. Vendors delay. Auditors need new guidance. Developers fear breakage more than they fear distant compromise. Show the scene and the tension becomes plain: a large institution knows a newer, stronger option exists, but continues with the older one because too many systems, contracts, and habits depend on the old pattern. Name the concept and it sharpens: standardisation as lock-in. Explain it, and the strategic implication follows. A standard can be both a public good and a brake on adaptation.

Security practice, then, is shaped less by what institutions *could* choose than by what their defaults quietly choose for them. A developer reaches for a familiar library because it is already bundled, already documented, already accepted by the build system. A systems engineer leaves a protocol setting unchanged because the vendor warns that stricter validation may disrupt older clients. A procurement officer approves a product because it cites recognised standards and passes known certification hurdles. None of these decisions is absurd. Together they form the real security posture of the institution. The abstraction of trust becomes visible behaviour: a software package imported without close inspection, a cipher suite left enabled for compatibility, a certificate validation rule inherited from an upstream platform, a library update postponed because the maintenance window is politically harder to win than the security case is to articulate.

Heartbleed remains important not because it proved standards are futile, but because it exposed the difference between using standard cryptographic components and understanding one's dependency on them. OpenSSL was common precisely because common tools reduce cost, accelerate deployment, and make encryption broadly available. That is a genuine achievement. Yet when the flaw became public, many organisations discovered they could not answer elementary questions quickly. Which servers relied on it? Which products embedded it indirectly? Which keys and certificates might have been exposed? Which suppliers had incorporated it into devices that could not easily be patched? The named concept here is dependency opacity. Explain it plainly and the lesson bites. Widely used standards and libraries spread security benefits efficiently, but they also spread uncertainty efficiently when something inside them fails. The implication is administrative as much as technical. Institutions that cannot map their inherited defaults do not truly know what their secure posture consists of.

A second example shows the same structure from another angle. In March 2021, Microsoft disclosed severe vulnerabilities affecting on-premises Exchange Server deployments, and organisations using those products had to patch urgently while also determining whether attackers had already exploited the flaws. This was not a story about cryptographic standards alone. It was a story about the power of default infrastructure inside institutions. A platform trusted as routine office machinery became a locus of concentrated risk because so many organisations depended on common software and common administrative assumptions. The visible behaviours were familiar: emergency guidance issued, vendor advisories studied, administrators searching logs, external responders brought in. The concept is shared operational dependence. Explain it, and the larger point emerges. Institutions often imagine their security posture as proprietary to themselves when much of it is borrowed wholesale from common components maintained elsewhere. The implication is uncomfortable. A weakness in a default can turn many separate organisations into one large target class.

This borrowed posture is not merely a technical fact. It has political consequences. Standards confer more than interoperability; they confer agenda-setting power. The body that defines acceptable algorithms, the platform vendor that ships the dominant defaults, the cloud provider that decides which cipher suites and key management options are easiest to use, the maintainer community that decides when an older primitive is deprecated - all help determine what other institutions can adopt without unusual cost. Engineering convenience therefore acquires a geopolitical edge. An organisation that controls a widely used library or protocol implementation can influence the cadence of migration, the terms of compatibility, and the practical meaning of "secure enough" across borders. This is not usually exercised as open coercion. More often it arrives through roadmaps, deprecation schedules, procurement expectations, platform support, and the subtle force of what comes pre-installed.

The lock being common property has another consequence: security becomes collective before institutions are ready to admit it. One organisation may spend carefully on cryptographic review and still depend on an upstream library maintained by a small team elsewhere. Another may comply with every formal requirement available to it and still inherit an outdated validation rule because a dominant vendor has not altered the default. Standards and libraries distribute competence unevenly. They allow smaller actors to benefit from knowledge they could never generate alone, which is one of their civilising virtues. But they also create strata of dependency in which the judgement of a few is amplified through the systems of many. The quiet politics of defaults begins here.

Consider what happens when a standard begins to age. Rarely does the world pause while everyone migrates neatly to a replacement. Instead, a long and uneven transition begins. New guidance appears. Some browsers, libraries, and operating systems tighten defaults. Large providers move earlier because they can absorb disruption. Smaller organisations lag because they depend on older devices, brittle software, or cautious procurement cycles. For a time, the standard is both accepted and suspect.

Administrators face a choice that is less technical than it sounds: preserve compatibility or enforce stricter trust. This is where "standard" shows its double face most clearly. The very thing that once gave confidence - widespread acceptance - now slows the withdrawal of confidence because so much remains built upon it.

That tension can produce bad habits of mind. Institutions start mistaking commonness for safety. They assume that if a library is widely used, someone else must have checked it thoroughly enough; if a protocol has a standard number and a familiar acronym, it must be mature enough to trust indefinitely; if a vendor default ships in millions of devices, changing it must be riskier than leaving it alone. Sometimes those assumptions hold well enough. Often they merely postpone responsibility. A familiar default can be well-reviewed, badly implemented, incompletely understood, or politically hard to replace. Those conditions are not mutually exclusive. They frequently coexist, which is one reason cryptographic governance produces such strange mixtures of elegance and squalor.

A credible limitation belongs here. Common standards and widely used libraries remain indispensable. Without them, secure communication would fragment into local improvisations, proprietary schemes, and repeated amateur errors of exactly the kind security history punishes. Shared standards allow review communities to form, interoperability to function, and vulnerabilities to be recognised in common rather than rediscovered separately by every institution. They make good practice portable. That matters enormously. One should be wary of any rhetoric that romanticises bespoke security as though uniqueness were a substitute for scrutiny. Custom cryptography and private protocols have a habit of becoming private embarrassments.

Yet that concession does not weaken the argument. It clarifies it. The problem is not standardisation itself but the institutional fantasy that standards remove the need for judgement. They do not. They relocate judgement into committees, maintainers, vendors, protocol designers, certification bodies, and default settings that most end users never see. A prudent institution therefore needs more than compliance with standards; it needs some grasp of how those standards are implemented, updated, inherited, and eventually replaced. When that grasp is absent, "using standard cryptography" becomes a talismanic phrase doing too much work.

Libraries make this especially plain because they embody security choices in code that developers consume almost as a raw material. A library decides which algorithms are easy to call, which parameters are discouraged, which legacy options remain available, which errors are recoverable, and how aggressively unsafe behaviour is fenced off. A well-designed library can save thousands of teams from subtle mistakes. A poorly designed or weakly maintained one can propagate them. The abstraction of risk here attaches to a concrete decision: which API a programmer reaches for, which option is enabled by default, whether the code fails loudly when validation is incomplete or quietly attempts compatibility. Many security outcomes begin in such apparently small interface choices. The politics of standards often enters the world through developer convenience.

The same is true of protocols. A protocol is not simply a technical agreement about message formats and cryptographic handshakes. It is a settlement between competing priorities: speed, compatibility, computational cost, privacy, auditability, recoverability, and administrative control. Once embedded in products and habits, that settlement becomes hard to revisit. Organisations build processes around it. Training materials assume it. Appliances support one version and not another. Older devices keep speaking the older dialect. A protocol, then, is never just a neutral pipe. It is an institutional memory encoded in software. Change the protocol and one quickly discovers how much of the surrounding world was relying on its old assumptions.

This is where the geopolitical layer becomes impossible to ignore. Control over standards bodies, reference implementations, hardware support, and platform defaults can shape the timing and direction of cryptographic change globally. A state or dominant firm does not need to dictate every outcome openly to exercise influence. It can shape which proposals gain legitimacy, which implementations become practically available, which certification paths are easiest, and which migrations are economically tolerable. For smaller countries, smaller firms, and public institutions with modest technical capacity, this means that strategic dependence may arrive under the bland language of interoperability and vendor support. The system works, but not on neutral ground.

The most revealing question, then, is rarely "Do we use standard cryptography?" Nearly everyone serious does. The sharper question is which standards, which libraries, whose defaults, under whose timetable, and with what room to dissent or migrate when confidence changes. The lock may be common property, but that does not mean everyone holds equal influence over who forges it, who repairs it, or when the whole building must accept a new one. That asymmetry is the quiet pressure building beneath ordinary engineering choices, and it will only become clearer as institutions discover how much of their security has always been written elsewhere.

## Where cryptography meets governance

In May 2021, Colonial Pipeline shut down operations after a ransomware incident that quickly became a national political story in the United States. Public attention turned to fuel supply, emergency response, and the spectacle of a private company suddenly cast as critical infrastructure in full view of government and markets. Yet beneath the headlines sat a quieter institutional fact. Decisions about access, segmentation, recovery, backups, vendor relationships, and the handling of sensitive systems had never belonged to one technical team alone. When the crisis arrived, the question was not simply whether the company used encryption or modern security tools. It was who had been allowed to decide what counted as acceptable risk before the emergency made those decisions visible.

The contract was the first clue.

Cryptography enters most institutions not as a philosophical commitment to secrecy or trust, but as a clause in a purchase, a control in an audit, a requirement in a tender, a standard in a procurement framework, or a feature in a product comparison. One team asks whether data will be encrypted at rest. Another asks whether certificates can be managed centrally. A legal office asks whether the supplier meets regulatory expectations. Finance asks what the secure option costs relative to the ordinary one. Operations asks whether stronger controls will slow service or break compatibility. A board asks for reassurance in language that can fit a paper pack. By the time the technology is deployed, its meaning has already been translated several times across people with different fears, incentives, and time horizons. That translation is governance.

This is why cryptographic choices cannot be understood as purely technical selections among algorithms and protocols. The visible act may look narrow: a key management service chosen, a hardware module approved, a signing process outsourced, a retention policy retained, a vendor default accepted. The named concept is decision rights. Explain it plainly, and the fog lifts. Decision rights concern who has authority to choose, approve, fund, delay, override, or inherit a security-relevant outcome. The implication is sharper than most institutional language admits. Security failures often emerge not because nobody cared, but because nobody owned the whole chain of choices that made the failure possible.

Procurement sits close to the centre of this chain because it turns abstract security aspirations into binding dependencies. Show the scene and the pattern becomes familiar. A public agency or large company issues a request for proposals requiring encryption, compliance with recognised standards, support for identity federation, and secure logging. Vendors respond with certifications, feature matrices, and assurance language polished for selection panels. The product that wins may indeed provide strong cryptographic functions. Yet the procurement itself may never ask whether the chosen design supports rapid algorithm migration, separates key custody properly, or allows the customer to audit critical cryptographic events independently of the supplier. The institution buys what it can compare. It often leaves unbought what it cannot easily score. The result is not irrational. It is governance under measurement pressure. The implication is that procurement often fixes tomorrow's security options long before tomorrow's threat model is taken seriously.

Compliance sharpens the problem in a different way. A compliance regime can be enormously useful. It turns vague good intentions into routines that can be inspected, attested, and enforced. It gives organisations a minimum floor. It creates a common language across sectors. But compliance also encourages substitution: the organisation starts treating proof of control as if it were control itself. A system passes review because encryption is present, keys are rotated on schedule, privileged access is documented, incident procedures exist, and vendors are certified. Each item may be true. The broader arrangement may still be brittle. A recovery key may be accessible to too many administrators. A signing process may depend on a small vendor team that nobody has stress-tested. A critical certificate may be accepted by legacy devices that cannot be updated quickly. Compliance records the existence of governance artefacts; it does not guarantee that the underlying decision rights are coherent. That distinction matters because institutions often discover it only in crisis, when documents are plentiful and authority is suddenly unclear.

A useful example came in 2017, when the Equifax breach exposed the personal information of a vast number of individuals and triggered investigations, public fury, executive fallout, and prolonged legal consequences. Much discussion focused on patching failures and neglected maintenance, correctly so. But the episode also showed how security governance fractures across ordinary corporate structures. Vulnerability management, data retention, legacy applications, third-party components, certificate handling, executive oversight, and legal accountability did not belong to one clean chain of command. The visible outcome was a breach. The governance lesson was more corrosive. Institutions frequently distribute responsibility for cryptographic and security-relevant choices across procurement, IT operations, software teams, legal functions, risk committees, and senior management without ensuring that those groups share a common picture of what they are protecting, for how long, and against whom. The named concept here is fragmented accountability. Explain it, and the implications are hard to ignore. When many parties hold pieces of the problem, each can act responsibly within its own remit while the institution as a whole drifts into irresponsibility.

This fragmentation becomes especially acute around keys, certificates, and identity systems. A developer team may integrate a cloud-based key management service because it reduces engineering burden. Security architects may approve the general pattern. Procurement may negotiate the commercial terms. Legal teams may review data processing implications. Operations staff may manage access roles. Internal audit may test whether key rotation occurs. Yet a simple question can still go unanswered: who decides, under pressure, whether a compromised key is rotated immediately at the cost of service disruption, or left in place until a maintenance window? That is not a cryptographic question in the narrow sense. It is a governance question disguised as a technical one. The institution must decide which costs it is willing to bear, who can authorise them, and what evidence counts as sufficient to act. If those answers are vague, good mathematics does not save the situation. Authority arrives too late.

This is where a vocabulary of institutional mapping becomes necessary. Not because jargon is attractive, but because precision prevents polite confusion. One useful distinction is between decision makers, implementers, and relying parties. The decision maker approves or mandates the control. The implementer builds, configures, or operates it. The relying party depends on it without necessarily understanding its details: a business unit trusting signed updates, a hospital relying on device certificates, a regulator relying on audit records, a citizen trusting a government portal. These roles often overlap, but not neatly. Another distinction lies between ownership of assets and ownership of mechanisms. A department may own the data but not the encryption service protecting it. A platform team may own the certificate infrastructure but not the business consequences of revocation.

A procurement office may own the supplier relationship but not the operational pain caused by a poorly timed migration. Once these lines are drawn, the central problem looks less mysterious. Institutions do not fail only because they lack controls. They fail because the right to choose, the burden to operate, and the exposure to consequence are routinely separated.

A second example helps show how this separation becomes strategic. In 2024, the publication of the first final post-quantum cryptography standards by NIST made it harder for large institutions to treat migration questions as a distant abstraction. One did not need to predict imminent cryptanalytic upheaval to see the governance problem. A bank, ministry, cloud provider, or university could not respond merely by instructing engineers to adopt new algorithms. Procurement would need to demand vendor support. Architects would need inventories. Operations teams would need testing windows. Legal and risk teams would need language for explaining residual uncertainty. Boards would need to approve expenditure before any public emergency compelled them to. The visible event was a standards milestone. The governance implication was larger. Readiness depends on whether an institution can align decision rights across teams that do not normally think in the same time horizon. Without that alignment, "migration" becomes a slogan attached to a budget dispute.

Still, a limitation deserves respect. Not every organisation can build perfect governance around cryptography. Smaller institutions live with constrained budgets, thin specialist staffing, inherited systems, and dependencies they did not choose. A local authority, hospital, or university may rely on common procurement frameworks and managed services precisely because doing everything in-house would be reckless. In such settings, distributed responsibility is not always a failure. It is often the only workable model. Centralisation can produce its own hazards: bottlenecks, brittle control, and an illusion that a single security office can meaningfully govern every detail of a complex estate.

That concession, however, should not be mistaken for absolution. The issue is not whether all authority must be centralised. It is whether authority is legible. A modest institution can still know who approves cryptographic exceptions, who controls key recovery, who accepts vendor claims, who owns retention schedules, who decides during a certificate incident, and who carries responsibility for migration when standards change. Large institutions often struggle more, not less, because scale allows ambiguity to masquerade as sophistication. Every committee believes the matter has an owner somewhere else. Every owner assumes the committee has harmonised the risk. The contract sits signed. The key lives somewhere. The audit passes. Then the first serious disruption asks a question nobody has rehearsed: who, exactly, gets to decide now?

Accountability complicates this further because it points in several directions at once. Legal accountability concerns obligations under regulation, contract, and public duty. Operational accountability concerns continuity, safety, and recoverability. Political accountability concerns public trust and reputational consequences. Technical accountability concerns whether the control actually performs as claimed. These forms of accountability do not always align. A legal team may prefer retention because documentation protects against future disputes. A security team may prefer deletion because retention enlarges exposure. A business unit may prefer broad access because service speed matters. A risk committee may prefer a familiar vendor because the paperwork is easier to defend. Each position can sound reasonable when voiced in isolation. Governance begins where isolation ends.

The contract returns here because it is rarely just commercial paper. It is a distribution map of power. Who has the right to audit a cryptographic module? Who can demand notice of deprecation or algorithm change? Who controls the root of trust? Who bears the cost of emergency migration? Who decides whether a supplier's recovery process is adequate? These are not incidental clauses. They define how much security discretion remains inside the institution after the purchase. A system can be cryptographically elegant and still politically submissive if the customer lacks the contractual rights to inspect, migrate, or contest essential trust functions. That is why procurement belongs inside security governance rather than outside it as a mere administrative prelude.

The same applies to compliance artefacts. Policies, assurance reports, certifications, and internal control registers are not worthless theatre; they are part of how institutions remember their obligations. But memory is not judgement. A control register may state that sensitive data is encrypted, keys are managed, and incidents are handled under documented procedures. The sharper question is whether those statements map to actual decision rights. Can someone force a rotation when evidence is ambiguous? Can a product team refuse a risky exception demanded for convenience? Can the organisation identify who has standing authority to weigh service continuity against cryptographic hygiene? If not, the institution possesses records of intent rather than a working system of governance.

This is why cryptographic maturity should be measured less by the elegance of adopted tools than by the clarity of institutional choice around them. The mature institution knows which teams own data, which teams own mechanisms, which teams own supplier leverage, which teams own incident authority, and where those responsibilities meet or collide. It knows who can grant exceptions, how long they last, and who must sign off when they touch long-lived secrets or shared trust anchors. It knows where compliance ends and operational judgement begins. Most of all, it knows that cryptography becomes politically serious the moment different parts of the organisation want different things from the same control.

The unresolved test is therefore brutally simple. When the institution next faces a cryptographic decision with real cost attached - replacing a trust anchor, refusing a risky compatibility exception, shrinking retention, demanding stronger vendor terms, or funding a migration before visible catastrophe - will it know who has the right to decide, who has to implement, who bears the consequence, and who is accountable when those interests clash? If the answer remains trapped somewhere between the contract, the audit file, and the org chart, the institution is not yet governing its cryptography. It is merely using it.

# Chapter 3

# Quantum Computing and Cryptanalytic Risk

What changes when a threat is serious enough to alter decisions, but not settled enough to justify certainty? That is the awkward place quantum computing occupies in strategic thought. For years, it could be treated as a specialist subject: important, technically fascinating, and safely fenced off from daily institutional judgement. That fence no longer holds. The reason is not that a single machine has arrived to sweep aside the cryptographic order in one theatrical gesture. The reason is that enough credible work has accumulated to make inaction a choice with consequences, even while the true pace, scale, and usability of future capability remain contested.

This produces a peculiar kind of pressure. Panic would be foolish. So would indifference. The public imagination tends to swing between those poles because it prefers clean stories: either quantum change is imminent and total, or it is remote and therefore irrelevant. Neither story respects how strategic environments actually shift. A capability can matter before it becomes routine. It can also matter unevenly, touching some assumptions much more directly than others. The hard part is not merely understanding the science at a high level. It is learning to think under conditions where signals are partial, incentives are mixed, and the cost of waiting may accumulate long before the evidence satisfies everyone.

The weather report is never enough.

That is because cryptographic risk does not arrive only through proof of a future machine. It arrives through altered expectations in the present. A standards body changes course. A major vendor adjusts its road map. A government agency reframes procurement language. A security team begins classifying data not only by sensitivity but by lifespan. These are not signs that the mystery has been solved. They are signs that the mystery has become too expensive to ignore. Once that threshold is crossed, quantum computing ceases to be a distant technical curiosity and becomes an intelligence problem in the broadest sense: who knows what, who claims what, who can act under uncertainty, and who mistakes the absence of complete proof for the absence of strategic movement.

The central tension lies here. Institutions need specificity because only some cryptographic assumptions are directly shaken by known quantum algorithms, and not all digital protections age at the same rate. Yet institutions also need judgement in the face of ambiguity, because no responsible organisation can wait for perfect visibility before deciding what to inventory, what to retain, what to migrate, and what to demand of suppliers. The trade-off is severe. Move too slowly and long-lived trust may rest on decaying foundations. Move too theatrically and scarce attention is wasted, compatibility is disrupted, and credibility is spent on fears that were never properly ranked.

That tension matters because computation is not merely a technical resource; it is a lever on bargaining power. A modest lead can be enough. Not a civilisational monopoly, just enough asymmetry to make some archives newly attractive, some identities newly forgeable, some signatures newly doubtful, or some forms of delay newly dangerous. The strategic value of such a lead depends on far more than the machine itself. It depends on who can integrate it into collection, throughput, targeting, secrecy, and institutional discipline. A laboratory milestone and an operational advantage are related, but they are not twins. The distance between them is where many bad public arguments live.

The stakes therefore extend beyond whether quantum computing eventually matures into a widely usable cryptanalytic tool. They extend to how organisations interpret contested evidence while the future remains cloudy. A ministry deciding how to classify records, a bank deciding how to structure migration options, a vendor deciding what to support by default, an intelligence service deciding what encrypted traffic is worth retaining: each faces a problem of timing as much as a problem of engineering. The temptation is always to wait for the horizon to become sharper. Serious institutions rarely have that luxury. By the time the fog clears, the slow work of adaptation may already be late.

The path ahead moves from the precise question of what quantum methods do threaten, and what they do not, into the harder problem of planning when credible signals arrive without a settled timetable. It then tightens around the uncomfortable fact that small capability gaps can yield disproportionate advantage when they are joined to patience, secrecy, and organisational competence. From there the focus turns outward to the politics of claims themselves: who speaks loudly, who stays quiet, and how public assertions about capability can mislead, reassure, or strategically shape the behaviour of others without ever fully revealing the truth.

This sequence matters because public language about quantum risk is often full of category errors. Technical possibility is confused with operational readiness. Research prestige is confused with deployable capacity. Standards urgency is confused with proof of imminent collapse. Scepticism is confused with prudence. So is excitement. A clearer frame is needed, not to drain the subject of drama, but to prevent drama from doing the thinking. The institutions that manage this best will not be those that predict the future most confidently. They will be those that can distinguish signal from theatre while still acting before ambiguity becomes an alibi.

The weather report is never enough because cryptographic risk is not just about what the sky may do; it is about what one has already left outside. That is the diagnostic pressure underlying everything that follows. Which existing assumptions deserve immediate doubt, which can still be treated as durable for now, and which public claims about progress should be read as evidence rather than performance? Until those questions are asked with some discipline, quantum computing remains either a slogan for panic or a lullaby for delay.

## What quantum changes, and what it does not

In August 2024, the US National Institute of Standards and Technology published its first final post-quantum cryptography standards in Gaithersburg, Maryland. The event did not resemble a cinematic crack in the foundations of digital security. No great archive flew open. No bank lost its ledgers in public. The practical outcome was quieter and, for that reason, more important. A leading standards body had moved from warning and competition to formal selection, which meant that a question once treated as partly speculative had become operational enough to shape procurement, implementation, and institutional timetables.

That shift matters because quantum risk is often discussed in a tone that encourages either melodrama or dismissal. One camp speaks as though all encryption were waiting for a single future machine to make it ridiculous. Another shrugs and notes, correctly, that large-scale, fault-tolerant quantum computers capable of breaking widely deployed public key systems do not yet exist in routine operational form. Both instincts miss the same point. Quantum computing does not threaten everything equally, and it does not need to arrive as a finished universal solvent to change strategic judgement.

The door is not falling off its hinges. Some locks are simply ageing faster than others.

The first task, then, is specificity. Quantum computing matters to cryptography because certain algorithms exploit properties of quantum systems to solve particular classes of problems more efficiently than known classical methods. That last phrase matters more than the hype usually allows. The threat is not "quantum" in the abstract, as though any machine using qubits automatically dissolves secrecy. The threat lies in concrete algorithmic consequences. Show the scene and the difference becomes visible. A system uses widely deployed public key cryptography to establish identity, exchange keys, or verify signatures. The named concept is algorithmic asymmetry. Explain it, and the strategic shape emerges. Some mathematical problems underlying familiar public key methods are believed to become tractable in principle for sufficiently capable quantum machines using Shor's algorithm, first described by Peter Shor in 1994. The implication is disciplined rather than apocalyptic. Public key systems based on those assumptions face a different class of future risk from systems that do not depend on them.

This is why the public conversation can become so sloppy. People say "encryption" when they mean several distinct things at once: key exchange, authentication, digital signatures, bulk data protection, password storage, integrity checks, archival assurance. Quantum computing does not press on all of these in the same way. The most widely discussed risk concerns public key cryptography built on integer factorisation or discrete logarithm problems, which underlie familiar schemes used for secure key establishment and digital signatures. If a sufficiently capable fault-tolerant quantum computer could run the relevant algorithms at meaningful scale, those schemes would lose much of the hardness on which their security relies. That is the real disturbance. Not all cryptography dies. Some assumptions do.

A second named anchor helps keep the picture honest. In 1996, Lov Grover described a quantum algorithm that can speed up brute-force search in a way often summarised as a quadratic improvement over classical search. The important point is not the slogan but the contrast. For symmetric cryptography, such as widely used bulk encryption, the best-known generic quantum advantage is much less devastating than what Shor's algorithm implies for certain public key systems. Show the practical consequence and the distinction becomes plain. A public key scheme may face the prospect of structural breakage under the right quantum conditions; a symmetric cipher may instead face pressure that can often be mitigated by larger key sizes and careful parameter choices. The implication is crucial. Quantum risk is not a single cliff edge. It is a differentiated pressure acting much more sharply on some mechanisms than on others.

That is what quantum changes. It changes the strategic status of some public key assumptions that have long been central to digital identity, key exchange, and signatures at scale. It changes the planning horizon for systems whose security depends heavily on those assumptions. It changes the urgency of migration for functions tied to long-lived trust, such as certificate hierarchies, software signing, device enrolment, and archival signatures. It also changes how institutions should classify data and trust relationships by lifespan. A message protected for a brief commercial interaction does not impose the same burden as a signed legal record, a root certificate, or a source identity that must remain safe for decades. The moment one stops saying "encryption" as though it were a single object, the problem becomes clearer and more manageable.

What quantum does *not* change is just as important. It does not make endpoints trustworthy. It does not solve implementation bugs. It does not erase the centrality of key management, access control, software supply chains, retention policies, or organisational confusion. A ministry can migrate to post-quantum algorithms and still expose sensitive records through weak administration. A company can fear future decryption while ignoring the fact that attackers usually prefer the cheaper route of stealing credentials, compromising devices, or poisoning update channels. The toothbrush in the glass still matters. By that I mean the ordinary, slightly embarrassing objects of security practice: passwords reused, keys mishandled, laptops left open, certificates forgotten, logs ignored, privileged accounts left sprawling across systems. Quantum computing does not rescue bad institutions from themselves, and it does not spare good institutions the work of governance.

That limitation is not a footnote. It is a discipline against fantasy. One can tell whether a discussion of quantum risk is serious by noticing what it leaves out. If it speaks only of future machines and never of migration complexity, legacy systems, key custody, certificate replacement, or inventory gaps, it is usually giving the reader a tale rather than an analysis. The practical burden lies in a mixed environment where some parts of the cryptographic estate are exposed to sharper long-term risk than others, while many immediate vulnerabilities remain stubbornly classical. The strategic implication is straightforward. Institutions need prioritisation, not theatre.

A useful example lies in software signing. Modern systems rely heavily on digital signatures to decide whether code should be installed, trusted, or executed with privilege. That trust can persist long after the code was first released. Show the scene and the concern becomes concrete. A vendor signs an update, devices verify the signature, and fleets of machines obey. The named concept is asymmetric trust concentration. Explain it, and one sees why quantum pressure falls unevenly. If the signature system used there rests on public key assumptions vulnerable to future quantum attack, then the problem is not merely that a message might be read one day. It is that authenticity itself may become contestable if old signatures can no longer be trusted or if migration of trust anchors lags behind operational dependence. The implication reaches beyond confidentiality into governance, archives, and control over software behaviour.

Another example makes the point from the defensive side. In August 2024, NIST's publication of final standards based on selected post-quantum schemes did not prove that existing public key infrastructure had suddenly become unfit. It did signal that leading institutions no longer regarded the matter as too distant for formal transition work. The visible behaviour attached to that judgement is revealing: vendors revising road maps, procurement language changing, engineering teams testing hybrid deployments, security leaders asking where vulnerable algorithms still sit in their estates. The concept here is threshold recognition. Explain it, and the strategic value is clear. Institutions do not wait for certainty in order to standardise replacements when the functions in question sit deep inside trust systems. They move when the cost of waiting begins to look less acceptable than the cost of preparation.

Still, there is a credible counterweight to panic. Quantum computing remains a demanding engineering field. Public announcements, laboratory milestones, and benchmark claims do not automatically translate into machines capable of defeating widely deployed cryptographic systems in operational settings. Error correction, stability, scale, control, and throughput all matter. A device that performs an impressive task under controlled conditions is not therefore ready to overturn global digital trust. This limitation deserves respect because bad analysis thrives on collapsing the distinction between possibility and capability. The history of computing is cluttered with people who mistook research significance for immediate practical revolution.

That caution should not slide into complacency. It should sharpen the hierarchy of concern. The right question is not whether all current cryptography is about to fail. It is which assumptions are worth doubting now because the consequences of late action would be severe. Long-lived secrets, public key identity systems, certificate hierarchies, software signing, and archival authenticity belong high on that list precisely because their migration is slow and their function is foundational. Short-lived confidentiality, especially where symmetric protection dominates and retention is limited, may justify a different tempo. This is not inconsistency. It is strategy.

The need for such discrimination becomes clearer when one compares public key exchange with symmetric bulk encryption. In many secure protocols, public key methods help establish shared secrets, after which symmetric ciphers do the heavy lifting for actual data transmission. Quantum pressure therefore bears especially on the handshake, the identity proof, the signature, the credential, the root of trust. The bulk data channel may remain comparatively stronger under larger keys and sound implementation. Show the system as a layered arrangement rather than a single encrypted blob, and risk prioritisation stops looking like timidity and starts looking like competence. Not every room in the house is on fire. Some rooms contain the fuse box.

This matters politically as well as technically. Organisations that hear "quantum breaks encryption" may waste effort in the wrong places, frightening leadership and confusing the public while neglecting precisely those components whose long-term authenticity or key-establishment role deserves earlier scrutiny. Organisations that hear "quantum is overblown" may preserve brittle trust structures far too long because they confuse the absence of immediate catastrophe with the absence of accumulating exposure. The strategic virtue lies in saying two things at once without flinching: some of the cryptographic assumptions that helped build the modern internet face a serious long-horizon challenge, and much of what keeps systems insecure remains stubbornly non-quantum, local, human, and administrative.

The toothbrush returns here because it is easy to buy futuristic anxiety as a substitute for ordinary discipline. A hospital with weak endpoint control, a government department with poor certificate hygiene, or a company with sprawling privileged access will not be saved by speaking eloquently about post-quantum transition. Yet a bank, cloud provider, or ministry that treats public key migration as an optional curiosity is also making a mistake, because trust systems with long institutional lives cannot be replaced overnight when confidence finally hardens. The challenge is not to choose between the future and the present. It is to refuse the childish hope that only one of them is real.

So the central lesson is narrow, almost austere. Quantum computing changes specific cryptographic assumptions, most notably around major families of public key methods. It does not abolish the importance of symmetric encryption, implementation quality, endpoint security, governance, or institutional readiness. It does not justify panic. It forbids vagueness. The serious question is therefore not whether one fears quantum computing in the abstract, but whether one can point to the exact places where future computational change would do the most institutional damage - and distinguish them from the many places where the older, duller failures remain the ones doing most of the work already.

## Capability uncertainty and planning under ambiguity

In October 2019, Google announced from Santa Barbara, California, that its quantum processor Sycamore had performed a computation that the company argued would take a classical supercomputer far longer to reproduce. The paper and the publicity around it were immediately followed by argument: about the comparison, about the meaning of the result, about whether a research milestone had been mistaken for something closer to practical advantage. The concrete outcome was not agreement. It was a widening circle of attention. A technical claim moved beyond laboratories and into policy offices, board briefings, procurement conversations, and the strategic imagination of institutions that did not need to settle the science in order to feel the pressure of it.

That pressure came from uncertainty itself.

This is the first mental adjustment serious organisations have to make when thinking about quantum progress. The question is not simply whether a decisive capability exists today in operational form. The question is how institutions behave when the available signals are incomplete, incentives to disclose are mixed, and the cost of waiting may prove higher than the cost of early preparation. In that sense quantum progress resembles an intelligence problem more than a clean engineering timetable. The relevant evidence is distributed across research papers, vendor claims, standards activity, state investment, classified programmes, benchmarking disputes, hardware road maps, talent flows, supply chain constraints, and silence. Some of that evidence is reliable. Some is strategic theatre. Most of it is insufficient on its own.

The temptation, under these conditions, is to demand prediction. Executives want dates. Procurement teams want milestones. Ministers want confidence intervals that can be converted into budget language. Journalists want a horizon that fits a headline. Yet forecasts in this domain have a poor habit of ageing badly, not because nobody understands anything, but because capability depends on a chain of conditions that do not mature at the same speed. A machine may improve in one dimension and stall in another. An approach that looks elegant in a paper may prove punishing in manufacturing. A benchmark may reveal genuine progress and still say little about operational throughput. Show the scene and the flaw in date-hunting becomes obvious. A board asks, "When will this break us?" The honest answer is less satisfying and more useful: the institution should care less about a guessed calendar point than about the conditions under which its own exposure becomes intolerable.

That is where thresholds matter. A threshold is not a prophecy. It is a decision rule. Name the concept, and one can stop pretending that foresight means clairvoyance. Explain it plainly and the idea is almost modest. An organisation identifies the exposures that would become unacceptable under a range of plausible futures, then prepares around those exposures before anyone can prove exactly when a breakthrough will occur. The visible behaviour tied to this approach is concrete: sensitive archives are classified by how long their confidentiality must survive; products are assessed for whether cryptographic components can be swapped; procurement language starts requiring upgradeability; software signing systems are reviewed because their trust life exceeds the comfort of static assumptions. The implication is strategic. Institutions can act intelligently under ambiguity without claiming knowledge they do not have.

This differs sharply from planning by forecast. Forecast-based planning asks for a date and then quietly treats the answer as a licence to defer until a later budget cycle. Threshold-based planning asks a harder question: what must be true before delay becomes irresponsible? That shift matters because cryptographic risk is unevenly distributed. A consumer interaction that expires in usefulness after a short interval does not deserve the same urgency as a trust anchor, a root certificate, an archive of legal records, or a repository of sensitive identities. If long-lived exposure is concentrated in a few classes of systems, then action can be prioritised without pretending that every corner of the estate faces the same horizon. The weather vane matters here. One does not need to know the exact hour of the storm to decide which roofs should have been repaired already.

A useful example sits in the standards process itself. In August 2024, NIST published its first final post-quantum cryptography standards. That event did not certify that existing public key systems had ceased to function overnight. What it did do was cross a threshold of institutional seriousness. Standards bodies do not move into final selection lightly, and major suppliers do not revise engineering road maps merely for philosophical amusement. The visible consequences followed familiar channels: vendors updated plans, implementers increased testing, procurement teams gained new language, and security leaders found it harder to explain inaction as prudence. The named concept here is signal aggregation. Explain it, and the strategic value becomes clear. No single announcement settled the future, but a cluster of signals became strong enough to justify transition work without requiring a universal consensus on timing. The implication is broader than quantum. Serious planning often begins when imperfect signals converge, not when uncertainty disappears.

A second example shows the same pattern from the other direction. In 2019, the Google Sycamore announcement prompted both excitement and rebuttal, including arguments from IBM about what classical computation might still accomplish under the comparison in question. The public disagreement was not a failure of analysis. It was evidence of the environment institutions must navigate. Signals are contested because the actors producing them occupy different roles, incentives, and audiences. A research group wants to communicate significance. A rival firm wants to preserve perspective and protect its own position. Governments may want to imply capability without revealing much. Investors may reward a tone of inevitability. Security officials may prefer guarded language because admitting concern can trigger costs before plans are mature. This is why capability assessment in quantum computing cannot be treated as a simple reading of the latest press release or paper abstract. The evidence is always travelling through incentives.

That phrase matters more than it sounds. Incentives shape what is published, what is delayed, what is benchmarked, what is omitted, and what is framed as progress. A laboratory may highlight coherence improvements and say little about manufacturing yield. A company may advertise error-correction milestones while understating the engineering burdens of scale. A state-backed programme may prefer quiet accumulation to public prestige, or the reverse. Even standards urgency can mislead if read too crudely. Early migration activity may reflect sound prudence under uncertainty rather than private certainty that catastrophe is near. The strategic analyst therefore has to read not just the content of signals, but the conditions under which they are produced. Capability uncertainty is never only a shortage of data. It is a problem of interpreting data made by actors with reasons to shape the story.

This is where the intelligence analogy earns its keep. Intelligence work rarely offers complete evidence neatly arranged in order of importance. It offers fragments, proxies, suspicious absences, partial disclosures, and a constant struggle to separate genuine signal from noise, posturing, or wishful inference. Quantum planning belongs in that family of judgement. Institutions have to compare public technical milestones, standards developments, supplier readiness, internal inventories, and the expected life of their own secrets without pretending any one input settles the matter. The decision is less "When will the machine arrive?" than "At what point do our current assumptions become too expensive to keep?" That is a harsher, and better, question.

A credible limitation belongs here. Not every organisation needs a bespoke intelligence-like capability to interpret quantum progress. Smaller institutions cannot reasonably track every research milestone or benchmark dispute while also managing ordinary security work. They should not be asked to behave like national laboratories in office clothing. Forecast scepticism also has its place. Some domains really do suffer from inflated claims, and institutions with limited budgets can waste enormous effort reacting to prestige contests that never mature into practical risk on relevant timescales. The discipline of refusing panic is part of sound planning, not a sign of laziness.

Yet that limitation does not rescue passivity. It points instead to a division of labour. Smaller organisations can use threshold planning precisely because it does not require omniscience. They do not need to predict the future of quantum hardware in detail. They need to know which of their data, signatures, dependencies, and supplier arrangements carry long-lived exposure; which services rely on public key assumptions that will be hardest to replace; and which procurement or architectural choices now would leave them trapped later. A hospital, university, or regional utility may not model the frontiers of error correction. It can still decide whether its vendors support cryptographic agility, whether its archives are over-retained, and whether its trust systems are too brittle to change under stress. Thresholds scale better than prophecy.

The deeper reason uncertainty creates pressure is asymmetry. The collector, the patient adversary, or the institution with more room to speculate can often act cheaply while the defender must prepare visibly and expensively. Storage is cheap. Migration is not. Quiet retention of encrypted material requires little public justification. Re-architecting trust systems, reviewing signatures, updating contracts, and testing hybrid deployments require meetings, budgets, outages, and executive consent. This means that even uncertain future capabilities can alter present incentives sharply. A defender who waits for certainty may be waiting for the one condition the environment will never honestly provide. The weather vane matters again. It does not forecast with perfect grace, but it tells you which way the pressure is moving.

That pressure becomes particularly difficult where the lifespan of the protected value exceeds the lifespan of institutional comfort. A software update signing system, a diplomatic archive, a certificate hierarchy, a store of biometric records, or a body of regulated legal communications all place different demands on planning. Some require protection against retrospective compromise. Some require continuity of authenticity. Some require both. Organisations that collapse these different horizons into one generic category - secure, encrypted, compliant - are not simplifying. They are blinding themselves to the very reason uncertainty matters. Threshold thinking restores sight by tying preparation to the life of the asset rather than to a guessed date on a research calendar.

Public claims complicate this further because they can themselves become strategic instruments. A state may emphasise progress to shape rivals' spending or to signal prestige. A company may soften timelines to avoid alarming customers or exposing weakness in its own migration posture. A standards body may sound urgent because delay is institutionally dangerous even when technical timelines remain debated. A listener who treats all of these voices as transparent reports from a neutral universe will be outmanoeuvred by actors who understand that ambiguity can be used. The right response is not cynicism. It is layered reading. Which claims come with visible commitments? Which are matched by procurement changes, engineering investment, standards activity, or revised validation practices? Which remain wonderfully dramatic and conveniently consequence-free?

This returns planning to a more sober footing. Thresholds should be tied to observable exposures and institutional friction, not to the emotional temperature of public claims. If a system cannot change its cryptographic dependencies without major disruption, that fact matters regardless of any contested forecast. If a body of data will remain sensitive for decades, that fact matters regardless of whether one believes a specific firm's road map. If a supply chain signs software with a trust model that cannot be rotated quickly, that fact matters now, not after headlines achieve unanimity. The organisation that understands this begins to govern uncertainty rather than merely endure it.

The weather vane is a humble object, and that is why it suits the subject. It does not pretend to know the exact shape of the storm or the precise minute the rain will begin. It shows motion early enough for roofs, shutters, and plans to be judged against changing conditions rather than comforting stillness. Capability uncertainty in quantum computing deserves exactly that sort of seriousness. The unresolved test is not whether an institution can win an argument about dates. It is whether it can name the thresholds beyond which its own cryptographic assumptions become too dangerous to keep - and act before the sky does the institution the discourtesy of becoming clear.

## Computational gaps and asymmetric advantage

In October 2019, when Google announced a quantum computing milestone from Santa Barbara, California, much of the public reaction focused on the headline question of whether a machine had done something classically impractical. Specialists argued over the comparison, the benchmark, and the meaning of the result. That argument was worth having. But a quieter strategic lesson sat beneath it. Even if one grants a genuine technical advance, the possession of a striking capability in a laboratory does not yet tell us who can turn that capability into durable advantage in intelligence competition. A prototype is not a pipeline.

That distinction matters because intelligence value is rarely produced by raw capacity alone. It is produced by the conversion of capacity into repeated, selective, timely use. A state, company, or research consortium may hold a narrow lead in computation and still gain little if it cannot decide where to apply it, feed it with relevant targets, protect the method, integrate the results into operations, and sustain the whole arrangement without public ruin or internal confusion. The machine matters. The organisation matters more than enthusiasts like to admit.

This is why a small capability lead can matter disproportionately. Strategic advantage does not always require universal dominance. A narrow edge, if kept secret and used against high-value material, may produce returns far beyond its apparent size. Show the scene and the idea becomes less abstract. An actor does not need to read every encrypted message in the world. It may be enough to read a small class of diplomatic traffic, verify the authenticity of a small class of signatures, or exploit a narrow window in a supply chain that touches a few critical systems. The named concept is selective superiority. Explain it, and the logic sharpens. Intelligence gains often depend less on total coverage than on being first, quiet, and well-targeted. The implication is severe. Even modest computational asymmetry can matter greatly if the targets are strategically rich.

This point is often lost because public discussion gravitates towards grand thresholds. People ask whether quantum computing, or any major computational shift, will "break encryption" as though the only meaningful outcome were a universal event. Intelligence history is less theatrical. Partial access can be enough. Temporary access can be enough. Access to the right subset can be enough. A capability that is too expensive, delicate, or scarce for routine mass deployment may still be priceless when directed at selected archives, leadership communications, technical design repositories, or identity systems. The value lies in discrimination, not merely scale.

The difference between possession and application is therefore central. Possession refers to the technical existence of a capability under controlled conditions. Application refers to the ability to use it against real targets, with enough speed, reliability, secrecy, and throughput to influence decisions beyond the laboratory. That second condition is much harder. It requires acquisition priorities, target selection, skilled personnel, secure facilities, supporting software, error management, legal or political cover, and often a tolerance for using a rare capability sparingly rather than noisily. The strongest algorithm in the hands of a disorganised institution behaves like a brilliant map locked in the wrong drawer.

The archive rewards patience.

That short sentence captures a large part of the strategic picture. A collector that stores encrypted material over time, classifies it carefully, and revisits it when capabilities improve may gain more from a small computational edge than a less disciplined rival with theoretically similar hardware. Organisational patience compounds technical capacity. The visible behaviours tied to this claim are not glamorous. They include long-term storage, metadata indexing, careful preservation of intercepted material, strict compartmentation, and decisions about which targets deserve scarce processing resources. These are managerial acts, not feats of pure science.

Yet they often decide whether a technical lead produces real advantage or merely an impressive conference presentation.

A useful historical analogue lies at Bletchley Park during the Second World War. One should be careful with analogies, but this one earns its keep. Breaking encrypted traffic was never just a matter of abstract brilliance. It depended on a disciplined system of interception, triage, machine support, analyst labour, operational secrecy, and integration with decision-making. The named concept here is throughput. Explain it plainly and the old lesson becomes contemporary. It is one thing to prove that a class of messages can be attacked in principle. It is another to process enough of them, fast enough, with enough reliability, that the result affects real operations. The implication travels well into the present. Computational gaps matter most when paired with institutions that can turn possibility into routine, selective exploitation.

This is why a small lead can be asymmetric in effect. Suppose two actors sit near one another in technical sophistication. One has a slight edge in hardware, software integration, error handling, or access to specialised talent. By itself, that sounds modest. But if the better-positioned actor also has clearer target priorities, better retention practices, more disciplined security, and a tighter route from technical success to operational use, the strategic difference widens quickly. The raw computational gap may be narrow. The intelligence gap becomes broader because the superior organisation wastes less of the advantage it has. One side owns a faster engine. The other side also knows which road leads somewhere worth reaching.

The example of Google's 2019 Sycamore announcement helps here precisely because it illustrates the gap between demonstration and deployment. The public saw a benchmark contest about whether a certain quantum task outpaced a classical comparison. Even granting the significance of the experiment, nothing about that event established an operational ability to defeat major cryptographic systems at scale. The machine performed a specialised task under controlled conditions. That matters scientifically. It does not automatically produce intelligence value. The visible difference between those two states is everything around the hardware: target data, algorithms relevant to the target, error-corrected stability, sustained operation, secrecy, staffing, and the organisational judgement to use the capability where it matters most. The implication is sobering. A lab success is a signal, not a harvest.

A second example comes from standards rather than spectacle. In August 2024, NIST published its first final post-quantum cryptography standards. That move did not certify that adversaries already possessed large-scale cryptanalytic quantum systems. What it did reveal was institutional recognition that the cost of waiting had become too uncomfortable for organisations with long-lived trust obligations. Show the scene and the point becomes clear. Standards bodies, vendors, and security teams were reacting not to proven universal breakage but to the possibility that narrow or emerging capability gaps, if exploited against selected targets, could impose unacceptable future costs. The concept is anticipatory adjustment. Explain it, and the strategic implication follows. Large institutions do not wait for universal proof when even partial asymmetry could damage root certificates, software signing systems, archives, or other hard-to-replace trust structures.

This also explains why public observers often underestimate the importance of secrecy around capability. An actor that gains a small but valuable computational advantage has strong reasons not to advertise it broadly. Quiet use preserves access. Loud boasting teaches others where to harden. In intelligence competition, the most valuable lead is often the one that survives without forcing visible countermeasures. That means outsiders should be careful when reading the absence of dramatic disclosure as evidence that no meaningful asymmetry exists. A capability that is too limited for public triumph may still be perfectly suited to silent use against a narrow but important target class.

Still, any serious account needs a limitation. Not every small capability lead produces strategic transformation. Some laboratory advances remain awkward, fragile, and too expensive to apply meaningfully outside demonstration settings. Some advantages are neutralised by poor target access, strong operational security, or the simple fact that the protected material is no longer useful by the time it could be exploited. Some institutional cultures are so slow, compartmented, or politically constrained that technical progress does not translate into action. This matters because the subject attracts a certain kind of fever dream in which every incremental benchmark is treated as if it were already an intelligence revolution. That is nonsense in a lab coat.

Yet the limitation strengthens the main argument rather than weakening it. It tells us what to examine. The real question is never only "Who has the machine?" It is "Who can convert the machine into repeatable advantage against selected targets without exhausting secrecy, throughput, or political patience?" That question points away from fetishising the hardware and towards institutional capacity. Can the actor store relevant material long enough? Can it prioritise which material matters? Can it maintain the specialists needed to interpret results? Can it hide the source of insight? Can it exploit partial access without alerting the target too quickly? These are organisational tests. They decide whether a computational edge remains a scientific trophy or becomes an intelligence weapon.

The phrase *operational throughput* deserves emphasis because it captures the awkward bridge between science and strategy. Throughput is not just speed. It is the whole chain by which raw technical capability turns into sustained useful output. A system with poor throughput may prove a concept beautifully and still fail strategically because it cannot handle enough tasks, enough targets, or enough uncertainty to matter in real time. A system with excellent throughput may turn a modest technical lead into disproportionate effect because it wastes less time, misclassifies fewer targets, and routes successful results into decisions more efficiently. When institutions speak vaguely about "capability", they often blur this distinction. Serious analysis should not.

The organisational side of throughput can be almost embarrassingly ordinary. Hiring matters. Security clearance processes matter. Budget continuity matters. Internal competition between agencies or departments matters. So do data retention rules, procurement of supporting hardware, integration with existing analysis tools, and the willingness of leadership to protect a fragile capability from premature operational overuse. None of this has the glamour of quantum theory, but glamour is a terrible guide to strategic relevance. A technically sophisticated state or company can still mismanage a computational lead into impotence through bureaucracy, secrecy dysfunction, or lack of analytical discipline. Another can turn a narrower lead into greater effect through patience and institutional coherence.

This is also why defenders should resist the false comfort of asking whether an adversary can apply a capability *everywhere*. It may not need to. The attacker who can exploit selected trust relationships, selected archives, or selected signature chains may already have enough to produce coercive leverage, intelligence insight, or operational access far out of proportion to the apparent scale of the breakthrough. Small gaps become dangerous when they intersect with high-value concentration points: root stores, update-signing systems, diplomatic archives, identity databases, design repositories, or authentication paths used by many others. The bridge appears again. A narrow crossing can still carry a great deal of strategic traffic.

The quiet risk, then, lies in confusing technical equality with strategic equality. Two institutions may read the same papers, buy similar equipment, and speak the same public language of innovation. One will still outperform the other if it can classify targets better, integrate results faster, keep secrets longer, and concentrate effort where the payoff is highest. The computational gap may be real but modest. The asymmetric advantage emerges in everything that surrounds it. That is why organisations assessing cryptanalytic risk should look beyond benchmark headlines and ask a rougher question. If a rival gained only a slight lead, where in our own trust structure would even that slight lead yield an outsized return?

The archive rewards patience, but only when patience is married to selection and organisation. That is the unresolved pressure here. When institutions imagine future computational competition, are they still picturing a race for the biggest machine, or are they prepared to face the nastier possibility that a comparatively small lead, quietly applied through superior throughput and sharper institutional discipline, could matter long before the public story of a decisive breakthrough ever arrives?

## Public claims, secrecy, and credibility

In October 2019, Google announced from Santa Barbara, California, that its quantum processor Sycamore had performed a computation beyond the practical reach of a classical rival under the terms the company set out. The result was immediately debated. IBM disputed the comparison. Researchers argued over what had been shown, what had not, and what sort of future the announcement really pointed towards. The concrete outcome was not a settled verdict about cryptanalytic danger. It was something strategically more interesting: a public claim had forced governments, firms, standards bodies, and security professionals to decide how much weight to assign to a statement made under conditions none of them could fully verify from the outside.

That is the central difficulty in this domain. Capability claims matter before they are conclusive. They shape procurement, regulatory language, investor expectations, talent flows, standards work, and internal security planning long before outsiders can test every implied consequence for themselves. A government ministry does not wait for laboratory access to ask whether its long-lived records may need stronger protections. A platform vendor does not revise road maps only after an adversary kindly publishes a complete technical dossier. A major firm hears the claim, compares it with other signals, and begins to decide whether silence would be prudence or merely drift. The announcement becomes part of the environment.

This gives public claims about quantum progress a peculiar power. They are neither pure evidence nor empty performance. They are attempts to shape belief under uncertainty. Show the scene and the pattern becomes recognisable. A company publicises a milestone, a state hints at strategic investment, a standards body accelerates formal work, a rival offers a cooler interpretation, and financial or political audiences start reading these moves as clues to hidden capability. The named concept is credibility management. Explain it, and the strategic stakes sharpen. Actors speak not only to describe reality, but to influence how others price risk, allocate resources, and imagine future advantage. The implication follows quickly. One should hear capability claims as interventions as well as reports.

This is why overstatement and understatement can both be rational. A firm may overstate progress because prestige attracts capital, talent, contracts, and influence over the agenda of what counts as urgent. A state may overstate progress because ambiguity itself can unsettle rivals, encourage wasteful countermeasures, or support a broader story of national competence. Yet understatement has its own attractions. An intelligence actor with a promising capability gains little from educating its targets too early. A company far from operational maturity may also prefer restraint if noisy claims would invite scrutiny, regulation, or commercial commitments it cannot honour. The paradox is plain enough. Revealing too much teaches adversaries. Revealing too little fails to shape their behaviour. The bridge sways.

That bridge is the quiet motif worth keeping in view, because credibility in this space is always a crossing between incompatible aims. An actor wants to be believed, but not fully inspected. It wants influence without overexposure. It wants urgency when urgency helps, patience when patience preserves advantage. A public claim therefore arrives carrying at least two questions. Is the underlying technical content sound? And what secondary purpose does the act of saying it serve? Those questions are not cynical. They are elementary hygiene when the topic involves strategic technology, prestige competition, and genuine secrecy.

The Google announcement remains useful because it showed all of this in compressed form. The technical paper mattered. So did the branding of "quantum supremacy", which was rhetorically vivid enough to travel well beyond specialist circles. The argument that followed was revealing in its own right. Public disagreement did not make the original milestone meaningless. It revealed how claims are filtered through institutional interest. Google had reasons to emphasise significance. IBM had reasons to preserve perspective. Researchers had reasons to disentangle benchmark theatre from practical application. Policymakers had reasons to ask whether the existence of serious debate should delay action or sharpen it. The visible behaviour attached to those motives was not abstract. It showed up in speeches, vendor positioning, internal briefings, conference panels, and standards urgency. Credibility was being negotiated in public.

The same logic applies to states, only with more shadows. Governments speak about advanced technology under layered incentives: deterrence, domestic legitimacy, budget competition, alliance signalling, industrial policy, and concealment of actual strengths or weaknesses. Some claims are made loudly because public prestige is the point. Others are made obliquely, through procurement plans, research funding, white papers, standards engagement, or strategic ambiguity in official testimony. Show the scene and one sees why simple truth-testing often fails. A state may sound cautious because it knows more than it can safely say. Another may sound triumphant because it needs influence more than it possesses capability. The concept here is informational asymmetry. Explain it plainly and the implication is unavoidable. Outsiders must interpret not only what is said, but who can afford to say it, who benefits from saying it, and what consequences the statement seems designed to produce.

This helps explain why standards activity can be a stronger signal than rhetoric, while still falling short of proof. In August 2024, NIST published its first final post-quantum cryptography standards. That move did not certify that any adversary already possessed routine large-scale quantum decryption capability. It did something both more modest and more consequential. It told the world that a major public institution judged the long-run transition problem serious enough to formalise replacements, shape implementation, and push migration decisions into the present. The visible consequences were concrete: vendor road maps changed, implementation work gained legitimacy, procurement teams acquired new language, and security leaders could justify investment without pretending to know the exact future. The named concept is institutional signalling. Explain it, and the strategic lesson becomes clear. Standards urgency often reflects prudent threshold-crossing rather than secret certainty, but it still alters the behaviour of others because public institutions rarely move this way for amusement.

That distinction matters because many observers misread urgency as prophecy. A standards body accelerating work is not necessarily whispering that collapse is imminent. It may be responding to the opposite fact: that migration takes so long, and trust structures run so deep, that waiting for certainty would be irresponsible. Public claims of urgency therefore need careful reading. Some are attempts to shape behaviour in advance of danger. Some are attempts to attach prestige to work that remains distant from practical deployment. Some are both. The serious question is whether the claim is backed by visible commitments. Has the speaker changed standards language, funding priorities, implementation guidance, or procurement expectations? Or has the speaker merely released another polished sentence into the air and gone home for tea?

A second example makes the credibility dilemma more concrete. In intelligence history, capabilities that matter most are often those least likely to be advertised directly, because their value depends on continued ignorance by the target. That logic plainly carries over to cryptanalytic possibilities. If an actor ever acquired even a narrow but valuable advantage against selected cryptographic targets, public triumph would usually be the least intelligent use of it. The visible evidence might instead be indirect: odd urgency in migration, unusual standards pressure, subtle shifts in collection priorities, or silence where one might otherwise expect loud boasting. This does not mean every quiet move conceals a dramatic secret. That way lies feverish nonsense. It does mean that absence of public revelation cannot be treated as absence of strategic concern.

A credible limitation belongs here. Not all public claims are strategic masks for hidden reality. Many are sincere accounts by researchers or institutions trying to communicate progress within the ordinary incentives of science and technology. A paper may simply be a paper. A benchmark may simply mark a genuine technical achievement. A standards timetable may reflect patient consensus-building rather than buried intelligence drama. One should resist the temptation to turn every announcement into a code that only the suspicious can decipher. That temptation flatters the interpreter and usually produces rubbish.

Yet the limitation does not rescue naivety. The point is not that all claims are propaganda. The point is that all claims in this space are *positioned*. Even honest statements are made from somewhere, for someone, under constraints that affect tone, emphasis, and omission. A company courting investment will not sound like a cautious archivist. A defence ministry will not sound like an open research seminar. A standards body will not speak like a venture-backed start-up unless something has gone very wrong with the refreshments. Reading such claims intelligently means comparing them against the speaker's institutional role, the costs of being wrong, and the observable actions that follow.

This is where credibility becomes more social than technical. A claim gains force not merely because it is true in some narrow sense, but because the surrounding institutions make it costly to ignore. A major vendor changes its implementation strategy. A regulator revises expectations. A procurement framework starts asking different questions. An alliance partner pressures for migration planning. A large platform deprecates an older primitive. These are public acts. They are legible. They do not prove the most dramatic hidden capability, but they do alter the burden of disbelief. The abstraction of trust becomes visible in calendars, contracts, code branches, standards meetings, and budget requests. That is where serious readers should look.

The bridge sways again here. If states and firms reveal too much about capability, they may trigger the very adaptations that destroy the value of their advantage. If they reveal too little, they may fail to deter risky behaviour, fail to justify necessary migration, or fail to shape the standards environment in which future competition will occur. The balance is especially delicate in cryptographic matters because success is often silent and defensive adaptation is painfully slow. A public claim must therefore do several jobs badly rather than one job perfectly. It must imply seriousness without full disclosure, invite adjustment without uncontrolled panic, and preserve enough ambiguity to avoid giving away the method. No wonder so many statements in this field sound like they were written by a committee trapped in a lift.

This has direct consequences for how institutions should interpret announcements. The right response is not credulity or reflexive dismissal. It is structured scepticism. What exactly is being claimed: a theoretical result, a laboratory milestone, a deployment capacity, a standards judgement, or a policy threshold? Who benefits if others overreact? Who benefits if others stay sleepy? What corroborating moves accompany the statement? Are vendors changing defaults? Are standards bodies moving? Are procurement requirements shifting? Are implementation teams being told to prepare? Each question ties abstract credibility to visible behaviour, which is the only way to avoid mistaking either hype for evidence or caution for insight.

Public claims also matter because they can create self-fulfilling pressure. A repeated narrative of impending quantum danger, even if technically overstated at the margin, can accelerate funding, standards work, talent recruitment, and organisational planning. A repeated narrative of remoteness can do the opposite, slowing migration and protecting incumbents whose systems are not ready to change. That does not make the narratives arbitrary. It shows how belief and preparation interact. Announcements help govern tempo. They tell institutions whether to treat the bridge as stable enough for delay or shaky enough to cross while there is still light.

The deeper lesson, then, is not to hunt for a single trustworthy voice that will end ambiguity. No such voice exists. Credibility here emerges from triangulation among public claims, institutional moves, technical substance, and the incentives shaping both speech and silence. The actor that sounds most confident may be compensating for weakness. The actor that sounds most restrained may be hiding strength, or simply uncertainty handled by adults. The standards body that moves fastest may be prudent rather than alarmist. The quietest signal may be a contract clause rather than a headline.

The unresolved test is therefore sharper than "Whom should we believe?" It is this: when a state, company, or standards institution speaks about quantum progress, can we tell whether it is trying to describe capability, shape behaviour, preserve secrecy, protect prestige, or do all four at once? Until that question is asked with some discipline, public claims will keep exerting influence precisely because they are hardest to read where the stakes are highest and the bridge is already moving underfoot.

# Chapter 4

# Harvest Now, Decrypt Later Dynamics

What is a secret worth if it cannot be read yet? The question sounds almost mischievous until one notices how much modern power depends on the answer. A diplomatic cable that is unreadable today may still be worth storing if its relevance persists into a later negotiation. A personnel record may appear dormant until a future clearance decision, blackmail attempt, or influence operation gives it new life. A design file may sit harmlessly encrypted for years and then become newly valuable the moment a rival closes a technical gap. The puzzle is not whether unreadable data has value. It is why so many institutions still behave as though unreadable and harmless were close cousins.

They are not.

Encryption encourages a natural, and often dangerous, simplification. If the data is protected now, people infer that the problem has been addressed. The underlying image is a locked drawer: inaccessible, settled, dealt with. But the lock only speaks to the present condition of access. It says much less about the duration of the promise, the changing value of what sits inside, or the incentives facing anyone patient enough to collect the drawer itself and wait for better tools. A secret can remain unavailable and still be under threat. That is the peculiar cruelty of delayed exposure. The harm begins long before the reading begins.

This changes the strategic meaning of retention. Data storage is often treated as an administrative convenience, a compliance habit, or an operational insurance policy. Keep the records. Preserve the archive. Save the messages in case they matter later. Those impulses are understandable. They are also exactly what can turn retention into a weapon. The actor that collects encrypted material today is not always making a technical bet alone. It is making a temporal bet: that some information ages well enough to justify patience, and that its owner will be slower to minimise, migrate, or rethink what has been kept. The locked drawer becomes worth stealing not because it opens immediately, but because the contents may still matter when it finally does.

That is the tension at the centre of the chapter. Institutions retain data to preserve continuity, accountability, convenience, and memory. Adversaries collect data for future optionality. Both are acting under uncertainty. One side calls it good administration. The other calls it opportunity. Between them lies a contest over time horizons. Confidentiality turns out not to be a permanent state but a duration claim, and many organisations make that claim without ever deciding how long they truly need it to hold.

The stakes reach well beyond technical embarrassment. When old data becomes newly readable, the damage is rarely confined to the original moment of collection. Relationships can be reinterpreted. Archives can be mined for leverage. Routine records can be combined with later disclosures to redraw networks of trust, obligation, vulnerability, and intent. A long-retained dataset can acquire meanings it did not possess at the moment it was created. That is why the most dangerous information is not always the most dramatic. It is often the data that keeps its relevance while changing its use. A sealed envelope can become more explosive with age, not less.

This has consequences for how institutions judge value. Many security decisions still revolve around present sensitivity: what would hurt if exposed now, what must be protected during this transaction, what would cause immediate scandal or loss. That frame is too narrow. Some information decays quickly and can be treated accordingly. Some ripens. The same record can move from operational trivia to strategic asset when political alignments shift, when identities are linked across datasets, or when an apparently minor personal detail becomes a handle for coercion. A serious institution therefore has to think not only about present confidentiality, but about future compromise multipliers - the conditions under which ordinary retained material becomes significantly more dangerous later.

The path ahead follows that logic from collection to consequence. It begins with the simple but unsettling reason unreadable data is still worth taking, then turns to the different lifespans of secrets and the way those lifespans alter the meaning of protection. From there the argument widens into the institutional damage caused by retroactive exposure, where alliances, contracts, and private assurances can all be weakened by information that was once considered safely buried. The sequence matters because the threat is easy to caricature as either speculative paranoia or mere data hygiene. It is neither. It is a strategic contest over the afterlife of information.

A paper file helps keep the issue honest. A note scrawled for a meeting may deserve to be discarded by evening. A signed personnel record may need handling very differently because its relevance persists, mutates, and accumulates context long after the ink dries. Digital systems encourage us to forget this distinction because storage is cheap and retrieval is frictionless. The result is a culture of preservation without much discrimination. That culture is a gift to any actor willing to think in decades rather than quarters.

The diagnostic question, then, is harsher than whether a system encrypts properly. It is whether an institution knows which of its secrets must survive time, which can safely perish, and which archived materials would become strategically dangerous if tomorrow's capabilities were applied to yesterday's records. Until that question is faced directly, retention will keep masquerading as prudence even when it has already become a form of exposure.

## Why data retention becomes a weapon

In June 2015, when the United States Office of Personnel Management disclosed the breach of highly sensitive personnel and security-clearance records in Washington, D.C., the public immediately grasped the scale of the embarrassment. What took longer to settle in was the strategic character of what had been taken. These were not merely contemporary credentials or short-lived administrative files. They were background investigations, family details, foreign contacts, financial vulnerabilities, fingerprints, and the slow bureaucratic record of who could be trusted with secrets. The concrete outcome was not a single moment of exploitation. It was the creation of a reserve.

That reserve could age well.

This is the logic that makes data retention a weapon. Information does not need to be readable now in order to be worth collecting now. It only needs a plausible future in which its contents remain valuable and the cost of unlocking or correlating them falls. The common image of encryption as a closed box can obscure this. If a file is encrypted, many institutions behave as though the danger has been suspended. Yet encryption is not a permanent condition. It is a promise about duration under particular assumptions. The box may remain shut today and still be worth stealing because its contents will matter tomorrow.

Once that point is seen clearly, the strategic logic of "harvest now, decrypt later" ceases to look exotic. Show the scene and it becomes almost banal.

A collector intercepts traffic, copies archives, or exfiltrates records even when direct exploitation is not immediately possible. The named concept is deferred utility. Explain it, and the behaviour turns rational rather than melodramatic. Storage is relatively cheap, patience can be institutionalised, and some categories of information retain or even increase their value over time. The implication follows with uncomfortable force. The future readability of data is only one part of the problem. The future usefulness of data is the other, and in many cases it is the more stable half of the equation.

This is why long-lived secrets attract patient collection. Diplomatic cables may remain relevant because alliances, grudges, negotiating positions, and private assessments do not evaporate simply because a meeting has ended. Design files may continue to matter because engineering choices, supply dependencies, and research paths carry value long after a product cycle moves on. Identity records may become more dangerous with age because they can be combined with later disclosures, organisational changes, or personal vulnerabilities. Legal archives may preserve leverage precisely because institutions rely on continuity of record and cannot simply wish away their own documented past. The abstraction of risk becomes visible here in a simple behaviour: somebody keeps the file because one day it may still be worth opening.

A contrast helps. Consider an ephemeral chat used to coordinate a routine task between colleagues. Its confidentiality may matter intensely for a short interval. After the task is complete, the message may lose most of its strategic significance unless it contains something unusually revealing. Now consider a personnel database holding addresses, family links, previous employers, disciplinary history, travel patterns, financial strain, security vetting notes, and the internal judgements that determine who can approach restricted work. The first item is a spark. The second is dry timber. Both may be encrypted. Only one almost guarantees future interest from a patient collector because the passage of time can deepen rather than diminish its utility.

This difference exposes a bad institutional habit. Many organisations still classify sensitivity largely by present embarrassment or present operational disruption. They ask what would hurt if exposed now, what would create immediate liability, what would cause headlines, what would force executive explanation by Friday afternoon. Those are not foolish questions. They are incomplete ones. A patient adversary does not think chiefly in press cycles. It asks whether the information can be joined to other information later, whether it helps map a network, whether it reveals enduring weakness, whether it preserves evidence of private disagreement, whether it offers a future coercive handle once circumstances change. This is how retention becomes weaponised: the value lies not only in what the data says today, but in what it can be made to say later.

The 2015 Office of Personnel Management breach remains a stark illustration because the records taken had exactly this enduring character. Background investigation files were not merely historical snapshots. They recorded habits, affiliations, relationships, disclosures, and vulnerabilities that could assist future screening, targeting, coercion, or counterintelligence mapping. The named concept here is time-shifted intelligence value. Explain it plainly and one sees why such material is different from an intercepted password reset link or a short-lived transaction token. The records can be mined years later against an altered political landscape, a changed organisational chart, or a newly surfaced source. The implication is severe. A dataset can become more exploitable as context accumulates around it.

A second example makes the same point from a different domain. In corporate life, design files, source repositories, merger documents, and legal working papers often remain useful well beyond the quarter in which they were created. An unreleased product design may still illuminate capability, manufacturing choices, or future commercial strategy years later. A legal archive may preserve internal views about risk, compliance, pricing, or negotiation positions that become valuable in later disputes. A source-code archive can reveal technical debt, security posture, architecture, or past shortcuts long after the codebase evolves. Show the scene and the strategic temptation is obvious. An adversary does not need immediate publication or instant exploitation. It may simply want the option to return later, once the material can be compared with new evidence or new capabilities.

This also explains why retention habits inside defending institutions matter so much. Storage often appears prudent because deletion feels irreversible and administrators are trained to fear the accusation that something needed was destroyed too soon. Compliance functions reward preservation. Legal teams prefer records that can be retrieved. Operations teams like logs for troubleshooting. Executives like the reassurance that everything can be reconstructed after a dispute. Each of these preferences is understandable. Together they can produce a data estate swollen far beyond what strategic prudence would recommend. The visible behaviour is easy to recognise: backups kept by default, chat histories preserved out of inertia, archives duplicated across vendors, old personnel files retained long after active need has faded, cryptographically protected material kept indefinitely because encryption is assumed to neutralise the danger. That assumption is where the weapon begins to form.

The phrase *confidentiality is a time-bound promise* should therefore be taken literally. Confidentiality does not exist in the abstract any more than freshness does. It exists over an interval. A payment instruction may need secrecy for moments or hours. A merger negotiation may require secrecy for months. A covert relationship, a legal privilege file, or a security-clearance record may require protection for years or decades. Yet many technical and administrative systems flatten these distinctions. A system encrypts data and records that it has done so. A procurement team verifies that encryption at rest is enabled. An audit notes that traffic is protected in transit. The organisation then quietly acts as though all sensitive information has been given the same kind of security, when in reality only some of it has been given the right duration of security.

This matters because collection and retention operate on different sides of an asymmetry. The collector can be opportunistic. It can gather broadly, index cheaply, and wait to see which materials ripen. The defender must be selective in advance. It must decide which data should exist at all, which should be segmented, which should be deleted, which should receive the strongest long-term protections, and which should never be pooled with neighbouring datasets because future correlation would magnify the damage. One side buys options. The other side has to reduce them. That imbalance is what turns retention into a strategic matter rather than a mere administrative convenience.

The role of correlation deserves special attention here. Old encrypted material rarely remains dangerous only in isolation. Its value often lies in combination. An old personnel file gains power when combined with later breach data, public records, location traces, financial leaks, or social graphs. An archived diplomatic cable becomes more revealing when read alongside subsequent events, shifting alliances, or private messages exposed from another source. A legal memo becomes more coercive when paired with evidence of later contradiction. The named concept is cumulative exposure. Explain it, and the weaponised character of retention becomes clearer. Time does not merely preserve data. It furnishes new interpretive tools for it.

Still, a credible limitation must be acknowledged. Not all retained encrypted data becomes strategically meaningful, and not every institution storing large volumes of information is thereby inviting future catastrophe in equal measure. Some records genuinely lose value quickly. Some archives contain mostly administrative residue with little long-term intelligence or coercive utility. Some encrypted stores remain difficult to access for reasons that go beyond cryptography, including segmentation, destruction policies for key material, or the simple irrelevance of the contents once the underlying activity has passed. This matters because the subject attracts sloppy maximalism. One can begin to sound as though every preserved file is a time bomb and every retention policy a gift to an adversary. That would be lazy analysis.

Yet the limitation clarifies rather than weakens the central claim. The question is not whether *all* retained data becomes a weapon. It is whether institutions can distinguish between data that merely accumulates and data that matures into leverage. That distinction requires more than a generic sensitivity label. It requires thinking about longevity, future correlation, political usefulness, personal vulnerability, technical replicability, and institutional dependence on continuity. The discipline lies in naming what kinds of information retain strategic value after their immediate business purpose ends. Without that naming, retention continues by default, which is precisely the condition a patient collector hopes to find.

A further complication is that data can change category without changing content. A routine employee record may acquire intelligence value when the employee later enters sensitive work. An ordinary contact list may become politically valuable once an organisation is accused of influence operations. Design documentation may become strategically significant when supply chains tighten or a technology acquires defence relevance. Private correspondence that once looked merely embarrassing may later become coercive if a public figure's position changes or a negotiation turns hostile. The file itself has not transformed. The world around it has. That is why present value is such an unreliable guide to future harm.

Legal archives illustrate this with special sharpness because institutions often preserve them as though duration were automatically protective rather than dangerously cumulative. Contracts, draft positions, privileged communications, due diligence materials, internal risk assessments, and negotiation histories all embody a peculiar blend of continuity and vulnerability. They are kept because institutions need memory, evidence, and defensibility. They are also precisely the sorts of material that can expose contradiction, hypocrisy, bargaining thresholds, or known weaknesses when reinterpreted later. A patient adversary understands this perfectly well. It does not need to publish everything. It may only need to read enough to know where pressure can be applied.

The strategic consequence is that retention decisions can no longer be treated as neutral technical housekeeping. They are choices about future attack surface. To keep a secret is not only to preserve its utility for oneself; it is also, in some cases, to preserve its future utility for an adversary who may gain access later by means not yet available. This does not mean institutions should embrace a childish cult of deletion. Many records must be preserved for legal, scientific, operational, or public reasons. It does mean they should stop treating preservation as an uncomplicated virtue. The locked drawer is not safer because it remains in the house indefinitely. It may simply be ripening in place.

That brings the argument back to the contrast between ephemeral chat and personnel databases. The former may be sensitive in the moment and nearly worthless later. The latter may look dull in the moment and become far more consequential later. Security language often privileges what feels dramatic now over what can become dangerous slowly. A mature institution reverses that reflex. It asks not only what would sting if exposed this week, but what would still matter after a decade, what could be recombined with future data, and what retained records would give an adversary a patient route to coercion, impersonation, or influence. That is the real logic of harvest now, decrypt later: not the romance of a future breakthrough, but the mundane certainty that some secrets age into better weapons than others.

The unresolved question is therefore exacting and unpleasant in equal measure. When an institution keeps encrypted data because storage is cheap and deletion is awkward, is it preserving what it truly needs - or quietly building a library of future leverage for whoever proves patient enough to wait?

## Which secrets have long half-lives

In June 2015, when the United States Office of Personnel Management disclosed the breach of sensitive personnel and security-clearance records in Washington, D.C., much of the first reaction focused on exposure in the present tense: who had been affected, what had been taken, how embarrassing the failure was, what damage might follow immediately. That reaction was understandable and incomplete. The most unsettling feature of those records was not simply that they were sensitive at the moment of theft. It was that they would remain interpretable, combinable, and coercively useful for years. A background investigation does not expire like a boarding pass.

Some secrets ripen slowly.

That is the point institutions resist because it disrupts the tidy habit of valuing information according to immediate pain. A leaked password reset token may cause instant trouble and then become worthless. A diplomatic assessment, a personnel file, a design archive, or a private legal memorandum may sit quietly for years and then become far more dangerous when joined to later events, later disclosures, or later computational capabilities. The difference is not merely one of content. It is one of half-life: the period over which the information remains actionable, interpretable, or politically combustible. Once that frame is adopted, data classification begins to look less like a filing exercise and more like a problem of strategic time.

The language of half-life is useful precisely because it resists the false simplicity of "sensitive" and "not sensitive". Show the scene and the weakness of those labels becomes obvious. An internal operations chat about a temporary software fault may matter intensely for a day and then hardly at all. A record of who authorised access to a restricted programme, who reported foreign contacts, who signed a controversial policy draft, or who approved a risky acquisition may remain live long after the original context has faded from memory. The named concept is durability of value. Explain it, and the strategic implication follows. Security cannot be judged only by present sensitivity because some information decays quickly while other information accumulates meaning as time supplies new context.

A useful way to bring order to this is to think in four broad families of secrets: operational, commercial, political, and personal. These are not rigid boxes. They are lenses for understanding why some kinds of information age differently from others. Operational secrets concern the mechanics of how something works or moves: procedures, schedules, system diagrams, access routes, inventories, incident plans, and technical dependencies. Commercial secrets concern advantage in markets: product designs, pricing logic, customer relationships, supply arrangements, acquisition plans, source code, and research directions. Political secrets concern decision, influence, and statecraft: diplomatic cables, internal assessments, policy disagreements, negotiating red lines, coalition strains, and intelligence reporting. Personal secrets concern the intimate terrain of identity and vulnerability: health, family links, finances, habits, correspondence, travel, biometrics, and the private disclosures from which trust and coercion are both made.

Each of these categories carries a different temporal logic. Operational data often has a short active life when tied to immediate procedures, but parts of it can persist longer than administrators assume. A network map may become outdated in detail and still remain valuable because architectures evolve by accretion rather than pure reinvention. A contingency plan may be superseded and still reveal institutional instincts, dependencies, and likely fallback choices. A maintenance schedule may look trivial until it reveals windows of vulnerability. The abstraction of operational secrecy becomes visible in familiar decisions: who may enter which system, when updates occur, where backups travel, how quickly emergency modes are invoked, which devices cannot be patched without downtime. These details may seem local. They often outlast the moment of their creation.

Commercial secrets have a more uneven half-life. A draft marketing slogan may deserve the dignity of oblivion. A product roadmap, source repository, engineering decision log, or supplier dependency file may age into strategic gold. A competitor reading old design files can learn not only what a company once intended, but what constraints shaped its choices, where it cut corners, which components it trusted, and what future directions remained plausible. That is why commercial archives can remain dangerous well after a launch window closes. They preserve patterns of judgement. A merger file or due diligence folder may seem stale after the deal is done, yet years later it can still reveal valuation assumptions, regulatory anxieties, internal doubts, or pressure points useful in negotiation and litigation. The secret survives because the institution that created it continues to live under the shadow of its own recorded choices.

Political secrets often possess the longest and strangest afterlives because they are embedded in relationships rather than transactions. A diplomatic cable may lose immediate urgency and retain immense value as a record of who trusted whom, who doubted whom, and what each side privately believed. Internal policy memoranda can become toxic not merely because they contain opinion, but because they preserve the contrast between public posture and private reasoning. Intelligence assessments may become newly valuable when later events expose which judgments proved right, which sources remained protected, and which alliances were more brittle than their public ceremonies suggested. Political information lives inside memory, and memory is where institutions are easiest to embarrass and hardest to repair.

Personal secrets form the most volatile category because their significance changes with biography. A routine personnel record may look mundane until the person concerned rises into a sensitive post. A family detail may look harmless until a relative becomes vulnerable. A disclosed financial pressure may appear stale until a later crisis makes it freshly exploitable. A record of private correspondence may sit quietly for years and then become coercive once a career, candidacy, appointment, or legal dispute alters the surrounding incentives. This is why personal data so often acts as a bridge between the other categories. It can help interpret political networks, operational access, and commercial loyalties. The person is the point where systems touch.

The Office of Personnel Management breach remains instructive because the stolen records moved across all four categories at once. They were personal because they contained intimate disclosures, political because they mapped trusted access to state activity, operational because they illuminated how clearance systems worked, and indirectly commercial because they could aid targeting of contractors and supply chains tied to sensitive work. The named concept here is category drift. Explain it, and one sees why some datasets are far more dangerous than they appear at first glance. A single archive need not belong neatly to one type of value. It can migrate across them as institutions change, people move roles, and new information becomes available to combine with it.

A second example can be found in large stores of corporate e-mail and legal archives exposed through breaches or disclosure disputes. At first sight such material looks commercial or legal. Over time it often becomes political and personal as well. A negotiation thread reveals more than price. It exposes temper, trust, internal factions, hidden assumptions, and patterns of escalation. A legal archive preserves not only formal advice but the institution's private map of risk, fear, and acceptable compromise. A personnel discussion inside that archive can later shape reputations, succession contests, regulatory disputes, or public scandal. Show the scene and the instability of classification becomes obvious. The same dataset slides from one category to another not because its contents changed, but because the world acquired new reasons to read it differently.

This is why risk cannot be assessed only by today's value. Present value is too narrow and too flattering. It encourages the institution to ask what would hurt immediately, what would make headlines, what would disrupt this quarter, what would generate legal exposure right now. Those are the questions of a creature trapped in the present tense. Long half-life secrets demand another question: what becomes more dangerous later because other things will happen around it? That later danger often comes from what may be called a future compromise multiplier. A multiplier is any feature of data that increases its eventual leverage when combined with time, new capability, or new context.

The most important multipliers are not mystical. They are visible. A dataset becomes more dangerous when it links identities across domains, when it captures relationships rather than isolated facts, when it preserves internal contradiction, when it contains credentials or trust markers, when it maps dependencies, when it records vulnerabilities that persist, or when it can be merged with public records and later breaches. A roster is a multiplier if it identifies who belongs where. A travel archive is a multiplier if it reveals patterns and routines. An engineering log is a multiplier if it shows where the system was known to be weak. A personnel file is a multiplier if it records debts, disclosures, and associations that can be revisited later. These are not simply secrets. They are indexing systems for future pressure.

The danger becomes sharper when one remembers that time does not merely preserve data; it often improves the tools available to interpret it. A file that meant little on its own when first stolen may become richly legible once later leaks, public disclosures, machine analysis, or organisational changes provide new anchors. Personal records can be paired with location histories. Diplomatic notes can be compared with voting patterns and private meetings. Source repositories can be mined against later product flaws. Legal drafts can be measured against public denials. The same archive acquires a second life because the surrounding information environment has matured. Half-life, in this sense, is not just about how long the secret survives. It is about how the world learns to read it better.

Still, a limitation is necessary. Not every secret with a long half-life deserves equal alarm, and not every institution can classify perfectly for future context it cannot fully know. Some operational data genuinely decays into irrelevance. Some commercial material loses strategic force because the market moves too quickly. Some personal data becomes useless because the person leaves the field or the institution no longer matters. It would be foolish to pretend that every old file is an unexploded shell. That habit leads to indiscriminate retention under the guise of caution or indiscriminate panic under the guise of sophistication. Both are forms of confusion.

Yet the limitation strengthens the need for typology rather than weakening it. The point is not to predict the exact future meaning of each record. The point is to identify which classes of information are most likely to carry durable or migratory value. That can be done without prophecy. One can ask whether the data ties people to systems, whether it records decisions with long institutional tails, whether it reveals dependencies that are slow to change, whether it preserves contradiction between private and public positions, whether it exposes identities that may become more important later, and whether it can be easily joined to other datasets. These are ordinary questions. They are also strategically clarifying.

The four-family typology also helps correct a common mistake: assuming that personal data is somehow softer or less geopolitical than operational or political material. The truth is nastier. Personal information often provides the most efficient route into every other domain because institutions are staffed by human beings, not incorporeal departments. A security vetting file can illuminate political access. A contact list can illuminate commercial partnerships. A travel record can illuminate operational rhythm. A health disclosure can become coercive in a political context. The secret changes category because people carry their vulnerabilities across institutional boundaries wherever they go.

The filing cabinet returns here because it is a good antidote to abstraction. A thin folder marked 'routine' may, under certain circumstances, warrant no special drama. Under another, the same folder may become the missing piece that explains who had access, who knew, who hesitated, who benefited, or who can now be pressured. Institutions are often very good at asking which folder matters today. They are markedly worse at asking which folder will matter once other folders, leaks, crises, and technologies begin to talk to one another.

That is the real lesson of long half-lives. Some secrets decay; some survive; some mutate. A mature security posture does not treat these as poetic observations but as classification problems with institutional consequences. It asks not only what is sensitive, but what remains linkable, what remains interpretable, and what grows in coercive or intelligence value when context changes. The hardest question, therefore, is not whether a dataset is important right now. It is whether the institution can recognise the future compromise multipliers hiding in material that still looks, at first glance, too ordinary to fear.

## Strategic consequences of retroactive exposure

In June 2015, when the United States Office of Personnel Management disclosed the breach of sensitive personnel and security-clearance records in Washington, D.C., the immediate public concern centred on theft in the present tense: who had lost privacy, which agencies had failed, what damage might follow in the next news cycle. The more serious question sat behind it. What happens when records taken years earlier remain useful long after the original breach has faded from public attention? A clearance file is not merely a snapshot. It is a lever with a long memory.

The past can be reopened.

That is the distinctive threat posed by retroactive exposure. Ordinary breach language encourages people to picture harm as immediate and visible: money stolen, service disrupted, files dumped online, reputations damaged in a burst of scandal. Retroactive exposure works differently. Information collected under one set of assumptions about secrecy becomes readable, interpretable, or exploitable under another. The material may be old; the pressure it creates can be entirely current. A secret does not need to remain fresh in order to remain dangerous. It needs only to remain legible enough to alter a relationship, discredit a claim, expose a contradiction, or identify a vulnerability at the wrong moment.

This makes retroactive decryption strategically distinct from routine disclosure. Show the scene and the difference becomes clear. An alliance has functioned for years on the assumption that private assessments, negotiation positions, and candid internal judgements would remain confined to those who made them. Later, older encrypted records become accessible. The named concept is a delayed coercive value. Explain it, and the implications widen quickly. The harm does not depend on immediate publication. It can arise from selective revelation, quiet blackmail, subtle pressure in negotiation, or the mere fact that one side now understands how the other privately weighed costs, loyalties, or fears. Trust erodes not because people spoke candidly, but because they discover that candour has an afterlife.

Alliances are especially vulnerable to this kind of afterlife because alliance politics depends heavily on managed discrepancy between what partners say publicly and what they admit privately. Diplomats flatter, hedge, reassure, and bargain in different registers at once. Defence planning assumes frank discussion behind closed doors. Intelligence sharing often rests on the expectation that private doubts will not be replayed later as instruments of humiliation. When older communications become newly readable, the resulting damage rarely looks like a single dramatic betrayal. It looks like a slow leak of confidence. A partner becomes less willing to speak plainly. A channel once used for candid assessment becomes sterile. A government delays sharing because its officials no longer believe that their private reasoning will remain bounded by time. The visible behaviour is restraint. The strategic cost is poorer coordination.

Contracts suffer in a related way. A contract is not merely a signed document; it sits atop internal drafts, negotiation notes, side assessments, legal reservations, pricing assumptions, and risk calculations. If the surrounding materials become accessible long after the agreement is executed, the formal document may remain valid even as the relational basis for it weakens. Show the scene and the danger is plain. One party learns, years later, that the other privately anticipated a defect, doubted a representation, or viewed a key clause as a temporary expedient. Name the concept and the problem sharpens: retrospective asymmetry. Explain it, and one sees why old data can destabilise present obligations. The exposure may not void the contract. It may instead alter bargaining power in renewal, litigation, regulation, or political oversight. The legal text stays fixed. The interpretive battlefield changes.

This is why blackmail belongs in the conversation, though it should be understood broadly rather than melodramatically. Blackmail in strategic settings is not always a crude demand accompanied by a lurid threat. It can take the form of quiet reminders, calibrated disclosure risk, or a private demonstration that someone knows more than they should. A decades-old record of undisclosed contacts, debts, medical vulnerability, extramarital conduct, internal disagreement, or ethically dubious judgement may gain force precisely because the subject thought the relevant moment had passed. The named concept here is revived leverage. Explain it, and the mechanism is simple enough. Retroactive exposure restores the present value of past secrecy. The implication is chilling. Time does not necessarily dissolve vulnerability. It can preserve it until the moment it becomes politically or personally maximally useful.

The same logic enables disinformation, and here the danger becomes more subtle. When old authentic data becomes available, it does not need to be published truthfully to be weaponised. It can be edited, sequenced misleadingly, stripped of context, mixed with forged material, or released in fragments that encourage false inferences. Authenticity becomes a raw material for manipulation. A partial archive of genuine correspondence can support a false narrative more effectively than a wholly fabricated document ever could, because the presence of real material lowers scepticism and raises confusion. The sealed envelope has been opened, but not in a way that produces clarity. It produces contest over what the archive means. That contest can be exploited to discredit institutions, damage public trust, and force defensive energy into argument about the past rather than action in the present.

A useful example lies in the broad pattern revealed by the 2016 disclosures surrounding the Democratic National Committee and John Podesta in the United States. Publicly reported e-mail disclosures did not need to be entirely novel in substance to prove politically potent. Their force came from timing, sequencing, selective exposure, and the difficulty of maintaining clear public interpretation once authentic internal material entered a hostile information environment. The relevance here is not that the material had been protected by future-vulnerable encryption in the specific technical sense. It is that older private communications became instruments in a later political contest. The named concept is temporal repurposing. Explain it, and the broader lesson emerges. Data collected or revealed under one strategic context can be redeployed under another, with effects that depend less on the original secrecy breach than on the later environment into which the material is introduced.

A second example returns to the Office of Personnel Management breach. Those files contained not only direct identifiers but the sort of contextual material that can support future targeting, social mapping, and counterintelligence pressure. The strategic consequence was not exhausted by the original compromise. A record of foreign contacts, finances, past disclosures, family ties, or behavioural vulnerabilities can become more valuable as careers advance, access changes, and organisations evolve. Show the scene and one sees why retroactive exposure is so corrosive. A person who was minor at the time of data theft may later become significant. An old disclosure once judged manageable may later become discrediting in a different office, administration, or public climate. The implication is severe. Institutions do not merely lose secrets; they lose control over the future timing of vulnerability.

This timing problem matters for deterrence because it changes where harm is expected to appear. Traditional security thinking often seeks immediate, attributable effects: a system outage, a public leak, a measurable theft. Retroactive exposure often produces indirect and delayed harms instead. A negotiator softens a position because they fear what the other side may know from older records. An official declines a posting because they suspect past disclosures could surface. An ally withholds candour. A firm accepts worse terms in settlement because it cannot predict what internal archives might reveal if the dispute escalates. None of these outcomes may be publicly legible as the consequence of long-stored data becoming newly exploitable. Yet each is strategically real. The damage is behavioural before it is cinematic.

This is one reason retroactive exposure so often escapes adequate political attention. Bureaucracies reward response to visible crises. They are less adept at recognising changes in conduct caused by quietly altered expectations. A security team can report a breach. It struggles to report the years of self-censorship, narrowed trust, and defensive bargaining that follow once people believe the past may no longer remain buried. The abstraction of institutional trust, therefore, needs to be tied to behaviours we can actually notice: fewer written candid assessments, more oral communication, shorter distribution lists, increased compartmentation, reluctance to record dissent, excessive retention of deniable ambiguity, or defensive over-lawyering in negotiation. These are adaptations to the possibility that yesterday's protected record may become tomorrow's instrument.

A credible limitation needs airing. Not every old dataset, even if exposed, produces dramatic strategic harm. Context decays. Some relationships end. Some people leave office. Some records become meaningless because the systems, products, or disputes they describe no longer matter. Retroactive exposure can also be blunted by the abundance of data in modern life; not every archive has the coherence or salience required to support coercion or persuasive disinformation. This matters because a certain fevered style of analysis treats every retained encrypted record as a guaranteed future catastrophe. That is not serious thinking. Many old files are just old files.

Yet the limitation clarifies rather than softens the central claim. The strategic problem lies with records whose meaning persists or can be revived through correlation, changed context, or changed capability. A personnel file, diplomatic archive, signing history, legal memorandum, design repository, or internal negotiation record has a different future profile from disposable chat about a lunch meeting. The point is discrimination. Institutions must learn which categories of data preserve leverage across time and which do not. Without that discrimination, they drift into one of two equally childish positions: hoard everything because deletion feels frightening, or shrug because the future feels too speculative to govern.

The deterrence lens becomes useful here because it asks not only whether harm can occur, but how the expectation of harm changes behaviour now. An actor contemplating long-term collection or future decryption is encouraged when targets retain richly interpretable archives, preserve unnecessary identity data, depend on durable signatures they cannot migrate cleanly, or treat old encrypted records as inert simply because they remain unreadable for the moment. The actor is discouraged when those same targets reduce retention, compartment long-lived secrets, rotate trust anchors effectively, and design systems so that old material ages badly from the attacker's point of view. Deterrence in this domain does not chiefly mean threatening punishment after exposure. It means shrinking the later payoff from having collected the material in the first place.

This is where early migration and minimisation enter, not as fashionable slogans but as ways of changing the future value of the archive. Early migration matters because long-lived trust systems - signatures, certificate hierarchies, archival protections, protected identities - cannot be replaced at speed without institutional pain. Minimisation matters because the most elegant encryption regime in the world cannot protect data forever if the institution keeps more than it truly needs for longer than it can confidently defend. The visible behaviours attached to these ideas are prosaic: shorten retention schedules, separate identity data from routine operations, reduce the spread of sensitive archives, map where long-lived secrets reside, replace brittle signing arrangements before crisis dictates the timetable. None of this is glamorous. Strategy rarely is when it works.

The sealed envelope returns here for a final reason. The danger of retroactive exposure is not simply that someone one day reads what should have remained shut. It is that the delayed opening changes present relationships in ways nobody can easily count. Partners trust less. Institutions speak less plainly. Individuals become easier to pressure. Authentic old material becomes feedstock for later deception. Contracts and archives remain on the shelf, yet the world around them has shifted because someone else may now know what was once safely folded inside.

The hardest question, then, is not whether old encrypted records might eventually be opened. It is whether the institutions depending on those records have asked what happens after opening no longer belongs to the past tense alone: which relationships would bend first, which private contradictions would become leverage, and which forms of public trust would prove weaker than they looked once the sealed envelope started circulating as a weapon rather than a memory.

# Chapter 5

# Standards Governance and Cryptographic Power

What decides whether a cryptographic choice becomes part of the world's wiring rather than just a clever proposal in a paper? The answer is rarely mathematics alone. A standard begins as a technical settlement, but once it is built into chips, cloud services, developer libraries, procurement templates, audit language, and user expectations, it stops behaving like a suggestion. It becomes a habit with legal documents attached. The difficulty is not merely that people depend on it. The difficulty is that they forget they are depending on it until change becomes painful.

That pain is the real clue. A protocol can be widely criticised and still survive because older devices cannot negotiate anything better, because vendors have little appetite for costly rewrites, because buyers fear disruption more than latent weakness, or because compliance still recognises the old vocabulary. A technically cleaner replacement may exist and still fail to spread. The lock is not just on the door. It is in the supply cupboard, the training manual, the factory line, and the contract renewal notice. Once a standard reaches that point, questions about security become inseparable from questions about power.

This is why standards governance deserves more seriousness than it usually receives. People often talk about cryptography as though the important struggle ends once experts identify a sound algorithm and publish the details for scrutiny. That matters enormously, but it is only part of the story. A standard must be selected, implemented, licensed, accelerated in hardware, maintained in software, explained to auditors, accepted by buyers, and tolerated by legacy systems. Trust attaches itself not only to proofs and peer review, but to process, stewardship, and the surrounding institutions that decide what counts as acceptable for everyone else. Technical confidence and institutional confidence do not always move together.

The central tension lies here. Open standards and shared implementations make modern digital life possible because they allow strangers, firms, states, and devices to communicate without negotiating from scratch each time. Yet the same shared arrangements concentrate influence. Whoever shapes the standard, controls a dominant implementation, holds key intellectual property, or writes the certification language can affect what others can deploy, when they can migrate, and what kinds of security become practical rather than merely admirable. Cryptography, in that sense, is a public good with private chokepoints and state interests threaded through it.

That tension matters because states are not neutral custodians of secure communication. They have a dual role that cannot be wished away. They want reliable protection for finance, infrastructure, administration, military command, and civic trust. They also value intelligence advantage, strategic access, and the option to preserve asymmetries where possible. Those incentives do not always collide openly, but they do pull in different directions. A state may champion strong standards in one forum while quietly preferring ambiguity in another. A firm may market trust while resisting changes that would weaken its control over an installed base. A standards body may pursue procedural legitimacy while depending on participants whose interests are not purely technical. The result is not necessarily corruption. It is politics in its ordinary clothes.

The stakes reach further because standards are never just documents. They harden into reference code, silicon support, default settings, approved modules, procurement requirements, and inherited assumptions inside organisations that did not participate in their creation. A secure option that cannot be integrated into a major product line, certified under prevailing regimes, or supported across mixed fleets may be available in theory and absent in practice. Likewise, a widely deployed option may continue to dominate long after its limitations are understood because too many systems need to keep talking to one another for anyone to force a clean break. Shared communication creates collective safety and collective drag at the same time.

This is why coordination is such a burdensome part of security. Interoperability sounds benign until one notices that partial adoption can widen exposure rather than reduce it. A mixed environment of old and new trust assumptions often creates downgrade paths, awkward compatibility exceptions, and false confidence that migration is already underway simply because some visible component has changed. Weakest-link dynamics enter quietly. The organisation with the strongest policy on paper may still depend on a supplier, partner, or device fleet that keeps an older standard alive. What looks like a technical detail is often a governance verdict delivered by network dependence.

The route ahead follows that verdict from the way standards settle into infrastructure, through the legitimacy struggles around how algorithms are chosen, into the uncomfortable reality that national security interests and public communications security are bound together rather than cleanly opposed. From there the focus moves below the level of abstract selection into implementations, patents, and the practical control exerted by those who can make a standard deployable or leave it stranded. The argument then widens into interoperability, where coordination failures acquire strategic weight, before tightening around assurance regimes that can certify presence without really measuring adaptability, upgrade paths, or the politics of key control.

A spare part left on a workshop shelf can clarify the whole problem. It may look trivial until a machine breaks and everyone discovers that only one supplier makes the compatible replacement, the old model cannot accept the newer fitting, and the paperwork for switching was never approved. Standards governance works much the same way. The hardest question is not whether a protocol or algorithm looks respectable in isolation. It is who can change it, who cannot, who profits from delay, and which institutions will discover too late that their security posture was built less on sovereign choice than on inherited dependence they never properly mapped.

## How standards become infrastructure

In April 2014, when the Heartbleed vulnerability in OpenSSL became public, organisations across the world discovered a truth they had managed not to think about for years: a single widely used cryptographic library, maintained outside most of their own walls, had become part of their basic operating condition. Servers needed patching, certificates needed replacing, passwords needed resetting, and many administrators found themselves asking a humiliating question far too late. Where, exactly, are we using this thing? The concrete outcome was not merely emergency repair. It was sudden recognition that a component chosen for convenience and interoperability had hardened into infrastructure.

The interesting part was how ordinary that hardening had been.

Standards rarely arrive wearing a crown. They appear as sensible agreements: a protocol version, an algorithm suite, a library default, a certificate format, a transport rule that makes one system talk to another without custom negotiation. Engineers adopt them because they work, vendors support them because customers ask for compatibility, auditors like them because they are recognisable, and buyers prefer them because nobody wants to explain why their product speaks a dialect only three machines on earth can understand. Then, after enough products ship and enough habits settle, the standard stops feeling like a choice at all. It becomes the floorboards.

That transformation from choice to floorboards is the central fact. A standard is not just a technical specification sitting politely in a document repository. It becomes infrastructure when it is embedded in products, build systems, silicon support, procurement language, maintenance routines, compliance expectations, and human reflexes. Show the scene and the mechanism becomes plain. A network appliance ships with a default protocol stack. An enterprise integrates it. A vendor support agreement assumes certain cipher suites. An audit framework recognises those suites as acceptable. Training materials and internal playbooks are written around them. A later attempt to change the standard is no longer a neat engineering substitution. It is a disturbance to contracts, schedules, certifications, staffing, and service continuity. The named concept is infrastructural entrenchment. Explain it, and the strategic implication follows. Security choices become sticky not because nobody knows better, but because too many other things now depend on the old answer.

This is why changing standards can be costly even when the underlying technical change looks straightforward on paper. Engineers like clean diagrams. Institutions inhabit dirty ones. A new protocol version may be mathematically sound, publicly reviewed, and supported by capable software. Yet if old industrial controllers, hospital devices, transport systems, vendor appliances, or embedded modules cannot negotiate it properly, the migration ceases to be a technical preference and becomes a political fight over downtime, risk ownership, capital spend, and acceptable breakage. The abstraction of efficiency becomes a visible decision: does the institution tolerate temporary incompatibility, buy replacements early, pressure the supplier, or keep the old standard alive until the last fragile system can limp across the line? Most organisations answer with delay because delay spreads pain more thinly than forced replacement. Path dependence is born in exactly that mood.

A useful example is the persistence of older versions of Transport Layer Security and related protocol support long after better understood options existed. Public browsers, major platforms, and large providers have repeatedly tried to retire older versions, yet the process has always been slowed by legacy dependencies: ageing medical equipment, industrial systems, old operating systems, network appliances, and business software that was never designed for frequent cryptographic renovation. The visible behaviour is familiar. Security teams want stricter settings. Operations teams warn of broken connections. Business owners fear service complaints. Vendors offer cautious upgrade windows. The named concept here is compatibility drag. Explain it, and the point sharpens. A protocol remains alive not because experts still admire it, but because the installed world cannot shed it without paying a price many institutions would rather postpone. The implication is brutal in its simplicity. Weakness can persist because replacement is socially harder than risk.

This persistence has a strategic consequence that people often underestimate. Once a standard becomes infrastructure, it starts distributing power unevenly. The vendor that controls an implementation, the platform that sets the default, the procurement authority that blesses one profile, and the regulator that defines acceptable compliance can all shape what others are realistically able to deploy. A nominally open standard may therefore live inside a highly unequal environment of adoption. "Available" is not the same as "usable at scale". A secure option may exist in principle and still fail because the device fleet cannot support it, the supplier will not warranty it, the audit regime has not yet caught up, or the cost of testing it across mixed environments is politically impossible to justify this quarter. The standard begins as shared technical language and ends as a map of dependence.

The history of cryptographic standards is full of this quiet accumulation. A cipher suite becomes default because it is well supported. That support attracts more users. More users create more demand for compatible hardware acceleration, training materials, certification guidance, and vendor tooling. Those investments then reinforce the standard's position even if a stronger alternative appears. The process resembles a footpath across grass. Nobody planned a road at the start. Enough people walked the same route, and suddenly there it was. Show the scene and one sees why security improvement is not merely a matter of persuading experts. It is a matter of redirecting traffic once the path has already hardened. The implication is broader than cryptography. Standards governance is inseparable from temporal inertia.

This is also why organisations routinely misdescribe their own security posture. They imagine that they "use strong cryptography" or "follow recognised standards", as though these were fresh, active judgements continuously renewed by careful scrutiny. Often they are inherited defaults frozen by prior procurement. A team may not know why a certain library was selected ten years ago, only that many systems now rely on it. An appliance may still ship with a legacy compatibility mode because the vendor found it easier to preserve old business than force customers into replacement. A compliance report may validate encryption at rest while saying little about whether the underlying cryptographic components can be changed cleanly when assumptions shift. The institution sees a control. The adversary sees a fossil.

Heartbleed illustrated this in humiliating miniature. The technical flaw mattered, obviously. Yet the deeper scandal was that so many organisations could not promptly answer basic dependency questions. Which systems used OpenSSL directly? Which used it through another product? Which certificates and keys might have been exposed? Which devices were too old or too obscure to patch quickly? The named concept is hidden centrality. Explain it, and the strategic lesson becomes unmistakable. A standard or implementation can become so ordinary that nobody notices how central it is until failure produces a scramble of belated cartography. The implication is that infrastructural status is often discovered only by breach, not by design.

A second example can be found in the persistence of older cryptographic and communication profiles inside specialised equipment. Hospitals, industrial plants, aviation systems, shipping networks, and utility environments often run devices with long service lives, limited update mechanisms, and certification burdens that make frequent change deeply unattractive. The protocol or algorithm profile inside such devices may have been respectable when adopted and awkwardly obsolete years later. Yet the standard survives because the device still functions, replacement costs are high, and system owners fear operational disruption more than an abstract future compromise. The secure alternative may be known. It may even be available. But if the vendor has not integrated it, if the test regime is expensive, or if downtime would interrupt critical work, the infrastructure stays as it is. Here path dependence is not a theory. It is a maintenance decision repeated until it becomes strategy.

Still, a credible limitation must be respected. Not all standards are prisons, and not all persistence is evidence of negligence. Some standards endure because they remain sound, interoperable, and economically sensible. Stability has real value. Frequent cryptographic churn can itself create vulnerabilities through rushed implementation, inconsistent migration, and operator error. A mature institution should not replace core standards merely to prove that it can move furniture around. That would be security by nervous fidgeting. Common, well-vetted standards often protect the world precisely because they are boring enough to be widely understood and well tested.

Yet that concession does not weaken the core argument. It sharpens the criterion. The problem is not stability as such. The problem is inability to distinguish justified stability from inherited drag. A sound standard that remains fit for purpose is an asset. A decaying standard kept alive because too much of the estate would break, too many suppliers would object, or too many audits still reference yesterday's assumptions is something else. It is infrastructure exercising power over judgement. The institution no longer asks, "What do we trust?" It asks, "What can we afford to stop trusting?" That is a much harder question, and far closer to reality.

This is where legacy devices matter as more than mere technical irritants. They are political actors in metal and plastic. A legacy device does not speak in meetings, but it shapes budgets, procurement road maps, maintenance windows, and risk appetite with surprising force. A manufacturer with a large installed base of older equipment can slow migration simply by making compatibility costly. A hospital administrator faced with replacing expensive devices early may accept weaker settings for longer. A utility operator may preserve an older protocol because the alternative requires field visits across geographically dispersed assets. The standard persists because the surrounding infrastructure is not just digital. It is capital, geography, warranty, labour, and fear of interruption.

The phrase *path dependence* sometimes sounds overly academic, but its meaning here is concrete enough to touch. Past choices narrow present options. A library chosen for convenience shapes what later products can integrate easily. A protocol profile blessed by certification becomes the path vendors optimise for. A hardware accelerator supporting one set of algorithms makes others slower or more expensive to deploy. A training programme teaches one operational rhythm and leaves alternatives underdeveloped. These are not abstractions floating above the institution. They are accumulated decisions that turn one route into the road and other routes into mud. Once enough wheels have gone through, the road starts telling people where they are allowed to drive.

This is why standards governance and cryptographic power belong together. The actor who influences the standard early does not only win an argument in a meeting room. It may shape hardware support, software defaults, procurement norms, certification language, and the practical tempo of future migration. Long after the technical debate appears settled, that influence survives in the infrastructure itself. The standard becomes a kind of slow force. It does not coerce dramatically. It narrows the field of realistic movement. Organisations then call this narrowing pragmatism, when often it is simply inherited dependence dressed in sensible shoes.

A more honest vocabulary would therefore treat standards not as neutral recommendations but as frozen negotiations with long afterlives. They embody trade-offs between security, speed, compatibility, cost, and governance. Once embedded widely enough, those trade-offs stop behaving like arguments and start behaving like conditions of existence. That is why even technically straightforward change can feel institutionally impossible. The floorboards are load-bearing now.

The hardest test comes when a standard still works well enough to keep everyone calm while quietly becoming too expensive to trust indefinitely. At that point the question is no longer whether a stronger option exists. It is whether the institution can identify where the old standard lives, who depends on it, which suppliers can move, which devices cannot, and who will bear the political cost of admitting that a former best practice has become a present constraint. Until that map is drawn, standards will keep pretending to be technical conveniences long after they have become infrastructure in the full strategic sense of the word.

## The politics of algorithm selection

In September 2013, *The New York Times*, ProPublica, and The Guardian reported allegations drawn from documents disclosed by Edward Snowden that the United States National Security Agency had pursued programmes aimed at influencing or circumventing aspects of global cryptographic practice. The technical details were debated, the evidence arrived in fragments, and not every public inference drawn at the time proved equally sound. The concrete outcome, however, was unmistakable. Confidence in parts of the standards process itself was damaged. Engineers, civil society groups, governments, and firms began asking a harsher question than whether an algorithm was mathematically clever. They asked who had shaped it, under what process, and for whose benefit.

That question altered the room.

Algorithm selection is often described as though it were the cleanest part of cryptographic governance: experts compare proposals, analyse security proofs, test performance, debate trade-offs, and eventually settle on a scheme judged suitably strong and practical. Much of that description is true. It is also incomplete. Algorithms do not enter the world as naked mathematics. They arrive through competitions, committees, institutional reputations, opaque or transparent design choices, national interests, vendor incentives, and public narratives about legitimacy. The trust they receive therefore has two layers. One is technical confidence: the belief that the construction resists known attacks under stated assumptions. The other is institutional confidence: the belief that the process by which the algorithm was advanced, reviewed, and selected was credible enough to justify dependence at scale. The seal matters. So does the hand that pressed it.

This distinction matters because a sound algorithm can still fail politically if its selection process looks compromised, and a politically celebrated algorithm can still fail technically if process esteem outpaces scrutiny. Show the scene and the problem becomes less abstract. A standards body endorses an algorithm after consultation and expert review. The underlying mathematics may be respectable. But if design parameters seem insufficiently explained, if key contributors appear unusually close to a state agency with conflicting incentives, or if the review process looks hurried, selective, or overly deferential, suspicion enters the adoption environment. The named concept is process legitimacy. Explain it, and the strategic implication follows. Cryptographic trust depends not only on whether the algorithm deserves confidence, but on whether the community judging it appears to have earned the right to ask for confidence.

The Dual_EC_DRBG controversy remains the clearest illustration. In the mid-2000s, the National Institute of Standards and Technology included Dual_EC_DRBG as an approved deterministic random bit generator in a standard. Researchers had already raised concerns about its efficiency and unusual structure. After the 2013 reporting and subsequent public debate, those older concerns were read in a darker light, especially because the generator's design included constants whose origins had not been explained in a way that satisfied broader trust. NIST later reopened public comment and revised its guidance. The technical story is subtle, and one should avoid reducing it to a cartoon. Yet the governance lesson is sharp. The issue was not only whether a backdoor had been proved beyond all doubt in public. It was that the perception of unexplained influence became corrosive enough to weaken institutional confidence in the selection process itself. The implication travelled far beyond one generator. Once process legitimacy is punctured, even innocent design decisions are forced to live under a cloud they may not deserve.

This is why openness matters, but also why openness is not a magic spell. Open publication, public comment, reference code, and academic scrutiny can all improve the quality and credibility of algorithm selection. They widen the review community, diversify criticism, and make it harder to smuggle extraordinary weakness through quiet authority alone. That is the usual public argument, and it is mostly right. Yet openness by itself does not settle trust. A design can be public and still badly understood. A review process can be open and still dominated by narrow communities, uneven incentives, or participants who lack the time to inspect a complex proposal deeply. The visible behaviour that turns openness into real assurance is not mere publication. It is sustained adversarial scrutiny, explicit response to criticism, transparent explanation of design choices, and a willingness to revise or abandon prestige projects when doubt remains serious enough.

That last point matters because algorithm selection is not only a scientific exercise. It is also a social test of whether disagreement can be handled without institutional defensiveness. When a standards process responds to credible criticism by widening review, clarifying rationale, and exposing hidden assumptions, confidence tends to grow even if the algorithm changes or is replaced. When the process closes ranks, treats scepticism as nuisance, or leans too heavily on authority, confidence shrinks even if the mathematics eventually survives scrutiny. The named concept here is procedural resilience. Explain it, and its strategic value becomes clear. Institutions earn trust not by pretending to be infallible, but by demonstrating that their selection processes can absorb challenge without collapsing into prestige protection.

The Advanced Encryption Standard competition offers a useful contrast. NIST's public selection process for AES, culminating in the choice of Rijndael in 2000, is often cited as a stronger model precisely because it combined open submission, public cryptanalysis, comparative evaluation, and a legible rationale for selection. One should not romanticise it; no process involving expertise, institutional authority, and international participation is free from politics. Still, the visible structure mattered. Competing designs were openly discussed. Performance and security trade-offs were aired. Criticism was part of the process rather than an external insult to it. The result was not merely technical acceptance. It was broader institutional confidence that the algorithm had survived a procedure people could inspect. That confidence helped AES become more than a winning design. It became a globally usable standard because enough actors judged the route to its selection credible.

This contrast helps separate technical confidence from institutional confidence without pretending the two are unrelated. Technical confidence concerns whether the algorithm, as analysed, appears sound against known attacks within defined assumptions. Institutional confidence concerns whether the community can trust the pathway by which those analyses were solicited, weighed, and translated into a standard. The first lives in proofs, cryptanalysis, reductions, implementation studies, and performance benchmarks. The second lives in governance: who was heard, how decisions were explained, whether parameter choices were justified, whether conflicts of interest were visible, whether review was wide enough, and whether the process can survive later scrutiny without turning evasive. The mathematics may be beautiful. The institution may still ask too much of reputation.

This matters because perceptions of influence can be as damaging as actual weakness. In cryptography, perception is not a cosmetic problem appended to an otherwise objective reality. It alters adoption, interoperability, procurement, diplomatic trust, and the willingness of states or firms to depend on shared standards. A government that suspects undue influence in a standards process may hesitate to adopt the result even if no technical flaw has yet been demonstrated. A vendor may avoid integrating an algorithm because customer confidence looks fragile. A standards body may find future selections harder because earlier opacity infected later judgments by association. The visible behaviours are easy to identify: procurement delays, duplicate internal evaluations, pressure for domestic alternatives, fragmented adoption, and the growth of parallel trust communities that no longer accept the same centre of authority. Perception, in other words, produces infrastructure effects.

This is one reason algorithm selection is unavoidably political even when the algorithms are not partisan objects in the vulgar sense. States possess genuine and conflicting incentives. They want strong public cryptography because finance, government administration, critical infrastructure, military operations, and social trust all depend on it. They also have reasons to preserve intelligence advantage where possible. Firms have their own cross-pressures: market trust, implementation cost, patent position, brand prestige, and dependence on regulatory acceptance. Academic participants may seek elegance, publication, or disciplinary influence. Civil society groups may prioritise transparency and rights-protective governance. None of these motives automatically corrupts the process. But they guarantee that algorithm selection cannot be treated as a purely innocent tribunal of mathematics. The participants bring interests to the table. The table does not become neutral merely because the subject is algebraic.

A credible limitation needs emphasis here. The fact that algorithm selection has political dimensions does not mean every standard is tainted or every winning design is the creature of hidden manipulation. That style of suspicion quickly becomes sterile. Most modern cryptographic selection processes involve many serious people acting in good faith, and many standardised algorithms have withstood extensive scrutiny while serving the world remarkably well. It would be childish to read every design choice as covert statecraft or every unexplained parameter as a smoking pistol. Paranoia is not analysis. It is often just vanity with a trench coat.

Yet the limitation strengthens the case for institutional seriousness rather than weakening it. Because many processes are conducted in good faith, the integrity of those processes becomes even more valuable and even more worth protecting. Because not every concern masks a conspiracy, institutions must show clearly how they distinguish routine design judgement from decisions that warrant deeper explanation. Because most standards do not collapse into scandal, the few moments when legitimacy is called into doubt can have disproportionate effects on trust for years afterwards. The response should not be indiscriminate suspicion. It should be disciplined scrutiny tied to visible process features.

One of those features is the handling of parameters and unexplained choices. Cryptographers know how much can ride on seemingly small details: constants, curve selections, implementation guidance, randomness assumptions, side-channel considerations, and performance trade-offs. For outsiders these can look like technical clutter. For trust they are often the hinge. When a process explains such choices clearly, allows independent reconstruction where possible, and documents why alternatives were rejected, institutional confidence strengthens because outsiders can see the reasons even if they cannot reproduce the entire intellectual labour themselves. When explanations are thin, delayed, or defensive, doubt spreads because people are forced to rely too heavily on authority in a domain where authority alone has already proved a dangerous idol.

Another feature is who gets to criticise without being marginalised. Open peer review sounds noble until one notices how easily prestige, funding, access, and committee culture can narrow who feels entitled to speak frankly. A process dominated by a small club may remain technically sophisticated and still lose legitimacy if outsiders come to view it as self-referential or too entangled with particular state or corporate interests. By contrast, a process that tolerates rough criticism, publishes objections, and answers them substantively rather than ceremonially signals something more valuable than harmony. It signals that the institution believes its choices can survive daylight. The seal is not hidden in the drawer.

This has direct implications for later questions of verification and trust. Verification is never only a matter of checking whether code conforms to a specification or whether an algorithm remains unbroken by current public knowledge. It also involves judging whether the institutions asking others to rely on a standard have behaved in ways that merit durable confidence. That is why technical audits cannot substitute for legitimacy, and legitimacy cannot substitute for technical scrutiny. The two forms of confidence must reinforce rather than replace one another. Where they separate too far, trouble begins: perfect process can elevate weak ideas, and strong mathematics can be stranded by mistrust.

The broader strategic point is almost severe in its plainness. Cryptography works socially only when enough people accept not just the equations but the stewardship of the equations. An algorithm selected in the cloud may remain technically competent but politically unusable. An algorithm chosen through a respected process may gain global adoption not because everyone has personally verified every theorem, but because they trust the community and institution that organised the contest of reasons. This is not a corruption of science by politics. It is what science looks like once it becomes infrastructure for strangers.

The seal returns here because it captures the problem exactly. When a document is sealed, one judges not only whether the wax is hard, but whether the seal itself belongs to an authority one accepts as genuine. Algorithm selection asks for the same two judgements at once. Is the design sound? And is the authority asking others to trust it, behaving in a way that deserves assent rather than reluctant dependence? The harder question for institutions is not whether they can produce a mathematically respectable winner. It is whether they can keep the process so legible, open to challenge, and free from corrosive ambiguity that a later generation will still regard the seal as one that was lawfully and intelligently pressed.

## National security incentives and public goods

In September 2013, after reporting by *The New York Times*, ProPublica, and The Guardian drew on documents disclosed by Edward Snowden, a familiar but usually muffled tension became impossible to ignore. The United States government, like other states, depended on strong cryptography to protect military operations, diplomacy, finance, and ordinary state administration. It was also alleged to have pursued ways of preserving intelligence access against protected communications. The concrete outcome was not merely controversy about particular programmes. It was a wider loss of innocence about the state's role in cryptographic order. The same hand was on the shield and the lockpick.

That is the central fact any serious account must face. States are not just guardians of secure communication, nor are they simply predators circling it. They are both builders and trespassers, patrons and opportunists, standard-setters and exception-seekers. Cryptography, from a public point of view, behaves like a public good. It protects payment systems, hospitals, military command, energy infrastructure, civil administration, journalism, private commerce, personal safety, and the ordinary dignity of being able to communicate without constant fear of intrusion. Yet the institutions most capable of organising, funding, and legitimising strong cryptographic standards are also the institutions that may benefit from asymmetry, ambiguity, or selective weakness when intelligence gains are at stake. The shield and the lockpick belong to the same ring.

This dual role can confuse public debate because people prefer moral tidiness. They want the state to be either the guarantor of secure communications or the enemy of them. Reality is more awkward and therefore more useful. Show the scene and the conflict sharpens. A government ministry funds standards work, supports secure infrastructure, and urges stronger protection for finance and critical services. At the same time, intelligence agencies inside the same state seek access, exploit implementation weakness, preserve collection routes, or resist designs that would close too many doors at once. The named concept is institutional cross-pressure. Explain it, and the implication follows. Cryptographic policy inside a state is rarely the expression of one unified will. It is the negotiated outcome of organisations with overlapping authority and genuinely conflicting missions.

This helps explain why cryptography should be understood as a public good with contested stewardship rather than as a neutral technical domain. A public good is something from which many benefit and from which exclusion is difficult or undesirable once the system depends on it. Secure digital communication plainly fits that description. The stability of banking, health records, logistics, taxation, defence supply chains, cloud services, and even everyday messaging depends on widespread availability of trustworthy cryptographic mechanisms. When those mechanisms are strong, interoperable, and broadly adopted, the benefits spill across society. Fraud falls. Identity systems function more reliably. Sensitive commerce becomes possible. State operations themselves become more resilient. The visible behaviours tied to this public good are mundane: transactions clear, updates verify, archives remain intact, and officials can exchange sensitive information without resorting to absurd improvisations. Public goods often look boring when they work. That is part of their value.

Yet stewardship becomes contested because the public interest in strong, widely available cryptography does not erase the strategic interest some arms of the state may have in exceptions, edge cases, or delayed transitions. A domestic security service may focus on investigative access. A foreign intelligence service may prize continued collection against external targets. A defence ministry may want uncompromised security for its own systems. A trade ministry may care about export competitiveness and international trust in national technology firms. A finance ministry may fear systemic fragility if communications security weakens. These are not fanciful tensions. They are structural. The state does not approach algorithm selection, standard setting, or implementation guidance as a single serene mind. It approaches them as a crowded room.

The Snowden-era reporting remains useful because it exposed how damaging perceptions of this crowded room can be even when outsiders do not know every technical detail. The controversy around Dual_EC_DRBG, for instance, did not merely raise a narrow question about one random number generator. It raised a broader one about whether standards processes influenced by state actors with intelligence interests could still command confident public trust. Show the scene and the trouble becomes obvious. A standards body approves a design. Later, allegations and design anomalies together make outside observers suspect that national security interests may have bent the process. Name the concept and the wound becomes legible: stewardship mistrust. Explain it, and one sees the wider implication. When states appear to treat cryptographic standards as venues for strategic manoeuvre rather than trustworthy public goods, they do not merely endanger one algorithm. They weaken confidence in the institutions needed to maintain shared security for everyone.

This is why the state's dual role cannot be analysed as hypocrisy alone. Hypocrisy is too easy a word. The more difficult truth is that the incentives are real on both sides. Strong public cryptography genuinely serves state interests. A government that undermines the cryptographic baseline too broadly may expose its own agencies, industries, citizens, and armed forces to costs far exceeding any selective intelligence gain. This is one reason states so often sound divided rather than merely duplicitous. They are divided. The foreign intelligence officer, the central bank official, the public procurement authority, the cyber defence planner, the police investigator, and the trade negotiator do not face the same losses from the same technical choice. The lockpick that delights one office may terrify another.

The 2016 confrontation between Apple and the Federal Bureau of Investigation over access to the iPhone used by one of the San Bernardino attackers made this tension unusually visible. Public attention focused on a specific device and a specific dispute, but the strategic importance lay deeper. One part of the state argued from the need for investigative access in a particular case. The company argued that creating a tool to bypass security protections would establish a dangerous precedent and weaken trust in a class of products used by millions. Whatever one thinks of the legal and moral arguments, the visible structure was unmistakable. A state seeking lawful access in one instance collided with the broader public-good logic of preserving general confidence in secure devices. The named concept here is local gain versus systemic cost. Explain it, and the recurring pattern becomes clear. National security and public security do not always sit neatly on opposite sides; sometimes a state actor pursuing one form of security degrades another.

This helps explain why public arguments about encryption often become strangely theatrical. Governments may frame access demands as narrow, exceptional, and responsible. Firms may frame resistance as a defence of universal trust. Civil liberties groups may frame the issue as one of rights and democratic accountability. Security practitioners may focus on technical spillover and institutional precedent. All of them are seeing something real. None of them sees the whole field alone. The state's incentives pull standards in different directions not because officials are confused about what cryptography does, but because they are trying to optimise for different security goods at once. Some of those goods can be jointly advanced. Some cannot.

A second example lies in post-quantum standardisation. The move by NIST in August 2024 to publish its first final post-quantum cryptography standards reflected, among other things, a recognition that long-run public security required formal migration pathways away from vulnerable assumptions. That choice clearly served the public-good side of state stewardship. It gave vendors, governments, and critical sectors a shared basis for preparation. Yet even here the dual role remains. The same state that benefits from a widely strengthened cryptographic baseline may still preserve strong incentives to collect aggressively while transitions remain incomplete, uneven, or selective. Show the scene and the contradiction dissolves into reality. A state can sincerely promote stronger standards and still exploit legacy weakness where it remains. The implication is uncomfortable but necessary. Strengthening the commons does not require a state to abandon all interest in advantage around the edges of the commons.

This is one reason states often behave so ambivalently around openness. Open review, public competitions, and transparent standards processes can improve both technical quality and institutional legitimacy. They also reduce the room for quiet manipulation. States that sincerely want strong public cryptography should therefore favour openness. Many do, much of the time. Yet openness can limit flexibility, expose preferred pathways, and reduce opportunities for selective advantage. The result is a recurrent pattern of partial openness: enough transparency to sustain legitimacy, enough opacity to preserve manoeuvre. That balance can hold for a while. It rarely survives scandal gracefully.

A credible limitation should be acknowledged. Not every state approaches cryptographic stewardship with the same capabilities, institutional culture, or balance of incentives. Small states without major signals intelligence ambitions may approach standards quite differently from large intelligence powers. Some states depend so heavily on imported technology and external trust that they have strong reasons to prioritise open, broadly trusted standards over any fantasy of covert influence. Others may lack the organisational coherence to pursue a consistent line at all. It would be foolish to speak of "the state" as though all governments behaved with identical intentions or tools.

Yet this limitation reinforces the broader argument rather than softening it. The point is not that every state is equally manipulative. The point is that the structure of incentives is widely present wherever governments must both secure their own systems and pursue security or intelligence advantage in a world of contested information. A realistic model of institutional behaviour therefore asks not whether a state is good or bad for cryptographic stewardship, but which organs of the state have more influence over which decisions, in which contexts, and under what political constraints. That is a more demanding question. It is also more useful than pieties about neutrality.

The idea of contested stewardship helps here because it avoids two opposite mistakes. One mistake is naive faith: the belief that standards blessed by state-linked institutions can be accepted as pure public service without regard to incentive structure. The other is childish cynicism: the belief that every state role in cryptography is merely a cover for sabotage. Both positions flatten reality. Stewardship is contested precisely because states really do supply essential public goods in this field. They fund research, convene review, coordinate procurement, defend critical infrastructure, and help stabilise interoperable trust. They also house actors whose mandate pushes towards selective access, strategic ambiguity, or preserved asymmetry. The contest is not external to the state. It runs through it.

This has practical implications for how standards politics should be read. When a government advocates a particular algorithm, implementation profile, certification rule, or transition schedule, the relevant question is not only whether the technical proposal appears sound. It is also whether the process around it makes room for countervailing scrutiny strong enough to offset the state's own mixed incentives. Are alternative views heard? Are design rationales explained? Are implementation consequences aired publicly? Are external researchers able to test and criticise without being treated as irritants? These are not decorative norms. They are the working conditions under which contested stewardship can still yield something like public trust.

The same is true of national rhetoric around secure communications. A state that speaks forcefully in favour of stronger public cryptography may be acting out of genuine recognition that the baseline matters for everyone, including itself. It may also be shaping markets, export expectations, procurement alliances, or diplomatic positioning. A state that argues for exceptions may be responding to real investigative frustrations while underestimating the systemic cost of generalising its own convenience. Neither possibility erases the other. The serious observer learns to read the shield and the lockpick together.

That is the realistic model of institutional behaviour the subject demands. States will continue to sponsor, depend upon, and publicly defend strong cryptographic standards because those standards underpin social and economic order. States will also continue to value selective insight, lawful access, covert advantage, or exploitability where they think the gain outweighs the public cost. The balance between those impulses will vary by country, agency, moment, and threat environment. But the tension itself is not temporary. It is structural.

The hardest question, then, is not whether cryptography is a public good. It plainly is. The harder question is who can be trusted to steward that public good when the institutions most capable of maintaining it also contain actors with reasons to bend it, delay it, or preserve strategic gaps around its edges. Until that question is faced without sentimentality, public debates about standards will keep mistaking conflicted guardianship for either betrayal or benevolence, when in truth it is usually both at once.

## Implementations, patents, and ecosystem control

In April 2014, when the Heartbleed vulnerability in OpenSSL became public, organisations across the world were forced into an awkward admission. They had not merely adopted cryptographic algorithms. They had inherited a software implementation, with all its maintenance burdens, funding fragilities, coding mistakes, and hidden centrality. The immediate outcome was a scramble to patch servers, replace certificates, and work out which systems depended on a library many decision-makers had barely noticed until it failed noisily. The algorithmic foundations of modern encryption had not suddenly been disproved. A shared implementation had become the point of strategic weakness.

That distinction changes everything.

Cryptographic discussion often flatters itself by speaking at the level of algorithms. Which scheme is stronger, faster, cleaner, more elegant under public scrutiny? Those questions matter. They are not enough. An algorithm that exists only in a paper, or in a reference implementation too awkward for industry to use safely, is not yet part of the world's security. The real contest takes place in codebases, chips, software development kits, instruction sets, licensing terms, certification regimes, procurement catalogues, and vendor road maps. The lock is described in mathematics. It is built in factories, repositories, and contracts.

This is why "available" and "deployable" are not synonyms. Show the scene and the difference becomes almost embarrassingly concrete. A standards body approves a sound new cryptographic option. Researchers publish analyses. A reference implementation appears. Yet major vendors hesitate because the code is immature, hardware acceleration is missing, patents create uncertainty, existing modules cannot be re-certified quickly, or the integration cost threatens service deadlines. The named concept is implementation friction. Explain it, and the strategic implication becomes clear. Security outcomes are shaped not only by what can in principle be used, but by what large and risk-averse institutions can actually integrate into real products without commercial, legal, or operational pain becoming intolerable.

Reference code sits at the heart of this problem. It is often treated as a convenience, a kind of generous appendix to the real achievement of algorithm design. In practice it can determine whether a standard lives or stalls. A good reference implementation lowers the cost of adoption, clarifies intended behaviour, exposes performance realities, reveals edge cases, and gives downstream developers something concrete to test against. A bad one can do the reverse. It can mislead implementers, conceal side-channel problems, normalise unsafe defaults, and create a false impression that a standard is ready for broad deployment when it is still closer to a lab artefact than to production infrastructure. The abstraction of trust becomes a visible decision here: which code is imported, who maintains it, how quickly issues are patched, whether the implementation is readable enough to audit, and whether downstream teams treat it as illustrative or canonical. Those details often decide more than the algorithm's public reputation does.

Heartbleed made this painfully obvious. OpenSSL was not merely one library among many. It had become embedded across servers, appliances, operating systems, products, and services because it was available, broadly compatible, familiar to developers, and cheap to adopt. That was a success by one measure. By another, it was a concentration of risk hiding in plain sight. The named concept here is infrastructural implementation dependence. Explain it, and one sees why the event mattered strategically. A cryptographic baseline used by countless organisations had been shaped not just by standard selection, but by the fortunes of a particular implementation community. The implication reaches far beyond that one flaw. Whoever controls, funds, or quietly neglects major implementations can influence global security posture even when the underlying algorithms remain sound.

Hardware acceleration deepens this pattern. Modern systems do not merely choose algorithms; they choose what their processors, secure elements, hardware security modules, mobile chipsets, and network devices can perform quickly and efficiently. Once an algorithm or mode benefits from widely deployed hardware support, it becomes easier to adopt, cheaper to scale, and more attractive to vendors under delivery pressure. Another option may be technically admirable and still struggle because it runs too slowly on existing hardware or requires new silicon support that will not arrive until several procurement cycles have passed. Show the scene and the problem looks less abstract. A vendor comparing two secure designs chooses the one already accelerated by the chips in its current product line. The other remains "supported" in documentation but absent in shipping devices. The named concept is performance-governed adoption. Explain it, and the strategic implication follows. Control over hardware support can shape which cryptographic options become normal, and therefore which security futures remain realistic.

This is why post-quantum transition has exposed so many uncomfortable truths about implementation power. A post-quantum scheme may be standardised and publicly endorsed, yet still encounter major deployment resistance if libraries are immature, message sizes stress existing protocols, secure elements cannot handle the new operations cleanly, certification regimes lag, or hardware vendors have not yet incorporated efficient support. The visible behaviour is familiar: cautious roll-outs, hybrid deployments, product lines segmented by what they can afford to absorb, and a long period in which the new option is technically real but commercially awkward. The secure option exists. Vendors cannot integrate it at scale without rewriting more of their stack than budgets or customers will presently tolerate. That is not an intellectual failure. It is ecosystem control exerting itself through ordinary engineering constraints.

Patents and licensing rules add a quieter but equally consequential layer. A cryptographic design can be open in spirit and still unattractive in practice if implementers fear future royalty demands, licensing disputes, or ambiguous intellectual property claims. Large companies may absorb that uncertainty with legal teams and negotiated agreements. Smaller firms, public institutions, open-source maintainers, and cross-border collaborations often cannot. The result is a market-shaped filter on adoption. A design that is technically strong but legally awkward may remain marginal while a less elegant but clearer alternative spreads. The named concept is legal deployability. Explain it, and the point becomes obvious. Security is not chosen in a vacuum. It is chosen under conditions where engineering time, warranty risk, export controls, indemnity language, and licensing exposure all press on the decision. The implication is blunt. A patent portfolio can influence security architecture even when nobody ever mentions the word "power".

A useful historical illustration lies in the old contest around elliptic-curve cryptography. For years, the mathematics offered real security and performance advantages, especially for constrained environments. Yet adoption was shaped not just by technical merit, but by concerns over patents, standardisation politics, implementation quality, and trust in selected curves. The result was not linear triumph. It was staggered, uneven integration influenced by exactly the sorts of ecosystem considerations that pure theory tends to ignore. Some actors moved quickly because the performance gains were compelling and their legal posture strong. Others hesitated because uncertainty around intellectual property, implementation risk, or institutional confidence made delay feel safer. The lesson survives. An algorithm can win the seminar and still lose the product cycle.

A second example can be seen in the persistence of cryptographic support inside embedded and industrial systems. A more secure option may be publicly documented, standards-compliant, and well-understood. Yet a manufacturer with long device lifetimes, tight margins, and limited update mechanisms may not integrate it because the required changes touch firmware, certification, testing, support contracts, and field maintenance. The old option persists not because engineers worship it, but because the vendor cannot fit the new one into the machinery of its business without opening costs it has no appetite to bear. Here the secure option fails through no obvious mathematical weakness. It fails because the surrounding ecosystem does not welcome it. Availability without deployability is a pamphlet, not protection.

This should temper romantic talk about open standards as though openness alone guarantees healthy adoption. Open standards are often essential. They reduce dependence on single vendors, widen review, and improve interoperability. Yet an open standard can still be captured indirectly if the dominant implementation is controlled by a narrow group, if hardware support is concentrated, if certification favours one stack, or if licensing complexity deters broad uptake. The visible signs of this kind of control are not dramatic. One codebase becomes the reference almost by habit. One vendor's SDK becomes the path of least resistance. One platform's support timetable becomes everyone else's practical calendar. The standard remains nominally open while its real route into the world grows narrow. That is ecosystem control in a suit and tie.

Still, a limitation deserves respect. Not every concentrated implementation base is unhealthy, and not every patent or hardware dependency is evidence of strategic manipulation. Some implementations become dominant because they are genuinely good, carefully maintained, and trusted through years of earned reliability. Hardware acceleration can reduce costs and widen access to stronger cryptography, not merely distort markets. Intellectual property can reward real innovation and fund development that might otherwise struggle. It would be lazy to treat every successful implementation as a cartel wearing a compiler's hat.

Yet that concession only sharpens the main argument. The issue is not whether concentration ever has benefits. The issue is whether institutions can distinguish beneficial concentration from dangerous dependence. A dominant implementation that is well-funded, transparent, independently audited, and replaceable under stress looks very different from one that is opaque, under-resourced, legally tangled, or inseparable from a broader vendor lock-in strategy. A hardware-supported option that accelerates strong cryptography broadly is not the same as one whose support is gated in ways that leave rivals or public institutions stranded. The same goes for patents: clear, fair, and predictable licensing conditions create a different deployment environment from ambiguous or strategically weaponised intellectual property. The problem is not that these forces exist. It is that they are so often smuggled into security discussion as though they were irrelevant side details.

This is also where ecosystem control becomes geopolitical. A state or bloc that hosts dominant chip designers, cloud platforms, mobile operating systems, certification labs, or widely used cryptographic libraries does not merely enjoy commercial success. It acquires the ability to influence the pace and shape of security migration elsewhere. It can make one cryptographic option easy to adopt and another expensive to integrate. It can define which reference implementations become authoritative, which hardware features are normal, and which certification paths are economically tolerable. Most of this influence is not exercised through overt command. It travels through procurement gravity, platform defaults, developer convenience, and the grimly persuasive force of what is already compatible with the rest of the world.

The result is that implementation choices can quietly decide whose security problems count. A large platform vendor may support a new standard because it can spread engineering cost across millions of users. A small manufacturer may lag because redesign threatens survival. A public agency may wish to adopt a safer configuration and find that its trusted suppliers, certified products, and legacy integration partners cannot follow without a budget increase nobody will approve. The technical option exists. The institution remains trapped. This is how cryptographic power often works in practice: not by denying the existence of a better tool, but by making its uptake too costly, too delayed, or too legally awkward for most actors to pursue.

The screwdriver matters here because it captures the issue better than grand talk of algorithms. Most people understand that owning a blueprint for a better lock is not the same as having the tools, spare parts, and permissions needed to install it on a working building without shutting the place down. Cryptographic standards often fail at precisely that stage. The better lock exists. The screwdriver is proprietary, the screw heads are incompatible, the building manager fears disruption, the warranty forbids improvisation, and the fire inspector has not yet approved the new fitting. Security talk that ignores these facts is not serious. It is a kind of ceremonial mathematics.

The strategic question, then, is not merely which algorithms deserve trust. It is who controls the route from abstract availability to ordinary deployment: whose code becomes canonical, whose hardware sets the tempo, whose patents shape caution, whose certification pathways decide what products can ship, and whose integration costs determine whether a secure option remains theoretical long after it has been standardised. Until institutions can answer that question about the systems they depend on, they do not really know what their cryptographic choices are. They know only what has been made easy for them to choose.

## Interoperability and the burden of coordination

In January 2020, Microsoft and the United States National Security Agency publicly disclosed a serious vulnerability in the Windows CryptoAPI, later tracked as CVE-2020-0601. The flaw could allow forged certificates to appear trustworthy to affected systems, undermining a mechanism millions of users never think about until it misbehaves. The immediate response was patching. The more enduring lesson concerned coordination. A cryptographic assurance is only as strong as the common rules by which many different systems agree to recognise it, and once those systems are spread across governments, companies, hospitals, factories, schools, and homes, even a straightforward fix becomes a collective exercise rather than a private one.

That is the awkward truth about interoperability. It sounds gentle, almost administrative, as though it merely meant devices getting along nicely. In reality it is the condition on which global digital communication rests. A browser trusts a certificate because operating systems, certificate authorities, software libraries, networks, and servers all share enough assumptions to complete the same ritual of verification. A payment clears because terminals, issuers, processors, and banks speak a common cryptographic language. A software update installs because the device, the platform, and the vendor all recognise the same chain of authenticity. Shared choices make this ordinary. Shared choices also make it fragile.

One broken connector can matter.

That short sentence captures more than it first appears to. Cryptography at scale is not merely a matter of choosing strong algorithms. It is a matter of ensuring that many different actors choose them in compatible ways, on compatible timetables, with compatible validation rules, fallback behaviour, and upgrade paths. Show the scene and the problem sharpens quickly. One organisation tightens certificate validation. Another still permits legacy exceptions. One vendor supports a newer protocol profile. Another preserves an older handshake because its customer base includes ageing devices. One government agency demands stronger settings in procurement. A contractor servicing critical infrastructure still depends on older modules that cannot follow without costly replacement. The named concept is coordination burden. Explain it, and the implication becomes hard to dodge. Security is often limited not by what the best participant can do, but by what the network as a whole can change together.

This is why global communications require shared choices in the first place. Without common protocols, naming rules, key exchange methods, certificate formats, and implementation expectations, each secure connection would become a bespoke negotiation. That would not merely be inconvenient. It would be unworkable at scale. Standards and shared libraries solve this by allowing strangers to interoperate securely without prior intimacy. Yet the same success creates a paradox. The more widely a cryptographic arrangement is adopted, the harder it becomes to alter without causing cascading friction. The abstraction of efficiency turns into visible dependence: devices shipped with one protocol stack, suppliers certified to one profile, auditors trained on one vocabulary, procurement frameworks written around one set of assumptions. What began as coordination in the service of security becomes, in time, a barrier to changing security.

This is where network effects enter. A cryptographic choice becomes more valuable as more participants adopt it, not merely because it is strong, but because it becomes the route by which others can still talk, transact, update, and authenticate. Network effects are often discussed in commercial language, but their security consequences are profound. If most of the relevant ecosystem supports a particular protocol or certificate logic, outliers face pressure to conform even when they know the arrangement is ageing badly. The visible behaviour is familiar. Product teams keep legacy support alive to avoid breaking customers. Operators delay retirement of older settings because too many external connections still rely on them. Partners accept weaker modes because refusing them would sever necessary communication. The implication is severe. Cryptographic strength can be subordinated to the gravitational pull of the installed base.

A useful example lies in the long retirement of older versions of Transport Layer Security. Major browsers, cloud providers, and enterprise security teams understood for years that older protocol versions and older configuration patterns imposed avoidable risk. Yet retirement was not simply a matter of flipping a switch. Legacy devices, embedded systems, middleboxes, old operating systems, industrial equipment, and brittle business software kept demanding compatibility. The scene repeated across sectors. Engineers proposed deprecation. Business owners warned of outages. Vendors pleaded for time. Customers discovered systems they had forgotten still spoke the old dialect. The named concept here is inherited interoperability debt. Explain it, and the broader lesson becomes plain. Every decision to preserve compatibility accumulates future coordination cost. The implication is not that deprecation was mistaken. It is that deprecation in a networked world is governance by deadline, not a mere technical preference.

This helps explain why partial adoption can be worse than none. At first glance that sounds perverse. Surely some movement towards stronger cryptography is always better than complete stasis. Often it is. But partial adoption can create dangerous transition zones if the system continues to accept old and new modes in ways that permit downgrade, confusion, policy inconsistency, or misplaced confidence. Show the scene and the problem becomes concrete. A service proudly announces support for a stronger cryptographic suite, yet still permits weaker modes for compatibility. Clients and servers negotiate to the lowest common denominator because that is how the mixed environment remains connected. Administrators believe migration is under way. Attackers see a wider surface of protocol complexity, negotiation edge cases, and fallback behaviour. The named concept is transition fragility. Explain it, and the implication follows. Improvement that preserves too much of the old world can create new routes to failure while convincing institutions that they have already become safer.

The Apple and FBI dispute in 2016, though not a narrow protocol coordination case, also illuminated the politics of interoperability from another angle. One of the reasons firms resist exceptional-access demands is that modern security is rarely compartmentalised by wish alone. A mechanism created for one lawful context can reshape expectations across the whole product line because customers, regulators, and foreign governments start asking whether the same accommodation exists elsewhere. That is coordination pressure in institutional form. Once a shared platform serves millions of users across jurisdictions, any cryptographic deviation becomes hard to keep local. The named concept is scalability of exception. Explain it, and the relevance to interoperability becomes clearer. A networked system is not a set of isolated bargains. Changes made for one segment can propagate trust consequences across all segments because common platforms are built to behave consistently.

A second example can be drawn from software updates and code signing. A vendor may be ready to strengthen its signing infrastructure, rotate trust anchors, or change certificate requirements. Yet customers with air-gapped environments, slow qualification cycles, regulated devices, or dependent third-party products may not be ready to verify the new chain cleanly. If the vendor moves too quickly, some clients fail to update and drift into insecurity through stagnation. If the vendor moves too slowly, others remain exposed through obsolete trust. The visible decision becomes agonisingly practical. Should the vendor preserve the old signature pathway a little longer, maintain dual trust, or force a break and accept operational pain? The abstraction of coordination becomes a calendar filled with incompatible obligations. The implication is plain. Migration is not just a technical activity. It is a negotiation among actors whose risk lies in different directions.

This is why weakest-link dynamics loom so large. In a tightly coupled environment, the most cautious or technically capable participant cannot fully determine the security of the whole. A bank may harden its interfaces and still depend on a payment partner using outdated cryptographic modules. A hospital may improve its central systems and still communicate with legacy medical devices that cannot support stricter validation. A government ministry may modernise internal trust anchors and still exchange documents with contractors whose software support lags. The weakest link here is not always the sloppiest organisation. It is often the least upgradable participant. That distinction matters because it shifts blame into structure. Weakness persists not only where people are careless, but where coordination costs distribute power unevenly across a network.

Still, a limitation deserves candour. Not every instance of partial adoption is harmful, and many successful migrations require overlap periods in which older and newer schemes coexist. Dual support can be prudent when carefully bounded, monitored, and time-limited. Abrupt global transitions are often impossible and sometimes reckless. A system that tried to purge all legacy compatibility overnight would cause failures severe enough to undermine confidence in the migration itself. This matters because criticism of partial adoption can become glib, as though security engineering were merely a morality play in which brave reformers are thwarted by cowards clinging to the past. Real systems are crueller and more ordinary than that.

Yet the limitation clarifies rather than weakens the core point. The question is not whether overlap ever occurs. It is whether overlap is governed as a temporary burden or normalised as a permanent habitat. A disciplined migration uses coexistence to narrow options over time, measure who remains on legacy paths, and make the cost of delay legible. An undisciplined migration uses coexistence to postpone conflict until it becomes embedded and therefore politically harder to resolve. The visible behaviours differ. In the disciplined case, inventories improve, deadlines tighten, exceptions are counted, and remaining dependencies are named. In the undisciplined case, the old support path quietly becomes indefinite because no one wants to own the disruption of ending it. That is how coordination burden turns into security stagnation.

The deeper strategic issue is that interoperability creates shared fate across sectors that do not govern themselves together. Finance, healthcare, energy, defence supply, telecommunications, logistics, education, and consumer technology all depend on overlapping cryptographic plumbing, yet they move at different speeds, answer to different regulators, and face different tolerances for downtime. The same protocol upgrade or certificate policy change can look urgent to one sector and almost impossible to another. That mismatch produces systemic exposure. A faster-moving sector cannot fully leave the slower behind if the two must continue exchanging trusted data. Network effects thus become political effects. One sector's legacy becomes another sector's attack surface.

This is why migration planning cannot be left to isolated technical teams inside single organisations. A security office may know perfectly well what should change and still fail if suppliers, customers, regulators, certification labs, insurers, and dependent partners are not moving on a compatible path. The burden of coordination therefore belongs inside strategic planning, not as an afterthought once technical choices have been made. The serious questions are blunt. Which partners must change together? Which legacy dependencies create mandatory overlap? Which fallback modes create the greatest downgrade risk? Which sectors can tolerate enforced breaks, and which cannot? These are not glamorous questions, but they decide whether shared cryptography behaves like a commons or a trap.

The motif of the connector returns here because it remains stubbornly apt. A system can be composed of individually excellent parts and still fail because one connector remains old, proprietary, brittle, or badly timed. Modern cryptography at scale works through connectors: protocols, certificate chains, validation rules, update channels, key exchange expectations, identity bindings. Their strength depends not only on local correctness but on collective synchrony. The connector no one wanted to replace becomes the one everyone must route around, and routing around in security usually means living with extra complexity, extra exceptions, or extra silence about what remains unresolved.

The hardest question, then, is not whether a stronger cryptographic option exists. It is whether the institutions that must rely on one another can move in enough concert to make the stronger option real without leaving behind a long, dangerous shadow of compatibility paths, downgrade openings, and silently stranded participants. Until that question is answered with more honesty than most migration plans can bear, interoperability will remain both the great enabler of secure communication and the quiet reason that secure communication so often changes too slowly to deserve its own confidence.

## Assurance, audits, and what they miss

In December 2020, when the SolarWinds compromise became public, many of the affected organisations had not been operating in a vacuum of standards, controls, and audit discipline. They had policies. They had security reviews. They had suppliers with formal assurances. Yet malicious code still travelled through a trusted update channel into systems whose owners believed, with some institutional justification, that they were behaving responsibly. The immediate story concerned software supply chains. The deeper lesson concerned assurance itself. A ticked box can look like a lock.

That illusion is expensive.

Assurance regimes exist for good reasons. They help buyers compare products they cannot fully inspect, give regulators and boards a common language for minimum expectations, and force organisations to document controls that might otherwise remain performative or absent. An audit can reveal neglected basics. A certification can stop truly poor products from masquerading as competent. A checklist can create discipline where rhetoric once stood. None of this is trivial. The trouble begins when institutions mistake these tools for something they are not. Assurance can show that a control exists, that a process was followed, or that a product met a stated profile at a stated moment. It cannot, by itself, guarantee that the control answers the right threat model, that the process will survive crisis, or that the product can adapt when assumptions change.

This is the central weakness of audit culture in cryptographic settings. Show the scene and it becomes obvious. An organisation passes a review because sensitive data is encrypted at rest, keys are held in an approved service, privileged access is documented, backups are retained, and incident procedures are written down. The named concept is static assurance. Explain it, and the gap appears. The audit establishes the presence of security artefacts under existing criteria. It says much less about whether the arrangement can survive a forced key rotation, a broken trust anchor, a compromised supplier, a future algorithm change, or a conflict between operational continuity and cryptographic hygiene. The implication is severe. Many institutions are certified for yesterday's danger while improvising against tomorrow's.

This is not a defect in auditors as a class. It is a structural problem. Audit frameworks need stable criteria. They work by making expectations legible, repeatable, and comparable across many organisations. Threats, by contrast, are unruly. They evolve unevenly. They arrive through combinations of technical and organisational weakness that no checklist can fully anticipate. The more dynamic the threat environment becomes, the greater the temptation to cling to what can still be measured neatly. Encryption at rest can be attested. Upgrade paths are harder. Documented key rotation intervals can be checked. The political authority to rotate keys under ambiguity is harder. A certificate can show that an algorithm is approved. The institutional ability to replace that algorithm across dependent systems is harder. Assurance therefore gravitates towards what is countable, even when the most serious risks are architectural, temporal, or governance-based.

A familiar example is compliance that validates encrypted storage while ignoring key escrow risk. The visible scene is unremarkable. A company stores sensitive records on encrypted volumes, uses approved cryptographic modules, and satisfies the relevant control language for protecting data at rest. The check passes. Yet the same organisation may maintain recovery mechanisms, administrative overrides, escrowed secrets, or centralised key access pathways that dramatically enlarge the population capable of recovering the data. The named concept here is compensating vulnerability. Explain it plainly and the problem becomes sharper. The system meets the formal requirement for encryption while introducing side paths that may matter more strategically than the encryption itself. The implication is not that encryption at rest is useless. It is that assurance focused on the presence of a control can miss the way surrounding design choices hollow it out.

This is why key lifecycles matter so much. Cryptography is often presented as a choice among algorithms, protocols, and products, but the decisive question in many institutions is less glamorous: how are keys generated, distributed, rotated, recovered, retired, and destroyed? A review that confirms a strong algorithm while skimming over key custody has secured the door handle and ignored who owns the spare keys. The key exists over time, and its security story changes over time. A key that is safe enough during ordinary operation may become dangerous if backups are too broad, if recovery is poorly governed, if mergers alter administrative boundaries, if staff turnover leaves old privileges intact, or if future migration requires touching systems nobody has inventoried properly. The abstraction of trust becomes a series of visible acts: who can authorise export, which logs are reviewed, whether old keys linger in escrow, whether revocation is rehearsed, whether retirement is actual rather than ceremonial.

The same problem appears in certification of cryptographic products. A device, module, or service may be certified against a recognised profile, and that certification may be meaningful within its stated scope. But scope is the mischievous word here. The product may be assessed under assumptions that exclude the way it will actually be deployed, the integration decisions customers will make, or the cross-system dependencies through which real compromise often travels. Show the scene and the limitation becomes plain. A hardware security module is certified. Procurement treats the certificate as reassurance. Yet the integration around it grants too many operators authority, or the surrounding application logic allows unauthorised use of otherwise protected key material, or the lifecycle support needed for future migration remains vague. The named concept is scope slippage. Explain it, and one sees why certification alone so often disappoints. It proves something true and narrower than buyers later imagine.

A useful example lies in the recurring gap between secure software development attestations and software supply chain exposure. Before a widely publicised compromise, organisations may point to code review practices, penetration tests, signed releases, and vendor assurances as evidence of a serious posture. After compromise, it becomes clear that signed releases were built through brittle pipelines, dependencies were not fully mapped, access to build systems was too broad, or the organisation lacked a credible plan for rotating trust once the release chain itself became suspect. The SolarWinds case remains instructive in precisely this sense. The problem was not that formal assurance had no value. It was that the most consequential weakness emerged in the living system of dependencies and trust transitions rather than in the neat categories those assurances had emphasised. The checklist looked at the document. The compromise walked through the process.

A second example can be found in the persistence of old cryptographic configurations inside regulated or critical sectors. Healthcare, industrial control, and transport systems often operate under regimes where certification and compliance are themselves heavy burdens. A product validated years earlier may remain deployed because recertification is costly, operational downtime is feared, and replacement budgets are politically difficult. The very assurance mechanism that once improved security can then slow change by rewarding stasis. The named concept is certification drag. Explain it, and the strategic implication becomes uncomfortable. Assurance frameworks designed to establish trust can end up preserving legacy trust longer than prudence allows, because the route to revalidation is too painful for institutions already under strain.

This should not be heard as an argument against assurance. That would be adolescent. Mature systems need shared baselines, external scrutiny, and documentary evidence that controls exist. Procurement without assurance becomes guesswork. Regulation without assurance becomes mere exhortation. Boards and publics alike need some legible way to distinguish disciplined institutions from theatrical ones. The real issue is what assurance claims to measure and what audiences imagine it measures. A certificate is not prophecy. An audit is not a strategic theory. A passed control is not a guarantee that the threat model is still fit for purpose.

A credible limitation deserves emphasis here. Some assurance regimes are improving. Certain modern frameworks pay more attention to secure development lifecycles, software composition, incident reporting, and key management practices than earlier generations did. Many auditors are acutely aware that controls age and that organisations game checklists when incentives encourage it. In sophisticated environments, certification can drive meaningful upgrades rather than merely decorate procurement files. This matters, because it would be unfair and inaccurate to paint the entire assurance landscape as hollow ritual.

Yet even the better regimes face the same basic problem: they tend to privilege what can be standardised before they fully capture what must remain adaptive. Threat models evolve faster than audit cycles. Cryptographic migrations unfold across supplier chains, budget periods, and legacy estates that no certification badge can magically reconfigure. A strong assurance process may tell you that a product uses approved encryption, isolates certain key operations, and logs administrative events. It may still say little about how rapidly the system can replace an algorithm under pressure, how many hidden dependencies still rely on the old trust anchor, or whether a recovery mechanism built for continuity creates an exploitable central point of failure. The safer institution is not always the one with the thickest assurance pack. It is often the one whose assurance materials are tied to changeable realities rather than fixed abstractions.

This is why upgrade paths should be treated as first-class assurance objects rather than optional engineering niceties. A system that cannot change its cryptographic assumptions under controlled conditions is not truly well assured, no matter how handsome its present documentation. Show the scene and the difference is practical rather than philosophical. One supplier can describe how keys are rotated, how trust anchors are replaced, how deprecated algorithms are retired, how clients are inventoried, how exceptions are governed, and how emergency transitions are rehearsed. Another supplier can only point to current compliance with recognised profiles. The first offers evidence of future survivability. The second offers a certificate framed in the present tense. The implication should be obvious. Assurance that ignores migration is assurance without a clock.

The same is true of key lifecycles. A system does not become safe merely because its keys are generated inside approved hardware or because rotation occurs on a fixed schedule. The important questions concern authority and reversibility. Who can trigger recovery? Under what audit trail? Can old key material be proven destroyed? How are escrow mechanisms governed? What happens during an acquisition, a legal dispute, a ransomware incident, or a shift in algorithm policy? Does the institution know which records remain decryptable under which past keys? These are not decorative details. They are the parts of assurance most likely to matter when the polite world of compliance collides with the impolite world of crisis.

This suggests a more realistic model of audit maturity. A mature regime does not stop at verifying that controls exist. It asks whether the controls can age, fail, and be replaced without leaving the institution blind or trapped. It looks for dependency maps, transition governance, retention discipline, rehearsed revocation, and credible minimisation of unnecessary trust concentrations. It treats exceptional-access pathways, escrow arrangements, and fallback modes as assurance subjects in their own right rather than as secondary implementation details. Most importantly, it recognises that a control validated under one threat model may become dangerously flattering under another. The institution that hears this and responds, "But we are compliant," has already missed the point.

The checklist returns here because it remains a useful symbol of both the promise and the failure. A checklist can focus attention, create discipline, and catch neglect. It can also become a substitute for thought when passing it starts to matter more than understanding why the boxes exist. Cryptographic governance is especially vulnerable to this substitution because so much of the subject sounds technical enough to intimidate non-specialists and routine enough to comfort specialists. Between those two moods, a great deal of strategic blindness can flourish.

The harder question is therefore not whether a system can pass an audit today. It is whether the audit would still mean much after a supplier compromise, a forced key rotation, a broken trust anchor, a legal demand for escrow use, or a standards shift that makes yesterday's approved configuration tomorrow's inherited liability. Until assurance can answer that kind of question with something more convincing than paperwork, institutions will continue mistaking administrative cleanliness for cryptographic readiness - and discovering the difference only when the spare keys, the old certificates, and the migration plan all turn out to live in different drawers.

# Chapter 6

# Key Management as State Capacity

What is the true centre of gravity in a cryptographic system: the elegance of the algorithm, or the small collection of secrets that decide who may actually use it? The question sounds technical until it is placed inside an institution. A ministry may mandate strong encryption. A bank may deploy certified hardware. A cloud provider may advertise impeccable controls. Yet if one administrator account, one recovery process, one escrow pathway, or one inherited access rule can unlock too much of the system, the real distribution of power looks very different from the architecture diagram. The mathematics may be sound. Authority may still be dangerously concentrated.

That is why keys deserve to be treated not as implementation detail but as assets of state-like importance. They are the points at which trust becomes operational. A key can authorise decryption, validate software, bind identities, recover archives, rotate systems, or silently preserve an emergency path no one mentions until crisis arrives. Institutions often speak as though they possess cryptography when what they really possess is a patchwork of key custody arrangements, access decisions, and recovery habits accumulated over years of procurement, mergers, staff changes, and vendor dependency. The lock may be impressive. The keyring tells the truth.

A safe is only useful if someone can open it, and that blunt fact drives much of the politics of security. Keys must be generated somewhere, stored somewhere, moved under some procedure, recovered under some exception, and destroyed at some point that is almost always later than planned. Each of those verbs introduces governance. Each creates an opportunity for convenience to disguise itself as prudence. Institutions centralise authority because centralisation feels efficient. They preserve fallback access because continuity feels responsible. They keep old keys longer than they should because deletion feels irreversible. Slowly, a security design intended to distribute trust can be bent back into a few powerful hands.

The tension at the centre of this chapter lies there. Strong cryptography appears to promise impersonal protection grounded in mathematics, but key management drags the whole matter back into administration, hierarchy, procurement, and human judgement. A secure hardware module may reduce one class of risk while binding an institution more tightly to a supplier, a certification pathway, or a lifecycle support decision it does not truly control. An identity system may formalise access while also multiplying the number of insiders, contractors, and inherited privileges able to authorise sensitive actions. An exceptional recovery path may look narrow in policy and expansive in failure. The more seriously one takes key management, the less plausible it becomes to describe security as a feature of tools alone.

That matters because compromise rarely requires defeating the strongest mathematics in the room. It often requires locating the account, process, or institution that already has permission to act. A silently powerful administrator role, a poorly governed certificate authority, an escrowed recovery mechanism, or an acquisition that leaves old trust relationships half-retired can each do more practical damage than a theoretical break in a well-chosen algorithm. The resulting harm is not merely technical. It reveals something about institutional capacity itself: whether the organisation knows where authority sits, who can exercise it, how quickly it can be withdrawn, and what happens when competing needs for secrecy, recoverability, and oversight collide.

The stakes therefore extend beyond cyber hygiene into the language usually reserved for statecraft. Key management is one of the clearest tests of whether an institution can govern concentrated power without either dispersing it into chaos or consolidating it into silent fragility. That is true for governments, certainly, but also for banks, universities, hospitals, cloud providers, and manufacturers whose products now carry cryptographic responsibility far beyond their own walls. The ability to generate and guard keys is only the beginning. The harder task is to preserve legitimacy around who may use them, under what constraints, with what audit trail, and with what capacity to adapt when yesterday's trust arrangement becomes today's risk.

The route ahead moves from the key itself as the real strategic asset, to the specialised hardware meant to protect it and the new dependencies that protection can create, then into the thicket of identity and access where insiders, contractors, and organisational change complicate every neat custody diagram. From there the argument turns towards escrow and exceptional access, where the promise of limited recoverability collides with the reality that every additional path into a secret changes deterrence, trust, and failure conditions for everyone linked to the system.

A spare key in a drawer captures the whole subject better than most white papers do. It may exist for entirely sensible reasons. Emergencies happen. Staff leave. Systems fail. Legal duties intrude. Yet the presence of the spare key alters the meaning of the lock, and the governance of the drawer often matters more than the engineering of the lock itself. Institutions like to imagine that they are debating technical architecture when they are often really deciding who gets to open the drawer, who gets told it exists, and who bears the consequences if its use becomes routine.

That is the diagnostic pressure underlying everything that follows. When an institution claims to have secured its most important systems, is it describing the strength of its cryptography, or the discipline with which it governs the small number of keys, accounts, and recovery paths that make the cryptography live in practice? Until that distinction is faced without euphemism, security will continue to be praised in public while authority remains concentrated in places too quiet, too convenient, and too politically awkward to name.

## Keys as the real assets

In December 2020, when the SolarWinds compromise became public, much of the first commentary focused on software supply chains, stealth, and the unsettling reach of a poisoned update channel. But buried inside the technical drama was a simpler and more durable lesson. The crisis was not, at root, about the failure of encryption theory. It was about trust being exercised through privileged paths, signed artefacts, and systems that already possessed the authority to act. The decisive question was not whether the mathematics was elegant. It was who held the keys, literal or institutional, to make a machine obey.

That is usually where the real story lives.

Cryptography is often discussed as though the algorithm were the jewel and everything else the velvet lining. That flatters our taste for abstraction. It also misleads. Institutions do not secure themselves by admiring strong algorithms. They secure themselves by governing keys: the secrets that permit decryption, validate signatures, authenticate devices, unlock archives, and authorise changes that other systems will accept as legitimate. A weak algorithm is obviously dangerous. A strong algorithm paired with badly governed keys is often worse, because it encourages false confidence while concentrating decisive power in places few people inspect closely enough.

The spare key tells the truth.

That is the quiet motif worth keeping in view. A building may have excellent locks, reinforced doors, and a respectable alarm system. The real security question often turns out to be where the spare key lives, who knows about it, who can copy it, and what happens when the trusted custodian leaves in a hurry. Show the scene and the concept becomes almost embarrassingly plain. A company encrypts sensitive records with approved methods. Those records are only accessible through an administrative service account used for recovery, maintenance, or automated processing. The named concept is concentrated trust. Explain it, and the strategic implication arrives quickly. Whoever controls the account, the credential, or the pathway around ordinary access rules may effectively control the whole protected estate. The institution may describe itself as cryptographically mature. In practice, it has centralised power into one quiet corner.

This is why keys, not algorithms, are the real assets institutions must govern. Algorithms are shared intellectual infrastructure. They are selected, standardised, implemented, and, in many cases, publicly scrutinised. Keys are different. They are local, specific, and loaded with authority. They decide who can read, who can sign, who can impersonate, who can recover, and who can replace trust itself. The visible actions that attach to them are not abstract. Somebody generates them. Somebody stores them. Somebody rotates them. Somebody recovers them after failure. Somebody decides when they are retired or destroyed. Each verb is a governance problem disguised as technical routine. The implication is harsh but clarifying. Security hinges less on choosing admirable mathematics than on managing a lifecycle of authority without losing track of where it sits.

Generation comes first, and institutions often treat it far too casually. A key generated badly may never recover its dignity. If the process uses weak randomness, occurs on a compromised machine, depends on unclear custody, or leaves unnecessary copies behind, later procedural neatness cannot fully redeem the original sin. Show the scene and it is not glamorous. A deployment team creates credentials in haste on a general-purpose workstation because the hardware module is delayed. Temporary becomes permanent. Copies linger in build systems, ticket attachments, administrator laptops, or automated scripts. The named concept is origin contamination. Explain it, and the lesson becomes obvious. A key inherits trust from the circumstances of its birth. If those circumstances are muddled, the rest of the lifecycle starts from damaged ground.

Storage is where institutions most often confuse encryption with security. Storing keys "securely" sounds straightforward until one asks what that phrase means operationally. A key may live in a hardware security module, a cloud key management service, an operating system keystore, a secrets manager, an application configuration store, a backup, a recovery envelope, or the memory of a running process. Each location alters the attack surface. More importantly, each location reveals something about the institution's actual priorities. Does it optimise for strict separation of authority, for convenience of automation, for rapid recovery, for broad administrative access, or for minimal operational friction? Trust becomes visible here in access permissions, audit logs, export controls, and whether emergency procedures are narrow exceptions or sleepy old customs. A key stored under tight technical control but surrounded by sprawling administrative privilege may be secure only in the way a safe is secure when the combination is taped beneath it.

Rotation sounds virtuous because it suggests movement rather than stagnation. In practice it is where many institutions discover whether they have been governing trust or merely admiring it. A key that cannot be rotated without panic was never properly governed in the first place. Show the scene and the problem emerges quickly. A certificate authority needs to replace a signing key. Downstream devices, legacy applications, third-party integrations, old archives, and forgotten validation scripts all depend on the existing chain. The planned rotation becomes an institutional stress test. The named concept is latent brittleness. Explain it, and the strategic implication follows. Good key management is not proven when nothing changes. It is proven when trust can change without the organisation collapsing into improvisation, exception-making, and denial. Rotation is therefore not a maintenance chore. It is a measure of state capacity in miniature.

Recovery introduces a sharper political problem. Institutions need ways back into their own systems when failure, loss, or legal obligation intervenes. Recovery is not foolish. It is unavoidable. Yet every recovery path creates a second story about who really controls the secret. A key recoverable by one administrator, one team, one escrow service, or one emergency procedure is no longer governed solely by ordinary access rules. It is governed by the exceptions as well. The abstraction of resilience becomes a visible decision: how many people can invoke recovery, under what evidence, with what delay, under whose authorisation, and with what independent review. The implication is severe. Every recovery mechanism is a declaration about where ultimate trust lies when ordinary trust fails.

This is why destruction matters so much and is so often sentimentalised instead of verified. A retired key that continues to exist in backups, exports, old appliances, archived virtual machines, or "just in case" administrator folders is not retired in any strategic sense. Institutions speak fondly of key destruction the way empires speak of demobilisation while leaving the barracks stocked and the railways ready. Show the scene and the weakness is ordinary. An old key is replaced, but legacy backups remain decryptable under it and nobody has a reliable inventory of where those backups sit. The named concept is ghost authority. Explain it, and one sees how past trust continues to cast power forward. Destroying a key is not only a cryptographic act. It is an act of institutional forgetting, and institutions are often bad at forgetting what once made life convenient.

A useful example of silent trust concentration is the privileged administrator account that can access a central key management layer or approve the use of signing material across systems. On the surface, the arrangement may look like good order. Centralisation reduces duplication, simplifies oversight, and makes recovery faster. Yet the same design can create a single human or service identity whose compromise defeats layers of otherwise admirable engineering. The account becomes the spare key in the drawer. The named concept here is administrative sovereignty. Explain it, and the danger becomes clear. The institution may have distributed applications, segmented networks, and certified modules, but one identity can still unify trust into a single point of strategic failure. The implication reaches beyond technology. A state, bank, or cloud provider that does not know where such identities exist has not truly mapped its own power.

The 2011 compromise of DigiNotar remains a sharp reminder from the public key world. The immediate issue was a certificate authority whose failure enabled fraudulent certificates to be issued. But behind the headlines lay the same deeper truth: what mattered was not only algorithmic soundness but control over key material and signing authority. Once those functions are compromised, dependent systems continue trusting the wrong thing with unnerving obedience. The visible outcome in that case was browser distrust and institutional collapse. The broader lesson is that key compromise often defeats strong cryptography not by solving hard mathematics, but by stepping into the place where trust was already meant to reside. The lock did not fail first. The authority to mint accepted keys did.

A second example sits in cloud infrastructure, where institutions often rely on centrally managed key services to protect storage, databases, and application secrets. This can be sensible and disciplined. It can also create a powerful illusion. A customer sees encryption at rest enabled across many systems and infers broad safety. Yet the real security posture depends on who can administer the key policies, export or reassign privileges, invoke recovery, integrate automated workloads, or access logs that are themselves governed by the same authority structure. The strong option is present. So is an administrative plane whose compromise can neutralise much of what "encryption enabled" was meant to reassure. The point is not that cloud key services are somehow fraudulent. It is that key governance always sits above the feature list, deciding whether the feature is shield or costume.

Still, a limitation deserves fairness. Algorithms do matter, deeply. No sane institution should pretend that key discipline can rescue fundamentally broken cryptography. A weak primitive, poor protocol design, or flawed randomness source can sink a system even under excellent governance. Likewise, some key concentrations are unavoidable. Complex institutions need recovery paths, automated services, and central trust functions. The fantasy of perfectly distributed, frictionless trust is just that: fantasy in a smart tie. Mature governance does not eliminate concentration. It identifies, constrains, audits, and plans around it.

That concession strengthens the main point rather than weakening it. Because concentration cannot be abolished, it must be governed with unusual honesty. Institutions need to know which keys anchor critical trust, which identities can authorise their use, which recovery routes bypass normal controls, which systems still rely on old material, and which political or operational pressures encourage exceptions that quietly become permanent. Key management is where cryptography stops being a theory of secrecy and becomes an organisation chart with privileges attached. The real asset is not only the secret bitstring itself, but the institutional arrangement that determines who may cause it to act.

This arrangement also explains why insider risk is so stubborn. Much security language imagines threat as external assault against a defended perimeter. Keys reveal how often the more consequential problem lies with legitimate authority used badly, inherited too widely, or retained too long. An insider, contractor, merged-team administrator, or compromised service identity does not need to break the cryptography. They need only occupy the place from which the cryptography is normally made to obey. The strategic consequence is that access reviews, separation of duties, acquisition hygiene, and identity governance belong inside cryptographic thinking, not in a separate filing cabinet marked human resources and awkwardness.

The spare key returns here for one final reason. People often think security fails when the lock is picked. Much of the time it fails because the wrong person is standing in front of the right drawer with ordinary permission and no one has noticed how much power has accumulated there. That is the unresolved test keys impose on institutions. When they claim to have secured their most important systems, can they actually show where the decisive key material is born, where it lives, who can rotate it, who can recover it, who can prove it destroyed, and which quiet administrator account might still be carrying half the state's trust in its pocket?

## Hardware security modules and their trade-offs

In March 2021, researchers disclosed serious vulnerabilities in devices made by Thales and used as hardware security modules in a range of institutional settings. The findings did not mean that specialised cryptographic hardware was a sham, nor that software-only key protection had suddenly become preferable by default. They did mean something more awkward. A technology purchased precisely to reduce trust in ordinary computing environments had itself become a site of concentrated trust, specialised expertise, vendor dependency, and difficult operational judgement. The box meant to narrow risk had become a new object of politics.

That is the recurring truth about hardware security modules, or HSMs. They are attractive because they address a real weakness in institutional cryptography: keys living too openly inside general-purpose systems. A carefully designed HSM can generate keys internally, prevent raw extraction, enforce access policies, sign or decrypt inside a protected boundary, and produce audit trails that make ordinary abuse harder. Those are not cosmetic gains. They can be decisive. But the moment an institution moves its highest-value secrets into specialised hardware, it is no longer merely buying stronger protection. It is buying a relationship: with a vendor, with a supply chain, with a lifecycle, with certification claims, with operational complexity, and with the people who will administer the machinery when something breaks at the least convenient hour.

The box is never just a box.

That motif matters because secure hardware often arrives wrapped in a form of reverence that obscures governance. A rack-mounted device or cloud-backed equivalent can look like an answer rather than a design choice. Show the scene and the problem becomes easier to see. A bank, ministry, or cloud provider moves signing keys or master encryption keys into an HSM. Policies are written. Administrators are designated. Procurement records that "hardware-backed key storage" is now in place. The named concept is transferred trust. Explain it, and the strategic implication is clear. The institution has not removed trust from the system. It has moved trust into a smaller, more specialised domain whose failure modes are harder to inspect and often harder to change once contracts, applications, and recovery procedures depend on it.

The appeal is understandable. General-purpose servers are noisy, porous, and managed by too many hands. Malware can scrape memory. Debugging practices leak secrets. Service accounts accumulate power. Administrators improvise. HSMs promise discipline where ordinary computing promises convenience. They create a narrower place in which key generation, signing, decryption, and policy enforcement can occur. That narrowing matters. It can frustrate whole classes of attack by making key extraction much harder and by separating cryptographic authority from the systems merely requesting it. The abstraction of security becomes visible in specific controls: a key cannot be exported in plaintext, a signature requires policy-defined approval, audit logs capture administrative actions, and tamper responses exist for certain classes of intrusion. For institutions with real key concentrations, these are substantial advantages.

Yet advantage arrives with dependence. A secure hardware estate is not only a technical architecture. It is also a procurement commitment. Which vendor built the device? Which firmware version does it run? How long will the model be supported? What happens when a vulnerability is found in the management plane or the physical module? How difficult is migration to another manufacturer? Can the institution test updates without risking outage to payment systems, certificate services, or signing infrastructure? These questions are not side notes. They are the beginning of strategic seriousness. A device that reduces exposure to one class of attacker may increase exposure to a different class of institutional risk: being trapped in someone else's lifecycle.

Supply chain trust enters here with unusual force because HSMs are trusted precisely where ordinary compromise would be intolerable. Show the scene and the stakes sharpen. A root key is generated in hardware. Firmware updates come from the vendor. Replacement units are shipped through a chain of manufacturing, distribution, and installation. Documentation explains administrative procedures, but the customer cannot inspect every component, fabrication step, or firmware path directly. The named concept is concentrated unverifiability. Explain it, and the paradox emerges. Institutions choose HSMs to reduce the number of places trust must be extended, yet in doing so they may extend very deep trust into the vendor's design practices, update discipline, manufacturing controls, and long-term solvency. The implication is neither panic nor piety. It is a demand to see secure hardware as an ecosystem of dependence rather than a magical object.

A useful example can be found in the broad role HSMs play in payment systems and certificate infrastructures. These are environments where raw key exposure would be especially dangerous, so specialised hardware is often entirely sensible. But once the hardware sits inside a critical path, its weaknesses become strategic. A vulnerability in the device firmware, a flaw in administrative separation, or a migration problem during product retirement can ripple through systems that were built around the assumption that the HSM would remain the stable heart of trust. The institution did not merely adopt stronger key storage. It organised time, staffing, procurement, certification, and incident response around the continued credibility of a small number of specialised boxes. The lock improved. The cupboard holding the spare parts became more important.

That cupboard matters because lifecycle support is where secure hardware often becomes a governance problem rather than a technical one. An HSM model does not live forever. Firmware ages. APIs change. Certification statuses lapse. A vendor may merge, change strategy, discontinue products, or shift support terms. Meanwhile the institution has tied signing services, archive access, code release pipelines, certificate issuance, or transaction processing to the device's behaviour. When replacement looms, the issue is rarely just buying the new model. Keys may need transfer under tightly controlled conditions. Applications may depend on old APIs. Compliance regimes may require revalidation. Downtime windows may be politically impossible. The named concept here is lifecycle entrapment. Explain it, and the strategic point becomes unmistakable. Secure hardware that cannot be replaced gracefully is not a fortress. It is a slowly hardening constraint.

This is one reason operational complexity deserves more candour. HSMs are often described as though they simply reduce risk by adding a hardened layer. In practice they add procedures, roles, ceremonies, recovery rules, vendor dependencies, and failure scenarios that ordinary teams may handle poorly if the institution has bought the gadget without investing in the governance. Key ceremonies, administrative quorum rules, audit review, backup modules, disaster recovery replication, firmware maintenance, role segregation, and emergency procedures all impose real burdens. Those burdens can be good. They force seriousness. They can also produce brittle workarounds when organisations tire of the friction. The visible signs are familiar: shared administrator knowledge, emergency overrides quietly normalised, poorly rehearsed recovery routines, under-trained operators, or a cloud-based HSM service treated as if outsourcing had dissolved all local responsibility. Complexity never vanishes. It migrates to wherever the institution is least inclined to look.

A second example lies in cloud-based key management services that offer HSM-backed operations under a managed model. These services can be highly effective. They spare customers some of the pain of running hardware estates and often bring strong engineering discipline to scale. But they also change the political geometry of trust. A customer using such a service depends on the provider's implementation, regional availability, access controls, audit features, incident handling, and migration path. The customer may gain operational simplicity while losing some visibility and bargaining power over the deeper cryptographic substrate. The named concept is managed opacity. Explain it, and the implication follows. Outsourcing the box does not remove the need to govern it. It merely changes who must be trusted to govern it well, and under what contractual or jurisdictional terms.

Still, a limitation should be acknowledged. It would be foolish to react to these trade-offs by implying that HSMs are overpraised ornaments or cynical theatre. Used well, they remain among the most important institutional tools for reducing key exposure, enforcing strong custody rules, and separating cryptographic authority from ordinary compute. For signing services, certificate authorities, major payment infrastructure, and high-value key hierarchies, specialised hardware often makes excellent sense. Many catastrophic failures would be easier, not harder, in a world without such devices. The point is not to sneer at secure hardware. It is to stop fetishising it.

That concession clarifies the argument rather than weakening it. The question is not whether secure hardware is good. The question is what kinds of risk it displaces, what kinds it introduces, and whether the institution is honest enough to govern the new pattern rather than celebrate the purchase order. A mature organisation does not ask only whether keys are inside hardware. It asks which vendor controls the path of updates, how replacement will occur, how many people can administer the module, how disaster recovery works, whether application teams depend on quirks of one manufacturer's interface, whether procurement has created practical lock-in, and whether the box has become too critical to question. Those are the terms on which hardware stops being gadgetry and becomes state capacity.

Identity and access complicate the matter further because HSMs never act in a vacuum. They act on behalf of administrators, services, certificate authorities, signing workflows, and applications whose identities must themselves be governed. An HSM that enforces perfect non-exportability can still be misused if too many identities can ask it to sign, decrypt, or unwrap on demand. The institution then congratulates itself on protecting the key while ignoring that authority has merely shifted from key possession to command over the module. The difference is real and valuable, but not complete. The same administrative sprawl that plagues other systems can colonise the HSM environment too if nobody has the patience to map who can authorise which operation, under what conditions, and with what independent review.

This also explains why supply chain questions cannot be reduced to espionage melodrama. One need not imagine fantastical tampering at the factory gate to see the strategic importance of secure hardware provenance. Ordinary issues suffice: patch quality, documentation errors, support withdrawal, opaque firmware components, poor administrative tooling, weak customer guidance, or a vendor's inability to sustain secure engineering over the lifetime its customers require. These are not cinematic failures. They are more dangerous for being prosaic. Institutions often prepare for the extraordinary compromise and neglect the ordinary exhaustion of lifecycle discipline that leaves them with secure hardware they cannot confidently update, replace, or audit.

The politics of procurement therefore belongs at the centre of this topic. When an institution chooses an HSM platform, it is also choosing an upgrade rhythm, a support relationship, a contractual dependence, a certification route, and often a set of assumptions about future interoperability with cloud platforms, software stacks, disaster recovery sites, and regulators. Procurement language that asks only whether the device is certified or supports required algorithms is asking an impoverished question. The richer one is whether the hardware can survive time: standards change, mergers happen, vendors falter, cloud strategies shift, and institutions discover that the secure option they bought was only secure under a static picture of the world that no longer exists.

The box returns here because it remains a stubbornly useful corrective to fantasy. A locked box can indeed protect what matters. It can also become the one object everyone is afraid to move, the one supplier everyone is afraid to offend, the one lifecycle everyone is afraid to accelerate, and the one administrative enclave everyone assumes somebody else understands. Hardware security modules are powerful precisely because they narrow trust. They are dangerous when institutions mistake that narrowing for simplification.

The unresolved test is therefore not whether an organisation has adopted secure hardware. It is whether it knows what political, operational, and supply-chain commitments now live inside that adoption: who can administer the modules, who can replace them, whose firmware is trusted, whose road map dictates timing, which applications cannot live without them, and what happens when the gadget that was purchased to reduce risk quietly becomes one of the most consequential forms of dependence the institution has ever signed for.

## Identity, access, and insider risk

In July 2011, when DigiNotar collapsed in the Netherlands after the discovery of fraudulent certificates issued from its systems, public discussion quite reasonably focused on browsers, certificate authorities, and the exposed fragility of internet trust. Yet beneath the visible drama sat a plainer institutional fact. Certificates do not issue themselves. Someone, or something acting for someone, held the authority to request, approve, sign, administer, or fail to detect the use of that authority. The collapse was not only a story about cryptography. It was a story about who inside an organisation could make cryptographic trust move.

That is where the real difficulty begins.

Keys are often described as strategic assets, and so they are. But assets do not act alone. They are surrounded by identities, permissions, workflows, exceptions, escalations, mergers, contractors, administrators, and service accounts that determine when the key may be invoked and by whom. A protected key inside fine hardware is not much comfort if too many people can instruct the hardware to sign, decrypt, or recover. A root certificate held under careful technical custody still becomes dangerous if the surrounding identity system grants issuance authority too loosely or preserves inherited privileges nobody has fully mapped. The lock may be exquisite. The badge reader decides who reaches the door.

This is why identity and access belong inside key management rather than sitting off to one side as an administrative annex. Show the scene and the point becomes concrete. An organisation says its most important secrets are held in approved key stores, access is role-based, and administrative actions are audited. The named concept is delegated authority. Explain it, and the deeper question surfaces. Which identities can trigger key use, create subordinate credentials, approve certificate issuance, recover stored secrets, or alter policy? Are those identities personal, shared, automated, inherited, or vendor-managed? The implication is severe. In institutional cryptography, the decisive weakness often lies not in exposure of the key material itself, but in the web of identities allowed to exercise its power.

That is what makes insider risk so stubborn. The phrase often conjures melodramatic images of disloyal employees skulking through sensitive systems with malicious intent. Such people do exist, but the more common and more dangerous problem is quieter. It is the normal insider: the administrator with too much standing privilege, the contractor whose account outlives the project, the support engineer granted emergency access that becomes routine, the acquired subsidiary whose legacy trust relationships are half-integrated and half-forgotten, the automation account nobody quite owns because everybody depends on it. Insider risk in cryptographic settings is not chiefly about dramatic betrayal. It is about the cumulative expansion of who can legitimately cause secrets to yield.

The badge matters more.

That short sentence is deliberately plain because institutions tend to over-glamorise the machinery and under-scrutinise the authorisation. A highly protected signing key, for example, is only as well governed as the system deciding whose request to sign should be honoured. If multiple teams can issue requests through loosely separated workflows, if human approval rests on tickets that can be socially engineered, if a service account can generate certificates without strong contextual checks, or if a merged identity directory leaves overlapping roles in place, the formal custody of the key may remain pristine while the practical power attached to it grows dangerously diffuse. The implication is not that key stores are unimportant. It is that key custody without identity discipline is a stately façade with weak hinges.

This becomes clearer when one distinguishes between possession and authorisation. Possession concerns where the key lives and whether it can be extracted. Authorisation concerns who can cause cryptographic actions to occur without ever touching raw key material. Modern institutions often improve the first while neglecting the second. They move keys into hardware security modules or managed key services, congratulate themselves on non-exportability, and then permit a wide or murky set of identities to invoke those keys through administrative consoles, APIs, recovery procedures, and delegated workflows. The named concept here is indirect control. Explain it plainly and the risk sharpens. One need not steal the crown if one can whisper convincingly enough to the chamberlain.

A useful example lies in certificate issuance after an acquisition. The scene is almost tediously realistic. A large company acquires a smaller one. The acquired organisation has its own certificate authority, identity directory, administrative conventions, and legacy applications. Integration is urgent because business continuity matters more this quarter than perfect trust hygiene. So temporary bridges are built. Old administrators retain some privileges while new teams learn the terrain. Cross-certification or delegated issuance is configured. Shared service accounts appear to smooth the transition. A year later, nobody is fully certain which identities can still request or approve certificates across the combined estate. The named concept is merger residue. Explain it, and the broader strategic point emerges. Organisational change creates cryptographic ambiguity unless authority is deliberately re-mapped, reduced, and retired. The implication is brutal in its ordinariness. Acquisitions and restructurings are key management events whether institutions treat them that way or not.

A second example can be drawn from the broader pattern of software supply chain incidents. The 2020 SolarWinds compromise showed how devastating it can be when trusted software release paths are abused. That was not simply a matter of one signing key living in the wrong place. It was also about build systems, developer access, release authority, and the identities able to influence what a signing process would bless. The relevant lesson for identity and access is straightforward. Cryptographic trust follows workflow trust. If insiders or compromised insider-equivalents can shape what is submitted to a trusted signing or issuance process, the institution may preserve the key perfectly while still producing perfectly authenticated harm. The badge reader again.

This is why contractors deserve more respect as a source of institutional complexity. Contracting is not an aberration. It is normal state and corporate life. External personnel maintain systems, integrate products, operate managed services, support critical infrastructure, and provide specialist knowledge the permanent organisation does not possess internally. None of that is inherently reckless. The trouble begins when contractual boundaries are mistaken for security boundaries. A contractor with system-level access, certificate administration rights, deployment privileges, or key recovery responsibilities does not become less consequential because their payroll sits elsewhere. The visible behaviour attached to this abstraction is easy to identify: vendor accounts retained for support, jump boxes shared across clients, emergency access granted under service-level agreements, outsourced operations teams working under broad delegated authority. The implication is uncomfortable but basic. Outsourcing work often means outsourcing part of the trust boundary.

The problem deepens with identity systems because they are built for continuity and convenience as much as for strict separation. Single sign-on, federated identity, role inheritance, privileged access management, and account recovery all make large institutions manageable. They also create places where cryptographic authority can accumulate invisibly. A person changes role yet keeps one old group membership. A service principal is granted broad scope because the narrower alternative caused failures during deployment. A backup administrator receives temporary privilege during an incident and never quite loses it. An old contractor identity is reactivated for a quick fix because creating a new one would take too long. None of this looks like sabotage. It looks like work. That is precisely why it matters. The most dangerous insider risk often wears the face of ordinary organisational patience running out.

Still, a limitation is necessary. Not every insider with broad access is a latent catastrophe, and not every complex identity estate is evidence of institutional negligence. Large organisations cannot function on purist fantasies of perfect least privilege at all times. Emergencies happen. Support requires access. Automation depends on service identities. Mergers cannot be integrated by magic over a weekend. A serious account must resist the adolescent temptation to sneer at all compromise as moral failure. Reality is thicker and more burdensome than that. Institutions need access paths in order to survive.

Yet that concession strengthens the argument rather than weakening it. Because some complexity is unavoidable, institutions need a better framework for mapping who can authorise cryptographic actions and under what conditions. The key question is not whether every exceptional path can be eliminated. It is whether every such path is known, justified, time-bounded, and legible. A mature organisation can answer a set of rough but revealing questions. Which human roles can request key usage, certificate issuance, or recovery? Which service identities can do the same without immediate human review? Which external parties hold such authority by contract? Which inherited roles survive from acquisitions or old systems? Which approvals rely on weak signals such as ticket possession rather than independent confirmation? Which emergency routes bypass ordinary controls? This is not bureaucratic fussiness. It is political cartography for trust.

That cartography matters because insider risk is often about adjacency rather than direct power. Someone may not be able to extract a root key and still be able to issue a subordinate certificate, alter a signing workflow, approve a recovery request, modify a policy, or introduce code into a trusted build path. Institutions frequently think in terms of raw possession and miss these chains of influence. The named concept here is authorisation adjacency. Explain it, and one sees why the map must include more than the final holder of the key. It must include the people and systems capable of moving requests, granting approvals, changing policy, or populating the inputs that trusted cryptographic processes later authenticate. The implication is that insider risk cannot be measured by counting a few privileged humans at the top of the hierarchy. It has to be traced through the routes by which trust is made to act.

This also explains why identity failures and cryptographic failures so often travel together during incidents. A response team may discover that the key store itself remains intact while the identity provider, access broker, service account inventory, or administrative federation around it is a small opera of accumulated exceptions. In such a setting the institution can neither revoke cleanly nor reassure honestly, because it does not know the full social perimeter of its own cryptographic power. Systems continue running, but the organisation is governing trust by folklore. That is a far more common condition than public security language likes to admit.

The badge returns here because it remains a better symbol than most key diagrams. People imagine cryptographic authority as a property of sealed machines and carefully handled secrets. Much of the time it is a property of access decisions: who can enter the room, who can tell the machine what to do, who can approve the emergency request, who kept their privileges after the reorganisation, who still appears in a group nobody has reviewed since the merger. The machine matters. The badge reader decides whether the institution truly knows itself.

The unresolved test is therefore not whether an organisation can state that its keys are well protected. It is whether it can name, without bluffing, the full set of identities and workflows that can authorise those keys to act, including the contractors, acquired teams, service accounts, emergency paths, and inherited exceptions that ordinary org charts politely forget. Until that answer becomes legible, key custody will remain less a matter of cryptographic design than of administrative myth.

## Escrow, lawful access, and unintended exposures

In February 2016, the dispute between Apple and the Federal Bureau of Investigation over access to an iPhone used by one of the San Bernardino attackers turned a technical argument into a public test of institutional imagination. The immediate issue looked narrow: could a device maker be compelled to assist in bypassing protections on a specific phone? The concrete outcome was broader. Even before the legal and technical details had settled, the argument exposed a deeper fracture in how people understood cryptographic systems. One side looked at a hard case and saw an exceptional access problem. The other looked at the same case and saw the beginning of a reusable pathway.

A door built for one room rarely stays there.

That is the central problem with escrow and lawful access proposals. They are usually framed as bounded instruments designed for specific, legitimate purposes: a recovery path for unusual circumstances, a controlled override for tightly supervised cases, a carefully governed exception inside a system that otherwise remains secure. Sometimes the motive is investigative. Sometimes it is framed as business continuity, compliance, or institutional resilience. The details vary. The structural issue does not. Once an additional access path is introduced into a cryptographic system, it stops being merely an answer to a single use case. It becomes part of the architecture. That means it must be governed, implemented, tested, protected, audited, updated, and defended against every actor for whom its existence might prove interesting.

The phrase *lawful access* can therefore obscure more than it reveals. It names the intended authority condition, not the engineering consequences. A cryptographic system does not understand legitimacy in the moral or procedural sense. It understands whether an access path exists, how it is invoked, who can authorise it, and what material or infrastructure must be preserved to make it work. Show the scene and the shift becomes plain. A service is designed with end-to-end protections, then modified so that under special circumstances another party can recover or unlock protected information. The named concept is architectural exception. Explain it, and the broader implication follows. The exception must now be treated as part of the system's normal threat surface, not as a noble thought floating above it.

This is why escrow is never only about storage of a spare secret. It is about the institutional chain built around that spare secret. Who holds escrowed material? Under what separation of duties? How are requests authenticated? How is abuse detected? How long is material retained? What happens during staff turnover, vendor collapse, merger, incident response, or cross-system migration? Does the recovery path depend on one central service, multiple trustees, hardware modules, jurisdictionally distributed infrastructure, or an application-level capability embedded in products? Each answer creates a different class of failure. The abstraction of recoverability becomes visible in tickets, consoles, approval flows, audit trails, break-glass accounts, sealed recovery packets, and the inevitable pressure to make emergency access smoother than yesterday's clumsy version. The implication is direct. Escrow does not add one feature. It adds a governance ecosystem.

A useful historical anchor sits further back. The Clipper chip debate in the 1990s in the United States revolved around a proposal for encrypted communications with government-access mechanisms built into the system. The particular technical and political circumstances belong to their own time, and no direct jurisdictional lesson need be drawn here. What matters is the structural insight the debate surfaced and never really lost. The named concept was key escrow, but the underlying concern was systemic spillover. Explain it plainly and the issue becomes durable. A special-access mechanism does not remain special merely because its designers say it will be tightly constrained. It alters the distribution of trust, the value of compromise, and the incentives of every actor who knows the mechanism exists. The implication persists across generations of technology. The argument is rarely only about one state's lawful process. It is about what happens to a cryptographic system once it must be built to yield under additional conditions.

This becomes especially sharp when one considers deterrence. A system without escrow presents one kind of target profile. A system with escrow presents another. The difference is not abstract. If a highly protected communication channel can only be accessed by defeating endpoints or stealing live credentials, an adversary faces one set of costs and uncertainties. If the same system includes an exceptional-access path, escrow repository, or recovery authority, a new class of targets appears: trustees, administrators, request-verification mechanisms, policy engines, hardware modules, or insiders with authority to trigger the exceptional path. The named concept here is shifted attack economics. Explain it, and the strategic point becomes uncomfortable. Escrow may be justified internally as a controlled concession to necessity, but it also creates concentrated assets and procedures that can look extremely attractive from outside. Deterrence changes because the adversary no longer needs to attack only the original user or endpoint. The door built for one room starts redrawing the floor plan.

A brief example makes the point clearer than slogans do. Imagine an institution that encrypts archival records strongly but keeps a recovery mechanism so that a small authorised office can regain access if the original holder is unavailable. On paper this may appear prudent. The archive remains protected, operations remain recoverable, and a lawful or emergency pathway exists. Yet now the institution must protect not only the archive and its original keys, but the recovery office, its personnel, its identity system, its hardware, its procedures, its backups, its approvals, and the long-lived material necessary to prove that a request is real. If any of those elements weaken, the cryptographic promise weakens with them. The issue is not that recovery is irrational. It is that recovery broadens the attack surface and lengthens the list of people and systems whose integrity becomes decisive.

The same dynamic appears in more public disputes over secure messaging, device encryption, or enterprise key recovery. Proposals for exceptional access are often presented as if they could be cleanly limited to rare, highly supervised cases. That aspiration should be treated seriously, not mocked. Hard cases exist. Institutions do face legitimate pressures to recover data or assist under lawful process. Still, aspiration does not cancel architecture.

Once engineers must preserve a capability for exceptional entry, they face recurring pressures to make it reliable, scalable, supportable, and administratively usable. Those pressures tend to push against narrowness. A mechanism that works only in ideal conditions will be denounced as unhelpful. A mechanism that works across product lines and deployment contexts will require more integration and more shared infrastructure. The named concept is operational expansion. Explain it, and the implication becomes obvious. Systems built for rare use have a habit of becoming normalised because institutions hate brittle exceptions.

This is one reason unintended exposure is not merely a side effect but a near certainty in complex organisations. A narrowly intended access path interacts with logging systems, identity providers, cloud administration layers, incident response tools, vendor support channels, and compliance obligations. It may require storage of long-lived recovery materials. It may create metadata about requests that becomes sensitive in its own right. It may alter product design so that a central authority has powers users did not previously need to think about. It may affect cross-border trust, internal employee behaviour, customer procurement choices, or partner willingness to share. None of these consequences requires malice. They arise because institutions are dense, and new powers spread through dense systems in ways that policy language usually understates.

The Apple-FBI dispute remains instructive here not because it proves one universal conclusion, but because it dramatised the difference between case-specific intuition and system-level analysis. Many people heard the facts and thought, reasonably enough, about one phone. Others thought about the precedent of building software able to reduce a security control for future use. The named concept is scope creep by design. Explain it, and the larger concern emerges. A tool or pathway created for one use acquires meaning within an ecosystem of repeatability. The practical question stops being "Can this be done once?" and becomes "What must exist, be preserved, and be governable so that this can be done when demanded again?" That change in question is where much of the disagreement really lives.

A second example arises in enterprise settings where key escrow is sometimes built into email, document management, or device administration systems for continuity reasons. These arrangements are often justified by sensible operational concerns: employees leave, regulated records must remain accessible, litigation holds apply, and organisational memory cannot depend entirely on individual custodians. Those reasons are real. Yet they also create a class of systems in which access depends on central authorities, administrative consoles, and long-lived recovery rights. The visible behaviours are familiar: legal or compliance teams request access, administrators execute a workflow, logs are generated, and business continues. The institutional cost is less visible. Users know the system contains an override. Attackers know it too. Trust changes because the system no longer promises only strong cryptography. It promises strong cryptography plus managed exception. That is a different security object.

Still, a limitation deserves fair treatment. Not every recovery or exceptional-access mechanism is equally reckless, and some forms of escrow can genuinely solve hard problems in narrowly bounded settings. Enterprise archives, regulated records, and operational recovery can create obligations that pure user-controlled secrecy does not satisfy well. It would be unserious to pretend that all such pressures are fraudulent or that any form of recovery is automatically equivalent to systemic sabotage. Institutions sometimes need ways back into their own records. Technical design should not be judged by ritual purity alone.

Yet the limitation clarifies rather than weakens the argument. The right question is not whether any access path beyond the original custodian is thinkable. The right question is what new failure modes are introduced when such a path is added, and whether the institution has the discipline to name and govern them honestly. Does the mechanism create a new concentration of authority? Does it depend on long-lived escrow material? Does it expand insider risk? Does it complicate migration? Does it alter vendor lock-in? Does it generate pressure for broader applicability once one class of case is accepted? Does it degrade trust in the system among users, partners, or foreign customers? These are not side issues. They are the main event.

That is why deterrence and trust must be considered together. A cryptographic system deters attack partly by making secrets difficult to obtain and by limiting the number of viable routes to them. Add an exceptional path, and the institution may gain a lawful or operational convenience while simultaneously signalling that access has become a governed possibility rather than a structural impossibility. That changes attacker calculation. It may also change user behaviour. People write less candidly. They shift to other channels. They assume that "secure" now means "secure unless the right office asks", which is a socially and strategically different proposition. The lawfulness of the intended use does not erase these effects. The system's lived meaning has changed.

The door built for one room returns here because it captures the illusion at the heart of many escrow proposals. Architects of exceptional access often speak as though they are adding a carefully labelled internal door that only authorised people will ever use. Real institutions do not keep doors in such moral isolation. Doors require keys, hinges, maintenance, inspection, signage, staff training, emergency procedures, and records of use. Other people notice them. Someone eventually proposes using them for a slightly different reason. Another team builds its workflow around them. A supplier starts supporting them in a standard way. An attacker changes the map. The technical move and the institutional move become impossible to separate.

The unresolved test, then, is not whether exceptional access can be described in reassuring language. It is whether the people proposing it can state, without euphemism, what new assets must be protected, what new identities gain decisive power, what new dependencies become permanent, what new attack routes are created, and how the system's deterrent value changes once those routes exist. Until those answers are faced directly, escrow will continue to present itself as a neat answer to a narrow problem while quietly rearranging the trust structure of the whole building.

# Chapter 7

# Public Key Infrastructure and Brittle Trust

What does it mean for a system to be trusted by millions when almost nobody using it could name the authorities, files, validation rules, or expiry dates on which that trust actually depends? The question sounds specialist until the moment a browser warning appears, a certificate fails unexpectedly, or a trusted service begins to look uncertain for reasons most users cannot see. Public key infrastructure, or PKI, enables ordinary digital trust at enormous scale. It also does so by hiding an extraordinary amount of concentrated power inside routines that feel almost trivial when they work.

That is the paradox. The modern network depends on chains of trust that must be widely shared to let strangers transact, update software, authenticate services, and exchange sensitive information without having to reauthenticate their identities each time. Yet the same chains rely on a relatively small number of trust anchors, naming conventions, certificate authorities, and validation behaviours. A root store entry, a naming mismatch, an outdated certificate, or a stale device can therefore become more than a technical nuisance. It can become a strategic event. The passport may look routine. The issuing office is not.

The quiet danger of PKI is that it succeeds by making dependence feel natural. A user sees a padlock, a signed update, an authenticated session, or a device joining a trusted system and infers that the machine itself has somehow generated confidence. In reality, confidence has been delegated through institutions, software defaults, and administrative decisions that can be targeted, coerced, misconfigured, or simply left to age badly. The chain is long enough to distribute trust and short enough to break. That combination gives PKI its power and its brittleness at once.

This brittleness is not an incidental flaw sitting beside an otherwise stable architecture. It is part of the architecture. Certificates bind names to keys, but names live inside human systems of ownership, dispute, jurisdiction, and administration. Revocation exists, but revocation depends on clients checking, networks responding, devices updating, and operators behaving sensibly under pressure. Expiry creates discipline, but it also creates abrupt failures when old assumptions linger in hardware, software, or forgotten fleets. The more one looks closely, the less persuasive the image of PKI as neutral plumbing becomes. It is political infrastructure disguised as convenience.

That matters because trust in this environment is not only a matter of whether cryptography is mathematically sound. It is a matter of who gets to vouch, who gets to revoke, who gets to name, and who bears the pain when trust has to move. A compromised certificate authority can do more than issue a bad certificate. It can briefly rearrange reality for every relying party that accepts its word. A stale endpoint can keep old danger alive long after central systems have done the right thing. A root transition can be perfectly justified and still fail if the institution planning it imagines the world consists only of servers and not of printers, appliances, mobile devices, embedded systems, and long-lived software that missed the memo years ago.

The stakes are therefore larger than browser hygiene or administrator embarrassment. PKI sits underneath finance, software distribution, government services, cloud platforms, industrial networks, internal enterprise trust, and a growing range of machine-to-machine relationships that no human ever directly sees. When trust degrades here, the first signs may be modest: a failed validation, a compatibility exception, a temporary override, a device that cannot check revocation properly. But quiet degradation is exactly what makes the system strategic. Institutions often lose trust not through a single spectacular break, but through the accumulation of exceptions, stale dependencies, and brittle transitions that teach administrators to click through warnings and engineers to preserve old assumptions because the alternative is operational pain.

That is why this chapter turns from the concentration of trust in certificates and naming, to the awkward reality that revocation, expiry, and checking often behave worst when pressure is highest, and then to the even harsher problem of moving trust anchors without imagining that the only things needing care are cleanly managed servers in well-run data centres. The argument tightens as it moves. A compromised authority reveals how much power sits in mundane validation rules. Degrading operational discipline shows how trust quietly rots at the edges. Migration forces the final admission that replacing trust is always harder than declaring it replaced.

A house key offers a better image than most technical diagrams. It is small, ordinary, easy to overlook, and decisive. It works because many surrounding assumptions hold at once: the lock has not changed unexpectedly, the door still fits the frame, the person using it is entitled to enter, and the spare copies are where someone thinks they are. PKI works in much the same way. Certificates, roots, revocation lists, firmware stores, and client behaviour all have to align just well enough that ordinary trust remains boring. The trouble begins when one part changes and the rest of the house keeps behaving as though nothing has happened.

The hard question, then, is not whether public key infrastructure can create trust at scale. It plainly can. The harder question is what kind of world has been built when that trust depends on anchors that can be undermined, operational checks that fail quietly, and migrations that punish any institution foolish enough to think that naming a new root is the same thing as moving an entire fleet to believe in it. That is where brittle trust stops being a technical phrase and starts sounding like a description of political order itself.

## Certificates and naming as geopolitics

In August 2011, browser makers began revoking trust in DigiNotar, a Dutch certificate authority, after the discovery that fraudulent certificates had been issued and reportedly used to intercept communications, including for Google users in Iran. The public-facing symptom was simple enough: browser warnings, broken trust, a company in collapse. The strategic meaning was more severe. A piece of infrastructure most users never noticed had briefly become a route to broad impersonation. The passport office had been compromised, and the borders kept opening until others rushed to change the rules.

That episode remains useful because it strips away the comforting fiction that certificates are merely technical paperwork. A certificate does two things at once. It binds a public key to a name, and it asks the world to accept that binding as trustworthy. The first task belongs to mathematics. The second belongs to institutions. Once those institutions are embedded in browsers, operating systems, corporate trust stores, and device firmware, they cease to be neutral clerks. They become strategic actors, whether they wanted the role or not.

The seal on the document matters.

That small image captures the heart of public key infrastructure better than most diagrams do. A seal is meaningful only because people accept the authority behind it. So it is with certificates. When a browser accepts a certificate, it is not engaging in some pristine act of mathematical reason detached from power. It is trusting that a root authority, a chain of intermediates, a naming convention, and a validation routine have all behaved as expected. Show the scene and the political character becomes obvious. A device shipped in one country, using software maintained in another, may rely on root certificates chosen by vendors, validation rules written by distant engineers, and naming systems governed under yet other institutions. The named concept is delegated sovereignty. Explain it, and the implication follows. Public key infrastructure distributes the practical power to define authenticity across a relatively small set of organisations whose decisions can shape global communications.

That is why certificate authorities and naming systems concentrate power so effectively. They sit at the point where the abstract possibility of secure communication becomes an operational yes or no. A certificate authority can say, in effect, "this key belongs to this service", and if enough relying parties accept the claim, the statement becomes reality for millions of users. Naming systems perform a similarly decisive role. A service is not merely a server with a key. It is a server bound to a name that users, software, and institutions recognise as meaningful. The abstraction of trust becomes visible here in a few plain behaviours: a padlock appears, a session starts, a warning is suppressed, a signed update installs, a login page looks ordinary enough to obey. The implication is severe. Whoever can influence naming and certificate issuance can influence what counts as genuine.

This is where geopolitics enters, not as melodrama but as structure. Trust anchors can be targeted because they are valuable. They can be coerced because they sit inside legal and political jurisdictions. They can be undermined because users and institutions depend on them long before they understand them. A state need not seize control of the internet to gain leverage over trust. It may be enough to pressure a certificate authority, influence a registration process, compromise a validation pathway, or exploit the fact that most users cannot distinguish an authentic certificate chain from a fraudulent one that their software has been tricked into accepting. The named concept here is authenticity chokepoint. Explain it, and the strategic lesson sharpens. Public key infrastructure offers global scale by narrowing where authenticity must be vouched for. Narrowing creates efficiency. It also creates targets.

The DigiNotar case made this plain. Fraudulent certificates were reportedly generated for major services, including Google, and were reportedly used in attacks associated with users in Iran. One compromised authority briefly widened the space in which interception could masquerade as legitimacy. The key point is not merely that one company failed. It is that the system had granted that company the power to make statements about identity that many machines would honour automatically. The visible consequence was not just technical confusion. It was strategic vulnerability embedded in ordinary trust behaviour. The implication reaches far beyond one certificate authority. Whenever trust is centralised enough to be convenient, it is centralised enough to be worth subverting.

A second example can be found in the repeated disputes over state-issued or state-linked trust anchors in browsers and operating systems. One need not claim that every such root is compromised to see the structural point. If a root certificate is widely trusted, the institution behind it gains a form of quiet geopolitical reach. It does not need to act overtly for the rest of the world to factor in the possibility of legal compulsion, covert pressure, or strategic influence. The named concept is latent coercibility. Explain it, and the damage of perception becomes easier to understand. A trust anchor may be technically competent and still generate unease if others believe it operates inside a political environment where demands for access, secrecy, or deference could distort the role it is meant to play. The implication is that trust in PKI is never purely technical. It is inseparable from confidence in the independence, resilience, and political surroundings of the institutions involved.

Naming systems deepen this problem because names are not natural facts. They are governed identifiers. A domain name exists because a chain of administrative and legal arrangements says it exists. Certificate validation then builds on that chain, binding cryptographic authority to a naming order that is already political. Show the scene and the point comes into focus. A service appears under a familiar domain. The certificate matches. The browser approves. Yet the entire interaction depends on a prior world of registration, delegation, dispute resolution, and governance. Name the concept and the ordinary act becomes less innocent: operational legitimacy. Explain it, and one sees why control over names can become strategic leverage. If naming is contested, redirected, or administered under pressure, the certificate chain may remain technically correct while the broader reality it confirms has already been bent.

This is one reason mundane validation rules matter so much. Outsiders tend to hear phrases like hostname matching, trust store configuration, certificate transparency, intermediate chaining, or revocation behaviour and assume these are mere implementation details. In strategic terms they are the rules by which an institution decides whom to believe at machine speed. A device that accepts an unexpected intermediate certificate, a corporate network that inserts its own trust anchor for inspection, an appliance that does not validate names strictly, or a fleet that retains stale roots for compatibility can all turn tiny-seeming decisions into channels of leverage. The named concept is rule-mediated power. Explain it, and the implication is plain. Strategic access often enters through ordinary validation logic because ordinary validation logic determines what gets treated as unremarkable.

Corporate interception products offer a useful illustration. Many enterprises install their own trusted certificates on managed devices so that encrypted traffic can be inspected within corporate networks for security or compliance purposes. This can be lawful, disclosed, and operationally justified in its own setting. It is also a reminder that trust anchors are not only external geopolitical artefacts. They are internal instruments of governance and control. Once a device accepts a local authority as trusted, that authority gains enormous practical power over what the user experiences as authenticated communication. The visible behaviour is almost too mundane to notice: pages load, sessions establish, inspection occurs without warnings. The implication is not that such arrangements are automatically abusive. It is that PKI trust is always a political allocation of authority, even inside a single organisation.

Still, a limitation deserves emphasis. Certificate authorities and naming systems are not somehow illegitimate merely because they concentrate power. Without some trusted naming and issuance framework, secure communication at internet scale becomes absurdly difficult. People cannot manually verify every key for every site, service, update channel, and device they use. Shared trust infrastructure exists because the alternative is chaos, fragmentation, or endless bespoke arrangements that would fail most users and institutions far more badly. Concentration is not the bug from which the whole system could be purified. It is part of the reason the system works at all.

That concession sharpens the real issue rather than softening it. The question is not whether trust concentration should exist. The question is how visible, contestable, replaceable, and governable it is. A trustworthy certificate regime is not one that pretends power has been abolished. It is one that makes power legible enough to be audited, constrained, challenged, and if necessary withdrawn. A naming system deserves confidence not because it floats above politics, but because its governance and dispute mechanisms are robust enough that strategic pressure does not quietly become routine. The same applies to trust anchors. Their safety lies not only in cryptographic competence but in the surrounding ecology of transparency, accountability, distribution, and the practical ability of relying parties to stop trusting them when trust is no longer deserved.

This is why compromised or controversial certificate authorities produce such disproportionate consequences. They do not merely fail in their own corner. They reveal how many other institutions have outsourced a portion of their authenticity judgements to entities they barely understand. A bank, a ministry, a cloud provider, a university, a browser vendor, and an ordinary user may all be relying on the same small set of trust decisions without sharing the same legal environment, threat model, or political assumptions. The weakness is not that any one of them is foolish. It is that global interoperability requires shared authority, and shared authority always carries the possibility that one party's trust becomes another party's exposure.

The seal on the document returns here for a final reason. People often think the danger lies in a forged seal. Sometimes it does. Just as often the greater danger lies in no longer knowing whether the office issuing seals can withstand pressure, scrutiny, and compromise strongly enough for its word to remain worth taking at face value. Certificates and naming systems are geopolitics in precisely that sense. They decide, quietly and constantly, which claims about identity the digital world will treat as ordinary truth. The uncomfortable question is not whether those decisions involve power. It is whether the institutions making them are sturdy enough, and limited enough, that the rest of the world can keep living with the answer.

## Revocation, expiry, and reality

In September 2021, a root certificate used widely through Let's Encrypt expired, and the consequences rippled far beyond the tidy logic of certificate lifecycles. In San Francisco, the organisation had long publicised the relevant dates and transition paths. On paper, expiry was doing exactly what public key infrastructure says it should do: ending trust on schedule so that old assumptions would not persist forever. In practice, older Android devices and other stale systems struggled because they could not follow the newer trust path cleanly. The visible outcome was not a dramatic break in cryptography. It was a reminder that time behaves differently in theory and in fleets.

That is the awkward truth about PKI safety. It depends not only on elegant chains of trust, but on small operational details that have to work under stress, across uneven devices, with mixed software ages, patch habits, network conditions, and human tolerance for warnings. Revocation must be checked. Expiry dates must be honoured. Clients must update. Validation must fail sensibly. Certificates must be replaced before panic, not after. None of this sounds glamorous, which is precisely why it causes so much trouble. Trust usually decays in quiet ways first.

The milk in the fridge turns slowly.

That modest image suits the subject because revocation and expiry rarely fail in grand, cinematic gestures. They fail through staleness, delay, fallback, and the organisational temptation to treat yesterday's trust as good enough for one more quarter. Show the scene and the problem becomes plain. A certificate authority is compromised, or a certificate should no longer be trusted, or a root is nearing the end of its life. The named concept is trust freshness. Explain it, and one sees the strategic burden. Public key infrastructure does not merely require that trust be established; it requires that trust be withdrawn, renewed, and revalidated on time. The implication is harsh. A system can be cryptographically sophisticated and still behave like spoiled inventory if its operators cannot keep trust current.

Revocation is the purest expression of this difficulty. In theory it sounds straightforward. If a certificate is compromised, misissued, or no longer trustworthy, relying parties should stop accepting it. In practice, that requires a chain of awkward conditions to hold. Clients must know where to check. They must be able to reach the relevant service or carry fresh revocation information locally. They must know what to do when the answer is unavailable. Software designers must choose whether failure to check means failure to connect or merely a shrug and a warning nobody reads. Show the scene and one sees why operational convenience corrodes security here so easily. A browser or device confronted with uncertain revocation status may be tempted to continue rather than block the user. The named concept is fail-open trust. Explain it, and the strategic implication follows. Systems designed to preserve usability under degraded conditions can turn revocation from a safeguard into a polite suggestion.

This is not a purely theoretical annoyance. The broader history of browser security is littered with uncomfortable lessons about revocation mechanisms proving slow, unreliable, inconsistently enforced, or too brittle under network failure to serve as the decisive line of defence people imagined. Certificate revocation lists can grow stale. Online status protocols can fail or be blocked. Applications can cache old answers too long or skip checks entirely in edge conditions. The visible behaviours are mundane: a network path times out, an endpoint has no current connectivity, a user clicks through, an appliance runs old firmware, an administrator disables strict checking because too many business workflows break otherwise. The implication is larger than the mechanics. Trust mechanisms are judged in calm weather, then quietly reinterpreted under operational pressure.

Expiry appears cleaner because it is built into the certificate itself. A date arrives, and trust should end. No external lookup required. No ambiguity about whether the certificate is still current. Yet expiry has its own reality problem. Certificates do not expire inside a vacuum; they expire inside estates full of stale devices, forgotten services, embedded systems, pinned assumptions, old dependencies, and administrators who discover the calendar only when the outage begins. The 2021 Let's Encrypt root expiry illustrated this with unusual clarity. The certificate event was entirely predictable. The breakage still arrived because prediction is not the same thing as fleet readiness. The named concept here is temporal mismatch. Explain it, and the lesson becomes difficult to ignore. Trust can end on schedule while systems depending on that trust remain marooned in the past.

Long-lived certificates deepen the trouble because they flatter institutional laziness. A certificate with a generous lifetime can feel efficient. Fewer renewals mean less operational friction, fewer opportunities for accidental outage, and less administrative labour. Those are real benefits. They are also seductive. The longer a certificate lives, the longer compromised assumptions can persist, stale ownership information can go unchallenged, and forgotten dependencies can hide under the apparent orderliness of "still valid". Validity is not vitality. A long-lived certificate can be formally acceptable and strategically stale at the same time. The milk may still sit within its printed date while the household has plainly stopped noticing who bought it, why it is there, or what else it now touches in the fridge.

A useful example sits in old internal certificates used across enterprise fleets. Such certificates may support device management, internal APIs, middleware, printers, industrial equipment, or management consoles. Because they are internal, organisations often treat them with a fatal mixture of familiarity and neglect. Renewal windows are pushed back. Old roots remain trusted "just in case". Devices unable to update cleanly are tolerated because they still function. Then, when an expiry, revocation, or emergency distrust event arrives, the institution discovers that the hardest problem is not issuing the new certificate. It is discovering all the quiet places still depending on the old one. The named concept is hidden reliance. Explain it, and the strategic point becomes obvious. PKI degrades not only through external compromise, but through internal forgetfulness.

Stale devices are where all these neat theories go to sulk in the corner. A modern server estate may handle certificate renewal gracefully, use automated issuance, and support current trust chains. The organisation still lives with phones that no longer receive updates, appliances purchased under old support terms, medical or industrial devices with long certification cycles, branch office systems running frozen software, or offline environments where trust data moves only when someone remembers to carry it. These devices often matter precisely because they are hard to replace. The visible behaviour is painfully familiar. Security teams know what the correct trust posture should be. Operations teams know which assets cannot follow it without budget, downtime, or regulatory pain. So exceptions accumulate. The strategic implication is not merely technical debt. It is legacy exposure built into the trust fabric itself.

The problem becomes more severe under stress because revocation and expiry are often invoked at the very moment an institution is already least capable of elegant action. A certificate authority compromise, a misissued certificate, a suspected interception event, or a rushed root distrust decision rarely occurs when all systems are calm, fully inventoried, and lovingly maintained. It occurs when administrators are already triaging, vendors are issuing hurried guidance, executives want continuity, and the temptation to preserve service by relaxing validation grows strongest. The named concept is crisis-induced trust erosion. Explain it, and one sees why PKI safety cannot be judged solely in nominal conditions. The real test is what organisations do when the safe path and the easy path part company under pressure.

Still, a limitation must be stated clearly. Expiry and revocation are not foolish mechanisms. They remain indispensable. Without expiry, trust would become dangerously sticky by default. Without revocation, compromise would often have to be endured until formal validity happened to run out. Modern automation has also improved parts of the picture. In some web and cloud environments, frequent certificate renewal, better tooling, and shorter lifetimes have made certain classes of expiry failure more manageable than they once were. It would be lazy to speak as though all PKI operations remained trapped in the same old amateur hour.

Yet that concession strengthens the core argument rather than weakening it. The issue is not whether revocation and expiry are conceptually sound. The issue is whether institutions can operationalise them across uneven reality rather than only inside clean diagrams. Automation works best where systems are current, reachable, well-inventoried, and built with replacement in mind. The very sectors most likely to carry long-lived strategic exposure - critical infrastructure, legacy enterprise environments, regulated fleets, mixed vendor estates, specialised devices - are often the ones least able to rely on the smoothest forms of automated trust hygiene. A modern web stack and a forgotten industrial controller may share a root store problem while living in radically different operational worlds. That difference matters more than the standards document wants to admit.

This is why revocation, expiry, and stale trust should be read as governance signals rather than merely technical episodes. When an organisation repeatedly extends old certificates, delays root replacement, weakens validation to preserve uptime, or discovers unknown dependencies only during incident response, it is revealing something about how it governs time. It is choosing continuity over freshness, sometimes wisely, often habitually. The abstraction of risk becomes a series of visible decisions: whether to block service when revocation checks fail, whether to keep old roots trusted for compatibility, whether to shorten certificate lifetimes and absorb the overhead, whether to fund device replacement before the next forced transition, whether to inventory endpoints rather than merely servers. Each choice teaches the institution what kind of trust decay it is willing to tolerate.

A second useful example lies in cross-signed and transitional certificate arrangements designed to smooth migration. These can be prudent and often necessary. They also create a dangerous kind of half-success. The institution sees a bridge and assumes it has solved the problem. In truth it may only have delayed confrontation with the older endpoints, stale trust stores, or buried dependencies that still cannot cross to the new side unaided. The named concept is transition masking. Explain it, and the implication sharpens. Transitional trust can preserve continuity while concealing the depth of legacy exposure, leaving organisations more surprised later precisely because the first stage appeared to work.

This quiet degradation is what makes PKI brittle in practice. Trust rarely disappears all at once. It thins. Checks are skipped. Old devices remain. Exceptions multiply. Validation becomes contextual rather than strict. The certificate is still technically valid, the revocation service is flaky, the fallback mode is tolerated, the endpoint has not been touched in years, the expiry date is on someone else's calendar. Each individual compromise feels manageable. Together they create a trust system that still performs legitimacy while quietly accumulating doubt. The milk in the fridge still looks serviceable until someone finally smells it.

The strategic lesson is therefore less about certificates themselves than about the pace at which institutions can refresh belief. A public key infrastructure that cannot revoke credibly, expire cleanly, and move stale devices off old assumptions in time is not merely untidy. It is structurally vulnerable to the kind of legacy exposure that adversaries, accidents, and future trust transitions exploit mercilessly. The hard question is not whether a certificate has technically expired or a revocation mechanism formally exists. It is whether the institution relying on them can tell, before the outage or the compromise, which parts of its estate are already living on expired assumptions while the interface still smiles and says everything is secure.

## Migration of trust anchors

In September 2021, Let's Encrypt's DST Root CA X3 expired, and a problem that had looked like tidy certificate housekeeping became a lesson in the politics of old devices. The replacement path had been known well in advance. Engineers had discussed it, documentation existed, and the basic logic of public key infrastructure had not changed. Yet older Android systems and other stale clients struggled because they could not all follow the new chain cleanly. The visible result was not the collapse of encryption. It was a distributed reminder that replacing trust is never only about the certificate authority's servers. It is about the endpoints that have to believe the new story.

That is the central difficulty in migrating trust anchors. A root certificate may seem like an abstract object, a cryptographic foundation stored in software and blessed by administrators. In practice it behaves more like civic plumbing. It sits in browsers, operating systems, enterprise appliances, mobile devices, embedded systems, industrial controllers, corporate trust stores, update mechanisms, and management tools. One can generate a new root, sign the right intermediates, publish the right guidance, and still fail strategically if the installed world cannot absorb the change. The old keyring still opens too many doors.

This is why trust-anchor migration is one of the clearest tests of institutional realism in security. Show the scene and the mistake becomes obvious. A security team plans root replacement carefully on the server side, validates the new chain, updates central systems, and congratulates itself on orderly progress. The named concept is server-side illusion. Explain it, and the trouble appears at once. Public key infrastructure is not only what servers present; it is what endpoints accept. A fleet containing new laptops, old phones, line-of-business appliances, branch-office systems, printers, handheld scanners, industrial gateways, offline devices, and outsourced services does not migrate by decree. The implication is severe. A trust-anchor change that ignores endpoints is not a migration plan. It is a staged outage with optimistic paperwork.

Trust anchors are especially awkward because they are meant to sit low in the stack, below ordinary human attention, and therefore often below ordinary inventory discipline as well. Institutions usually know a lot about their major applications and public-facing services. They know much less about every trust store, certificate pin, embedded root, custom validation behaviour, or stale firmware instance spread across years of procurement and mergers. The abstraction of trust becomes visible only when it breaks: a device refuses connection, an update fails, a service cannot authenticate, a monitoring tool fills with certificate errors, a remote site goes dark because some forgotten dependency still lives under the old root. The named concept here is distributed dependence. Explain it, and the strategic lesson sharpens. Root trust is not concentrated where organisations most like to look.

This is why rotating a root certificate across a heterogeneous fleet is not merely a technical exercise. It is a coordination problem among actors with very different clocks. Browsers update quickly. Managed desktops can often be pushed. Cloud workloads can usually be rehearsed. Embedded devices may not update cleanly at all. Industrial systems may require careful maintenance windows. Regulated medical equipment may face change-control burdens that make even straightforward trust-store updates politically difficult. Offline or intermittently connected systems may receive changes only through clumsy physical processes. A root replacement therefore moves at the pace of the slowest tolerable participant, not the speed of the most disciplined team. The implication is as annoying as it is true. The weakest endpoint often becomes the timetable.

The Let's Encrypt root expiry episode is useful precisely because it was not an exotic state plot or a revolutionary cryptanalytic event. It was a fairly legible trust transition colliding with old reality. Cross-signing arrangements and compatibility strategies prolonged service for many systems, but they also demonstrated the limits of elegant PKI theory when faced with devices living outside normal update culture. The named concept is compatibility scaffolding. Explain it, and one sees the deeper point. Transitional measures can reduce pain, but they can also mask how much of the estate remains dependent on the old anchor. The organisation sees continuity and may mistake it for completed migration. The old keyring remains in use, simply tucked behind a nicer label.

A second example can be found in enterprise environments where mergers or platform changes force internal certificate hierarchy replacement. The outward story often sounds manageable. An old internal root must be retired; a new hierarchy will be introduced; servers will be updated; clients will trust the new chain. What actually happens is messier. Legacy appliances have hard-coded certificate assumptions. Thin clients in remote offices have not checked in. Mobile device management policies differ by operating system generation. Contractors connect through unmanaged endpoints. VPN gateways, device management tools, and monitoring products each validate certificates in slightly different ways. Show the scene and the migration problem stops looking like PKI maintenance and starts looking like institutional archaeology. The named concept is trust sediment. Explain it, and the implication follows. Old anchors sink into layers of operational history that no central diagram fully captures.

This is why endpoint inclusion is not a pedantic afterthought but the heart of the task. Servers are the easiest part because they are visible, managed, and usually touched by the people writing the migration plan. Endpoints are where policy meets entropy. They are owned by different teams, purchased in different years, patched unevenly, and used under conditions far less tidy than server administrators like to imagine. A trust-anchor migration that counts only what is centrally administered counts only what is least likely to surprise. The strategic exposure lies with what remains peripheral, unmanaged, forgotten, or inherited. A printer in a warehouse, a scanner on a loading dock, a diagnostic workstation in a clinic, a legacy VPN client on a director's old laptop - these are not romantic adversaries of progress. They are where trust transitions go to become expensive.

The problem becomes worse under stress because root replacement is often attempted for reasons that do not permit leisurely perfection. A certificate authority may lose credibility. A root may be nearing expiry. An organisational split or acquisition may demand rapid trust separation. A post-incident response may require replacing anchors whose continued use now looks intolerable. In such conditions the institution is not merely migrating. It is migrating while under pressure to preserve service, reassure leadership, and avoid teaching users to click past warnings. The named concept is crisis migration. Explain it, and the danger becomes obvious. Under stress, organisations are tempted to preserve compatibility too long, extend trust too widely, or accept insecure temporary paths because the visible cost of breakage is immediate while the strategic cost of a messy transition feels delayed. That is exactly how brittle trust survives.

Still, a limitation deserves honesty. Not every trust-anchor migration is a near disaster, and modern automation has made many certificate operations vastly better than they were in earlier eras. Managed fleets, current browsers, coordinated cloud environments, automated issuance, and central device management can reduce the pain substantially where they are actually present. Some root transitions are handled with impressive discipline. It would be lazy to imply that PKI migration is always a theatre of incompetence and panic. Many institutions do parts of it very well.

Yet that concession clarifies the real point rather than weakening it. The question is not whether some systems can migrate cleanly. The question is whether the institution knows where clean migration ends and heterogeneous reality begins. A mature trust-anchor transition plan includes inventory, endpoint classes, unmanaged or intermittently connected devices, third-party services, certificate pinning, custom trust stores, offline recovery paths, communication plans, fallback boundaries, and a timetable for retiring transitional compatibility rather than merely announcing it. The visible sign of maturity is not a beautifully worded migration memo. It is the ability to name which endpoints still depend on the old anchor and what will happen to them when patience runs out.

This is also where weakest-link dynamics reappear. A central team may complete the root rotation correctly and still be forced to preserve old trust because a small but critical class of endpoints cannot move. That preservation is not neutral. It extends the life of old assumptions, maintains attack surface, and creates opportunities for ambiguous or duplicated trust paths. An adversary need not defeat the new anchor if the old one remains live in just enough corners to matter. The named concept is anchor overhang. Explain it, and the strategic implication becomes clear. The danger of legacy trust does not disappear when the new root is deployed. It persists as long as the old root remains necessary somewhere the organisation cannot afford to neglect.

A subtler problem lies in human behaviour. Trust-anchor migration is not only about certificates and devices. It is also about the narratives institutions tell themselves. Teams like to say that the new root is "rolled out" once central services present it. Leadership likes to hear that migration is "complete" once the visible systems remain up. Users learn bad habits if warnings proliferate during messy transitions. Help desks start advising workarounds. Temporary trust exceptions become invisible norms. These social adaptations matter because PKI ultimately depends on sustained habits of acceptance and refusal. If a migration teaches the organisation that warnings are noisy but harmless, the damage may outlast the technical transition itself. The old keyring still opens too many doors, and people stop checking which one they are using.

This is why trust-anchor migration should be understood as governance over time rather than one replacement event. The institution has to manage overlap carefully, define when transitional chains will end, identify who can authorise exceptions, and keep endpoint reality in view long after the server-side dashboards look green. It must decide how much pain to accept now to avoid carrying dangerous compatibility into the future. That decision is partly technical, but mostly political. Which business unit will tolerate downtime? Which regulator will permit revalidation delays? Which vendor will support older devices? Which executive will own the cost of replacing gear that still functions except for the inconvenient matter of believing the wrong root? Migration decisions become power decisions the moment old trust becomes expensive to keep.

The old keyring returns here because it captures the subject more honestly than elegant diagrams of certificate chains. Replacing a trust anchor is not like swapping one equation for another. It is like changing the master keys for a city while many buildings are inhabited, some locks are forgotten, some doors are jammed, and several property managers insist they were never told the date. The mathematics may be immaculate. The practical task is civic and stubborn.

The unresolved test is therefore not whether an organisation can issue a new root certificate. It is whether it can say, before the deadline hardens into incident, which endpoints will still refuse the new trust, which transitional crutches are prolonging old exposure, who owns the ugliest corners of the fleet, and when the old anchor will truly stop being part of reality rather than merely part of the documentation. Until those answers are credible, root migration remains less a ceremony of renewal than a contest between clean design and the long memory of the installed world.

# Chapter 8

# Secure Communications and Metadata Competition

What does it mean for a message to be secure if the content is unreadable but the pattern of contact remains legible, the device at one end is compromised, and the system quietly falls back to weaker behaviour the moment conditions worsen? The question sounds fussy until one notices how much modern confidence rests on a partial answer to it. People see a lock icon, an encrypted tunnel, a promise of end-to-end protection, and infer that secrecy has been achieved in the broad human sense. Usually something narrower has been achieved: one class of interception has become harder. Much else may still be visible, governable, or breakable under pressure.

That gap matters because secure communications are usually sold through the language of content. Can outsiders read the message? Is the call encrypted? Has the transport been protected? Those are important questions. They are not the whole terrain. Communications systems live inside devices, backup routines, identity layers, timing patterns, routing decisions, network constraints, and organisational demands for recovery or oversight. Once those layers are restored to view, the ordinary contrast between "secure" and "insecure" begins to look much too coarse. The envelope may be sealed while the postmark does most of the damage.

The postmark gives a lot away.

That is the chapter's central tension. Communications security is indispensable and yet persistently incomplete. Transport protections make interception harder and deserve their status as basic civic hygiene. End-to-end designs can shift power away from intermediaries and restore meaningful privacy in environments otherwise built for extraction and surveillance. But the same systems produce new struggles over usability, recovery, policy control, and institutional accountability. Metadata continues to reveal structure even when content is hidden. Constrained links and old hardware keep weaker assumptions alive in places far from the polished world of consumer apps and cloud dashboards. Crisis conditions then arrive and punish every design that relied on calm networks, current software, and patient users.

The stakes therefore extend beyond technical neatness into the architecture of power. A society that can protect content but not patterns may still expose journalists, dissidents, military units, supply chains, and ordinary citizens to forms of inference that are politically potent even without plaintext. A company that deploys strong end-to-end protection may still find itself in conflict with its own compliance, archive, or incident-response expectations. A military or critical-infrastructure network that secures routine communications may still stumble when radio links degrade, satellite windows narrow, or emergency fallback strips away verification in the name of continuity. The problem is not that encryption fails. The problem is that communications systems are judged too often by their best case.

That is why the strategic contest around communications is not only about who can read content. It is also about who can map relationships, predict movement, exploit transition states, shape defaults, and take advantage of the moment when an institution values restored service more than preserved assurance. Metadata is useful because life itself is patterned. Networks are revealing because organisations repeat themselves. Fallback modes are dangerous because crises tempt people to accept unverified substitutes for trusted channels. Once that is understood, communications security starts to look less like a solved problem of stronger ciphers and more like an ongoing struggle over what kinds of visibility the system still permits.

The argument therefore moves from the strong but limited protections offered by common transport security into the harder politics of end-to-end systems, where security for users can collide with the supervisory instincts of institutions. From there the focus widens to metadata, where timing, location, and social structure create their own intelligence field even when content remains sealed. The line then runs beyond familiar internet settings into satellite, radio, and other constrained environments, where update cycles are slow and old assumptions linger in hardware that cannot be wished into modernity. It closes against disruption itself, where censorship, jamming, outage, and emergency procedure reveal whether the whole design was robust or merely graceful under ideal conditions.

A map folded in a pocket can explain the deeper issue. It may never reveal the exact conversation, yet it shows routes, choke points, distances, timing, and the habits of movement that make later interpretation possible. Secure communications systems often resemble that map more than their advertising admits. They can protect the words while still exposing the rhythm. They can secure the link while leaving the endpoint soft. They can function admirably on ordinary days and then betray their own priorities the moment stress, interruption, or governance pressure forces them to choose between continuity and strict trust.

The hardest question, then, is no longer whether a communication channel is encrypted. It is whether the people relying on it understand what remains exposed, who still holds power over recovery and fallback, and what the system will do when conditions cease to be normal. Until that question is faced directly, secure communications will keep being praised as a finished achievement while the real contest shifts to everything the lock icon never promised to hide.

## Transport security and its limits

In April 2014, when the Heartbleed vulnerability in OpenSSL became public, organisations around the world were forced into an awkward admission. The lock icon in the browser had not been lying, exactly. Transport Layer Security was still doing what it was designed to do in principle: establishing encrypted channels between clients and servers. Yet a flaw in widely used implementation code meant that protected memory contents could be exposed from systems people believed were securely communicating. The immediate outcome was a patching scramble, certificate replacement, and a belated effort to map where vulnerable code had spread. The channel was encrypted. The system was not safe.

That episode still matters because it punctures a lazy but persistent idea: if communications are encrypted in transit, then the strategic problem has been solved. It has not. Secure transport protocols do something both essential and limited. They protect data moving across networks against a range of interception and tampering risks. They help establish who is at the other end, negotiate keys, and create a protected tunnel through untrusted infrastructure. They are among the great quiet achievements of the modern digital order. But a tunnel is not a destination. Once data reaches an endpoint, passes through a compromised device, is copied into logs, synced into backups, or handled by a badly configured application, the strategic promise narrows sharply.

That is the core tension. Transport security is necessary because open networks invite interception, manipulation, and impersonation. It is insufficient because communications do not live only in transit. They live in endpoints, storage systems, identity frameworks, user habits, administrative tooling, and fallback paths. Show the scene and the distinction becomes plain. A user sends a message over a secure channel. The named concept is link protection. Explain it, and one sees its exact value: outsiders on the network path should not easily read or alter the content. The implication, however, arrives immediately. If the user's phone is compromised, if the receiving server stores the plaintext insecurely, or if a synced backup copies the message into a weaker environment, the secure link has merely protected one segment of a longer and more vulnerable journey.

This is why common secure transport protocols deserve both respect and scepticism. Protocols such as TLS have transformed ordinary communications security. They protect web sessions, APIs, software updates, financial transactions, and much else besides. Without them, the modern internet would be little more than a scavenger's paradise. Yet their success invites a dangerous inflation of confidence. Once transport encryption becomes a default, institutions begin to speak as though the word *secure* belongs to the whole system rather than to the path segment the protocol actually governs. The abstraction of trust then drifts upward. A board hears that traffic is encrypted. A procurement team notes secure transport in the product sheet. An audit confirms encryption in transit. The organisation quietly infers that confidentiality, integrity, and authenticity have all been solved in a larger sense than the protocol itself ever promised.

Endpoint compromise is where this inflated confidence most often collapses. Secure transport works by encrypting communications between endpoints. It does not make the endpoints wise, clean, or incorruptible. A phone infected with spyware, a laptop running a hostile browser extension, a server with weak administrative boundaries, or an application exposing decrypted content to the wrong process can all nullify the practical value of transport security without breaking the transport protocol at all. The message arrives safely, then dies on the kitchen table. The named concept here is endpoint supremacy. Explain it, and the strategic lesson is bracing. In communications security, the endpoint usually matters more than the wire. A nation-state, criminal group, or insider who can compromise devices and applications has little need to attack the tunnel if the tunnel faithfully delivers secrets into open hands at either end.

A useful example lies in secure messaging that is undermined by device backups. Messaging apps may use strong transport protection, and some may use stronger content protection as well, yet users or institutions often enable cloud backups, local sync, or device migration features for entirely understandable reasons. Messages that were difficult to intercept on the network can then appear in weaker storage contexts governed by different access controls, different retention rules, or different legal and administrative pathways. Show the scene and the problem is almost too ordinary to notice. A user trusts the message because the chat app advertises strong encryption. The phone then backs up content to a cloud account whose protections, retention logic, or account recovery model are very different. The implication is not that the transport protection was fake. It is that communications security is only as strong as the least-governed point where the content is allowed to rest.

Downgrade risk reveals another limit. Modern transport protocols often negotiate security features dynamically: versions, cipher suites, extensions, certificate paths, resumption behaviour, and fallback options. This flexibility makes interoperability possible, especially during transitions. It also creates opportunities for a connection to become weaker than either side ideally intends. A system designed to support old clients, tolerate misconfiguration, or preserve service during partial migration may accept a less secure version or weaker handshake path under the wrong conditions. The named concept is negotiated weakness. Explain it, and the strategic implication becomes obvious. A protocol that is secure in its strongest profile may be much less reassuring in the mixed reality of compatibility settings, old devices, middleboxes, and emergency exceptions. Transport security is not just what the protocol can do. It is what it actually negotiates under pressure.

This is where configuration pitfalls become politically important. Technical people know that protocol safety depends heavily on exact choices: certificate validation, hostname checks, accepted protocol versions, cipher suite ordering, client authentication behaviour, session resumption, logging, proxying, and policy enforcement at network edges. Non-technical leaders often hear only that the organisation uses modern secure transport. That phrase hides a multitude of sins. A badly configured reverse proxy, a load balancer preserving old protocol support for one legacy application, a corporate inspection device inserting its own trust anchor, or a monitoring appliance terminating secure sessions in the wrong place can all transform a well-designed transport scheme into a patchwork of quiet exceptions.

The visible behaviour attached to this abstraction is familiar: warnings suppressed, compatibility preserved, legacy clients still supported, internal interception normalised for "security purposes", and administrators hoping nobody asks too closely which links are secure in the narrow sense and which are merely believed to be.

A second useful example lies in the history of TLS transitions themselves. The retirement of older protocol versions and weak configurations did not happen in one clean act of expert consensus. It took years of browser changes, server updates, industry guidance, patching, and reluctant concessions to the stubborn life of old devices and enterprise dependencies. The scene mattered because it showed that a stronger transport protocol does not instantly replace a weaker one just because the technical case is clear. Organisations had to weigh breakage against exposure, compatibility against confidence, and migration cost against abstract future risk. The implication extends beyond the specific versions involved. Transport security at scale is governed by institutional willingness to stop tolerating weak negotiation, not simply by the existence of better standards.

Still, a credible limitation should be acknowledged. None of this means transport security is overpraised or somehow marginal. Without strong encryption in transit, the rest of the conversation collapses into far cruder forms of vulnerability. Open Wi-Fi networks, hostile intermediaries, ISP-level observation, routine tampering, credential theft, session hijacking, and commodity interception would all be much easier and more common without secure transport. For banking, web browsing, software distribution, remote administration, and cloud services, transport protection remains indispensable. It is not some decorative minimum. It is civilisational plumbing.

That concession strengthens the larger argument rather than weakening it. The real danger lies not in trusting transport security too much, but in misdescribing what exactly it secures. The tunnel is necessary. The tunnel is not the whole road. Once this is accepted, a better strategic vocabulary becomes available. Instead of asking whether communications are encrypted, institutions can ask where plaintext appears, where backups travel, which proxies terminate sessions, which clients still negotiate older modes, which administrative tools can observe decrypted traffic, and how many users confuse secure transit with durable secrecy. These are not pedantic questions. They determine whether a communication channel is merely well-protected against one class of attack or genuinely positioned within a larger system that deserves confidence.

The issue grows sharper in institutional settings because transport security often serves other organisational purposes besides privacy. Companies inspect traffic for malware, data loss, and compliance. Governments route communications through managed gateways. Cloud architectures terminate secure sessions at multiple layers for scaling and monitoring. None of this is automatically reckless. It does mean that transport encryption frequently operates inside systems that intentionally decrypt, inspect, log, transform, and re-encrypt data as part of normal business or state routine. The named concept is managed exposure. Explain it, and the strategic lesson becomes plain. Transport security can protect a link while still feeding a large apparatus of internal visibility. The link may be safe from outsiders even as the content becomes legible to a significant set of insiders, tools, and retained records.

This is one reason the phrase *encryption in transit* can be so misleading when treated as a strategic claim rather than a technical one. It encourages a path-based view of secrecy in situations where the real contest may centre on endpoints, metadata, backups, cloud tenancy, or policy-controlled interception. The ordinary user thinks about whether the message is protected while crossing the network. The serious adversary thinks about where the message will be easiest to obtain once it arrives, who can be tricked into negotiating down, and which "temporary" configuration exception has already become part of the institution's hidden normal.

The milk crate in the delivery van offers a quieter metaphor than the lock icon. The crate may be sealed securely during transport. That matters. If the receiving warehouse leaves it open overnight, if an inventory clerk copies its contents into the wrong ledger, or if a second truck with weaker rules takes it the last mile, the success of the original delivery protection remains real and strategically incomplete. So it is with transport security. It does one hard thing very well. It cannot stop other parts of the system from behaving foolishly, generously, or under pressure.

That is the forward test. When an institution says its communications are secure, does it mean that packets are encrypted on the wire, or does it understand where content reappears, where negotiation can weaken, where backups quietly betray the promise, and how many ordinary operational choices still sit outside the tunnel waiting to turn a good protocol into a flattering story?

## End-to-end encryption and institutional control

In March 2017, the United Kingdom government introduced the Investigatory Powers Act, and one of the broader public arguments surrounding the period turned on a deceptively simple question: if a messaging service cannot read what its users say to one another, who is really in control of the system? The concrete legal debates were specific to one jurisdiction, but the strategic problem was much wider. End-to-end encryption had shifted a crucial point of power. Intermediaries could still route, store, suspend, charge, and design. They could no longer assume they would also be able to inspect content as a matter of routine architecture.

That shift was not merely technical. It was political.

End-to-end encryption changes communications by changing where trust resides. In a conventional service model, the provider is not just the courier. It is often also the reader, the archivist, the compliance partner, the moderator of last resort, the recovery agent, and the point through which institutions can seek access or oversight. In an end-to-end design, the provider still matters enormously, but the content itself is meant to remain intelligible only to the communicating endpoints. That sounds like a neat upgrade from weaker transport security. In practice it rearranges authority across the whole system. The provider loses one kind of power. The endpoint gains it. So does whoever controls the endpoint.

The phone becomes the safe.

That image matters because end-to-end encryption is often praised as though it removes trust from the system entirely. It does not. It relocates trust away from intermediary platforms and into devices, identity verification, local storage, backup settings, key recovery schemes, contact management, and the social habits by which users decide whether the person on the other end is really who they claim to be. Show the scene and the difference becomes obvious. A service provider cannot read the message in transit or at rest on its own servers. The named concept is intermediary blindness. Explain it, and the strategic implication follows. The provider is less able to betray, monitor, monetise, or casually surrender content. At the same time, the provider is less able to rescue, supervise, moderate by inspection, or comply with demands for broad content visibility. The burden of trust has not vanished. It has moved into a narrower, more personal, and often more fragile domain.

That relocation is why end-to-end encryption so often collides with institutional instincts. Organisations like visibility. They like archives, compliance review, discovery processes, incident response access, fraud investigation, user support, continuity during staff turnover, and the ability to reconstruct what happened after a dispute. Those desires are not always sinister. Many are tied to ordinary governance and legitimate responsibility. Yet end-to-end designs frustrate them by making content unavailable to the very intermediaries institutions are used to treating as operational choke points. The abstraction of control becomes visible here in practical frustrations: a compliance team cannot search message content centrally, a service provider cannot restore a user's history without access to their keys, a corporate administrator cannot easily inspect staff communications without redesigning the system, and a state authority cannot assume that service providers hold the plaintext by default. The implication is profound. "Secure" for the communicating parties can mean "less governable" for the institutions around them.

This is one reason usability becomes strategically important rather than merely ergonomic. In end-to-end systems, features that look like convenience - account recovery, multi-device sync, backup restoration, contact migration, key change notifications, device pairing - are often the points at which security posture is quietly rewritten. A user who loses a phone does not care, in the first instance, about architectural purity. They care about whether messages, contacts, and identity can be recovered without catastrophe. A product designer who ignores that will build a noble system with miserable adoption. A product designer who solves it carelessly may reintroduce central weaknesses through cloud backups, escrow-like recovery, or invisible trust transfers. The named concept here is recovery pressure. Explain it, and the central trade-off emerges. End-to-end encryption is strongest when recovery is hard; it is most usable when recovery is easier. Most real systems try to inhabit the unhappy middle.

A useful example lies in secure messaging services that protect messages between devices but allow optional or default cloud backups outside the end-to-end model. The visible story told to users may still be "your messages are secure". Often that is partly true. Messages may be secure against network interception and against routine provider-side reading inside the primary channel. Yet once backups are created under different keys, different recovery rules, or a cloud account governed by a different access model, content may become reachable through other paths. The point is not that the original end-to-end design was fraudulent. It is that the endpoint safe has acquired a side door because users, quite reasonably, expect not to lose their lives' communication history when a device falls into a river. The implication is not merely technical embarrassment. It is an institutional lesson in what convenience demands from secrecy.

A second example comes from enterprise collaboration systems, where organisations increasingly want both the marketing reassurance of strong encryption and the managerial reassurance of recoverable visibility. Employers need to investigate harassment claims, maintain records, preserve discoverable material, meet regulatory expectations, and ensure continuity when staff leave. End-to-end designs complicate all of this. Show the scene and the tension becomes concrete. A corporation deploys a secure communications platform. Employees assume private protection. The company then wants message archiving, supervisory access, or organisational key retention for legal and operational reasons. The named concept is governance override. Explain it, and the strategic implication is sharp. A system cannot simultaneously maximise user-exclusive control and institutional oversight without making hard choices about who ultimately holds the keys, whether on paper or in software. The friction is not an unfortunate side effect. It is the architecture speaking honestly.

This is why end-to-end encryption changes organisational power even when nobody is arguing about criminal investigations or grand constitutional questions. It narrows the intermediary's role as a content authority and widens the importance of device integrity, user identity assurance, and client-side design. The endpoint becomes the decisive location. That helps ordinary users against platform overreach and bulk interception. It also magnifies the consequences of endpoint compromise. Spyware, malicious device access, coerced unlocking, compromised backups, and account recovery abuse all become more important because they now sit closer to the only places where plaintext reliably exists. The phrase *secure messaging* therefore needs care. A system can be strongly end-to-end encrypted and still expose users badly if the phones are weak, the identity checks are casual, or recovery settings quietly put copies of the conversation elsewhere.

Still, a credible limitation deserves emphasis. End-to-end encryption is not automatically the right answer for every institutional communication environment. Some settings genuinely require shared access, durable organisational archives, controlled supervision, or recoverable records as part of their core purpose. A hospital team coordinating clinical action, a regulated financial firm handling sensitive transactions, or a public body subject to strict recordkeeping obligations may need communication systems that preserve forms of institutional access by design. It would be unserious to pretend that every operational context can be remade in the image of the most privacy-maximising consumer messenger. Organisations are not simply large individuals with expense accounts. They carry duties that private chat between friends does not.

Yet that concession clarifies rather than weakens the main argument. The point is not that all systems should maximise endpoint-exclusive secrecy. The point is that one must be honest about what is being traded away when institutional control is added back in. A product that offers central supervision, searchable archives, or account-level recovery may still be entirely defensible for its purpose. It is not meaningfully the same security object as a system where intermediaries are blind by design. Confusion begins when organisations want the political and marketing prestige of end-to-end language while also demanding the operational privileges of traditional intermediaries. They want the safe and the spare master key, the private room and the inspection window. Security discourse becomes mushy at exactly that point.

This is where corporate compliance and user safety can genuinely diverge rather than merely appear to. For a corporation, safety may mean evidential access, retention, recoverability, insider oversight, and the ability to reconstruct events after a dispute or attack. For a vulnerable user - a journalist, dissident, abused partner, organiser, whistleblower, or merely an ordinary person living under the wrong local power - safety may mean that nobody beyond the communicating endpoints can retrieve the content at all. The same design choice can therefore count as prudent governance in one context and dangerous exposure in another. The named concept is audience-relative security. Explain it, and one sees why debates over end-to-end encryption become so heated. The parties are not always disagreeing about facts. They are disagreeing about which user the system is ultimately meant to protect from whom.

This also explains why end-to-end encryption has become a symbolic battleground. It is not just another technical feature. It is a statement about where power should sit in a communications system. A provider that adopts it signals reduced willingness or ability to act as a universal interpreter of user content. A government or organisation that resists it often signals not simple hostility to privacy, but attachment to older models in which intermediaries remain governable chokepoints. Neither side should be romanticised. Platforms may invoke privacy while leaving metadata rich and backups weak. Institutions may invoke safety while understating how much new exposure their preferred oversight requires. The right analysis starts by refusing both fairy tales.

The phone as safe returns here for a final reason. A safe gives privacy by narrowing who can open it. It also shifts responsibility onto whoever possesses it, maintains it, and remembers the combination. Lose the combination, and recovery becomes hard. Give a second key to an institution, and the safe is no longer purely yours. End-to-end encryption works the same uncivil little trick on modern communications. It empowers users by reducing intermediary visibility. It burdens them, and the institutions around them, with harder choices about recovery, oversight, and what happens when the endpoint itself becomes the weak point everyone quietly suspected it always was.

The difficult question, then, is not whether end-to-end encryption is good. It plainly can be. The harder question is which kind of control a system is willing to surrender, and to whom, when it claims to be secure: the control of the intermediary, the control of the organisation, or the control of the user once convenience, compliance, and crisis begin asking for the spare key.

## Metadata as an intelligence target

In June 2013, when documents disclosed by Edward Snowden drew public attention to large-scale communications surveillance by the United States National Security Agency, one of the most revealing admissions in the public debate concerned a category of information many people had barely considered. The issue was not always the content of calls or messages. It was often the records around them: who contacted whom, when, for how long, from where, and in what pattern. The concrete outcome was not merely a controversy about one government. It was a wider recognition that secrecy had been misunderstood. A sealed letter can still advertise its route.

That recognition matters because modern security culture still tends to flatter itself with the language of content protection. If the message body is encrypted, if the call is secured, if the file is unreadable in transit, people infer that privacy has been meaningfully preserved. Sometimes it has. Sometimes what has been preserved is only one layer of it. Metadata does not usually reveal the sentence, the argument, or the exact attachment. It reveals the map around them. For intelligence work, coercion, commercial prediction, and institutional control, that map can be enough.

The envelope still speaks.

That small phrase captures why metadata deserves strategic attention rather than technical footnote status. Metadata is not simply "data about data" in some dry archival sense. In communications systems it often includes timing, duration, frequency, location, recipient patterns, network paths, device identifiers, account associations, and behavioural regularities. Show the scene and the point becomes obvious. A journalist speaks to a source at odd hours before a sensitive story breaks. A military unit's devices begin communicating from an unusual area in a recognisable pattern. A corporate executive's travel and message rhythm changes just before a merger announcement. The named concept is relational exposure. Explain it, and the implication sharpens. Even when content remains unreadable, metadata can reveal structure, intent, priority, and vulnerability with surprising force.

This is why intelligence services, law enforcement bodies, advertisers, platform firms, and hostile private actors alike value metadata so highly. It scales well. It can often be collected more cheaply than content. It lends itself to correlation, automation, and long-term storage. Most importantly, it preserves social and organisational structure. Content tells you what was said. Metadata often tells you what matters. If one person contacts a hundred numbers in an hour, that is one sort of pattern. If three rarely connected officials begin communicating repeatedly in a narrow window, that is another. If a phone spends every weekday near one office and every evening at one residence, the content of its messages may be almost secondary to the regularity of its path. The abstraction of risk becomes visible in repeated behaviour.

A useful example lies in location patterns inferred from encrypted network usage. A phone may use secure protocols for messaging, browsing, and application traffic. The content may be protected strongly in transit. Yet the network still sees timing, endpoint relationships, and often enough routing or radio-layer information to infer movement and routine. Show the scene and one sees why secrecy is broader than content. A person repeatedly connects from one district in the early morning, another building during office hours, and a third location late at night, with sudden deviations before specific events. The named concept here is mobility inference. Explain it, and the strategic implication follows. A protected message stream can still yield a behavioural portrait detailed enough for surveillance, coercion, targeting, or prediction without anyone ever reading the messages themselves.

This is not merely a state intelligence concern. It is a broader property of digital life. Corporate systems infer performance, intent, and risk from internal communication graphs. Platform companies infer friendships, influence, and routines from usage patterns. Criminal actors can derive extortion opportunities from contact networks and temporal habits. A hostile employer can learn who is organising. A domestic abuser can infer movement from device behaviour. A foreign service can identify likely intermediaries, couriers, or aides by watching changes in communication density rather than by decrypting content. The same pattern appears across scales because metadata preserves relationships, and relationships are where power usually lives.

The intelligence value of social graphs deserves special emphasis. A social graph is not just a list of contacts. It is a model of association, hierarchy, trust, and centrality. Who communicates with whom, how often, in what clusters, and at what moments of stress can reveal more than many institutions care to admit. Show the scene and the stakes become plain. An organisation may protect internal messages rigorously, yet a graph of communication spikes around certain individuals can still identify managers, coordinators, vulnerable connectors, or hidden channels between teams. The named concept is structural intelligibility. Explain it, and one sees why metadata often survives attempts to hide content. The graph can show where authority, influence, and sensitivity are likely to reside long before content becomes necessary to confirm the details.

A second example lies in military and intelligence history, where traffic analysis has long mattered even when messages themselves remained unreadable. One need not romanticise old cryptology to grasp the lesson. Sudden changes in volume, routing, or radio activity can indicate mobilisation, command shifts, supply activity, or crisis response. The exact order may remain concealed. The shape of readiness becomes visible anyway. The digital version of this has only grown richer. Modern metadata includes not only who spoke and when, but which devices moved together, which services lit up simultaneously, which locations suddenly generated unusual encrypted traffic, and which accounts changed behaviour after a breach, arrest, or leadership transition. The implication is sobering. Metadata often gives an adversary enough to ask the right question, even when content would have given only the answer.

This is why coercion can emerge from metadata alone. People often imagine coercion as requiring damning text, explicit confession, or intimate imagery. Sometimes it requires only proof of association, timing, or contradiction between declared and observed behaviour. A politician who publicly denies contact with a fixer, a civil servant who secretly meets a journalist, an executive who repeatedly appears near a competitor's office, or an official whose device regularly joins an unusual cluster of contacts may become pressure-worthy long before anyone reads a single message. The named concept is pattern leverage. Explain it, and the mechanism becomes disturbingly clear. A behavioural pattern can be used to threaten exposure, imply deception, or destabilise trust even when its underlying content remains opaque. The envelope still speaks, and sometimes that is enough.

Prediction is the other great prize. Metadata enables forecasting because humans, institutions, and networks repeat themselves. A person goes to the same places, contacts the same circles, reacts to stress in recognisable ways, and follows rhythms that become machine-legible over time. Organisations do the same. They have calendars, escalation paths, press cycles, payroll rhythms, procurement seasons, command routines, and recurring crises. When these rhythms are mapped through encrypted network usage, the resulting predictions can be commercially useful, politically manipulative, or strategically dangerous. The content of the exchange may matter later. The timing of the exchange may already tell an observer what is about to happen.

Still, a credible limitation belongs here. Metadata is not omniscient. It can be noisy, ambiguous, and prone to overinterpretation. Correlation is not causation, and pattern analysis can mislead when analysts or systems impose too much meaning on incomplete traces. A burst of traffic may reflect an update, not a secret meeting. A co-location pattern may be accidental. A dense contact cluster may reflect logistics, not conspiracy. It would be foolish to speak as though metadata alone delivers perfect knowledge. The history of intelligence and policing contains plenty of cases where pattern confidence outran reality. Good analysis must keep that in view.

Yet this limitation strengthens the central claim rather than weakening it. Metadata does not need to be perfect to be powerful. It only needs to be good enough to narrow search, prioritise targets, pressure the vulnerable, or guide more intrusive collection. A social graph with a few errors can still identify a central broker. A location profile with gaps can still expose routine. A timing pattern can still predict when to watch more closely. Metadata often operates not as final proof but as force multiplier. It makes everything else cheaper, faster, and more discriminating. That is a strategic advantage even when content remains beyond reach.

This is why secrecy should be understood as a broader condition than unreadable text. A communication can be content-secure and relationship-exposed. It can be message-safe and pattern-loud. It can keep the words hidden while advertising the network, the schedule, the hierarchy, and the route. Institutions that speak only of encryption strength therefore risk flattering themselves. They protect the letter and forget the postmark, the sender, the recipient, the time, and the movement of the courier. In strategic settings, those surrounding facts can be precisely what an adversary needs.

The implications spread into product design and governance quickly. Systems that minimise metadata collection, reduce logging, limit retention, blur contact patterns, and avoid centralising network maps are not merely polishing privacy optics. They are altering the intelligence value of the service. Systems that retain detailed logs indefinitely, expose rich traffic patterns to providers, or rely on central directories and constant synchronisation may offer strong content protection while quietly preserving a rich behavioural archive. The visible decisions are technical and administrative at once: what gets logged, how long it stays, which identifiers are stable, whether contact discovery is centralised, whether location-linked behaviour is stored, whether timing patterns are easy to reconstruct later. These are not implementation curiosities. They are choices about what kind of future observer the system is helping to create.

The envelope returns here because it remains the right corrective to content fetishism. People often think privacy fails only when someone opens the letter and reads the words. Much of the time privacy is already compromised when someone can see who sent it, where it travelled, when it arrived, how often similar letters move between the same hands, and which other envelopes tend to follow. Metadata is not a shadow version of the real thing. It is one of the real things. Sometimes it is the more valuable one.

The unresolved question, then, is not whether content can be encrypted. It is whether the people building and relying on communications systems understand how much of the social world remains inferable from timing, pattern, and relation alone - and what kinds of power are still available to those who can read the postmark even when the letter stays sealed.

## Satellite, radio, and constrained environments

In February 2022, as the Russian invasion of Ukraine began, a cyberattack disrupted modems used on Viasat's KA-SAT network across parts of Europe. Public reporting quickly focused on the immediate operational effects: communications were interrupted, remote management was impaired, and even users outside the core military theatre felt the consequences. The case mattered for another reason as well. It showed how communications in constrained environments do not fail like ordinary internet services. They fail through remote management channels, brittle update paths, specialised hardware, and systems that must keep working despite distance, intermittence, and the rude fact that somebody may be shooting at the infrastructure.

The internet encourages bad habits of thought. It teaches people to imagine secure communications as a problem of abundant bandwidth, frequent patching, dense infrastructure, and software stacks that can be changed more or less on demand. Satellite links, tactical radio, industrial wireless systems, maritime communications, aviation links, and remote field deployments do not live in that world. They live with intermittent connectivity, expensive or delayed updates, harsh physical conditions, long procurement cycles, and hardware expected to remain useful long after its designers have left the company or the ministry. The link is thin. The timeline is thick.

That difference changes everything.

Constrained environments force security into contact with logistics. Show the scene and the issue becomes plain. A secure internet service can rotate certificates overnight, push new client code, deprecate weak settings, and assume that most users will eventually reconnect and update. A radio network used in remote operations, a satellite terminal on a vessel, or a fielded industrial control device may see the world very differently. The named concept is operational latency. Explain it, and the strategic implication follows. In such systems, the delay between identifying a necessary security change and actually deploying it may be determined by ship schedules, maintenance windows, regulatory approvals, physical access, spare-parts availability, or simple radio silence. Legacy risk persists not because people are foolish, but because movement itself is slow.

This makes key distribution unusually hard. In rich network environments, key material can often be refreshed through frequent online contact, layered trust services, automated provisioning, and managed identity infrastructure. In constrained environments, those assumptions weaken quickly. A device may be intermittently connected, connected only through expensive links, or deliberately offline for long periods. The system may rely on pre-placed keys, narrow-band channels, limited secure storage, or manual rekeying procedures. Each of these can be entirely rational. Each also creates pressure to make keys live longer, recovery simpler, and changes rarer than ideal cryptographic hygiene would recommend. The abstraction of trust becomes visible in physical acts: a technician loads key material before deployment, a maintenance team carries updates to a remote site, a commander delays rotation because the field cannot absorb disruption, a satellite operator preserves older profiles because many terminals cannot all be touched in time. The implication is severe. Time and geography become security parameters.

Radio systems make this especially clear because they operate in an environment where communications are not merely intercepted but contested, jammed, imitated, and physically constrained. A radio link may have to balance encryption overhead against latency, interoperability, battery life, spectrum discipline, and the need for quick field operation by tired humans wearing gloves in bad weather. A mathematically cleaner design may lose to a cruder one if it cannot be loaded, maintained, or repaired under realistic conditions. The named concept here is fieldability. Explain it, and the strategic lesson becomes obvious. Security in constrained communications is always judged against whether the system can actually survive the conditions of use. A design that wins in theory and fails at the edge of human endurance is not more secure in the serious sense.

A useful example lies in maritime and offshore environments, where satellite connectivity is essential yet uneven, expensive, and tightly intertwined with specialised equipment lifecycles. A vessel may rely on terminals installed years earlier, maintained during limited service windows, and integrated with navigation, logistics, or safety systems not easily altered mid-voyage. The communications link may be encrypted and professionally managed, yet still depend on remote administration channels, stale firmware, or compatibility assumptions that would look absurd in a cloud environment. Show the scene and one sees why legacy persists. The ship cannot visit a patch window the way a browser visits an update server. The system must be serviced within the cadence of voyages, port access, vendor support, and physical replacement schedules. The implication is not quaint backwardness. It is strategic inertia built into the medium.

The Viasat disruption in 2022 illustrated this larger pattern brutally. Public reporting indicated that the attack targeted modem management mechanisms rather than defeating the idea of encrypted communications in some grand abstract sense. That matters. It showed that in satellite systems the decisive weakness may lie not in the protected payload but in the operational channels used to configure, control, and sustain the network. The named concept is management-plane fragility. Explain it, and the broader lesson emerges. A constrained communications system is only as resilient as the narrow set of functions through which updates, configurations, and trust relationships are maintained. If those functions fail, the link may remain physically present while its practical security and usability collapse.

Specialised hardware deepens the problem. Devices deployed in radio, satellite, remote sensing, industrial monitoring, and critical field operations often have long service lives and narrow certification envelopes. They may not accept frequent firmware changes. They may depend on chipsets or cryptographic modules whose support horizon is shorter than the deployment horizon of the system itself. They may be hard to test under new configurations without risking mission failure. The result is a strange asymmetry. The institution depends on highly durable hardware precisely where cryptographic assumptions and software dependencies may need more agility, not less. The box is built to last. The trust inside it may not be.

This is one reason constrained communications expose the fantasy that security can be reduced to standards compliance or current best practice. A terminal can be compliant when procured and problematic years later when new requirements emerge. A radio system can be strongly designed and still vulnerable because key loading procedures are clumsy, update channels are fragile, or interoperability with allies and partners preserves weak modes too long. A satellite platform can use respectable cryptography and still carry dangerous operational debt through remote management, vendor dependence, or the inability to re-provision fielded terminals quickly. The named concept is lifecycle divergence. Explain it, and the implication follows. In long-lived systems, the lifecycle of the hardware, the lifecycle of the threat, and the lifecycle of the cryptographic assumptions rarely stay politely aligned.

A second useful example comes from aviation and other regulated sectors, where communication systems often sit inside strict certification regimes. That certification may be essential for safety, but it also slows security adaptation. A change to cryptographic behaviour can trigger broader validation burdens because the system is not just a software service; it is part of an operational environment where failure has physical consequences. The visible behaviour is predictable. Older algorithms or trust arrangements remain in place because recertification is slow, replacement is costly, and downtime is politically intolerable. The implication is not that safety regulation is the enemy of security. It is that critical domains often preserve old trust assumptions longer than anyone would choose in a greenfield design. Legacy risk persists because the system is doing important work in the world, not because nobody read the white paper.

Still, a limitation deserves fairness. Constrained environments are not automatically less secure than mainstream internet services. In some respects they can be more disciplined. Closed deployments, tightly controlled physical access, narrower user populations, and mission-specific procedures can reduce certain classes of casual exposure. A radio network used by trained operators under strict doctrine may be less vulnerable to the sprawling human improvisation that plagues consumer and enterprise platforms. A satellite system designed for one narrow mission may avoid much of the commercial complexity that turns ordinary cloud software into a carnival of dependencies. It would be foolish to treat "remote" or "specialised" as synonyms for "careless".

Yet that concession sharpens the main argument rather than weakening it. The security of constrained environments depends less on fashionable tooling and more on whether institutions understand the physics, logistics, and governance of long-lived systems. A mature operator asks not simply whether encryption is present, but how keys are loaded in the field, how updates reach distant devices, how long unsupported hardware remains trusted, what fallback happens during outage, who can change management settings, how quickly fleets can be rekeyed, what dependencies sit in vendor hands, and how many emergency workarounds have become permanent doctrine. Those questions are not ancillary. They are the architecture.

This is where metadata and operational secrecy intersect too. Satellite and radio environments often reveal pattern even when content is protected. Transmission timing, power use, network presence, routing shifts, and activation patterns can expose movement, priority, and organisational rhythm. A constrained link is often easier to observe as a pattern than to understand as content. That means the difficulties of update and key management live alongside the difficulties of traffic analysis and jamming. The system is under pressure from both silence and visibility. It must remain secret enough and resilient enough, often with far less room for graceful adaptation than an internet-native service enjoys.

The long-lived nature of these systems also creates institutional amnesia. Procurement teams remember why the device was chosen. Years later the operators inherit the fleet without inheriting the full logic of the trade-offs. Vendors change hands. Support contracts lapse. Integration knowledge becomes folklore. A generation of engineers arrives having grown up in the world of cloud agility and assumes that everything important can be patched on Tuesday night. The constrained system resists that fantasy and is then blamed for being old. In truth it is revealing something about modern institutions: they are poor at remembering that the most critical systems are often the least able to change.

The thin link returns here because it is the right corrective to internet abundance. A thin link forces choices. What crosses first? Which updates wait? Which keys live longer? Which failures are tolerated because communication at all is better than elegant silence? Secure communications in constrained environments are governed by those choices, not by the most impressive slide in the design brief. The difficult question is therefore not whether a satellite, radio, or field system uses strong cryptography somewhere in its stack. It is whether the institution depending on it can still govern keys, updates, recovery, and trust across years of physical distance, operational stress, and hardware that may outlive the assumptions under which it was first blessed as secure.

## Resilience under disruption

In February 2022, as Russia's full-scale invasion of Ukraine began, communications systems across the region faced not merely heavy use but deliberate contest. Networks were disrupted, links were degraded, and operators had to keep information moving under pressure that was technical, physical, and political all at once. The immediate lesson was not that encryption had become irrelevant. It was harsher than that. Systems designed for orderly, validated, well-connected operation were suddenly being judged by what they did when the network was broken, the bandwidth poor, the timing urgent, and the old promise of "secure by default" had to compete with the brutal demand to communicate now.

Crisis changes the meaning of design.

That is the governing fact of resilience under disruption. Secure communications are usually evaluated in peacetime conditions: stable links, current certificates, reachable validation services, patient users, available support staff, and enough bandwidth or latency headroom for proper handshakes and verification. Under disruption, those assumptions begin to fail one by one. A revocation check cannot complete. A key server is unreachable. A certificate cannot be refreshed. A congested or jammed channel cannot tolerate the preferred protocol overhead. An operator, medic, engineer, or dispatcher faced with real-world urgency may choose the channel that works over the channel that reassures. At that moment, the fallback stops being a secondary feature. It becomes the real system.

This is why fallback modes so often prove to be the weakest link. In theory, a fallback exists to preserve service when preferred conditions vanish. In practice, it often preserves only part of the original security promise while quietly discarding the rest. Show the scene and the danger becomes obvious. A secure system cannot complete its usual authentication sequence because connectivity is intermittent or supporting infrastructure is down. The named concept is degraded trust. Explain it, and the strategic implication follows. To keep communication flowing, a system may skip verification, accept stale credentials, defer checks, reuse old keys, or route traffic through less trusted paths. The channel survives. The conditions that made it trustworthy may not. That distinction is where many real incidents begin.

The phrase *resilience under disruption* therefore deserves suspicion as well as admiration. Institutions often congratulate themselves for having backup channels, emergency modes, and continuity procedures. Those matter. Yet continuity and resilience are not synonyms. A system that continues operating by silently disabling its own core security properties is not fully resilient. It is functioning in a narrower and more dangerous sense. The abstraction of continuity becomes visible in specific decisions: whether expired certificates are tolerated during outage, whether identity checks are softened to speed access, whether old cryptographic modes are re-enabled because the new ones are too brittle under poor connectivity, whether manual overrides replace automated verification, whether messages are relayed through less trusted intermediaries because the direct path is gone. Each decision may be understandable. Together they redraw the attack surface.

Emergency protocols that disable verification to restore service are the purest example. The logic always sounds responsible at first hearing. A hospital cannot lose access to essential systems because a validation chain failed during a network incident. A utility cannot leave field teams disconnected because revocation checks time out under congestion. A military unit cannot wait politely for full certificate freshness while under active disruption. So a temporary bypass is added, or an emergency mode is documented, or an operational doctrine says that under severe conditions the system should accept a reduced assurance state rather than collapse. The named concept here is crisis exceptionalism. Explain it, and the larger problem appears. Once a system contains a documented path for bypassing normal verification, that path itself becomes part of the architecture to be protected, targeted, and inevitably expanded by future convenience. The implication is strategic rather than moral. Emergency trust exceptions do not stay purely hypothetical once users learn they are the most reliable feature in the room.

A useful example comes from industrial and utility environments, where availability has obvious primacy and secure remote management is often layered onto older operational technology. In ordinary conditions, central authentication and certificate-based trust may work well enough. Under outage, latency, or partial isolation, operators can face a cruel choice between strict validation and the ability to restore critical function. Show the scene and the pressure becomes concrete. A remote site is unreachable through its normal authenticated path. Engineers need to recover it quickly because downstream systems depend on it. Temporary credentials, manual trust decisions, or degraded connection modes appear. The immediate outcome may be entirely justified operationally. The strategic implication is that every such pathway accumulates institutional permission to weaken security when time hurts. Over years, those permissions become part of the true system even if the network diagrams keep pretending otherwise.

A second example lies in censorship and politically induced disruption. When states throttle connectivity, block certain services, or force networks into narrow and fragile channels, users and institutions often rely on whatever alternative still functions: mirror services, proxy chains, out-of-band messaging, improvised radio links, unofficial routing, peer-to-peer workarounds, or manually exchanged trust material. These methods can be lifesaving. They can also widen exposure to impersonation, traffic analysis, malicious intermediaries, and inconsistent key verification. The named concept is survival routing. Explain it, and the strategic lesson becomes clearer. Under censorship or jamming, people do not choose between ideal security and sloppy practice in the abstract. They choose between communication and silence. Adversaries understand this very well. They pressure the environment until people reveal which safeguards they are willing to abandon first.

This is one reason network degradation and active interference should be treated as security events in themselves rather than mere availability problems. Jamming, throttling, denial of service, certificate distribution failure, time source manipulation, route hijacking, and support-channel outage can all force a system into behaviours it would never select voluntarily under calm conditions. A communication system may remain technically encrypted and yet become far easier to subvert if disruption causes users to ignore warnings, trust cached states too long, or accept unverified counterparts because the verified service is too slow or unavailable. The envelope remains sealed, but the return address is guessed. In strategic terms that can be enough.

Metadata competition also intensifies during disruption. When content protection remains partly intact, adversaries may shift attention to who is still communicating, through which fallback route, at what times, and from which physical or network positions. A crisis often compresses communications into smaller sets of urgent contacts and emergency channels, making patterns more legible rather than less. A jammed network that forces certain units, activists, or responders onto backup links may inadvertently reveal hierarchies, movement, and priorities through the very act of preserving communication. The implication is that resilience must be judged not only by whether messages get through, but by what new observable structure the fallback creates.

Still, a credible limitation belongs here. Not every fallback is reckless, and not every degraded mode is evidence of poor design. Real systems need layered communication options because perfect assurance under perfect conditions is a fantasy luxury. There are settings in which refusing degraded communication would cause greater harm than accepting additional risk. A rescue team, emergency department, or field unit sometimes needs a channel that is less trusted than preferred but vastly better than silence. It would be childish to sneer at that reality from the comfort of a clean white paper. Security that cannot survive crisis is not mature security. It is decorative discipline.

Yet that concession sharpens the real issue rather than softening it. The question is not whether degraded operation should ever exist. The question is whether degraded operation is designed, bounded, and governed honestly. A strong system makes its emergency compromises visible, limited, and auditable. It decides in advance which properties can be weakened, for how long, under whose authority, and with what later recovery. It avoids pretending that emergency mode is simply normal mode with less paperwork. A weak system accumulates ad hoc overrides, undocumented exceptions, inherited compatibility hacks, and cultural habits of clicking through anything that delays restoration. Under calm conditions the difference may be hard to see. Under disruption it becomes the whole story.

This is where the idea of resilience has to be rescued from sentimentality. Real resilience is not just surviving disruption. It is surviving disruption without silently inverting the trust model. That may mean designing protocols whose verification can continue under constrained conditions, caching trustworthy material carefully rather than indefinitely, separating truly life-critical fallback from merely convenient bypass, rehearsing failure states, and inventorying where emergency modes exist before somebody hostile discovers them first. The visible behaviours attached to that maturity are plain: operators know what the system will relax and what it will never relax, emergency credentials are narrow and time-bound, degraded communications are logged and reviewed, and recovery from crisis includes restoring full assurance rather than normalising the weak state because nobody can face another migration. Those are governance decisions wearing technical clothes.

A deeper problem remains, though. Crisis conditions often do more than stress systems; they rearrange incentives. Institutions become impatient. Leaders want restoration before explanation. Users stop trusting warnings that appear during genuine emergencies. Engineers acquire prestige for bypassing friction and getting the link back up. A manual workaround that saved the day once becomes cherished folklore, then accepted doctrine, then permanent architecture. The fallback turns from contingency into culture. That is how strategic weakness settles in. Not through one grand blunder, but through a series of moments when everyone had a reason to prioritise immediate function and nobody owned the cost of leaving the emergency door in place afterwards.

The radio on the shelf explains the subject better than most dashboards do. In quiet times it is a backup. In crisis it becomes the centre of attention, and suddenly all the compromises made in its setup - who can use it, what it verifies, what it logs, how it identifies the other end, whether old keys still work - become decisive. Modern networks behave the same way. The backup path, the emergency mode, the trust bypass, the cached certificate, the manually approved peer: these are not side notes. They are the conditions under which institutions reveal what they truly value when the network turns hostile.

The hardest question, then, is not whether a communication system can keep operating under disruption. Many can. The harder question is what exactly it becomes when it does: which assurances remain, which disappear, who decides, and whether the restored service is preserving the mission or teaching the adversary that the surest way to weaken trust is simply to make normal trust impossible for long enough.

# Chapter 9

# Legacy Systems and Hidden Exposure

What does an institution fear more: a known weak system that still functions, or the disruption required to replace it? The honest answer explains more about modern security than most technical diagrams do. Old systems rarely remain because nobody knows they are old. They remain because they still do something essential, because replacing them touches too many other things, because downtime has visible owners while slow exposure does not, and because every organisation learns to live with yesterday's compromise when today's budget, staffing, and political patience run thin.

That is why legacy should not be treated as a mere residue of technical backwardness. It is a living settlement between risk, habit, procurement, dependence, and institutional memory. A temporary exception survives one quarter because the replacement window is missed. A vendor patch is delayed because a regulator must sign off. A protocol remains enabled because one fleet, one customer, one hospital machine, one transport controller, or one third-party appliance cannot move yet. After enough repetitions, the exception stops feeling temporary at all. It becomes part of the operating model. The old key still fits.

This matters because adversaries do not search for the newest and most elegant cryptography in an estate. They search for the oldest surviving trust assumption, the forgotten appliance, the unpatchable fleet, the replicated backup, the stale certificate chain, the hard-coded protocol setting, the archive whose classification logic belongs to another decade. Modern organisations often narrate themselves through their flagship systems and current standards. Their real exposure is usually distributed through the layers beneath: legacy devices, inherited dependencies, retained data, and quiet compatibility decisions that nobody wants to revisit until failure makes them impossible to ignore.

The central tension lies here. Institutions know, in broad terms, that legacy creates risk. They also know that replacing legacy creates cost, breakage, and accountability in the present tense. Security teams can describe the weakness. Operations teams can describe the pain of fixing it. Executives can usually see only one of those costs at a time. This is why legacy persists even in places full of intelligent, conscientious people. The argument is not between knowledge and ignorance. It is between different forms of damage, one immediate and attributed, the other delayed and easy to diffuse across time, teams, and future leadership.

That delayed damage is especially dangerous in cryptographic settings because old systems rarely fail in isolation. A protocol fossil in an industrial fleet can hold open a broader compatibility path. A long-lived medical or transport device can keep weak modes alive across an otherwise modern network. A replicated archive can preserve secrets long after their owners have changed roles, institutions, or assumptions about who might one day read them. A third-party appliance can carry embedded trust relationships nobody centrally remembers but everyone operationally depends upon. Legacy risk therefore behaves less like a museum exhibit and more like dry rot. It spreads quietly through connection, accommodation, and administrative fatigue.

The stakes are not only technical. They are strategic. A legacy estate teaches an adversary how an institution actually governs change. It reveals which systems are politically untouchable, which vendors hold leverage, which operations cannot tolerate interruption, which teams own dependencies without owning budgets, and which archives are retained because nobody has the standing to delete them. That is why legacy is a governance outcome before it is a technical condition. It reflects who can say no to replacement, who must absorb the operational risk of migration, and who benefits from preserving the old arrangement a little longer while the future grows heavier around it.

The path ahead follows that governance logic into the reasons old systems persist, then into the stubborn life of protocol fossils inside long-lived devices and specialised environments where updates arrive slowly or not at all. From there the argument turns to stored data, where backups, logs, and replicated archives outlive the classification assumptions under which they were first created, and finally into the harder practical work of mapping exposure across an organisation so that hidden cryptography, embedded dependencies, and responsibility lines become visible enough to prioritise. The order matters because legacy is not merely something found. It is something inherited, tolerated, and only sometimes fully seen.

An old key in a drawer captures the subject more honestly than most maturity models do. It was kept for a sensible reason. Then another. Then nobody remembered exactly which doors it still opened, only that throwing it away felt riskier than keeping it. Institutions treat old protocols, stale devices, retained archives, and inherited trust stores in much the same way. They know the key is old. What they do not know, or do not want to discover too quickly, is how much of the building still depends on it.

The difficult question, then, is not whether legacy exists. It always does. The harder question is whether an institution can identify where its oldest assumptions still exercise power, which exceptions have quietly become policy, and which hidden exposures would remain invisible until an adversary, an outage, or a forced migration turned the old key in a lock nobody realised was still connected to the rest of the house.

## Why legacy persists

In May 2017, the ransomware outbreak known as WannaCry spread across networks around the world, and among the most haunting images were those of the United Kingdom's National Health Service struggling with disruption across hospitals and clinics. The technical explanation quickly became familiar: old systems, missing patches, brittle dependencies. Yet the deeper story was not one of simple negligence or ignorance. These were institutions that knew, in broad outline, that ageing systems carried risk. They also knew that replacing them could interrupt care, consume scarce budgets, break integrated equipment, and demand a kind of cross-organisational coordination that modern institutions often find harder than they admit. The old machine stayed because the cost of change had a face.

That face matters.

Legacy systems do not persist because everyone involved is too foolish to recognise them as old. They persist because they continue to perform work that somebody, somewhere, depends upon, and because the burdens of replacement are distributed unevenly. The security team sees exposure. The operations team sees downtime. The procurement team sees delayed capital expenditure. The finance office sees an expensive project whose success will be hard to celebrate because the best outcome is that nothing visibly goes wrong. Senior leadership often sees all of these at once and reaches for the least politically combustible choice: preserve function, postpone upheaval, and manage the risk later. Legacy begins as yesterday's compromise and survives as today's truce.

That is the first point to make sharply. Legacy is not mainly a technical category. It is a governance outcome. Show the scene and the distinction becomes plain. A system is known to run outdated software or weak cryptographic settings. The named concept is institutional deferral. Explain it, and the logic hardens. Replacing the system requires business owners to accept interruption, users to relearn processes, regulators to approve changes, vendors to cooperate, and budget holders to fund work whose benefit is largely the avoidance of future embarrassment. The implication is severe. Old systems remain because organisations are built to reward visible continuity more reliably than invisible resilience.

This helps explain why "temporary" exceptions so often become permanent. In most institutions, an exception enters life with a sensible story. A device cannot be updated until the next maintenance window. A compatibility mode must remain enabled until a partner catches up. A legacy certificate is kept trusted because one department still relies on it. A protocol downgrade is permitted for one specific appliance. A retirement date is set, then softened, then postponed, then quietly forgotten once the person who made the original commitment changes roles. The exception survives because every review of it occurs under pressure from something more immediate: patient safety, customer service, revenue continuity, regulatory timing, supply chain delay, staff shortages, contractual obligations. The old key still works, and nobody wants to be the one who throws it away before proving beyond all doubt that no essential door still depends on it.

The organisational reasons are therefore more serious than laziness, though laziness can always be found if one enjoys easy villains. Cost matters, but not only in the narrow sense of purchase price. Migration requires testing, retraining, integration work, fallback planning, documentation, vendor engagement, and management attention. Risk of downtime matters, especially where systems support hospitals, transport, utilities, financial clearing, public administration, or other operations that fail loudly and publicly. Embedded dependencies matter because modern institutions are not built from clean modules. They are accretions of software, hardware, contracts, habits, and human workarounds. Replace one part and a dozen hidden assumptions wake up in protest. The abstraction of inertia becomes visible in ordinary behaviour: change boards rejecting upgrades, support teams insisting on backward compatibility, budgets split across silos, vendors extending support "for one more year", and leaders treating security debt as tolerable so long as service remains smooth this quarter.

A useful example lies in healthcare environments, where old devices and legacy operating systems have often remained in service not because administrators believed them ideal, but because they were tied to diagnostic machines, laboratory equipment, scheduling platforms, or records systems whose replacement implicated patient care and regulatory process all at once. The WannaCry episode exposed this brutally, but the deeper lesson was not restricted to ransomware. The named concept here is mission-coupled fragility. Explain it, and the strategic point emerges. A system becomes difficult to retire when its failure would interrupt essential work, even if everyone involved recognises that keeping it alive is itself a form of long-term danger. The implication is unsettling. Legacy often persists most stubbornly where institutions are performing morally or operationally indispensable functions, because those are the places least willing to gamble on disruptive change.

A second example can be found in industrial and transport settings, where control systems, telemetry devices, and specialised hardware can remain operational for years beyond the comfort horizon of modern security practice. A transport operator or utility may know that some communications profile or certificate arrangement is old. It may still preserve it because the device fleet is geographically dispersed, vendor support is narrow, re-certification is slow, and the risk of field failure during migration is judged worse than the quieter risk of continued exposure. Show the scene and the pattern becomes almost painfully ordinary. Security teams push for deprecation. Operations teams ask who will take responsibility if remote assets fail to reconnect. Procurement points to long replacement cycles. The named concept is infrastructural lock-in. Explain it, and one sees that legacy is rarely one bad decision. It is a continuing settlement between incompatible forms of prudence.

This is why institutional inertia points are worth learning to see. An inertia point is the place where a known improvement repeatedly stops moving because responsibility, cost, and operational pain are arranged in just the wrong pattern. It may be a vendor dependency, a regulatory review gate, a budget boundary, a support team with veto power, a merger-inherited system nobody wants to own, or a business process whose users have enough influence to delay change indefinitely. The problem is not that the institution lacks intelligence. The problem is that the institution distributes incentives such that somebody always benefits from keeping the old arrangement a little longer while the cost of future compromise remains distant and ownerless. Once this is understood, legacy starts looking less like decaying machinery and more like frozen politics.

The human side matters as well. Organisations remember outages vividly and exposures abstractly. If a migration fails, the pain is immediate, attributable, and humiliating. Leaders are called. Customers complain. Regulators may notice. If a weak protocol remains in place for another year without visible incident, the decision feels prudent, even if the adversary has simply not yet chosen to collect the dividend. This asymmetry of memory encourages conservatism in the worst places. Temporary extensions feel responsible because they avert known disruption. Over time, those extensions accumulate into a permanent architecture of tolerated weakness. The named concept here is asymmetry of blame. Explain it, and the implication becomes plain. Institutions fear being blamed for active breakage more than they fear being blamed for passive exposure, especially when passive exposure may not surface until after roles, administrations, or budgets have changed.

Still, a limitation deserves candour. Not every legacy system is an act of institutional failure. Some systems remain in service because they continue to perform adequately, because replacement would genuinely introduce more risk than it removes in the near term, or because their security can be managed acceptably through segmentation, compensating controls, and disciplined operational practice. It would be foolish to imply that every old system should have been ripped out yesterday by morally purified engineers with infinite budgets and no patients, passengers, or payrolls to worry about. Real institutions do not live inside that fantasy.

Yet that concession sharpens the argument rather than weakening it. The issue is not whether all legacy is indefensible. The issue is whether institutions can distinguish between controlled ageing and unmanaged drift. A mature organisation can say why a legacy system remains, what dependencies hold it in place, what compensating controls are active, what triggers would force replacement, who owns the risk, and when the exception will be reviewed again with real authority. An immature one uses language like "temporary", "until the next cycle", or "business critical" without ever converting those phrases into governed decisions. The difference is enormous. One posture is strategic patience. The other is sentimental hoarding in enterprise clothing.

The persistence of legacy also tells us something about cryptographic change more broadly. New algorithms, better key lifecycles, stronger verification, and cleaner trust models do not enter a vacuum. They enter organisations already full of systems that were built around earlier assumptions. That means every migration is also an argument with memory. The old key still works not only because the lock remains, but because habits, vendor contracts, training materials, fallback procedures, and business process documentation were all written when the old key was still respectable. The result is that institutions often continue protecting themselves according to the logic of the time in which the system was acquired rather than the time in which it is now being used.

This is why adversaries care so much about legacy. They understand a simple truth that defenders often prefer not to state aloud: the newest cryptography in an organisation is not always the most relevant. The relevant cryptography is the one still attached to something indispensable. If a hospital keeps an old protocol alive for one diagnostic fleet, if a manufacturer cannot update devices in the field, if a bank preserves an old certificate chain for an inherited application, if a ministry retains decades of archives under ageing assumptions, then the institution's real security perimeter is partly defined by those residues, not by the best practice slide in its annual report. Adversaries search for the oldest still-trusted component because that is where institutional compromise has usually been legalised by routine.

The old key returns here for one final reason. Nobody keeps it because they admire age for its own sake. They keep it because throwing it away feels riskier than preserving it, and because the institution has forgotten how to decide who should test whether the locks have truly changed. That is the unresolved pressure legacy exerts on governance. When an organisation says a system remains for business reasons, who has actually measured those reasons against the accumulating cost of exposure, who owns the timetable for change, and who will still recognise the old key as a strategic liability before somebody else proves, in the worst possible way, that it was never just sitting in the drawer?

## Protocol fossils and long-lived devices

In May 2017, when WannaCry disrupted hospitals across the United Kingdom, the public saw cancelled appointments, diverted ambulances, and systems that suddenly looked far older than the buildings around them. The immediate explanation pointed to ransomware and missing patches. The more revealing story lay underneath. Many affected environments depended on device fleets, support arrangements, and software baselines that had not aged at the pace of the threat. Machines built to scan, schedule, record, or monitor had become quiet carriers of old assumptions about trust, connectivity, and acceptable cryptographic weakness. The newest security guidance was irrelevant if the device in the room could not follow it.

Old protocols travel well.

They travel not because anyone admires them, but because industrial, medical, and transport systems are built to last, to interoperate, and above all to avoid unpredictable failure. A protocol that was respectable when a device was procured can remain embedded for years after its weaknesses are well understood. The result is what might be called a protocol fossil: an outmoded communications or cryptographic arrangement preserved inside living infrastructure because too many surrounding systems, procedures, and contracts still depend upon it. These fossils do not sit in museums. They direct trains, connect imaging machines, relay telemetry, authenticate controllers, and keep critical services legible to the people running them. That is why they are dangerous.

The first point to see clearly is that protocol fossils are not merely old code. They are institutional settlements. Show the scene and the issue becomes concrete. A hospital relies on a fleet of diagnostic devices purchased under a long capital cycle. The named concept is operational entanglement. Explain it, and the pattern sharpens. The devices speak an older protocol because the vendor designed them that way, the hospital integrated them with other systems on that basis, the regulatory pathway for substantial change is burdensome, and the budget for wholesale replacement competes with obvious clinical priorities. The implication is not that anyone failed to read the security bulletins. It is that the protocol remains because the organisation cannot alter one part of the chain without touching many others at once.

This is why interoperability constraints matter so much. In consumer software, it is at least imaginable that an update can be pushed and most users will absorb the change. In industrial, medical, and transport environments, systems are often expected to communicate with devices purchased years apart, certified under different assumptions, or maintained by different vendors with different support horizons. A protocol survives because it is the only shared language left across the estate. An operator may know that stronger options exist and still preserve the older one because the newer protocol would strand part of the fleet, interrupt service, or break an integration nobody can afford to lose. The abstraction of compatibility becomes visible in mundane decisions: leave the weak mode enabled, keep the old certificate trusted, preserve the legacy handshake, delay the deprecation notice, wait for the next maintenance outage. The old key still opens enough doors to stay on the ring.

Vendor lock-in turns this problem from engineering difficulty into strategic dependence. A long-lived device is rarely an isolated object. It is part of a support ecosystem involving firmware, configuration tools, management consoles, service agreements, spare parts, and approval pathways. If only the original vendor can update the device, certify the change, or explain the undocumented quirks in its communications stack, then the institution does not really control the tempo of security improvement. Show the scene and one sees why. A transport operator wants to retire a legacy protocol, but the signalling hardware vendor has not approved the replacement mode across the installed base. A hospital wants stronger certificate handling, but a manufacturer warns that modification could affect support status. The named concept here is supplier-governed security. Explain it, and the implication becomes obvious. A protocol fossil survives not merely because it is technically old, but because the institution is contractually and operationally dependent on the entity that fossilised it.

A useful example lies in medical imaging and diagnostic environments, where devices often remain in service for long periods and communicate with record systems, scheduling software, archives, and specialist workstations that have been built around their stable but ageing behaviour. One machine cannot be treated as a mere laptop with a screwdriver problem. It may have to remain available for patient care, preserve validated workflows, and satisfy regulatory expectations that make rapid modification unattractive. The visible behaviour is familiar. Network segmentation is used as a compensating control, older protocols are tolerated internally, and replacement is deferred because the device still performs its core clinical function. The implication is severe. An adversary does not need to defeat the strongest systems in the hospital if an older, indispensable device can still be reached and used as a pivot.

A second example appears in transport and industrial fleets that cannot receive updates easily, or at all. The phrase "device fleet that cannot receive updates" sounds absurd if one lives mainly inside app stores and browsers. In long-lived operational systems it is common. A fleet may be geographically dispersed, intermittently connected, dependent on local technicians, or tied to certification regimes that make frequent updates undesirable. Some devices may only be patched during service visits or planned overhauls. Others may be functionally unpatchable because their vendor no longer supports the line or because the cost of proving the update safe exceeds the value of doing so. The named concept is frozen trust. Explain it, and the strategic point emerges. These devices do not merely miss new security features. They preserve old cryptographic assumptions as an enduring condition of operation. The implication follows with a certain grim elegance. Adversaries search for the oldest, not the newest, encryption because the oldest is often the least moveable and the most quietly accepted.

This is where the chapter's argument becomes less about age and more about time horizons. A protocol fossil remains dangerous because it occupies two temporal worlds at once. In the world of procurement and operations, it is stable, familiar, supported enough, and too integrated to disturb casually. In the world of adversarial search, it is a known weak point embedded in a high-value environment. Those two worlds rarely meet in the same meeting room. Security teams describe exposure; operations teams describe dependency; finance describes capital planning; vendors describe support options; regulators describe safety; leadership hears a dispute about priorities. The protocol remains. The institution has not chosen weakness in the abstract. It has chosen continuity within a structure that makes weakness the cheaper political option.

One reason these fossils are so troublesome is that they often hide behind stronger surrounding systems. A modern network may enforce current transport protection, central identity controls, and improved monitoring, while one set of field devices, laboratory instruments, controllers, or embedded modules still speaks an older dialect through a carefully preserved exception. To outside observers the organisation looks modern. To an adversary it looks layered. The named concept here is perimeter misdirection. Explain it, and the lesson is sharp. Strong outer architecture can coexist with brittle interior trust if legacy protocols remain necessary somewhere deeper in the estate. The newest security controls become the wallpaper around an older weakness that still matters more.

Still, a limitation deserves honest attention. Not every old protocol in a specialised environment is a scandal waiting to happen. Some long-lived devices are well segmented, tightly monitored, physically constrained, and used in ways that reduce exposure materially. In certain cases the risk of aggressive modification can genuinely exceed the risk of controlled ageing, at least for a period. It would be childish to demand that every industrial controller, diagnostic machine, or transport subsystem be renovated on the rhythm of consumer software. Systems with physical consequences deserve caution, and security that ignores safety is not wisdom. It is vanity wearing a hard hat.

Yet that concession strengthens the main argument rather than weakening it. The issue is not whether every protocol fossil must be smashed immediately. The issue is whether institutions can tell the difference between managed legacy and institutional drift. A managed fossil is known, bounded, compensatingly controlled, and paired with a believable replacement or retirement path. An unmanaged one persists through vendor convenience, incomplete inventory, deferred budgets, undocumented dependencies, and the vague hope that segmentation or obscurity will carry the burden a little longer. The visible signs of the difference are plain enough. Does someone know which devices still require the older mode? Is there a schedule for testing alternatives? Are procurement terms pushing vendors towards updateability? Is there a plan for what happens when the next major trust change arrives? Those questions turn nostalgia into governance.

This matters because protocol fossils do not remain local. They shape surrounding design. If one critical fleet cannot move beyond an older protocol or certificate model, neighbouring systems preserve support for it. Monitoring tools learn to live with it. Gateways translate for it. Administrators stop noticing its presence because exception becomes routine. The fossil changes the habitat around it. That is why attackers search for it. They understand that weak protocols in critical systems often come with a cushion of tolerated exceptions, reduced scrutiny, and human reluctance to touch anything that still appears to work. The oldest encryption in the building is rarely there by accident. It is there because the institution has spent years learning not to disturb it.

A subtler problem is the way long-lived devices outlast the people who understood their original trade-offs. Engineers retire. Vendors merge. Documentation decays. Procurement files vanish into archives. What remains is a device that "must stay that way" because no one can safely reconstruct the full consequences of changing it. The protocol fossil then stops being merely old. It becomes mysterious. The named concept is inherited opacity. Explain it, and the strategic implication is stark. Once a system survives beyond the memory of the people who chose its design, its weaknesses become harder to challenge because authority has dissolved into folklore. No one owns the history strongly enough to revise it.

This also explains why modernisation programmes often stall at the device edge. An organisation may update servers, identity systems, cloud services, and public-facing applications while leaving behind a shadow world of operational technology, embedded appliances, and fielded instruments that still speak older protocols. Those systems remain coupled to critical work, yet their security life proceeds on a different calendar. The institution then starts living in two centuries at once: one where certificates rotate and cipher suites retire, another where the old modes survive in cabinets, control rooms, vehicles, and treatment suites because the world there cannot absorb rapid change without consequences someone else will have to explain. The risk does not disappear because it has moved out of sight. It becomes harder to govern precisely because it no longer looks like the rest of the estate.

The old key returns here because it explains the adversary's instinct perfectly. No burglar starts by admiring the newest lock on the front door if the service entrance still uses a mechanism installed two owners ago and patched ever since with polite excuses. Protocol fossils are service entrances for whole sectors. They persist inside systems people prize for continuity, and they acquire protection from the understandable fear of causing harm through change. That makes them strategically precious to anyone hunting for the oldest still-trusted path into a modern institution.

The unresolved question, then, is not whether outdated protocols survive in critical ecosystems. They plainly do. The harder question is whether the organisations depending on them can say which doors those old keys still open, which vendors control the pace of replacement, which devices cannot yet be moved, and how long they intend to let the oldest encryption in the estate define the terms on which the newest systems must still defend themselves.

## Data archives and long-term confidentiality

In June 2015, when the United States Office of Personnel Management disclosed the breach of security-clearance files and personnel records in Washington, D.C., public attention settled first on theft in the present tense. Who had lost data, whose records were exposed, what immediate damage might follow? The harder question sat in the archive itself. These were not fleeting transaction logs or disposable session tokens. They were records built to last: background investigations, family details, foreign contacts, financial pressures, fingerprints, and the bureaucratic memory of trust. Their danger was not exhausted at the moment of theft. It was preserved for future use.

Archives age differently.

That is the central problem of long-term confidentiality. Stored data does not merely sit still while the world moves on. Backups, logs, replicated archives, and retained records pass through changes in technology, politics, staffing, mergers, classifications, and adversarial capability. A file that looked properly governed when created may become newly exposed because the encryption around it ages, the key management around it drifts, the reason for keeping it is forgotten, or the surrounding data environment becomes rich enough to interpret it in ways the original custodians never anticipated. The archive becomes dangerous not because it changes, but because the world learns new ways to read it.

This is why stored data deserves a different form of analysis from data in transit or even from active operational systems. Show the scene and the distinction becomes plain. A live service may be patched, segmented, monitored, and eventually retired. An archive is often duplicated, copied into backups, mirrored across regions, exported into legal holds, replicated into analytics environments, and preserved in formats meant to survive ordinary system churn. The named concept is persistence asymmetry. Explain it, and the strategic implication follows. Defensive controls around active systems evolve, however imperfectly. Archives often remain protected by the assumptions of the day they were sealed. Over time, the living environment changes around them while the archive keeps trusting yesterday's arrangements.

Backups illustrate this with almost cruel clarity. Institutions usually think of backups as prudence made visible: the technical equivalent of good housekeeping. Keep copies. Preserve recovery. Ensure continuity after ransomware, disaster, or operator error. All of that is sensible. Yet backup logic also creates one of the most persistent forms of hidden exposure. A record deleted from the live system may remain in snapshots, offline stores, tapes, disaster-recovery images, cloud replicas, or outsourced retention services for months or years. The abstraction of resilience becomes visible in a string of ordinary actions: nightly replication, offsite storage, test restores, retention extension for legal caution, "temporary" duplication during migration. The implication is severe. Institutions often reduce present exposure in one place while preserving historical exposure in six others.

Logs create a related but subtler problem. They are generated for debugging, compliance, monitoring, incident response, billing, and system understanding. In the moment they seem technical rather than intimate. Over time they can become some of the richest archives an institution owns. Connection records, identity events, API calls, failed logins, geolocation hints, configuration changes, internal addresses, and system timestamps can reveal patterns of behaviour, network architecture, organisational rhythm, and human error more effectively than many more obviously sensitive records. The named concept here is secondary sensitivity. Explain it, and the problem becomes sharper. Data created as operational exhaust can later function as intelligence material, legal evidence, coercive leverage, or architectural guidance for an adversary. The log was never classified as highly sensitive because nobody first encountered it as a story. Time turns it into one.

Replicated archives are often more dangerous still because they multiply exposure while thinning ownership. A primary archive may be tightly governed. Its replicas may sit in analytics platforms, cold storage, vendor-managed environments, migration staging areas, reporting systems, or long-forgotten test repositories. Each copy may have travelled there for a legitimate reason. Few institutions maintain the same discipline over every copy that they claim for the source. Show the scene and the familiar pattern appears. A sensitive dataset is mirrored to support disaster recovery, then copied for testing, then partially restored into a new platform, then retained because deleting it feels risky, then inherited by a successor team that did not create it and does not fully understand its original classification. The named concept is custodial dilution. Explain it, and the strategic implication becomes impossible to ignore. The more an archive is replicated, the less likely it is that anyone can say with confidence who truly governs all of it.

This is where classification assumptions begin to decay. A dataset is usually classified at the point of creation according to what it means then. An internal negotiation file is judged according to the live transaction. A personnel archive is judged according to present roles. A technical design store is judged according to current product plans. Years later the surrounding conditions may have changed entirely. The negotiation may now illuminate a later dispute. The personnel file may concern people who have risen into more sensitive positions. The design archive may reveal vulnerabilities in still-supported systems or commercial strategies that matured in unexpected directions. The named concept is semantic drift. Explain it, and one sees why long-term confidentiality cannot be assessed by original labels alone. Archives often outlive not only their first systems but the first meanings assigned to them.

A useful example lies in legal and administrative archives. Institutions preserve contracts, internal memoranda, audit trails, board papers, draft positions, and decision records because continuity, accountability, and defensibility require memory. Sensibly so. Yet these stores frequently survive under assumptions that no longer fit their later strategic value. A due diligence archive from a past acquisition may later reveal internal doubts, dependencies, or bargaining thresholds. A personnel grievance file may later intersect with leadership change, litigation, or public controversy. A technical incident archive may later offer a roadmap to systemic weakness. The visible behaviour attached to this is deceptively dull: the archive remains in place because retention rules, legal caution, or administrative habit preserve it. The implication is that archives quietly become richer to outsiders even when insiders stop looking at them altogether.

A second example returns to the logic of harvest now, decrypt later. An adversary collecting encrypted stored data does not need to assume that all of it will be readable soon, or even ever. It only needs to assume that enough of it will remain valuable if readability improves or if surrounding data grows richer. A long-held archive of diplomatic records, design documents, identity files, or corporate correspondence can acquire increasing utility as other datasets leak, as public records expand, or as future computational capabilities change the cost of access. The named concept is future-readability risk. Explain it plainly and the strategic lesson emerges. Risk is not confined to whether a record is currently unreadable. It concerns the possibility that the record will become meaningfully readable while its contents still matter. That is a different clock, and many institutions do not govern against it well.

A practical framework for thinking about future-readability risk begins with three questions. How long does the information remain sensitive? How likely is it that the protection around it will weaken before that sensitivity expires? And how many copies, derivatives, or contextual companions exist that would increase the value of future access? This framework matters because it forces confidentiality to be treated as a duration problem rather than a static property. A routine operational message may not justify long-term concern. A replicated archive of legal, identity, scientific, diplomatic, or infrastructure data often does. The point is not to dramatise all storage. It is to separate data that decays quickly from data that remains combustible across institutional time.

This is also where retention minimisation becomes strategically serious. The phrase can sound like administrative tidiness, a polite cousin of records management. It is much more than that. Minimisation changes the future value of archives to an adversary by reducing volume, reducing context, reducing correlation opportunities, and shrinking the set of materials whose later readability would still matter. Show the scene and the effect becomes clear. A system deletes logs sooner when they no longer serve operational need, avoids replicating full sensitive datasets into test environments, strips identifying detail from long-term analytics stores, shortens backup retention where defensible, and segregates archives whose continued existence must be justified explicitly rather than inherited by default. The implication is strategic rather than hygienic. A smaller, more disciplined archive is not merely easier to manage. It is less useful to a patient collector.

Still, a limitation needs respect. Not every archive should be minimised aggressively, and not every form of long-term retention is evidence of institutional laziness. Scientific records, public archives, medical histories, legal obligations, safety investigations, historical accountability, and continuity of governance can all require durable retention. Some institutions have duties not to forget. It would be foolish to treat deletion as a universal virtue or to imply that every old record is an avoidable burden. The archive can be a public good as well as a liability.

Yet that concession sharpens the real issue rather than softening it. The point is not that retention is bad. The point is that retention without re-evaluation is dangerous. A mature institution does not ask only whether it once had a reason to keep a dataset. It asks whether that reason still outweighs the long-term confidentiality burden, whether the dataset's classification still reflects its modern meaning, whether the copies and backups are governed consistently, whether the encryption and key management around it can plausibly outlast the sensitivity of the material, and whether the archive has become richer through contextual accretion than its original owners ever intended. These are not archival niceties. They are security questions with a memory.

The archive also reveals something about institutional psychology. Organisations are better at creating records than at deciding what deserves to die. Creation is tied to caution, evidence, continuity, and the fear of losing something useful. Deletion requires confidence, cross-functional authority, and acceptance that some future convenience will be sacrificed for a reduction in future exposure. Those are harder virtues to organise.

So the archive grows. Backups accumulate. Logs persist. Replicas remain because somebody once needed them. What no one needed permanently becomes what no one can confidently dismantle. The old paper box stays in the cupboard because throwing it away feels more dangerous than letting it sit there quietly becoming important again.

The paper box is the right image here because archives often retain the aura of inert storage long after they have become strategic terrain. They look quiet. They are not quiet. They hold past identities, past secrets, past negotiations, past architectures, and past permissions in forms that may be reinterpreted by future machines, future investigators, future litigants, future adversaries, and future crises. A live system demands attention because it moves. An archive demands attention because it waits.

That is the unresolved test. When an institution says its data is protected, is it thinking only about the live systems it can see and patch, or can it also account for the backups, logs, and replicated archives that will remain long after today's classifications, encryption assumptions, and responsible managers have changed? Until that question becomes ordinary, long-term confidentiality will remain one of the easiest promises to make and one of the hardest to honour.

## Mapping exposure across an organisation

In April 2014, when the Heartbleed vulnerability in OpenSSL became public, organisations across London, New York, Singapore, and countless less celebrated server rooms discovered that they did not actually know where some of their most important cryptography lived. Administrators rushed to patch internet-facing services, then found themselves facing a nastier question. Which systems were using the vulnerable library through products they had not built, appliances they did not fully manage, or software stacks whose inner components had long ago disappeared beneath vendor branding and routine operation? The concrete outcome was not only urgent remediation. It was a revelation about institutional sight.

Many estates were partly blind.

That blindness is the real subject here. Institutions often speak about "their encryption" as though it were a coherent asset they have selected, understood, and governed. In reality, cryptography is usually scattered across an organisation in uneven and half-visible ways: embedded in web services, identity platforms, backups, mobile devices, databases, VPNs, industrial controllers, printers, cloud services, third-party appliances, code-signing systems, payment terminals, and management tools. Some of it is carefully administered. Some arrives by default. Some sits inside purchased products whose marketing language is far more legible than their trust model. The result is not mere technical clutter. It is a strategic problem of cartography. The organisation cannot prioritise what it cannot see.

The floor plan matters.

That quiet motif suits the problem because mapping exposure is not an abstract exercise in asset lists. It is a way of learning which doors exist, what locks they use, who holds the keys, and which corridors connect systems that are usually described as separate. Show the scene and the need becomes obvious. A security team is asked whether the organisation can migrate away from an ageing cryptographic primitive or identify where long-lived secrets depend on brittle trust. The named concept is cryptographic visibility. Explain it, and the implication becomes immediate. One cannot answer responsibly by naming only major applications or public-facing services. The decisive exposure may sit in a forgotten gateway appliance, a contractor-managed file transfer product, a storage array doing encrypted replication, or an old internal system whose certificates are renewed by habit rather than understanding. Mapping is therefore not bureaucracy. It is the precondition for serious choice.

This is why inventories deserve more respect than they usually receive. The word sounds deadening, almost clerical, which is one reason organisations underinvest in it. Yet an inventory is the first honest statement of what must be governed. It asks not simply which devices or applications exist, but which ones perform cryptographic functions, depend on certificates, terminate secure sessions, store encrypted archives, validate signatures, manage keys, or preserve old trust anchors. The abstraction of security posture becomes visible in a sequence of ordinary questions: where is encryption used, for what purpose, with which algorithms or trust stores, under whose administrative control, and with what replacement path if that component becomes untenable? The implication is harsh but clarifying. Institutions often discover that they have many more cryptographic systems than they have owners capable of describing them.

A useful example lies in third-party appliances. These are among the most deceptive components in a modern estate because they present themselves as bounded products while often containing dense internal security dependencies. A network appliance, storage controller, load balancer, industrial gateway, medical workstation, or security management console may terminate transport security, issue certificates, hold keys, or rely on embedded libraries long after the organisation has stopped thinking of it as a software system at all. Heartbleed made this brutally plain. The vulnerability was not only in "servers" in the generic sense. It also surfaced in appliances and products that used OpenSSL under the surface, sometimes in ways customers could not patch directly or even identify quickly. The named concept here is embedded trust opacity. Explain it, and the strategic lesson sharpens. A purchased box may carry cryptographic exposure on behalf of the institution even when the institution lacks the practical ability to inspect or modify it. The implication is that inventories must not stop at what internal developers built.

Dependency graphs are the next step because a flat inventory still lies by omission. Knowing that a system uses certificates, a cloud key service, or an embedded crypto library is useful. Knowing what else depends on it is what turns knowledge into prioritisation. Show the scene and the difference becomes clear. A certificate authority appears on an asset list. That tells you it exists. A dependency graph shows which user devices, VPNs, internal applications, code-signing processes, contractor connections, and remote sites would fail or weaken if that authority changed. The named concept is trust topology. Explain it, and one sees why so many organisations suffer during migration and incident response. They have lists of things. They do not have maps of consequence. The implication is large. Cryptographic exposure is rarely local. It moves through dependencies, and the most important system is often not the one with the most obvious label but the one whose failure would quietly propagate furthest.

A second named example comes from certificate-related incidents that exposed how hidden dependencies distort institutional judgment. When DigiNotar collapsed in 2011 in the Netherlands after fraudulent certificates were discovered, the public saw browser distrust and headlines about a compromised certificate authority. The deeper lesson for organisational mapping was that many relying parties had outsourced authenticity judgments to infrastructure they neither controlled nor monitored with anything like equal seriousness. Some systems could move away quickly; others could not. The named concept is asymmetrical dependence. Explain it, and the method becomes clearer. When mapping exposure, it is not enough to ask what cryptographic component exists. One must ask who depends on it, who can replace it, who cannot, and who will still be carrying it after official trust has supposedly moved elsewhere.

Responsibility lines matter because mapping without ownership becomes a kind of decorative archaeology. Many organisations can produce an asset spreadsheet after enough pressure. Far fewer can say who is answerable for each cryptographic dependency, who approves changes, who understands its upgrade path, and who bears the operational pain if it must be replaced. This is where the exercise turns from technical discovery into governance. A mature map links each meaningful use of cryptography to an accountable line of stewardship: not just a team name in a forgotten wiki, but a real decision route. Who owns the VPN gateway certificates? Who can retire the old protocol support in the file transfer service? Who controls the cloud key policies for archival storage? Who has authority over the trust store on managed devices? Who speaks for the vendor-managed appliance whose internal crypto no one can patch directly? The implication is severe. Exposure becomes strategically dangerous when institutions know the component but not the decision-maker.

This is why "with what upgrade path" is as important as "where is it used". A cryptographic component with a clean, tested migration path is not the same risk as one that can only be changed through vendor intervention, capital replacement, regulatory approval, or a maintenance window so narrow it exists mostly in legend. Show the scene and the contrast matters immediately. Two systems both rely on an ageing trust anchor. One can be updated centrally with rehearsed rollback and current client support. The other sits inside a third-party appliance serving a critical workflow and can only be modified through a vendor release scheduled for next year, assuming the product line remains supported. The named concept is upgrade asymmetry. Explain it, and the strategic value of mapping becomes obvious. Under constraints, the institution needs to know not only where weakness exists but where weakness is moveable. Prioritisation without this knowledge is little more than managerial theatre.

Still, a credible limitation should be admitted. No organisation can achieve perfect visibility. Large estates are too dynamic, outsourced, inherited, and layered for total cartographic mastery. Cloud services change beneath customers. Vendors underdocument internals. Shadow IT appears. Mergers import systems nobody fully understands. Engineers leave. Documentation ages. A map is always partly out of date the moment it is drawn. It would be foolish to promise a final, complete picture and call anything less failure. That standard would produce paralysis disguised as ambition.

Yet the limitation strengthens the case for method rather than weakening it. Because perfect visibility is impossible, organisations need maps that are good enough to support ranked decisions under uncertainty. The goal is not omniscience. It is progressive reduction of blind spots where consequences would be severe. That means starting with systems whose compromise, immobility, or hidden trust concentration would matter most: identity, key management, certificate issuance, archives, remote access, signing, externally exposed services, safety-critical operations, and vendor appliances in the middle of everything. The floor plan need not show every cupboard before it can reveal that the stairwell is on fire.

This is also where prioritisation under constraints becomes honest. Most institutions cannot replace all ageing cryptography, review every dependency, and retire all weak trust assumptions at once. Budgets, staffing, vendor cycles, and operational reality forbid it. A good exposure map therefore does not merely catalogue. It distinguishes between what is dangerous and moveable, dangerous and stuck, benign for now, and simply unknown but likely important. The visible outcomes are practical. A legacy gateway with many external dependencies rises in urgency. A contained internal service with short-lived data may fall. A third-party appliance with embedded cryptography and no clear owner becomes a governance problem, not just a technical one. A replicated archive with unclear key custody becomes a priority because future-readability risk is high. The implication is that mapping is how scarce attention stops being wasted on what is easy to discuss and starts flowing towards what is structurally consequential.

The method also changes how organisations talk to themselves. Without a map, debates about cryptographic risk become ideological or generic. Security teams say the estate must modernise. Business teams say operations cannot break. Vendors say support is coming. Everyone is right in the vaguest possible way. Once exposure is mapped, the conversation can become more exacting. Which systems still rely on the old root? Which appliances embed unpatchable trust assumptions? Which backups preserve long-lived secrets under outdated key governance? Which client fleets cannot accept the new chain? Which contractor-managed services terminate secure sessions in ways the institution has never properly reviewed? Exactness is not a luxury here. It is the difference between panic-driven migration and deliberate sequencing.

There is also a cultural gain. Institutions that map cryptographic exposure seriously stop treating encryption as a badge and start treating it as infrastructure. They learn that "uses encryption" tells them almost nothing. What matters is where the cryptography sits, what function it serves, what assumptions it depends on, and how gracefully it can change. That change in language is itself a form of strategic maturity. It replaces boastful generalities with locational truth. A team can say, not "we are secure", but "this archive depends on this key service, owned by this team, with this recovery route, and here is the replacement path if the current trust fails". That sentence has more value than many glossy assurance reports.

The floor plan returns here because it remains the right corrective to wishful thinking. An organisation can walk confidently through a building it has occupied for years and still not know which walls hide weak wiring, which doors use obsolete locks, or which rooms connect through passages only maintenance staff remember. Cryptographic exposure is much the same. The systems most likely to surprise are often not the ones that look dramatic from outside, but the ones embedded in ordinary operational life and therefore spared the scrutiny reserved for visibly sensitive platforms.

The hard question, then, is not whether an institution has some inventory somewhere. Many do. The harder question is whether it can point to its cryptographic dependencies as a living map of responsibility and change: where trust is anchored, where it is embedded, where it is outsourced, where it cannot yet move, and where a third-party appliance or inherited system is still quietly deciding the real pace of security for everyone else. Until that map exists in a form leaders can act on, hidden exposure will remain not merely a technical problem but a political one concealed inside the floorboards.

# Chapter 10

# Post-Quantum Migration Planning

What is the more dangerous mistake: moving too early towards new cryptographic arrangements, or waiting until certainty arrives? The question sounds technical until one notices how institutions actually change. A cryptographic standard can be selected in a meeting room. A real migration has to pass through codebases, vendors, procurement cycles, compliance language, legacy devices, customer contracts, testing regimes, and leadership attention. By the time certainty feels comfortable, the timetable for safe change may already have narrowed.

That is the first difficulty. People like to imagine cryptographic transition as a race to identify the winning algorithm and then install it as one might replace a broken lock. The reality is less tidy. Institutions do not simply adopt stronger mathematics; they expose the quality of their own governance. Some can change trust mechanisms with discipline, version systems cleanly, and stage risk across time. Others discover that their security posture has been built on hidden rigidity: hard-coded assumptions, vendor dependencies, brittle interfaces, and a culture that treats cryptography as fixed plumbing rather than a living system. The bridge matters less as an object than as a test of whether the organisation knows how to cross it without dropping half its cargo into the river.

That is why post-quantum readiness should be understood as a competence before it is understood as a destination. Readiness is not the possession of a preferred algorithm or a confident slide deck. It is the ability to alter cryptographic dependencies safely, repeatedly, and under imperfect conditions. It requires an institution to distinguish between liking a future standard and being able to deploy it across a messy estate without producing new weaknesses in the act of improvement. The crucial division is therefore not between old maths and new maths, but between systems that can change and systems that merely hope change will remain somebody else's problem for a little longer.

This changes the meaning of delay. "Waiting for the winner" can sound prudent, even sophisticated, as though one were resisting fashion and preserving scarce effort until the technical picture settles fully. Sometimes restraint is wise. Often it becomes a flattering excuse for not building the organisational machinery that migration will require regardless of the exact final standard mix. A system that cannot inventory its cryptographic dependencies, negotiate protocol changes cleanly, test mixed deployments, or pressure suppliers into supporting upgradeable designs will not become agile by learning one more acronym. It will simply arrive later at the same hard work, under worse conditions, with less room for error.

The stakes are therefore broader than post-quantum cryptography in the narrow sense. This chapter concerns whether institutions can engineer adaptability before necessity turns adaptation into crisis. Agility sounds graceful until one realises what it asks of real systems: modular interfaces, disciplined versioning, tolerance for parallel schemes during transition, careful testing of old and new clients together, and the willingness to pay design costs now for flexibility whose value will only become obvious later. Most organisations prefer immediate utility to optionality. That preference is understandable. It is also how future migrations become present emergencies.

This is where the subject stops being a matter for cryptographers alone and becomes a question of political economy inside technical systems. Vendors decide road maps. Large buyers decide what the market learns to treat as mandatory. Certification regimes translate standards into shipping behaviour. Procurement language can either reward upgradeable designs or trap institutions inside products that were never meant to change elegantly. The force of a standard is not merely intellectual; it is commercial, contractual, and administrative. A migration succeeds when these pressures align well enough that stronger cryptography can move from specification to ordinary use without vanishing into a swamp of exceptions and half-compatible estates.

The route ahead follows that institutional logic from the meaning of readiness itself, through the design discipline required for cryptographic agility, into the practical role of hybrid arrangements that can reduce transition risk without pretending to be a final resting place. From there the argument turns to testing, where many migrations fail not in theory but in integration, compatibility, and operational surprise, then outward to supply chains and procurement, where large organisations discover that buying power is one of the few levers capable of moving whole ecosystems.

It closes with communication, because cryptographic change that cannot be explained honestly to leadership, partners, and the public will always tempt either complacency or theatre.

A spare wheel offers a better metaphor than a silver bullet. Sensible people do not confuse carrying one with arriving safely, nor do they wait for a tyre to burst at speed before learning whether the boot opens and the jack still works. Post-quantum migration planning has the same awkward character. It is less about discovering a perfect future than about proving that the institution can continue moving when one of its current assumptions finally goes flat.

The hard question, then, is not which algorithm makes the neatest promise on paper. It is whether the organisation depending on that promise can change cryptography as a governed practice rather than a panicked event: across suppliers, across old clients, across constrained devices, across public explanation, and across the inconvenient stretch of time in which old and new must coexist without teaching the system to trust the weakest option simply because it is the easiest to keep alive.

## What post-quantum readiness means

In August 2024, when the National Institute of Standards and Technology published its first final post-quantum cryptography standards in Gaithersburg, Maryland, many observers heard the event as a finish line. The names were now formal. The algorithms had crossed from contest and draft into a more stable public status. For institutions outside the standards world, that can sound like the decisive moment: the winners are known, so the serious work can begin. The trouble is that the serious work began much earlier for anyone who understood what migration actually demands.

Standards do not move systems by themselves.

That is the first point to grasp if post-quantum readiness is to mean anything useful. A standard settles one part of the problem: which cryptographic constructions have been judged mature enough for formal adoption in a given process. It does not tell an organisation where those constructions must be inserted, which products in its estate can support them, which interfaces assume older handshakes, which devices cannot absorb larger keys or signatures gracefully, which vendors have no road map, or which archives, trust anchors, and protocols have been built on the flattering fiction that cryptography changes only when committees say so. The published standard is real. The deployment question is where institutions either reveal competence or discover they have mistaken selection for readiness.

The hinge on the door decides.

That quiet image is worth keeping close because post-quantum readiness is less like choosing a new lock and more like discovering whether the doors, frames, hinges, and people using the building can support the change without tearing the structure sideways. Show the scene and the distinction becomes obvious. A security leader asks whether the organisation is ready for post-quantum migration. The named concept is deployment capability. Explain it, and the strategic implication follows. Readiness is not primarily the possession of a preferred algorithm name in a policy binder. It is the capacity to change cryptography safely, repeatedly, and without losing control of the surrounding system. If a service cannot swap key exchange methods without breaking old clients, if an appliance vendor cannot update embedded cryptography on schedule, if archives depend on trust models nobody can map cleanly, then the organisation is not ready merely because it has chosen a future favourite.

This is why algorithm choice and migration capability must be pulled apart. People naturally fixate on the former because it is crisp, technical, and legible. Which scheme has been standardised? Which looks strongest? Which offers better performance trade-offs? Those are real questions. They are also the easiest part for many institutions, because they can be answered by deferring to respected processes, vendors, or external guidance. Migration capability is harder because it cannot be delegated so neatly. It lives in inventories, interface design, testing practice, version discipline, procurement leverage, client diversity, and the institutional habit of changing trust assumptions without panic. The abstraction of readiness becomes visible here in very ordinary things: can the team identify where public key cryptography is used, can it change libraries without rewriting business logic, can it negotiate new protocol modes without leaving old systems stranded, can it retire earlier assumptions after transition rather than carrying them indefinitely like sentimental luggage.

A useful example lies outside post-quantum cryptography in the narrow sense. In September 2021, the expiry of the DST Root CA X3 certificate associated with Let's Encrypt exposed how much of "migration readiness" depends on endpoints and operational reality rather than on central intention alone. The broad direction of trust change was known. Technical guidance existed. Yet older Android devices and other stale clients struggled because they could not all follow the new trust path cleanly. The named concept here is transition asymmetry. Explain it, and the lesson becomes immediately relevant. A central authority can move. The installed world may not. Post-quantum migration will reproduce that asymmetry at larger scale if institutions imagine that choosing the new primitive is the same thing as preparing the estate. The implication is uncomfortable but clarifying. Readiness belongs to the environment, not to the meeting at which a preference is declared.

A second example comes from the long retirement of older transport and certificate assumptions across enterprise and internet-facing systems. Organisations often "support" modern cryptography while preserving legacy modes, older libraries, or weak compatibility paths for clients they cannot yet abandon. That pattern has strategic meaning. It shows that migration succeeds or fails in coexistence, not in declaration. A protocol suite that can introduce stronger options while maintaining disciplined boundaries around fallback is very different from one that only pretends to modernise while silently negotiating down to the oldest surviving dependency. The named concept is staged adaptation. Explain it, and one sees why post-quantum readiness must be treated as a habit of controlled change. Institutions need proof that they can run transitions in phases, not just speeches about intending to do so someday.

This is where "waiting for the winner" becomes more dangerous than it sounds. The phrase carries a certain air of common sense: avoid premature investment, let the standards process mature, do not commit to a path that may change. There is wisdom in refusing panicked adoption. But the seductive mistake is to treat every form of preparation as premature merely because the final standard mix is still settling or implementation practice is still improving. Show the scene and the cost of delay sharpens. An organisation postpones inventories, leaves crypto hard-coded deep inside applications, buys products with no clear upgrade path, and tells itself that serious planning can begin once the standards landscape feels final enough. The named concept is preparatory procrastination. Explain it, and the strategic implication becomes plain. By the time the institution feels intellectually comfortable, it may already be operationally late, because the work it avoided was never really about predicting the exact winner. It was about making change possible at all.

This does not mean every institution should rush into visible migration before it understands the trade-offs. A credible limitation belongs here. Some systems should indeed wait before committing to particular implementations. Performance constraints, hardware limitations, immature vendor support, and interoperability uncertainty can make early production adoption unwise in specific contexts. There is no medal for bolting a fashionable primitive into a critical service before the surrounding engineering is ready. A botched migration can weaken security as surely as a delayed one. This subject punishes both vanity and sleepwalking with equal cheerfulness.

Yet that limitation strengthens the central point rather than weakening it. The disciplined alternative to premature commitment is staged preparation, not idle waiting. A mature institution can prepare without pretending to predict the entire future. It can locate cryptographic dependencies, demand upgradeability in procurement, design interfaces so algorithm changes do not require total rewrites, build testing environments for mixed deployments, map high-longevity data that must survive future decryption risks, and train leadership to understand that migration is a programme of capability rather than a single switch-flip event. These are actions in the present tense. None require false certainty about the exact shape of the final resting place. They require only the less glamorous admission that the ability to move is itself part of security.

This is why post-quantum readiness should be framed as institutional competence. Competence has three features worth naming. It is repeatable, meaning the organisation can alter cryptographic components more than once without treating each change as a once-in-history trauma. It is bounded, meaning transitions occur through known ownership lines, tested procedures, and visible risk acceptance rather than improvised exception. And it is social, meaning the competence is distributed across engineering, procurement, operations, architecture, leadership communication, and vendor management rather than living only in a few specialists who can explain lattices over coffee and then watch the organisation buy unupgradeable appliances anyway. The implication is almost severe in its plainness. An institution unready to change cryptography repeatedly is not ready for a post-quantum future, whatever algorithms it claims to admire.

The social part matters because readiness is often defeated by the shape of organisations rather than by the difficulty of the mathematics. Engineers may understand the need for agility while procurement still buys locked products. Security architects may design clean interfaces while product teams preserve old dependencies for commercial convenience. Leadership may ask for a plan while refusing the budget needed for staged testing. Vendors may advertise support while leaving upgrade details vague. The result is an institution that is rhetorically aligned with post-quantum preparation and operationally nowhere near it. The hinge on the door squeals again. The new lock will not matter much if the frame splits under installation.

This framing also changes how success should be measured. A serious institution does not ask only whether it has adopted a post-quantum algorithm somewhere visible. It asks whether it can describe where cryptography lives, which systems can accept change cleanly, which cannot, where hybrids will be needed, which archived secrets require longer time horizons, what supply-chain dependencies control the pace, and how many business-critical services still depend on assumptions no one has rehearsed changing. The visible behaviour of readiness is not a press release. It is an inventory, a test environment, an owned dependency map, procurement language with teeth, and the quiet absence of panic when the first major migration window opens.

The hinge returns here because readiness is rarely glamorous where it is real. It looks like interface discipline, replacement planning, version control, client inventories, staged rollout rules, rollback procedures, and honest communication about what is known and unknown. None of this carries the romance of breakthrough science. That is precisely why it matters. The institutions that perform it before urgency arrives will look merely sensible until the moment everyone else realises they have confused choosing a destination with building a road.

The difficult question, then, is not whether an organisation can name the emerging post-quantum standards it intends to trust. The harder question is whether it has already built the habits, ownership lines, and technical seams that would let it replace trust assumptions safely more than once - because the real future challenge is not picking the winner, but proving that the institution can keep moving after the race has stopped looking theoretical.

## Cryptographic agility and its design costs

In August 2024, when the National Institute of Standards and Technology published its first final post-quantum cryptography standards in Gaithersburg, Maryland, many organisations treated the moment as a question of selection. Which algorithms now counted as the serious ones? Which vendors would claim support first? Which road maps could be presented to boards without sounding either alarmist or asleep? Those were natural questions. They were also incomplete. The more revealing question was harsher and far less flattering: if the organisation needed to swap a cryptographic component across real systems, could it do so without quietly breaking everything around it?

That is the point at which cryptographic agility stops sounding like foresight and starts sounding like engineering debt with a better tailor. Institutions often praise agility as though it were a policy virtue, a sentence that can be inserted into strategy documents and procurement templates without changing how systems are actually built. Yet agility is not a declaration. It is a property of architecture. A service is agile only if its interfaces, state management, protocol negotiation, key lifecycles, logging, monitoring, error handling, client compatibility rules, and operational ownership are all arranged so that cryptographic change does not amount to partial demolition.

The hinge carries the weight.

That image matters because agility is frequently mistaken for the lock itself. People talk as though choosing a strong algorithm with future options attached were enough. It rarely is. Show the scene and the reality emerges quickly. A system depends on a cryptographic library for key exchange, certificates, signatures, and internal token validation. The named concept is substitution cost. Explain it, and the illusion disappears. If those functions are hard-coded into application logic, assumptions about key size are embedded in message formats, validation behaviour is scattered across services, and older clients cannot negotiate new modes cleanly, then replacing the algorithm is not a swap. It is a cascade of code changes, integration failures, and governance arguments about which part of the estate must absorb the pain. The implication is severe. Agility must be engineered before it is needed because once the pressure arrives, retrofitting it is often indistinguishable from rebuilding under duress.

This is why interface design sits at the centre of the matter. Cryptography is most brittle when it is treated as intimate application detail rather than a bounded service with disciplined assumptions. A well-designed interface does not make cryptography trivial. It does something more useful. It limits how deeply any one primitive, key format, or trust assumption is allowed to colonise the rest of the system. The abstraction of flexibility becomes visible in small, unfashionable decisions: whether APIs describe capabilities rather than specific algorithms, whether application logic depends on raw certificate structures or uses stable abstractions, whether key lengths and signature sizes are assumed in storage schemas and packet layouts, whether error handling distinguishes negotiation failure from total system failure. These choices sound pedestrian until the day they decide whether a migration is a managed evolution or a bloodbath in the release pipeline.

Protocol negotiation is where much of this either works or quietly collapses. A protocol suite designed for change can advertise supported options, agree cleanly on mutually acceptable modes, and retire older behaviour with disciplined boundaries. A badly designed one often relies on implicit assumptions, ambiguous fallback, or ad hoc compatibility hacks that accumulate like barnacles. Show the scene and the distinction becomes practical. Two endpoints attempt to communicate after one has added a stronger scheme. The named concept here is negotiation discipline. Explain it, and the strategic point follows. If the protocol was built to accommodate new choices, the change may be awkward but governable. If it was built around a single dominant assumption with only perfunctory thought for future variation, the introduction of new cryptography can trigger downgrade hazards, silent incompatibility, or support for weak coexistence paths that outlive their supposed temporary role. The implication is that agility is not the ability to add options alone. It is the ability to add them without teaching the system to trust the weakest answer simply because it remains the easiest one to keep alive.

A useful example lies in the evolution of transport security protocols. One reason TLS became far more governable than many earlier security mechanisms is that its later versions formalised negotiation and cipher suite handling in ways that made controlled evolution more realistic, even if never painless. That did not eliminate compatibility pain, misconfiguration, or weak deployment choices. It did show what cleaner extensibility can buy. A protocol suite designed to add new cipher suites and retire old ones with relative discipline does not remove politics, legacy, or inertia. It narrows the places where those problems can hide. The named concept is structured extensibility. Explain it, and the lesson becomes relevant far beyond TLS. Good protocol design cannot guarantee good migration, but poor protocol design can almost guarantee bad migration when the time comes.

Versioning discipline belongs in the same family of costs. Institutions often dislike explicit version boundaries because they look like friction. They force planning, client communication, deprecation schedules, and decisions about what the organisation is actually willing to support at any given moment. In the short term, loose compatibility feels kinder. In the long term, it becomes one of the most expensive forms of sentimentality in technical life. A system that cannot say clearly which version does what, which cryptographic assumptions belong to which generation of clients, and when older behaviour will cease to be accepted is not agile. It is merely permissive. The visible behaviour attached to this is familiar: APIs that never quite deprecate old fields, products that carry "temporary" legacy support for years, client libraries that suppress warnings for convenience, and operations teams forced to preserve older validation logic because nobody defined a clean end state. The implication is hard to evade. Agility without version discipline becomes drift.

The design costs are real, and they deserve candour because many organisations flatter themselves by praising agility while refusing to fund what creates it. Abstraction layers have to be built. Packet formats may need redesign. Storage schemas may need to stop assuming particular key sizes or signature lengths. Test environments must support mixed-mode operation. Monitoring systems need to understand multiple negotiation outcomes. Documentation has to improve. Product teams must coordinate with security engineers earlier than they might prefer. Vendor requirements have to be sharpened. None of this feels as immediately gratifying as shipping a feature or cutting infrastructure cost. The named concept is anticipatory expense. Explain it, and one sees why so many institutions postpone it. Agility demands paying in advance for a disruption whose exact timing and shape are uncertain. The implication is political as much as technical. Organisations with weak long-term discipline will always be tempted to borrow against the future by hard-coding the present.

A second example can be drawn from identity and signing systems. These are often more brittle than teams admit because cryptography leaks into user lifecycle, audit trails, certificate issuance, token formats, third-party integrations, and compliance reporting. A signature scheme is not merely a mathematical primitive inserted into a product; it is part of how legitimacy is represented and verified across a chain of systems. When such systems are designed without cryptographic agility in mind, later change becomes terrifying. A stronger signing method may affect payload size, validation libraries, device firmware, archive verification, or downstream tooling built by outside partners. The named concept is institutional coupling. Explain it, and the strategic point becomes plainer. What looks like a cryptographic change in one team's architecture diagram may actually be a change in the organisation's administrative bloodstream. Agility reduces that coupling not by making trust simple, but by making the boundaries of trust less entangled with unrelated assumptions.

Still, a credible limitation should be acknowledged. Agility is not an unqualified good in all forms. A poorly governed obsession with future flexibility can produce overly abstract systems, needless complexity, performance penalties, and configuration surfaces so broad that they create fresh attack opportunities. There is such a thing as designing for an imagined future so enthusiastically that one weakens the present. A system with many negotiation branches, too many modes, and endlessly extensible semantics can become harder to reason about, harder to secure, and easier to misconfigure. It would be foolish to treat flexibility as a sacrament. Some of the most secure systems are deliberately narrow.

Yet this limitation sharpens the central lesson rather than weakening it. The goal is not maximal flexibility. It is controlled replaceability. That means engineering just enough room for change that cryptographic evolution does not require heroic surgery, while preserving enough discipline that the system does not dissolve into optionality for its own sake. A mature organisation can state which parts of the design are intentionally stable, which are intentionally swappable, and how changes are introduced, tested, observed, and retired. It does not mistake a pile of knobs for preparedness. It treats agility as a carefully bounded capability, not a playground.

This is where institutional competence reappears. Cryptographic agility is not delivered by architecture diagrams alone. It depends on whether the organisation can align developers, security teams, product owners, procurement staff, vendors, and operators around a design philosophy that values replaceability before crisis forces the value upon them. An architect may understand the need for capability-based interfaces while procurement still buys appliances with opaque crypto stacks. A protocol team may define clean negotiation while client product teams keep old libraries alive forever because customer migration is awkward. A security office may demand post-quantum readiness while release engineering still lacks a test harness for mixed cryptographic modes. The hinge may be well designed in one room and missing entirely in the next.

The practical question therefore becomes less romantic and more exacting. Where, precisely, are cryptographic assumptions allowed to leak into business logic, packet formats, storage design, product contracts, and vendor commitments? Which systems can add or replace algorithms by changing bounded components, and which would have to be reworked at structural level? Which negotiation paths are explicit and testable, and which are accidents preserved by compatibility? Which versioning boundaries are real, and which are soft promises everyone hopes to avoid enforcing? These are not the questions of people waiting for the future to reveal itself. They are the questions of people deciding whether they will meet that future with architecture or with improvisation.

The hinge returns here for a final reason. When a door swings smoothly, attention goes to the lock, the handle, the key. Almost nobody admires the hinge. Yet the hinge carries the load, and when it fails the quality of the lock becomes a strangely academic subject. Cryptographic agility is built from such hinges: interfaces, negotiation rules, version boundaries, upgrade paths, and disciplined abstraction that feel tediously secondary until change becomes unavoidable. Then they become the difference between an institution that can move and one that discovers, too late, that its strongest algorithms were bolted into place by systems designed on the assumption that time would be more polite than it is.

## Hybrid schemes and transition strategies

In August 2019, Google announced that Chrome would begin experimenting with a hybrid key exchange in TLS that combined X25519 with a post-quantum candidate then known as HRSS. The public language around the trial was restrained, as it should have been. No one serious claimed that the future had arrived in perfect form. The concrete significance lay elsewhere. A major platform was not merely debating post-quantum cryptography in principle. It was testing what happened when old and new assumptions had to coexist inside real protocol machinery, across real clients, with real performance and compatibility consequences.

That is where transition becomes honest.

Hybrid schemes matter because they acknowledge a difficult fact that pure debates about "the next algorithm" often try to outrun. Institutions do not migrate from one clean world to another. They pass through an awkward interval in which confidence in existing methods is no longer intellectually sufficient on its own, while confidence in new methods is not yet operationally complete. A hybrid design responds to that condition by combining a classical mechanism with a post-quantum one so that the security of the overall exchange does not rest exclusively on either assumption. It is, in effect, a belt-and-braces strategy for an era when nobody sensible wants to bet the whole building on a single untested renovation.

The temporary bridge matters.

That image is worth holding because it captures both the strength and the limitation of hybrid schemes. A bridge is not the destination. It is what allows movement while the far side is still being built, inspected, or politically argued over. Show the scene and the logic becomes clear. A system wants to begin reducing future cryptanalytic risk without abandoning widely deployed classical methods overnight. The named concept is assumption stacking. Explain it, and the strategic implication follows. By requiring an attacker to defeat both the classical and the post-quantum component, or at least by avoiding immediate dependence on only one of them, the institution buys time and reduces the chance that one mistaken assumption will dictate the entire outcome. The implication is not that risk disappears. It is that risk is distributed more cautiously during transition.

This distribution is the best argument for hybrids. It recognises that post-quantum migration takes place under two forms of uncertainty at once. One concerns the future capability of adversaries against today's classical public-key systems. The other concerns the practical maturity, performance behaviour, implementation discipline, and deployment surprises of post-quantum schemes themselves. A hybrid arrangement says, in effect, that neither uncertainty should be allowed to rule alone. The abstraction of prudence becomes visible in protocol behaviour: derive shared secrets from both components, require successful processing of both paths, and preserve security so long as the combination is designed correctly and at least one of the assumptions holds as intended. In institutional terms, that can be an attractive proposition because it reduces the political temperature of migration. Teams do not have to pretend they have perfect faith in the new world in order to begin preparing for it.

A useful example lies in those early Google experiments and related work by major infrastructure actors such as Cloudflare in exploring hybrid key exchange for real network traffic. What mattered was not the specific candidate names alone, some of which changed as the field evolved. What mattered was the encounter between theory and deployment. Once a hybrid moved from white papers into protocol negotiations and live systems, awkward realities surfaced: larger messages, handshake complications, implementation complexity, middlebox behaviour, client compatibility, and the endless ingenuity of legacy infrastructure in objecting to progress. The named concept here is transition realism. Explain it, and the lesson becomes sharper. Hybrids are valuable not only because they may improve security posture during uncertainty, but because they force organisations to discover early what their systems can and cannot tolerate when cryptography starts to change materially.

That discovery has strategic value because the greatest failures in migration usually occur in integration, not in abstract mathematics. A hybrid design can expose whether packet formats assume older sizes, whether client libraries negotiate poorly when new options appear, whether hardware accelerators choke on unexpected patterns, whether logging and observability tools misinterpret the new flow, and whether partner systems silently drop or downgrade traffic when faced with unfamiliar structures. Those findings may sound mundane. They are not. They are what turns "post-quantum readiness" from a slide deck into an engineering verdict. The bridge is useful partly because it tells you which vehicles will fall through the planks before you try to move the whole convoy.

There is another reason hybrids appeal to serious institutions: they fit the psychology of staged change better than abrupt replacement does. Organisations cope more readily with layered transitions than with demands for sudden purity. A team can accept a hybrid TLS mode or hybrid certificate strategy as an incremental step while it inventories dependencies, negotiates vendor support, and prepares the estate for fuller change later. The named concept is institutional tolerability. Explain it, and one sees why hybrids often gain traction. They let security teams say something more measured than "trust the new primitive absolutely" and more responsible than "wait until uncertainty vanishes". In a domain where certainty arrives late if it arrives at all, that middle ground has real political utility.

Still, hybrids are not free gifts from the gods of prudence. They carry operational costs, and those costs deserve plain language rather than ceremony. Combining methods usually means larger handshakes, more code paths, more failure conditions, more testing burden, more complicated diagnostics, and more opportunities for implementation mistakes. A system that was already brittle under one cryptographic path does not necessarily become elegant by carrying two. Show the scene and the problem becomes plain. A service introduces a hybrid key exchange. Some older clients connect badly. Monitoring tools misclassify the new negotiation. A load balancer tuned for previous assumptions starts behaving oddly. Developers now have to reason not only about whether the hybrid is enabled, but about what happens when one component succeeds, the other fails, or the peer supports only part of the transition story. The implication is obvious but often underplayed. A bridge made of two materials can be stronger, but it can also be harder to inspect.

This is why hybrids should not be romanticised as the end state. They are often best understood as a bridge, not an endpoint, because carrying both classical and post-quantum machinery indefinitely imposes costs that many systems should not want to bear forever. Permanent hybridity can mean permanent complexity, permanent negotiation overhead, permanent compatibility puzzles, and permanent pressure to support older assumptions long after the organisation should have retired them. The named concept here is transitional overhang. Explain it, and the strategic danger appears. A temporary coexistence model can quietly become a new normal if institutions lack the discipline to define exit criteria. Then the bridge stops helping movement and starts becoming another piece of legacy infrastructure everyone is afraid to dismantle.

A second useful example comes from the more general history of cryptographic transitions in protocols like TLS. The world has repeatedly learned that introducing stronger options while preserving older support is both necessary and dangerous. Necessary, because clients and servers do not update in lockstep. Dangerous, because fallback and coexistence can preserve weak pathways longer than intended. Hybrids inherit this old lesson in a new form. They allow movement under uncertainty, but they also create a temptation to treat dual support as a comfortable resting place. That is precisely the temptation institutions must resist if they are serious about migration rather than theatre.

A credible limitation must also be admitted here. Not every system should adopt a hybrid approach immediately, and not every hybrid design will make sense in every context. Some constrained environments may struggle with message size or computational burden. Some devices may not have room for the added complexity. Some organisational estates are so poorly inventoried that adding hybrid support before visibility improves could simply deepen confusion. There is no virtue in stapling new cryptographic machinery onto a brittle system and calling the result strategic foresight. A hybrid deployed carelessly can fail in ways that neither old nor new paths would have produced alone.

Yet this limitation strengthens the real argument rather than weakening it. The point is not that hybrids are universally mandatory. The point is that where they are used, they should be used with the discipline appropriate to a bridge. That means clear scope, bounded purpose, visible testing, ownership of operational costs, and a defined sense of what successful passage looks like. A mature institution can answer sober questions. Which systems are suitable for hybrid deployment now? Which depend on legacy clients that require staged accommodation? Which performance envelopes can tolerate the added burden? Which vendors support the relevant combinations honestly rather than aspirationally? And crucially, what conditions will tell us that the bridge can eventually be dismantled? Without those answers, a hybrid is not a transition strategy. It is just more entropy wearing the clothes of prudence.

This is where transition strategies become a matter of governance as much as engineering. A hybrid scheme does not succeed because cryptographers approve its structure alone. It succeeds when architects define clean insertion points, protocol designers manage negotiation carefully, implementers avoid accidental downgrade or silent failure, operations teams understand what new telemetry matters, procurement teams demand credible vendor support, and leadership accepts that temporary complexity is being purchased to reduce strategic uncertainty. That is a lot to ask. It is also much closer to the truth than the fairy tale in which one simply "moves to post-quantum" by selecting a better algorithm and announcing the future has begun.

The practical pathway from theory to deployment therefore depends on treating hybrids as revealing instruments. They reveal where systems are rigid, where dependencies are hidden, where version discipline is weak, where testing is superficial, and where organisations confuse support claims with real readiness. A hybrid rollout that causes older clients to disable verification silently, or that forces awkward compatibility exceptions no one can later retire, has not failed merely as a technical tweak. It has exposed the institution's deeper inability to govern change across a mixed estate. That exposure is uncomfortable. It is also valuable, provided the organisation learns from it before larger commitments arrive.

The bridge returns here for a final reason. Sensible people do not build one in order to live on it. They build it to cross uncertainty while preserving movement and avoiding catastrophic commitment to either bank before the route is proven. Hybrid schemes serve the same purpose in post-quantum migration planning. They are useful because they reduce the risk of staking everything on one assumption too early. They are dangerous when they become a sentimental attachment or a permanent excuse to postpone the harder work of simplification after passage.

The hard question, then, is not whether hybrids are clever. Many are. The harder question is whether the institution deploying them knows why the bridge is there, what load it is meant to carry, where the weak joints are likely to appear, and when it will have the nerve to step off it rather than turning a temporary structure into the next generation of inherited complexity.

## Testing, validation, and failure modes

In September 2021, when the expiry of the DST Root CA X3 certificate disrupted connectivity for some older clients relying on Let's Encrypt trust paths, the cryptographic theory was not the problem. No dramatic mathematical collapse had occurred. The public key infrastructure had not suddenly forgotten how certificates work. What failed was integration across a mixed estate: newer systems moved on, older clients lagged, compatibility assumptions broke, and trust behaved differently depending on what sat at the far end of the connection. The event was a small masterpiece of operational embarrassment. It showed, once again, that secure migration tends to fail in the joins.

That is the hard lesson institutions dislike because it lacks glamour. People enjoy arguing about algorithms, proofs, and standards because those questions feel clean. Integration is mud. It involves stale clients, undocumented vendor behaviour, overloaded middleboxes, legacy firmware, configuration sprawl, and the humiliating discovery that a system described as modern is still quietly negotiating with something built to older assumptions. A cryptographic migration therefore does not really begin when a new primitive is selected. It begins when the old world and the new world are forced to speak to each other without lying.

The quiet break is worst.

That short sentence captures the danger better than any migration Gantt chart. A visible failure causes alarms, ticket storms, and executive attention. A quiet failure can leave the system looking healthy while its security properties degrade underneath. Show the scene and the issue becomes plain. A new cryptographic mode is deployed. Most clients work. Some older clients do not. Rather than failing closed, the service or the client silently drops verification, negotiates a weaker path, skips a freshness check, or accepts a trust state it would not normally tolerate. The named concept is silent security regression. Explain it, and the strategic implication follows. The migration appears successful in operational terms while actually teaching the estate to trust less than it claims. That is a more dangerous outcome than an honest outage, because it rewards everyone involved for not noticing.

This is why testing during cryptographic transition is a security activity rather than a mere quality assurance ritual. Quality assurance, in the narrow corporate sense, often asks whether the product still works for users. Security testing asks a sterner question: does the system still fail safely, validate correctly, negotiate honestly, preserve intended trust boundaries, and resist the temptation to degrade its guarantees when confronted with incompatible peers or stressed conditions? The abstraction of assurance becomes visible in exact behaviours. Does a client reject an unsupported certificate path or quietly accept a fallback? Does a protocol negotiation stop on mismatch or retreat to a weaker option? Does a device preserve signature verification under performance strain or disable it to maintain throughput? These are not "edge cases" in the dismissive sense. They are where migration reveals what the system truly values.

Performance surprises are often the first source of trouble because cryptographic change is rarely free in operational terms. Larger keys, longer signatures, additional handshakes, hybrid mechanisms, or different computational patterns may alter latency, memory use, bandwidth consumption, or CPU behaviour in ways that do not matter in a laboratory and matter immensely in production. A service may remain correct and still become operationally fragile if handshake costs rise enough to stress load balancers, mobile devices, thin clients, or constrained links. The named concept here is performance-induced insecurity. Explain it, and the point becomes uncomfortable. Once a new cryptographic mode makes the system slower or more failure-prone, pressure begins to mount for short-term fixes: session shortcuts, validation exceptions, narrower logging, older compatibility settings, or selective disablement in the very places the migration was supposed to strengthen. Performance, in other words, can become a political route back to weakness.

A useful example lies in the history of transport security transitions, where stronger protocol versions and tighter validation repeatedly encountered older devices, broken middleboxes, and compatibility machinery that had been quietly normalised. The result was not usually a dramatic rejection of improved security. It was something more ordinary and more corrosive: partial support, selective fallback, inconsistent enforcement, and systems that claimed a new standard while still carrying an older behavioural spine underneath. The named concept is staged incoherence. Explain it, and the lesson becomes relevant to post-quantum planning immediately. Migration does not fail only when the new primitive is wrong. It fails when the estate becomes internally contradictory - some parts enforcing new assumptions, others silently preserving old ones, with no one able to state clearly which trust guarantees actually survive end to end.

Interoperability breaks matter for the same reason. A cryptographic component never exists alone. It sits inside browsers, operating systems, proxies, hardware accelerators, mobile apps, firmware stacks, security appliances, vendor SDKs, cloud services, and business workflows that were often built by different people at different times with different incentives. Show the scene and the problem is instantly familiar. One side of the connection supports the new scheme; the other nominally does but only through a different library version; an intermediate appliance mishandles the negotiation; logging systems misreport the result; help desks classify the incident as random connectivity trouble rather than trust degradation. The named concept is cross-layer mismatch. Explain it, and the strategic implication becomes plain. A mathematically sound transition can fail because the layers around it do not agree on what "support" actually means.

A second named, checkable example can be found in the 2021 trust-path complications around older Android devices and the expiry of DST Root CA X3. The event has already become a useful teaching case precisely because it was not exotic. The broad trust transition was known. The challenge was real deployment across heterogeneous clients. Some environments could follow the intended path. Others could not. The visible symptom was service disruption. The deeper lesson was about validation behaviour under mismatch: which clients failed clearly, which failed oddly, and which workarounds institutions reached for in response. The implication is large. Even relatively well-signalled trust changes become messy when old clients, inherited assumptions, and real interoperability conditions are allowed to participate.

This is where misconfiguration becomes more than human sloppiness. During migration, misconfiguration often emerges from ambiguity rather than ignorance. Teams are forced to make decisions quickly about negotiation order, accepted modes, certificate chains, client compatibility, monitoring thresholds, trust stores, and rollback conditions. If the architecture was not designed for clean change, those decisions get made in distributed pockets of the estate. One service preserves old settings for an important customer. Another enables a hybrid path without fully instrumenting it. A gateway inserts a temporary override to keep traffic moving. A mobile client suppresses a warning because the alternative is broken user journeys. The named concept is fragmented adaptation. Explain it, and one sees how an institution can sincerely believe it is conducting one migration while actually running six different ones, each with distinct and partly hidden security properties.

The example of a rollout that silently disables verification on older clients captures the point almost too perfectly. It is the sort of behaviour most security policies would condemn if described in advance and most operations teams may tolerate in practice if the alternative is an outage affecting important users. A team might discover that older clients cannot validate the new signature path or handshake properly. Instead of failing hard, a client patch or proxy rule quietly relaxes verification to maintain compatibility. Users experience continuity. Metrics look acceptable. The migration dashboard stays green. The named concept here is compatibility laundering. Explain it, and the strategic danger becomes unmistakable. The organisation has translated a security failure into an operational success signal. That is precisely the kind of error adversaries do not need to create because institutions volunteer it under pressure.

Still, a credible limitation belongs here. Not every migration failure reflects poor engineering or institutional weakness in some simple moral sense. Complex estates genuinely contain old clients, regulated environments, constrained links, and vendor-controlled components that make perfect test coverage impossible. It would be childish to claim that every surprising integration issue should have been anticipated completely. Some uncertainty is irreducible. A migration that touches many layers will always discover things only by moving. That is normal.

Yet this limitation strengthens the main argument rather than weakening it. Because perfect foresight is impossible, testing must be treated as continuous security reconnaissance rather than a one-off gate before launch. A mature organisation assumes that cryptographic transition will reveal unknown dependencies and strange behaviours. It therefore designs tests to surface not only crash conditions but degraded-trust conditions. It tests older clients deliberately, not as an afterthought. It measures handshake failures, fallback rates, certificate validation anomalies, latency spikes, message-size problems, and the operational temptation to disable safety features. It rehearses rollback with the same seriousness as rollout. Above all, it asks whether the system continues to refuse what it should refuse, even when refusal is inconvenient.

This is why testing belongs in the strategic story of migration rather than in the basement of software process. Institutions that treat testing as security work build different habits. They preserve representative older clients instead of pretending the estate is fresher than it is. They involve operations, security, vendors, and business owners in defining what counts as unacceptable degradation. They instrument negotiation paths so that silent fallback becomes visible. They rehearse mixed-mode deployments and failure states. They insist on observing not just whether traffic flows, but how trust is being established while it flows. The floor under the migration is therefore not confidence in the chosen algorithm. It is confidence in the organisation's ability to notice when reality is quietly turning the new design into an older one wearing nicer language.

A deeper cultural issue lurks underneath. Institutions like successful migrations for the same reason they like tidy audits: success is legible, reportable, and politically calm. Trouble during testing can feel like delay, embarrassment, or loss of momentum. Yet the absence of trouble in a cryptographic transition is often less reassuring than people think. Sometimes it means the estate is unusually disciplined. More often it means the tests were too shallow, the client diversity too sanitised, the fallback behaviour too invisible, or the operational definitions of success too forgiving. The test bench that produces no friction may simply be flattering the migration rather than measuring it.

The hinge returns here because it suits the entire subject. People admire the new lock, the advanced material, the elegant cryptographic design. Then the door is hung, and the hinge starts to decide whether the thing can actually move under weight. Testing and validation are hinge work. They determine whether the migration can bear real traffic, mixed clients, awkward vendors, legacy devices, and the human appetite for convenience when the schedule slips. They are not ancillary. They are what tells you whether the institution is upgrading trust or merely relocating the place where it will next fail.

The unresolved question, then, is not whether a new cryptographic scheme can be proved sound on paper. It is whether the organisation deploying it can detect, before an adversary or outage does, the moment at which performance pressure, interoperability pain, or a well-meant compatibility fix causes the estate to keep operating while quietly abandoning the very verification it claimed the migration was meant to strengthen.

## Supply chains, vendors, and procurement leverage

In August 2024, when the National Institute of Standards and Technology published its first final post-quantum cryptography standards in Gaithersburg, Maryland, a certain kind of organisation made the same mistake at once. It treated the publication as a technical cue rather than a supply-chain event. Security teams read the algorithms. Procurement teams often did not yet rewrite the contracts. Vendors updated road maps selectively. Product managers waited for customer pressure. The standards existed, but existence is not deployment. Between the standard and the installed system stands a long line of sellers, buyers, certifiers, integrators, and support agreements.

That line is where power accumulates.

Cryptographic adoption does not spread through admiration alone. A standard may be elegant, publicly reviewed, and strategically urgent. It will still travel at the speed of vendor incentives unless large buyers and certification regimes make delay expensive. This is one of the least romantic facts in security, and one of the most important. People like to imagine that technical superiority eventually wins by force of reason. Usually it wins by getting written into product requirements, framework agreements, support renewals, sector guidance, and procurement clauses that turn "ought to" into "must provide by contract". The specification may begin the story. The purchase order gives it teeth.

This is why supply chains matter more than many institutions want to admit. Show the scene and the mechanism becomes obvious. A bank, ministry, cloud provider, hospital network, or telecom group decides it needs upgradeable cryptography as part of post-quantum preparation. The named concept is vendor-mediated readiness. Explain it, and the strategic implication follows. The organisation does not only depend on its own engineers. It depends on operating system vendors, network appliance makers, managed service providers, hardware suppliers, cloud platforms, software libraries, industrial equipment manufacturers, mobile device vendors, and consultants who configure the whole uneven stack. If even a few of these parties lag, obscure their timelines, or sell "future support" as a foggy promise, the buyer's internal readiness begins to collapse into external dependency.

A useful example lies in the long and uneven retirement of older transport security across the commercial internet. Stronger settings and newer protocol versions did not become widespread simply because experts preferred them. They spread because browser vendors, cloud platforms, enterprise buyers, and major service providers gradually made older support harder to justify commercially. The named concept here is induced coordination. Explain it, and the lesson becomes clear. Markets with many actors rarely move together out of goodwill. They move when enough influential participants narrow the acceptable range of options and make lagging behaviour costly in support burden, liability, compatibility, or loss of business. Post-quantum migration will obey the same political economy, only with more devices, longer lifecycles, and a wider field of partial dependence.

This is where procurement leverage becomes strategically interesting. Large buyers often underestimate how much cryptographic power they exercise when they ask the right questions early. If a major public agency, financial institution, or infrastructure operator requires that products support algorithm agility, defined upgrade paths, explicit post-quantum road maps, mixed-mode transition testing, and contractually visible deprecation commitments, vendors begin to re-order their priorities. Not out of charity. Out of revenue discipline. The abstraction of influence becomes visible in contract language: support for pluggable cryptographic modules, timelines for library updates, guarantees about certificate and key migration, test evidence for hybrid operation, disclosure of embedded third-party dependencies, and obligations to notify customers when a cryptographic component becomes unsupported. The implication is sharp. Standards translate into power when buyers convert them into conditions of sale.

A second example can be found in government and defence procurement more broadly, where standards have often shaped supply chains not by intellectual persuasion alone but through certification and acquisition rules. Once a requirement becomes part of what qualifies a product for purchase, vendors stop treating it as an optional engineering curiosity. The named concept is procurement coercion, though the word need not be taken pejoratively. Explain it, and the strategic reality emerges. In sectors where buyers are large, few, or highly regulated, demand can organise the market faster than public exhortation ever will. A supplier with vague road maps suddenly acquires deadlines when bids, framework memberships, or certification standing depend on clarity. The implication for post-quantum migration is practical: organisations that spend heavily but ask timidly will get vague promises and slideware. Organisations that specify upgradeability as a condition of trust will change what the supply chain learns to build.

Still, this leverage has limits, and serious institutions need to understand them. Not every buyer is large enough to move a market. Not every sector has concentrated purchasing power. Some organisations inherit products through resellers, managed platforms, or long-term outsourcing arrangements that blunt direct influence. Others are trapped inside support contracts or equipment lifecycles too rigid to renegotiate quickly. A rural hospital trust, municipal utility, or medium-sized manufacturer may know perfectly well what upgradeable cryptography would look like and still lack the market weight to demand it from powerful vendors. That is a real constraint. Yet it does not erase the broader argument. It shifts the level at which coordination must occur: industry associations, public procurement frameworks, insurer expectations, sector regulators, and shared certification language can all aggregate smaller buyers into something more consequential than their individual signatures.

This is why certification matters alongside purchasing. Certification regimes can be clumsy and slow, but they perform one vital economic function: they convert diffuse technical concern into legible market thresholds. A vendor may tolerate a few demanding customers. It cannot as easily ignore a certification expectation that affects broad sectors or public trust in its product class. The named concept here is market legibility. Explain it, and one sees why standards alone are weak until they pass through institutions that buyers and sellers actually use to sort acceptable from unacceptable offerings. If upgradeable cryptography, explicit migration support, and disciplined deprecation handling become certifiable expectations rather than merely nice talking points, the market begins to internalise them. The implication is that governance bodies, assessors, and procurement authorities often matter as much as cryptographers in determining the real tempo of adoption.

There is a more awkward layer beneath this: vendors often know much more about the cryptographic brittleness of their products than customers can easily see. They know which components are hard-coded, which libraries are ancient, which devices cannot absorb larger keys or altered handshakes gracefully, which firmware lines are near end-of-life, which dependencies are inherited from outside suppliers, and which product families will never be economically elegant to migrate. The customer sees a road map. The vendor sees the floorboards. This information asymmetry makes procurement language especially important, because general promises about "supporting future standards" are almost useless unless they force disclosure of architecture, lifecycle, and dependency realities. A serious buyer must therefore ask not only whether post-quantum support is planned, but whether the product can adopt new cryptography without full platform replacement, what customer actions will be required, which hardware generations are excluded, and how long dual support will persist before turning into a maintenance nightmare.

A credible limitation deserves emphasis here. Procurement leverage is not magic. A contract clause cannot force competence into a vendor that lacks the engineering capacity, organisational discipline, or supply-chain visibility to deliver what it promises. Nor can certification cure every hidden dependency. Some suppliers will overstate readiness. Some buyers will write requirements they cannot meaningfully verify. Some products will technically "support" new cryptography in laboratory conditions while remaining operationally poor fits in the field. It would be childish to imagine that the procurement office, having discovered the sacred phrase "cryptographic agility", can now summon trustworthy transition by paperwork alone. Contracts are scaffolding, not salvation.

Yet that limitation sharpens the core point rather than weakening it. Because procurement is not magic, it must be linked to verification and consequence. A mature organisation does not merely ask vendors whether they support post-quantum migration. It requires evidence of how. Can the vendor show mixed-mode testing? Can it identify which product lines support algorithm replacement without hardware refresh? Can it disclose where embedded third-party cryptographic components sit inside the stack? Can it describe failure handling on older clients? Can it commit to support windows and retirement dates in writing? These are not legal flourishes. They are methods of turning vague strategic intent into measurable supply-chain behaviour.

This also helps explain why coordination can be induced rather than awaited. Institutions often talk as though coordination were a natural phenomenon that arrives once enough actors feel ready. It rarely does. Someone has to make the first cluster of requirements economically unavoidable. Large cloud providers can do it. Major public-sector frameworks can do it. Financial infrastructure consortia can do it. Platform vendors can do it. Sometimes insurers and auditors do it clumsily, by making unsupported cryptography harder to justify. The point is that coordination is usually organised through incentives, not discovered like a spring flower in a forest of mutual goodwill. Post-quantum migration will follow the same script. The winners in strategic terms will not only be those with the strongest algorithms. They will be those who can align demand, certification, support, and purchasing into a coherent pressure field.

The vendor road map therefore needs to be read with healthy suspicion. A road map is partly an engineering statement and partly a political artefact. It signals seriousness, reassures customers, and buys time. Some road maps are real and precise. Others are elegant procrastination. A mature buyer learns to ask whether the dates are tied to product versions, certification milestones, migration tooling, and support obligations, or whether they merely float in future tense. The named concept is roadmap credibility. Explain it, and the practical takeaway becomes plain. Road maps deserve trust only when they expose dependency, not when they conceal it behind the smooth language of planned enablement.

There is also a geopolitical edge to all this. When a small number of vendors dominate cloud, operating systems, networking equipment, mobile platforms, or cryptographic hardware, their decisions shape not only commercial outcomes but the effective pace of security across whole sectors and countries. A standard may be publicly open; its path into practice can still be bottlenecked by firms whose support choices carry quasi-infrastructural force. That does not make those firms villains by default. It does mean that purchasing and certification decisions around them become forms of strategic coordination, not routine back-office administration. The contract is a policy instrument whether the signatories admit it or not.

The motif of the invoice belongs here because it punctures a certain kind of technological vanity. Engineers often prefer to think that security wins through technical merit. Policymakers prefer to think it wins through standards and guidance. Executives prefer to think it wins through strategic intent. Many of the most important victories are much duller. They happen when someone writes, prices, audits, and enforces the right requirement at the moment a supplier needs the business badly enough to change. The invoice moves the market.

The hard question, then, is not whether post-quantum standards exist or whether vendors say they support them. The harder question is which buyers are willing to convert standards into purchasing power, which certification bodies are willing to translate vague future-proofing into enforceable criteria, and which organisations still imagine they can outsource cryptographic readiness to suppliers without first making readiness a condition of being bought at all.

## Communications to leadership and the public

In August 2024, when the National Institute of Standards and Technology published its first final post-quantum cryptography standards in Gaithersburg, Maryland, many organisations confronted a familiar communications temptation. Some wanted to announce that they were now preparing for a revolutionary threat. Others preferred to say almost nothing, fearing that any public discussion would sound either alarmist or embarrassingly technical. Both instincts miss the real problem. Cryptographic change is difficult enough when it is engineered badly. It becomes far worse when it is explained badly.

Language can weaken trust.

That is not because leadership and the public are incapable of understanding difficult subjects. It is because institutions often present cryptographic change in one of two unhelpful forms. The first is theatrical urgency: a style that suggests present systems are on the verge of sudden irrelevance, that only heroic action can save the organisation, and that technical complexity should be excused because the future is arriving at a sprint. The second is anaesthetic vagueness: a style that wraps everything in terms like resilience, modernisation, and future-proofing until nobody can tell what is changing, why it matters, or what remains uncertain. Between panic and mush lies the only ground on which trust can actually be built.

The weather report matters.

That quiet motif is useful because good communication about cryptographic transition resembles a serious forecast more than a battle cry. A forecast does not pretend certainty where none exists. It does not deny risk merely because timing is hard. It gives people a time horizon, explains what kind of conditions may develop, states what is already being done, and leaves no confusion about whether carrying an umbrella means the sky has already fallen. Show the scene and the point becomes plain. A board asks whether post-quantum migration is urgent, whether customers should be told, and whether existing systems are still safe enough to trust. The named concept is calibrated explanation. Explain it, and the strategic implication follows. The institution must describe change in a way that is specific enough to guide decisions, honest enough to preserve credibility, and calm enough not to generate theatre that later ages badly.

Time horizons are the first responsibility. Much public and executive confusion arises because cryptographic issues are often framed as either immediate emergency or distant research curiosity. Neither category is adequate. Some risks concern data whose sensitivity may outlast current cryptographic assumptions. Some concern procurement and architecture choices being made now that will be difficult to alter later. Some concern present migration capability rather than present breakage. The visible behaviour attached to this abstraction is straightforward. Leadership wants to know whether to fund change this budget cycle. Customers want to know whether their information is currently exposed. Journalists and public audiences want to know whether this is a looming collapse or merely another piece of technical housekeeping. The implication is that communication must separate present exposure, future exposure, and present preparedness. Institutions that collapse those distinctions teach audiences either to panic too early or to stop listening altogether.

Residual risk is the next obligation, and it is where honesty usually becomes inconvenient. Organisations like to announce improvements in ways that imply finality. The system has been upgraded. The migration is under way. New standards are supported. All of that may be true and still misleading. A cryptographic transition rarely removes uncertainty in one clean motion. It changes the balance of assumptions, reduces some classes of future exposure, and may introduce temporary operational complexity while older and newer methods coexist. The named concept here is bounded improvement. Explain it, and one sees why trust depends on precision. People can live with residual risk if they feel it is being described candidly. They become cynical when institutions imply that a migration has solved "the quantum problem" or "secured future communications" in some total sense that no serious engineer would affirm in private.

This is one reason leadership communication must resist the temptation to turn technical migration into executive myth. Senior decision-makers are often offered one of two stories: either a looming catastrophe that justifies exceptional urgency, or a technical standards update that can be delegated out of sight. Neither is useful. Leadership needs a different story. The organisation is improving its ability to change cryptography safely over time; it is prioritising systems whose secrets have long horizons; it is pressing suppliers for upgrade paths; it is testing transitional designs; it is reducing future-readability risk where possible; and it is not claiming certainty about every timeline or every eventual winner. That narrative sounds less heroic than some would like. It is also much more governable. The named concept is managerial legibility. Explain it, and the implication becomes plain. Leaders make better decisions when they understand what kind of competence is being built, not when they are handed either apocalypse or jargon.

A useful example of poor communication can be found in the broader history of security announcements that oversold "military-grade encryption" or "unbreakable" protection. Those phrases work briefly as marketing because they convert uncertainty into swagger. They age terribly once the public learns that security always lives inside operational constraints, user behaviour, key management, and future change. The point is not to rehearse old slogans for sport. It is to see what they teach. When institutions promise absolute safety, every later nuance sounds like retreat. The implication for post-quantum communication is sharp. A transition should never be sold as the end of cryptographic vulnerability. It should be described as an effort to reduce a set of risks across meaningful time horizons while preserving room to adapt as evidence and deployment experience evolve.

A second useful example lies in the August 2024 publication of final NIST post-quantum standards. The event was significant and easy to distort. A careless institution could have told customers that "quantum-safe" security had now arrived in a finished state, or that immediate wholesale danger to all existing systems had finally been confirmed. A more credible institution would say something narrower and stronger: public standards have matured enough to support more concrete planning and staged deployment; current protections do not suddenly vanish; long-lived data and upgradeable systems deserve priority; some migration work can begin now, but it will unfold through procurement, testing, and system replacement over time. The named concept is milestone interpretation. Explain it, and the lesson is simple. Public trust improves when milestones are described as milestones rather than as theatrical chapter endings in a story that was never that neat.

The public dimension matters for another reason. Ordinary audiences do not need every technical detail, but they can detect evasion and overstatement with surprising accuracy. A comprehensible narrative therefore has to answer a few plain questions. What is being improved? Which kinds of information are most affected by the time horizon of the change? What remains secure under present practice? What remains uncertain? What practical commitments is the institution making about testing, supplier pressure, and future updates? The visible signs of seriousness are not dazzling. Dates for review. Clear descriptions of scope. Avoidance of miracle language. A willingness to say that migration reduces some risks without eliminating all of them. The implication is that clarity is not a concession to non-specialists. It is part of the institution's own security posture because it shapes how well customers, partners, and staff can judge credibility.

Still, a limitation should be acknowledged. Not every detail of cryptographic change ought to be publicly disclosed at full technical depth, and not every organisation can publish precise migration blueprints without exposing unnecessary information about system composition or supplier dependence. There is room for discretion. There is also room for staged disclosure as plans mature. The mistake would be to hear the case for candour and infer that all technical and strategic details must be laid on the table at once like a hardware catalogue at a county fair. Good communication is not maximal disclosure. It is proportionate truth.

Yet that limitation strengthens the main argument rather than weakening it. Because full detail is neither possible nor wise in every setting, the institution must become even more disciplined about the truth it does choose to tell. If some specifics cannot be shared, then the broader narrative must be even more exact about what is known, what is being acted upon, and what remains a matter of planning rather than accomplished fact. Ambiguity should not be used to smuggle in false reassurance. Nor should uncertainty be used as a permanent excuse for saying nothing intelligible. The weather report can omit the exact roof structure of every house in town and still tell people what kind of stormfront is moving in.

This becomes strategically important because communication about cryptographic change is not merely explanatory. It is also a form of signalling. An institution that communicates well signals that it understands the difference between technical adoption and operational readiness, that it can describe residual risk without collapsing into either panic or denial, and that it is building migration capacity rather than chasing headlines. That kind of signalling matters later for deterrence. Adversaries learn something when an organisation can demonstrate not only that it is aware of changing cryptographic conditions, but that it has the governance to respond coherently. Customers and partners learn something as well. The named concept here is credible preparedness. Explain it, and the implication emerges. Credibility grows when communication reflects real institutional discipline rather than aspirational marketing.

Poor communication, by contrast, creates two distinct hazards. The first is complacency. If leaders or users hear that a system is now "quantum-safe", they may infer that difficult legacy and migration questions have been settled when they have barely begun. The second is theatrical fear. If people hear that quantum progress means encrypted systems are essentially doomed, they may lose confidence in present protections that remain meaningful and necessary. Both errors harm governance. One delays practical preparation. The other corrodes confidence in the very systems institutions still depend upon while the transition is under way. Honest narratives are therefore not just public-relations niceties. They are part of the mechanism by which the organisation preserves operational steadiness while it changes.

This is why communicators need a disciplined vocabulary. Instead of saying that current encryption is "broken", say that some public-key assumptions face credible long-term transition pressure. Instead of claiming that new standards "solve" the problem, say that they provide a stronger basis for staged migration and future resilience. Instead of implying that change is merely technical housekeeping, say that it affects procurement, testing, and long-horizon data protection. Instead of promising certainty, describe scenarios, dependencies, and review points. These are not cosmetic differences. They teach the audience what kind of reality it is inhabiting: one in which uncertainty is governed rather than denied.

The weather report returns here because institutions often underestimate how much trust depends on tone as well as content. A good forecast respects the audience. It does not dramatise ordinary rain as the end of civilisation, and it does not pretend that gathering clouds are a matter of aesthetic interest only. It tells people what sort of world they are likely entering and what the current forecast can and cannot support. Communications about cryptographic transition need the same discipline. Leaders, customers, staff, and the public do not need propaganda. They need orientation.

The hard question, then, is not whether an organisation can produce a reassuring statement about post-quantum planning. Most can. The harder question is whether it can explain, in language strong enough to guide decisions and modest enough to survive contact with reality, what is actually being improved, what remains uncertain, how long the transition may take, and why the institution deserves to be believed when it says it is becoming more ready without pretending that readiness is already complete.

# Chapter 11

# Intelligence Competition and Cryptographic Incentives

What happens to intelligence competition when encryption works well enough that the message becomes harder to read, but the people, devices, suppliers, and timings around it remain within reach? The tempting answer is that secrecy wins and collection retreats. The truer answer is colder. The desire to know does not soften because cipher text becomes stubborn. It moves. It looks for cheaper surfaces, slower institutions, weaker endpoints, richer metadata, and the commercial actors through whom modern life now passes almost by default.

That movement matters because it ruins a sentimental picture of cryptography. Strong protection does not end competition. It reallocates effort inside it. A service that becomes harder to penetrate through direct decryption may become more attractive through compromised identity systems, poisoned update channels, or quietly acquired access to cloud administration. A target that no longer yields its content easily may still yield its pattern, its dependencies, its habits, and the people around it. The sealed letter remains valuable. So does the desk, the courier, the copy machine, and the person who knows where the spare key is kept.

This is the chapter's central tension. Cryptography raises costs for some forms of collection while increasing the strategic value of others, and the resulting contest is not only technical. It is organisational, commercial, and political. Intelligence services adapt because they must. Companies become terrain because they already sit between users and infrastructure. Internal discipline regains importance because when direct access grows harder, any avoidable weakness inside the institution grows more precious. What changes is not the appetite for knowledge but the route by which knowledge is pursued, hidden, defended, and explained.

The stakes are larger than tactical espionage. A state that cannot read protected traffic may seek leverage through software supply, administrative access, or vendor relationships. A company that advertises strong security may still become a point of strategic pressure if its cloud, telecom, or security tooling can be influenced from elsewhere. An organisation that believes encryption alone has made it safe may relax the very habits that matter most once adversaries turn their attention from the cipher to the surrounding system. The result is a harsher theory of competition: not an argument between secrecy and intrusion, but a struggle over where trust accumulates and how quietly it can be converted into access.

This is why secrecy about capability remains so valuable and so troublesome. An actor that knows what it can break gains from silence, because silence preserves future access and keeps the target behaving as though its protections still stand unchallenged. Yet silence also weakens deterrence, because an adversary rarely fears a capability it cannot detect. Reveal too much, and one teaches others where to adapt. Reveal too little, and one forfeits the chance to shape their behaviour in advance. The contest becomes as much about what can be signalled credibly as about what can be done covertly, which is why intelligence and public trust keep colliding in such awkward ways.

Commercial dependency deepens every part of this picture. Modern communications and data flows do not move only through state systems or self-contained private estates. They pass through cloud providers, telecoms, software vendors, managed security services, and update channels that combine convenience with concentration of power. These firms are not merely service providers in the background. They are strategic ground. Their infrastructure can be pressed, compromised, or quietly relied upon by multiple parties at once, and their contractual or jurisdictional position can complicate every clean distinction between private security and public power. A vendor's maintenance pathway or update channel can matter as much as a target's chosen algorithm, because it offers something intelligence competition has always prized: scalable access that looks routine until the moment it is not.

The route forward therefore moves from the practical redirection of collection effort away from protected content and towards endpoints, metadata, and supply chains, into the strange value of keeping offensive capability secret even while defensive credibility may require some degree of revelation. From there the focus settles on commercial actors as strategic terrain rather than passive infrastructure, before turning inward to the disciplines that still decide whether an institution can resist pressure once the algorithm itself is no longer the easiest place to attack. The order matters because it follows the path an adaptive adversary would be likely to take: around the lock, through the landlord, and then into the habits of the household.

A service corridor offers a better image than the front gate. People think first about the main entrance because it is visible, guarded, and symbolically important. Serious intruders often think about deliveries, maintenance access, side doors, contractor badges, and the staff routines that keep the building alive. Intelligence competition in an encrypted environment has much the same character. As the front gate hardens, the service corridor grows more interesting. That is not a reason to neglect the gate. It is a reason to stop pretending that a stronger gate ends the contest.

The difficult question, then, is not whether encryption changes intelligence competition. It plainly does. The harder question is where the competition goes next, who controls the surrounding pathways, and whether institutions can recognise that their real vulnerability may now lie less in the unreadable message than in the update channel, identity tier, vendor relationship, or internal lapse that tells an adaptive adversary exactly where to stop treating cipher text as the main prize.

## Collection priorities in an encrypted world

In June 2013, when documents disclosed by Edward Snowden brought the scale of contemporary signals intelligence into public view, one of the most enduring surprises was not that states wanted to know more than they said. It was where that desire to know had settled. Encryption had not ended collection. It had redirected it. Content remained valuable, certainly, but so did contact chains, device identifiers, cloud platforms, telecom relationships, software updates, and the sprawling administrative machinery through which modern communications pass before and after any message is read.

That moment remains instructive because it broke a childish story about secrecy. Many people like to imagine that once communications are strongly encrypted, the contest ends in favour of privacy and the eavesdropper slinks away to nurse its disappointment. Real intelligence services do not behave like offended schoolboys. They adapt. If cipher text becomes expensive to exploit directly, collection priorities migrate towards the places where meaning still becomes accessible: the endpoint where the message appears in plaintext, the identity layer that decides who may log in, the vendor that distributes trusted code, the metadata that reveals structure without content, the insider who already stands near the safe with a legitimate key.

The courier still matters.

That quiet motif is useful because it captures the central strategic correction. Intelligence competition is not organised around romance about breaking the hardest mathematical object in sight. It is organised around cost, scale, persistence, and the practical value of the information gained. Show the scene and the logic becomes plain. A target adopts strong public-key cryptography and modern secure transport. The named concept is collection substitution. Explain it, and the implication follows. The adversary does not stop caring. It simply asks where the same or adjacent value can be obtained more cheaply: through device compromise, credential theft, key management errors, software supply, identity infrastructure, or traffic analysis. Cryptography changes tactics, not appetite.

This is why endpoints become so important in an encrypted world. A message protected perfectly in transit must still become legible somewhere if it is to be useful to its intended recipient. Phones, laptops, servers, administrator consoles, archive systems, and cloud workloads therefore become natural priorities. The abstraction of secrecy becomes a visible sequence of events: a document is decrypted on a workstation, a chat appears on a handset, an email is indexed on a server, a file is opened in a managed cloud application. Each of these is a point at which intelligence collection can shift from mathematics to access. The implication is not that cryptography has failed. It is that intelligence follows utility. The ciphertext is one route to the information. The endpoint is often a better one.

This helps explain the growing strategic value of identity infrastructure. Rather than trying to crack well-protected communications directly, an actor may prefer to compromise the authentication layer that grants legitimate-looking access. The difference is profound. If one can steal, forge, or misuse credentials, session tokens, certificate issuance authority, or identity federation pathways, one may not need to read protected traffic on the wire at all. One can simply walk through the front door after the system has kindly decrypted everything for authorised users. A useful example is the recurrent attraction of identity providers, single sign-on systems, and directory services as high-value targets. The named concept here is authentication displacement. Explain it, and the strategic point sharpens. In a heavily encrypted environment, the question "Can I break the cipher?" may be far less attractive than "Can I become someone the system already trusts?"

Supply chains offer a related advantage because they transform individual access problems into scalable access opportunities. A compromised update channel, poisoned software dependency, abused certificate path, or malicious build process can place collection mechanisms near many targets at once. Show the scene and the economy of effort becomes obvious. Rather than penetrate a hundred endpoints one by one, an actor may seek the vendor, service, or maintenance pathway that those endpoints already depend upon. The named concept is trust concentration. Explain it, and the implication becomes severe. Modern systems defend content while simultaneously centralising trust in software distributors, cloud operators, device management systems, and security vendors. Intelligence collection adjusts accordingly. The vendor can become more interesting than the victim precisely because the vendor's routines are already treated as ordinary and legitimate.

A second named, checkable example lies in the 2020 SolarWinds compromise. Public reporting made clear that a trusted software update pathway could be used to distribute malicious code into sensitive environments. The case is often discussed under the heading of cyber intrusion, and rightly so. It is also a near-perfect illustration of collection priority in an encrypted world. The crucial move was not to defeat the strongest cryptography protecting each target's communications individually. It was to enter via a pathway that the targets themselves had already authorised to install code and shape system behaviour. The implication extends beyond that incident. Encryption of content does not reduce the intelligence value of trusted maintenance channels. It increases it, because those channels sit upstream of many protected systems and often enjoy operational legitimacy difficult to challenge in real time.

Metadata remains another major priority because it survives even when content protection improves. Who contacted whom, when, from where, how often, and in what pattern can reveal enough to guide targeting, infer hierarchy, expose movement, or anticipate decisions. Intelligence services have always prized such patterns, but an encrypted environment makes them even more attractive relative to direct content exploitation. The named concept is pattern efficiency. Explain it, and the strategic lesson becomes plain. Metadata scales, often costs less to collect than content, and can direct more intrusive methods towards the most promising targets. In practical terms, strong content protection can therefore make traffic analysis, social graph mapping, and location correlation more rather than less central to collection planning.

Still, a limitation deserves fairness. Strong cryptography genuinely changes the field. It raises costs, narrows some mass-interception options, reduces casual compromise, and forces adversaries into riskier or more expensive routes. It would be foolish to deny that. There is a tendency in some strategic writing to overcorrect, as though adaptation by intelligence services meant that encryption does not matter much. That would be nonsense. It matters enormously. A world with strong encryption is not the same as a world without it. Collection substitution is not frictionless, and many actors cannot afford the more invasive alternatives. Good cryptography is therefore still a decisive public good.

Yet that concession strengthens the deeper argument rather than weakening it. Because encryption works, the remaining collection priorities become more revealing of institutional weakness. If an actor abandons ciphertext and turns instead towards identity, supply chains, or endpoints, it is telling you where it expects the real system of trust to be softer than the mathematics. A strong cryptographic posture should therefore change defensive attention as well as offensive tactics. It is not enough to celebrate the unreadable channel while leaving device management, credential hygiene, software provenance, and metadata discipline to live by the shabby lights of administrative convenience. The courier still matters, and so does the office that hires him.

This is where the non-romantic view becomes essential. Intelligence organisations are not wizards obsessed with the purest technical challenge. They are bureaucracies under pressure to deliver knowledge. They compare routes to access the way logistics planners compare routes to a port: by reliability, cost, speed, deniability, and volume. If targeting identity infrastructure yields reusable access to mail, documents, cloud administration, and internal messaging, it may beat years spent trying to subvert a well-implemented cryptographic scheme directly. If compromising a telecom or cloud provider yields metadata and account insight at scale, that may prove more strategically fruitful than chasing isolated pieces of plaintext. The implication is disconcertingly ordinary. The cleverest method is often not the one that best flatters technical prestige, but the one that best suits the institution's appetite for regular, maintainable access.

Counterintelligence therefore returns to the centre of the story almost by stealth. Once collection priorities shift towards endpoints, identities, suppliers, and internal routines, organisational discipline becomes inseparable from cryptographic security. Compartmentation, logging, credential boundaries, insider screening, vendor governance, and suspicious update-path monitoring all become part of the same strategic picture. The abstraction of posture becomes visible in behaviour: who can issue a certificate, who can approve a software release, who can create a privileged account, who can enrol a device, who notices an unusual pattern in identity infrastructure, who reviews the vendor relationship that everyone assumes is too boring to threaten. The implication is not glamorous. It is that algorithms do not replace institutional hygiene. They expose its importance.

Commercial actors complicate this further because intelligence competition now runs through private infrastructure at extraordinary scale. Cloud providers, telecoms, security firms, managed service operators, and update platforms are not simply neutral carriers. They are terrain on which multiple states, criminal groups, and corporate actors all have incentives to exert pressure or seek advantage. This does not require melodrama about omnipotent conspiracies. Ordinary contractual access, lawful process, insider compromise, technical partnership, jurisdictional asymmetry, and supply-chain dependency already create enough strategic complexity. The target is not only the message but the ecosystem through which the message becomes useful.

The courier returns here because it remains the right corrective to fantasy. People often imagine intelligence collection as a contest between a secret message and a secret reader. In reality the most valuable action may take place around the courier's route, the depot where the parcel is sorted, the ledger that records delivery, the locksmith who copied the master key, or the clerk who stamps the paperwork granting ordinary passage. Strong encryption closes one route of entry. It does not close the building.

The real question, then, is not whether cryptography changes intelligence priorities. It clearly does. The harder question is whether the institution defending itself understands that the most likely substitute targets are the very systems it still treats as administrative support rather than strategic terrain: identity, endpoints, vendor relationships, and metadata-rich infrastructure. Until that is understood, organisations will keep congratulating themselves on unreadable cipher text while their actual adversaries walk past the mathematics and wait patiently by the courier's door.

## The value of secrecy about capabilities

In January 1917, in Room 40 of the British Admiralty in London, British cryptanalysts read the Zimmermann Telegram: a German message proposing that Mexico join the war against the United States. The intelligence value was obvious. So was the problem. If Britain simply announced that it had read the message, it risked exposing how much of Germany's diplomatic traffic it could already see. The solution was not silence and not plain disclosure. It was a carefully staged reveal, using a cover story that protected the deeper capability while still making the message politically usable. The contents mattered. The method mattered more.

That old episode remains sharp because it captures a rule that has not aged: if an actor can read something important, the knowledge itself becomes double-edged. One edge cuts outward, yielding intelligence, leverage, warning, or advantage. The other points inward, because every visible use of the capability risks teaching the target what to seal, reroute, replace, or distrust. A successful interception is therefore never just a success. It is also a decision about whether to spend access or preserve it.

The sealed window is valuable.

That phrase captures the paradox at the centre of intelligence secrecy. If one can see through the window and the people inside do not know it, the advantage may persist. If one announces the view too plainly, the curtain comes down. Show the scene and the logic becomes immediate. A state, service, or organisation gains the ability to read, infer, or monitor something an adversary believes to be protected. The named concept is access preservation. Explain it, and the strategic implication follows. Keeping quiet protects the stream of future insight, often at the cost of foregoing immediate signalling or public credit. Revealing the capability may produce a short burst of political or deterrent value, but it can also destroy the very route through which the knowledge became available.

This is why intelligence services conceal what they can break even when outsiders imagine that public proof would be useful. The common civilian intuition is simple: if an adversary knew that a communications channel, software pathway, or cryptographic assumption had been compromised, it would behave more cautiously and therefore be deterred. Sometimes that is true. More often the logic of collection runs the other way. A service that has gained access to a valuable stream of information usually wants the stream to continue. The abstraction of secrecy becomes visible in concrete behaviour: evidence is sanitised, sources are compartmented, operational decisions are justified through alternative explanations, and even internal audiences are told less than they might wish to know. The implication is severe. Intelligence success often depends on institutional restraint that can look irrational from the outside because the best proof of capability is often the proof that cannot safely be shown.

Bletchley Park offers the clearest example. During the Second World War, British codebreakers working against German Enigma traffic generated intelligence of extraordinary value, later known under the umbrella term Ultra. Yet the point of the operation was not simply to know. It was to keep knowing. That required exquisite secrecy. Show the scene and the burden becomes plain. If military action followed decrypted traffic too directly, the Germans might infer that their communications were compromised. If information was ignored too often, commanders would lose trust in the intelligence. The named concept here is operational masking. Explain it, and the strategic lesson becomes unmistakable. A capability can remain valuable only if its use is managed in a way that does not reveal its own existence too clearly. The implication is morally and strategically uncomfortable. Sometimes intelligence is not acted upon as directly as it might be because preserving future access outweighs immediate exploitation in the minds of those responsible.

The non-romantic view begins here. Intelligence services do not conceal capabilities because secrecy is mystically attractive to them. They conceal capabilities because hidden access can be more valuable than public proof. A cryptanalytic breakthrough, an endpoint compromise, or a supply-chain penetration that remains invisible can yield a continuing series of small advantages: policy insight, troop movement warning, procurement knowledge, negotiating leverage, or the ability to distinguish signal from noise in moments of crisis. Public revelation may provide one dramatic moment. Persistent secrecy can provide a hundred quieter ones. The sealed window keeps paying.

This makes the deterrence problem unusually awkward. Deterrence depends, at least in part, on the target believing that certain actions will fail or incur cost. Hidden capability works poorly for that purpose. An adversary cannot be reliably deterred by something it does not know exists. The named concept is invisible strength. Explain it, and the contradiction appears. The better a service is at preserving secret access, the worse it may be at publicly shaping behaviour through that access. This is why intelligence and deterrence sit uneasily together. One rewards concealment. The other often requires some form of revelation, or at least a credible hint. The implication is that actors must decide not only what they can do, but what kind of effect they value more: continuing secret access or outward influence on an adversary's choices.

The Zimmermann episode illuminates one answer to that dilemma: selective revelation. Britain did not simply burn the capability or keep the message permanently hidden. It sought a middle path, revealing enough to achieve a political effect while disguising enough to protect the broader cryptanalytic position. This is a recurring pattern. A service may disclose the result while concealing the route. It may leak confidence without exposing mechanics. It may share information with a narrow partner set while preserving public ambiguity. The named concept is managed disclosure. Explain it, and the strategic implication becomes clear. The question is rarely whether to reveal everything or nothing. The harder question is whether the capability can be used in a way that preserves uncertainty about its precise origin, scope, or persistence.

Still, managed disclosure is treacherous. It assumes the target will not infer too much, that allies or subordinates will keep discipline, that the explanation offered will remain plausible, and that the capability is not so distinctive that even limited use points back to its source. This is where many neat theories about signalling begin to wobble. A sophisticated adversary studies not only what was revealed, but what had to be known in order for that revelation to occur. The abstraction of credibility becomes visible in the adversary's analysis: who could have known this, through which route, with what technical means, and with what consistency over time? The implication is that even partial signalling teaches. An actor hoping to deter by hinting at hidden capability may end up educating its target about which walls to reinforce.

A second historical example shows the same logic under different conditions. The long secrecy surrounding parts of Allied codebreaking in the Second World War did not end with the war itself. For years afterwards, knowledge about what had been broken, and how, remained tightly controlled. That secrecy did not merely protect institutional prestige or old paperwork. It reflected a continuing belief that methods, assumptions, and analytic practices could retain future relevance if their history remained obscure. The named concept is temporal spillover. Explain it, and one sees that capabilities are not always bounded by the conflict in which they first proved useful. The implication is that actors may hide what they once could do not only to protect a current stream of access, but to preserve the ambiguity from which future access might grow.

A credible limitation belongs here. Secrecy does not always serve the holder best. There are cases in which withholding knowledge about a break or weakness allows harm to continue, prevents allies or domestic institutions from defending themselves, or forfeits a chance to shape adversary behaviour before damage spreads. A capability that remains perfectly secret may also remain strategically mute. Worse still, a service can become so attached to preserving access that it mistakes possession for influence. Hidden knowledge is not the same as changed outcomes. This limitation matters because it keeps the argument honest. Secrecy is valuable, but it is not sacred. An actor that never reveals anything may preserve access and still fail to alter the world in the direction it prefers.

That limitation strengthens the central argument rather than weakening it. Because secrecy has costs as well as benefits, the real dilemma is not whether concealment is good in the abstract. It is when to reveal, and to whom. The answer depends on the value of continuing access, the urgency of the threat, the plausibility of controlled disclosure, the probability that revelation will induce useful defensive or deterrent behaviour, and the likelihood that the capability can be regenerated by other means. These are not purely technical judgments. They are strategic judgments about time. Use the capability now and risk losing tomorrow's view, or preserve tomorrow's view and accept that today's target may continue acting under false confidence.

This temporal problem explains why internal audiences often become restless. Policymakers want proof. Military leaders want reasons for action. Publics want accountability. Partner services want sharing. Each demand pulls against the logic of access preservation. The service holding the capability therefore faces not only an external adversary but an internal audience management problem. The visible behaviours that follow are familiar: compartmentation, vague briefings, sanitised intelligence reports, and decisions justified by downstream effects rather than upstream collection. The implication is that secrecy about capabilities is never merely external concealment. It is also internal rationing of knowledge to prevent one's own side from accidentally burning what it values most.

This is where credibility becomes such a difficult word. Public credibility often asks for evidence. Operational credibility inside intelligence work often depends on not exposing the evidence too directly. A service may be entirely truthful in substance and still unable to prove that truth in ways outsiders find satisfying. That gap can breed suspicion, theatrical overstatement, or clumsy signalling designed to reassure without fully revealing. The result is a dangerous middle terrain in which states hint, imply, and posture around capabilities they cannot safely demonstrate cleanly. Sometimes this works. Sometimes it produces precisely the opposite effect, encouraging adversaries to test boundaries because the signal lacks verifiable weight. The sealed window remains useful, but its very invisibility complicates the effort to frighten anyone away from the building.

The sealed window returns here for a final reason. The person inside the room may behave very differently depending on whether they know they are observed. Intelligence secrecy tries to keep them natural. Deterrence tries to make them cautious. One wants the curtain open without the occupant realising it. The other wants the occupant to glance at the glass and hesitate. That is why the tension never resolves neatly. It is built into the purpose of the capability itself.

The hard question, then, is not whether actors conceal what they can break. They often do, and for good strategic reasons. The harder question is when preserving silent access ceases to be wiser than spending some of that secrecy to shape behaviour - and whether any revelation can ever be precise enough to deter effectively without also teaching the target exactly where the curtain no longer holds.

## Commercial actors as intelligence terrain

In December 2020, when the compromise of SolarWinds became public in Austin, Texas, the headlines quite reasonably focused on espionage, software updates, and the alarming reach of a poisoned supply chain. The deeper lesson was less theatrical and more enduring. The operation did not need to batter down every target's front gate one by one. It moved through a vendor pathway already trusted to enter. A mechanism built for maintenance became a route for collection. The delivery van had become the scene of the crime.

That episode remains a sharp starting point because it strips away a comforting illusion. Many institutions still imagine intelligence competition as something that happens between states, or between a state and a target, with private firms acting as neutral infrastructure in the background. That picture is no longer adequate. Cloud providers, telecoms, software vendors, identity services, managed security firms, and update channels are not merely service layers around the real action. They are part of the terrain on which access is won, hidden, defended, and sometimes quietly normalised. A modern organisation may own its data, set its policies, and deploy strong cryptography, yet still depend on commercial intermediaries for identity, storage, routing, administration, telemetry, and trusted code execution. The target is no longer just the message or the server. It is the relationship.

The service entrance stays busy.

That modest image is useful because commercial actors are often most important where they look least dramatic. They patch systems, distribute updates, authenticate users, move traffic, host workloads, terminate sessions, store logs, and provide support access. Show the scene and the strategic point becomes obvious. An intelligence service or sophisticated intruder looking at a hardened organisation must decide where access can be gained most cheaply and preserved most quietly. The named concept is intermediary concentration. Explain it, and the implication follows. The vendor serving a thousand customers may be more attractive than the customer with a thousand employees, because the vendor already possesses trust at scale. Where trust concentrates, pressure follows.

This does not mean commercial actors are secretly sovereign powers in disguise, nor that every cloud provider or telecom is a willing adjunct of intelligence competition. That would be melodrama in a respectable tie. The point is more structural. Modern systems rely on public-private arrangements in which technical trust, contractual obligation, and jurisdictional exposure overlap uneasily. A provider may be bound by service agreements, subject to regulatory and legal demands, dependent on multiple subcontractors, exposed to insider risk, and entrusted with functions that customers once kept in-house. The abstraction of dependency becomes visible in ordinary actions: a single sign-on provider authorises access across the estate, a managed detection service ingests sensitive telemetry, a telecom operator handles location-rich traffic, a cloud platform controls administrative boundaries, a security vendor pushes updates into privileged systems. The implication is severe. Security decisions made by the customer are no longer the whole security story.

Cloud providers are the clearest illustration because they collapse so many traditional boundaries at once. They host computation, store archives, manage keys, provide identity services, log activity, and often shape the practical meaning of network segmentation. A customer may encrypt data and still rely on the provider's control plane to define who can access which workloads, under what identity, from which region, and with what administrative visibility. The named concept here is platform dependence. Explain it, and the strategic lesson sharpens. In such environments, intelligence competition can shift away from defeating the customer's chosen cryptography and towards the cloud relationships surrounding it. The goal may be metadata, administrative access, support pathways, or influence over the management layer rather than direct compromise of content itself. The implication is not that cloud is uniquely unsafe. It is that cloud centralises power in ways that make it strategic terrain by design.

Telecoms occupy a different but equally consequential position. Even when content is well protected, telecom operators often sit close to routing, location, timing, subscriber identity, and traffic patterns. That makes them valuable not only for content collection where available, but for metadata, movement inference, and service shaping. Show the scene and the attraction is plain. A handset uses secure applications and modern transport protection. The named concept is transport adjacency. Explain it, and one sees why telecom infrastructure remains intelligence terrain. The operator may not hold the plaintext, but it can remain close to when, where, and how communications occur. The implication is broader than traditional wiretapping narratives. Intelligence advantage may come from mobility patterns, network relationships, roaming behaviour, and timing signals rather than the message body.

Security vendors form an especially awkward category because they are trusted precisely to reduce risk. Their products observe endpoints, inspect traffic, manage certificates, authenticate users, orchestrate updates, and provide incident response. In other words, they often sit near the most sensitive and operationally decisive layers of an organisation. The named concept is protective proximity. Explain it, and the paradox emerges. The closer a vendor stands to the system in order to defend it, the more strategically valuable that vendor becomes to anyone seeking access, influence, or intelligence at scale. This does not make security companies hypocrites or villains. It makes them important. A managed security service or endpoint platform that sees broadly across many environments can become a remarkable concentration of trust, telemetry, and administrative privilege.

The SolarWinds example is useful here not simply because it was dramatic, but because it illustrated how a vendor update channel can become a contested pathway. Customers trusted the update mechanism because refusing to trust it would mean refusing the maintenance model on which modern software depends. That is the ordinary tragedy of the matter. The named concept is routine entry. Explain it, and the larger implication follows. The most strategically valuable pathways are often the ones that already look normal. An update channel, certificate renewal process, identity federation, remote support tool, or telemetry feed does not need to look suspicious to matter. Its very normality is what grants scale and persistence. A vendor pathway becomes intelligence terrain not because it is exotic, but because it is woven into daily function.

A second useful example lies in identity services run or supported by major commercial platforms. Many organisations now rely on external or vendor-managed identity infrastructure to authenticate users, devices, applications, and administrators across large estates. This can be sensible and efficient. It also creates a concentration of failure and pressure. If identity is the new perimeter, then commercial identity providers become terrain on which strategic contest naturally converges. The visible behaviours are ordinary enough: federated sign-in, device enrolment, token issuance, multifactor workflows, conditional access policies. The implication is profound. Compromise or coercive pressure at that layer can yield access more efficiently than attacking encrypted traffic directly. When an organisation outsources much of its trust choreography, the dance floor changes owners.

Still, a credible limitation is necessary. It would be foolish to write as though dependence on commercial actors were always a strategic blunder. Most modern organisations cannot build and operate everything themselves, and many commercial providers deliver security, resilience, and expertise far beyond what their customers could sustain alone. A well-run cloud platform may be safer than a neglected private server room. A disciplined managed identity service may outperform a patchwork of local improvisation. A mature telecom or security vendor may absorb defensive burdens that would otherwise collapse under local incompetence. The point is not to sneer at outsourcing from the lofty hilltop of fantasy self-sufficiency.

That concession sharpens the real argument rather than weakening it. The issue is not whether public-private dependency should exist. It already does, and often productively. The issue is whether institutions understand the strategic consequences of the dependency. A mature customer asks not only whether the service works, but where the trust sits, what support pathways exist, what logging is retained, how updates are delivered, what subcontractors or embedded suppliers matter, how administrative access is governed, what contractual rights shape visibility and obligation, and what happens when the vendor's interests diverge from the customer's need for clarity. These are not legal questions in the narrow sense, nor purely technical ones. They are governance questions about who is really in the room when sensitive systems are maintained.

Jurisdictional and contractual pressures intensify the difficulty precisely because they are often both ordinary and opaque. A provider operates under multiple legal regimes, serves multiple customer classes, and may confront demands, obligations, or constraints its customers only partly understand. Even without naming any specific law or claiming any universal outcome, the structural point holds. Commercial actors do not exist in a vacuum. They inhabit political and contractual environments that shape what they can disclose, resist, expedite, delay, or quietly accommodate. The named concept here is layered obligation. Explain it, and the strategic implication becomes plain. When an organisation entrusts critical functions to a commercial intermediary, it also inherits part of that intermediary's legal and contractual weather system. The customer may not control when that weather changes.

This is why public-private dependency complicates security decisions in ways that simple slogans cannot capture. "Trust the specialist" is too easy. So is "keep everything in-house." The real work is comparative and institutional. Which functions create the greatest concentration of trusted access? Which providers offer genuine transparency about architecture, support, and incident handling? Which dependencies can be diversified, and which have become too central to move easily? Which update channels, identity systems, and telemetry paths create silent concentrations of intelligence value? These are not anti-vendor questions. They are adult questions. They treat commercial relationships as part of the security perimeter rather than as neutral utilities outside it.

The service entrance returns here for a final reason. People like to imagine that important systems are breached through dramatic frontal assaults because it flatters the defenders. In reality, the service entrance is busy with cleaners, contractors, delivery staff, maintenance crews, support engineers, update packages, identity tokens, and monitoring feeds. It is exactly the sort of place a serious intruder studies patiently. Commercial actors matter because they manage much of that traffic now. Their trust is real. So is the strategic value of standing where that trust passes.

The hard question, then, is not whether cloud providers, telecoms, and security vendors are part of the security environment. They obviously are. The harder question is whether the institutions relying on them can distinguish between useful dependence and unexamined exposure: between a trusted service and a contested pathway, between operational convenience and strategic concentration, between buying expertise and quietly outsourcing part of the terrain on which intelligence competition is actually being fought.

## Counterintelligence and internal discipline

In June 2013, when Edward Snowden left Hawaii with a vast cache of highly sensitive National Security Agency material and then surfaced in Hong Kong, the public argument quickly turned to surveillance, secrecy, and the politics of disclosure. Beneath the spectacle sat a duller and more unsettling lesson. The organisation involved was not short of advanced cryptography, hardened networks, or technical sophistication. Yet a determined insider had still managed to collect, move, and reveal extraordinary volumes of protected information. The vault doors were real. So was the fact that someone inside the vault had learned how to walk through too many of them.

That case endures because it strips away one of the most persistent fantasies in security culture: the belief that strong encryption and modern cryptographic architecture can somehow compensate for weak internal discipline. They cannot. Cryptography can protect data against outsiders, raise the cost of interception, and narrow certain avenues of access. It cannot by itself decide who should see what, who should be able to copy what, who should be able to combine distinct compartments of knowledge, or who should notice when ordinary access stops looking ordinary. Those are not mathematical questions. They are institutional ones.

The badge opens the door.

That plain image is worth keeping close because counterintelligence in a cryptographically mature organisation often begins not with broken ciphers but with authorised presence. Show the scene and the problem becomes concrete. An employee, contractor, administrator, analyst, or engineer has legitimate access to one part of a system. The named concept is trusted adjacency. Explain it, and the strategic implication follows. Once someone stands near the data, the key store, the logging layer, the release pipeline, or the identity system with broadly accepted credentials, the remaining challenge for an adversary may be less about defeating encryption than about exploiting proximity, routine, weak oversight, or institutional complacency. The implication is severe. The strongest algorithm in the building is much less decisive if the badge reader, approval process, and audit culture remain sloppy.

This is why compartmentation still matters even in highly encrypted environments. Compartmentation is not simply the old spy novel idea of fragmented secrets and need-to-know access. It is a practical discipline for preventing any one person, team, or service role from assembling more of the picture than their task genuinely requires. The abstraction of control becomes visible in specific design choices: separate administrative roles, narrow permissions, segmented data access, strong boundaries between production and development, restricted visibility into archives, and differentiated oversight for identity, key management, and operational telemetry. The implication is straightforward. If an insider, coerced administrator, or compromised account can traverse too many compartments without resistance, then the institution has already translated cryptographic strength into a false sense of safety.

A useful example lies in administrative overreach. Many organisations centralise trust quietly through a small number of privileged accounts, support paths, or platform operators who can issue certificates, recover data, alter logging, enrol devices, or access encrypted stores through legitimate channels. This can be efficient. It can also be dangerous. The named concept here is privilege compression. Explain it, and the strategic problem sharpens. The more an institution compresses critical authority into a narrow band of highly trusted identities, the more it creates attractive targets for insider recruitment, coercion, blackmail, burnout, and simple abuse. Counterintelligence begins at the point of asking not merely who is technically authorised, but whether the pattern of authorisation has created concentrations of power out of proportion to the organisation's ability to supervise them.

Snowden's case illuminated this brutally. The public record revealed not some magical defeat of cryptography, but a deeper problem of access accumulation, oversight weakness, and the gap between formal controls and practical reality. The named concept is mission drift in access. Explain it, and the lesson becomes harder to shrug off. Roles expand over time. Technical staff receive broader visibility to solve operational problems. Contractors inherit responsibilities that were supposed to be temporary. Auditing grows noisy and then decorative. Data that was notionally compartmented becomes more reachable through convenience tooling, search functions, or cultural deference to cleared insiders. The implication extends far beyond any one case. An institution may believe it has protected secrets because those secrets are encrypted, classified, or segmented on paper, while the lived system quietly permits too much assembly by those already inside.

A second named example comes from Chelsea Manning's disclosures in 2010, which again showed that highly sensitive state information can move outward through an insider who is not defeating cryptographic protections so much as operating within a trusted environment whose controls were insufficiently restrictive or insufficiently observed. The strategic point is not to relitigate motives or politics. It is to observe a pattern. Where large volumes of sensitive information are accessible to insiders for legitimate work, the decisive question is not whether the files are encrypted at rest or transmitted securely in transit. It is whether the institution can detect unusual aggregation, copying, access patterns, and cross-compartment behaviour before ordinary access becomes extraordinary extraction. The implication is plain. Cryptography protects the container. Counterintelligence watches the hands.

This is where auditing becomes essential, but only if one treats it as a means of disciplined observation rather than ceremonial recordkeeping. Many organisations collect vast quantities of audit data and then behave as though the act of collection itself had solved the problem. It has not. Logs that nobody reads intelligently, alerts that drown in false positives, and dashboards that flatter administrators with activity graphs while failing to expose anomalous privilege use are forms of institutional self-soothing, not counterintelligence. The named concept is inert visibility. Explain it, and one sees the deeper risk. An organisation can generate perfect technical traces of misuse and still remain strategically blind if it lacks the analytical discipline, escalation norms, and managerial seriousness to act on what those traces reveal.

Compartmentation and auditing belong together because each compensates for the other's limits. Compartmentation reduces the damage any one insider or compromised identity can do. Auditing helps discover when those boundaries are being tested, bypassed, or quietly eroded. Without compartmentation, auditing can become little more than a detailed obituary for a system that granted too much power in the first place. Without auditing, compartmentation can decay into a static permission model no one notices has been undermined by exceptions, inherited roles, and administrative shortcuts. The badge opens the door; the log should tell you when the badge is wandering where it ought not to be.

Still, a credible limitation must be stated clearly. No serious institution can function if every trusted employee is treated as a latent traitor and every privileged action is slowed to paralysis by bureaucratic suspicion. Counterintelligence can become self-defeating when it destroys the trust, speed, and initiative that real organisations need in order to work. A military unit, hospital, intelligence service, or large technical enterprise cannot be run as a permanent internal sting operation without corroding judgment and morale. Total suspicion is not discipline. It is institutional acid.

Yet that concession strengthens the real argument rather than weakening it. The goal is not universal mistrust. The goal is structured trust. Structured trust means giving people enough access to do real work while designing systems that assume human frailty, coercion risk, divided loyalties, role drift, and ordinary temptation. It means using separation of duties where power would otherwise concentrate dangerously. It means reviewing privileged access as a living governance problem rather than a one-time approval. It means ensuring that auditing distinguishes meaningful anomaly from routine noise. It means building processes that can escalate concern without theatrical accusation. The implication is that mature counterintelligence is not paranoid. It is administrative realism.

This becomes especially important in commercial and hybrid public-private environments, where contractors, vendors, and managed service personnel often stand close to sensitive systems. An organisation may trust its own staff discipline while quietly expanding its exposure through external identities granted broad operational powers. The named concept here is perimeter outsourcing. Explain it, and the strategic issue becomes sharper. A vendor engineer, support contractor, cloud operator, or security service analyst can occupy a position functionally equivalent to an insider even when payroll and legal identity sit elsewhere. Counterintelligence therefore cannot stop at the boundary of formal employment. The institution has to map who can act, not just who belongs.

The same logic applies to cryptographic posture itself. Strong key management, well-designed identity infrastructure, disciplined certificate issuance, and careful backup governance do not replace internal discipline; they increase its stakes. The more an institution relies on cryptography to organise trust, the more valuable the people and processes governing cryptographic action become. A weak password reset path, an incautious recovery workflow, a support override, a certificate issuance shortcut, or an emergency administrative exception can turn mathematically strong systems into politically weak ones. The implication is not anti-technical. It is precisely the opposite. Technical strength concentrates the importance of the human and administrative chokepoints around it.

This is why counterintelligence should not be understood only as the dramatic search for a spy. Most of the time it is quieter. It is the discipline of preventing trusted access from widening unnoticed, of noticing when privilege use becomes behaviourally strange, of ensuring that no one role can both authorise and conceal sensitive action, of keeping archives, identities, and key systems from becoming soft internal monopolies. It is the refusal to let operational convenience become a standing excuse for dissolving boundaries that exist for a reason. The strongest institutions are rarely those with the most suspicious rhetoric. They are those whose routines make betrayal, coercion, and misuse harder to scale.

The badge returns here because it remains a better guide than most grand theories. People often imagine security as a contest between the outsider and the wall. Much of the serious work lies in asking who is already inside, what they can touch, who can watch them, and how quickly the organisation notices when its own trust model has been stretched beyond what discipline can carry. The badge opens the door, but it should not open every door, and it should never move without leaving a trail someone is truly prepared to follow.

The unresolved question, then, is not whether an institution uses strong cryptography. The harder question is whether its internal discipline is strong enough that trusted access remains meaningfully bounded, observable, and governable once the mathematics has already done its part - or whether the next serious compromise will again reveal that the cipher held while the institution around it quietly forgot how to watch its own hands.

## Chapter 12

# Deterrence, Signalling, and Credibility

Can a state, company, or institution deter an adversary from touching information it cannot prove the adversary has ever tried to steal, using capabilities it cannot safely display in full, in a domain where successful collection is often silent and attribution is often murky? The question sounds almost unfair, which is precisely why it matters. Deterrence in cryptographic affairs is often discussed with a confidence borrowed from other strategic settings, yet the underlying conditions are far less obliging. Visibility is patchy. Proof is selective. The most consequential moves may leave no public crater at all.

That mismatch has encouraged a great deal of loose language. People speak as though strong encryption automatically deters intrusion, or as though public statements about being prepared will somehow cause adversaries to retreat in respectful silence. Neither claim survives contact with reality. Some behaviours can be influenced. Some can be made costlier, less reliable, or less politically attractive. Others remain stubbornly hard to deter because they thrive on secrecy, deniability, and patience. Quiet collection, in particular, has a nasty strategic advantage: it often imposes little immediate visible harm, creates little public evidence, and therefore leaves the victim guessing whether deterrence has failed, succeeded, or never really engaged.

The lock on the door helps.

That modest image is useful because it keeps the subject grounded. A lock can deter some things. It can discourage casual tampering, increase the time and effort required for entry, and signal that intrusion will not be frictionless. It cannot by itself deter a patient observer from watching the house, learning the occupants' habits, or returning later with better tools. Cryptographic deterrence works in much the same way. It may credibly shape behaviour around broad interception, blunt manipulation, and certain coercive uses of stolen data by making those actions harder to scale, easier to expose, or less likely to succeed cleanly. It is much weaker against silent collection that remains unattributed and unadvertised. The central tension is therefore not whether deterrence exists, but what kind of behaviour it can realistically touch.

That question matters because policy and institutional strategy become unserious when they claim too much. If everything is deterrable, then any breach becomes evidence of failure. If nothing is deterrable, then investment in readiness, disclosure discipline, and visible resilience begins to look ornamental. Neither extreme is useful. The serious ground lies between them: some behaviours are responsive to cost, exposure, and demonstrated capacity to recover. Others are not easily moved by such signals because they are quiet, opportunistic, or too cheap to abandon. A mature institution must know the difference, not merely for analytical tidiness, but to avoid performing strength where only patience and repair are possible.

This is why signalling matters so much, and why it so often goes wrong. In military settings, deterrence is frequently imagined through visible weaponry or explicit red lines. In cryptographic settings, showing the secret often destroys its value. Revealing that one can read a channel, inspect a pathway, or attribute a method too precisely may simply teach the adversary what to change. Yet saying nothing leaves others uncertain whether any real capacity or resolve exists. The answer, more often than institutions prefer to admit, lies not in signalling secret powers but in signalling readiness: inventories kept current, migration capacity rehearsed, update paths demonstrated, damage containment practised, and public commitments tied to things the organisation can actually prove it will do under pressure.

That shift from secret capability to visible governance changes the meaning of strength. A resilient institution may deter not because it can promise invulnerability, but because it can show that tampering will be noticed, weak points will be migrated, stolen data will be rendered less useful over time, and recovery will occur faster than the adversary expects. Such signalling is less glamorous than boasting about hidden mastery. It is also more credible. Adversaries often study maintenance discipline more carefully than public rhetoric. They notice whether a target can rotate algorithms, retire trust anchors, limit blast radius, and communicate calmly under strain. Readiness, in that sense, becomes a language of resolve that does not require exposing the most sensitive details of how the institution sees.

The route ahead therefore runs from the difficult but necessary work of defining what behaviours can plausibly be deterred, into the question of how an institution can signal readiness without squandering its own security by overexplaining, and then into the danger that follows whenever incidents are read too quickly as evidence of strategic intent, hidden capability, or impending escalation. The order matters. Without realistic boundaries, deterrence becomes boastful fog. Without credible signalling, resilience remains invisible. Without caution about misperception, even honest defensive action can be misread as provocation or proof of something it was never meant to show.

A cracked mirror is the right secondary image here. Cryptographic incidents rarely reflect the whole reality cleanly. A breach may reveal poor hygiene rather than extraordinary hostile capability. A failed migration may look like sabotage when it is merely brittle design meeting old clients. A single successful intrusion may be treated as evidence that an adversary can read everything, while in truth it exploited one contingent weakness. The temptation to infer far too much from one broken reflection is strong, especially under political pressure. That temptation itself becomes dangerous, because institutions that mistake noise for proof may escalate rhetorically, overcorrect strategically, or signal a level of certainty their evidence cannot sustain.

This makes credibility the chapter's deepest concern. Credibility is not loudness. It is not the theatrical announcement that one takes cyber and cryptographic threats very seriously indeed, delivered with the usual polished gravitas and very little oxygen. Credibility comes from matching claims to demonstrable behaviour. If an institution says it can update rapidly, it must be able to point to update discipline. If it says it can contain damage, it must know where trust is anchored and how responsibilities are assigned. If it says a breach does not imply systemic compromise, it must show why without drifting into wishful mysticism. The lock on the door matters only if the frame is sound and the occupants know which windows are still open.

The difficult question, then, is not whether deterrence belongs in the cryptographic story. It does. The harder question is whether institutions can speak about it with enough realism to avoid hollow threats, enough openness to make resilience visible, and enough restraint to stop every ambiguous breach from being inflated into a strategic revelation. Only then does deterrence stop sounding like a borrowed slogan and start becoming a disciplined way of thinking about costs, signals, and the uneasy politics of being believed.

## What can be deterred in cryptography

In October 2013, when reports emerged that Belgian telecom operator Belgacom had been compromised in an operation later linked in public reporting to a state intelligence service, the strategic point was not merely that a network had been penetrated. It was that a communications system sitting near large volumes of traffic, routing data, and service relationships had become a contested instrument of influence. The case did not prove that all encrypted content had become futile, nor that deterrence had wholly failed. It showed something more exacting. Some actions in the cryptographic environment are noisy, scalable, and politically risky enough to be influenced. Others remain quiet, deniable, and stubbornly attractive despite improved defences.

That distinction matters because deterrence in cryptographic affairs is often discussed with the grand confidence of nuclear theory and the evidentiary discipline of a pub argument. Strong encryption is said to deter surveillance. Harsh public warnings are said to deter interference. Better standards are said to deter hostile collection. These claims usually contain a grain of truth wrapped in a loaf of wishful thinking. Cryptography can alter incentives. It does not abolish them. The task is therefore not to ask whether deterrence exists in some total sense, but to identify which behaviours are plausibly moved by visible costs, visible failure, and visible consequence.

The lock does some work.

That simple image is the right place to begin because a lock does not deter everything equally. It discourages certain intrusions because they become harder, slower, more obvious, or less scalable. It does not prevent someone from watching the house, bribing the caretaker, or copying a key elsewhere. Show the scene and the logic sharpens. A state, company, or organisation uses strong cryptography, disciplined key management, and visible migration practices. The named concept is selective deterrence. Explain it, and the implication follows. Some hostile acts become less appealing because they are more likely to fail noisily or to produce evidence that will trigger response. Other hostile acts remain tempting because they stay quiet, cheap, and deniable. The consequence is that deterrence in cryptography must be grounded in observable effects, not in slogans about total protection.

Tampering is one of the clearest behaviours that can sometimes be deterred. It is often easier to detect than passive collection, and detection matters because visible failure changes the political and operational cost of interference. A digital signature that fails, an update that no longer verifies, a certificate mismatch, an integrity alert, or an audit trail showing unauthorised change can all transform covert meddling into something riskier. The named concept here is evidentiary friction. Explain it, and the strategic point becomes plain. When cryptographic integrity mechanisms are well deployed and trusted operationally, they raise the probability that tampering will be exposed in a form others can act upon. That can deter broad, crude, or scalable attempts to alter data or software because the benefit no longer cleanly exceeds the reputational and operational cost of being caught.

Software update systems offer a good example. A signed update pathway does not make malicious interference impossible. It does make unsophisticated or mass tampering more difficult and, when detection works properly, more politically expensive. An adversary contemplating broad manipulation of a widely deployed update channel must now account not only for the technical challenge, but for the risk that a broken verification chain, unexpected signature, or widespread integrity failure will expose the action quickly and publicly. The implication is not that update ecosystems are safe by default. As incidents involving software supply chains have shown, trusted channels can still be abused. The deterrent effect lies in the increased need for stealth, precision, and upstream access. Tampering has not vanished. It has become costlier to do clumsily.

Broad interception can also be deterred to a degree, especially when the relevant systems make passive mass collection less fruitful and more operationally expensive. Strong transport security, authenticated endpoints, disciplined certificate validation, and rapid retirement of weak cryptographic pathways can make indiscriminate interception a less efficient strategy. The named concept is collection inflation. Explain it, and the meaning becomes clear. Broad interception becomes harder when one must either compromise more endpoints, obtain more trusted access, or tolerate much lower content yield. A state or large-scale intruder may still attempt it, but the economics worsen. Where deterrence is plausible, it arises not because adversaries become morally persuaded, but because the cost of scale rises and the visible signs of interference or failure multiply.

This matters especially for broad rather than narrow collection. A highly resourced actor may still target a few individuals or systems through endpoints, identities, or supply chains. Broad, routine interception across many users is more sensitive to cost and visibility. A security architecture that forces an interceptor away from easy mass collection and towards bespoke compromise has achieved something strategically important. It has not made itself unreadable in every circumstance. It has narrowed the range of cheap, scalable, plausibly deniable options. That is exactly the kind of behaviour deterrence can sometimes influence, because the adversary must now choose whether the additional investment, exposure, and maintenance burden are worth it.

Certain coercive uses of stolen data can also be influenced by deterrence, though here the mechanism is usually indirect. If an institution can show that data has been minimised, segmented, re-encrypted, rotated, or rendered harder to authenticate and weaponise, then some kinds of coercion become less attractive. The named concept is usability denial. Explain it, and the strategic effect appears. Stolen data is not equally useful in every form. A cache that is difficult to verify publicly, incomplete enough to weaken blackmail, old enough to be contextually muddied, or subject to rapid remedial action may still cause harm but may no longer deliver the same clean coercive leverage. The implication is that deterrence can sometimes operate not by preventing theft entirely, but by reducing the confidence that stolen material will convert smoothly into influence.

This is one reason why visible damage limitation matters. Suppose an organisation can credibly demonstrate that compromised credentials are rapidly revoked, sensitive archives are re-keyed, signing chains are rotated, and exposed material has limited enduring utility because of retention discipline or compartmentation. In that case, a hostile actor contemplating coercive release or manipulation must consider whether the data will still yield the desired pressure once the target responds. That is not full deterrence. It is deterrence of a narrower and more practical sort: discouraging some uses by reducing expected payoff. The lock does some work here too. It does not stop the theft retroactively. It alters what the theft can buy.

Still, the boundaries matter, and this is where quiet collection must be treated with cold realism. Quiet collection is hard to deter because it is often designed to remain below the threshold of visible failure, visible harm, and visible proof. An adversary who can collect without tampering, without broad disruption, without public signature, and without obvious operational consequence enjoys the strategic advantages of secrecy and deniability at once. The named concept is low-observability advantage.

Explain it, and the difficulty becomes unmistakable. Deterrence relies, at least in part, on an adversary perceiving that an action will be costly, attributable, or likely to fail. Quiet collection erodes each condition. If the target cannot detect it reliably, cannot attribute it confidently, and cannot demonstrate it persuasively, then threats of response become abstract and often unconvincing.

This is why policy claims about "deterring cyber espionage" or "deterring decryption" so often sprawl beyond what the evidence can sustain. Espionage conducted through discreet endpoint compromise, insider recruitment, supply-chain positioning, or long-term metadata collection may simply not present the sort of observable event on which deterrence feeds. The absence of noise is part of its value. The implication is not defeatism. It is analytical hygiene. Institutions can make such collection harder, more expensive, slower, and less scalable. They should not pretend that they can reliably frighten it away merely by declaring resolve.

A useful contrast can be drawn between broad tampering and quiet observation. A mass manipulation of software updates, a widespread certificate abuse event, or overt interference with integrity protections is more likely to trip alarms, trigger public blame, and impose visible political costs. A patient adversary quietly collecting metadata, compromising a few carefully chosen endpoints, or using a trusted maintenance path sparingly may escape those costs for long periods. The strategic lesson is almost embarrassingly simple. Deterrence works better against things others can see. It works poorly against things others can only suspect.

A credible limitation deserves emphasis here. Even among the behaviours that are more plausibly deterred, success is never guaranteed. Strong integrity protections do not always reveal tampering quickly enough. Broad interception may still be attempted by actors willing to bear higher costs. Coercive uses of stolen data may proceed even when its utility is imperfect, because imperfection does not always spoil political effect. It would be foolish to speak as though visible resilience mechanically produces adversarial restraint. Human institutions are too strange for such neatness, and hostile actors are often willing to gamble on ambiguity. The prudent claim is narrower. Some behaviours become less attractive under certain visible defensive conditions. That is already worth something.

Indeed, recognising these limits helps institutions communicate more credibly. A mature organisation does not promise to deter all hostile collection. It states that certain actions - broad tampering, widespread interception, some public coercive uses of stolen material - can be made less likely or less rewarding when integrity checks, rapid recovery, segmentation, and migration readiness are visible and believable. It also states that some hostile acts, especially quiet collection, remain difficult to deter directly and must instead be managed through detection, resilience, compartmentation, and long-term reduction of adversarial opportunity. That distinction sounds less heroic than many policy speeches prefer. It is also vastly more useful.

This realism matters because overclaiming deterrence creates two strategic hazards. The first is false comfort. Leaders may imagine that strong cryptography and firm public language have frightened away adversaries when those adversaries have simply shifted to quieter methods. The second is false crisis. If any breach is taken as proof that deterrence has collapsed entirely, institutions may lurch into overreaction, misattribute motives, or escalate on the basis of a poor theory of what was ever realistically deterable in the first place. A disciplined concept of deterrence helps avoid both errors. It anchors expectation to the kinds of hostile behaviour that produce observable effects and therefore can plausibly be influenced by visible readiness and visible consequence.

The lock returns here because it continues to say exactly what the theory should say. A lock can deter forceful, clumsy, or scalable intrusion. It cannot by itself deter watchfulness, patience, or betrayal from within. The same is true in cryptographic affairs. Strong protections, good governance, and credible recovery can discourage certain forms of tampering, raise the cost of mass interception, and blunt some forms of coercive exploitation. They do not make secret collection vanish into the moral night. That is too much to ask of any lock, however well made.

The hard question, then, is not whether cryptography can deter. It can, in bounded and practical ways. The harder question is whether institutions can name those bounds honestly enough to guide strategy: deterring what is visible, recoverable, and politically costly, while refusing to pretend that the quiet observer in the dark will always be frightened away merely because the front door has acquired a stronger bolt.

## Signalling readiness rather than secrets

In August 2024, when the National Institute of Standards and Technology published its first final post-quantum cryptography standards in Gaithersburg, Maryland, many organisations faced an awkward communications choice. They could imply that they were now prepared for a profound technical shift, or they could admit that a standard on paper and readiness in practice were not the same thing at all. The first option offered immediate reassurance. The second offered credibility. Most institutions, when pressed in public, are tempted to choose reassurance and call it strategy.

That temptation is dangerous because the most credible signals in cryptographic affairs rarely come from announcing hidden strengths. They come from visible evidence that an institution can adapt without panic. Secret capabilities are inherently difficult to use as public signals. Reveal too much, and one teaches an adversary where to change course. Reveal too little, and one sounds like a bureaucrat in a fine suit muttering incantations about resilience. The more useful alternative is often humbler. Show that the organisation knows what it owns, can change what it uses, and has rehearsed how to respond when trust assumptions shift. The spare key is not the point. The lock maintenance log is.

The drill matters more.

That plain sentence captures the chapter's strategic turn. Institutions often think of signalling through the language of secrets: what they can detect, what they might retaliate against, what they privately know. In cryptographic matters, that language is usually weaker than it looks. A hidden capability may remain strategically precious precisely because it cannot be displayed. Governance, by contrast, can often be shown without giving the game away. Show the scene and the distinction becomes clear. A ministry, cloud provider, bank, or public service wants to convince adversaries, partners, customers, and internal leadership that it is not an easy target for future cryptographic shock. The named concept is demonstrable preparedness. Explain it, and the implication follows. A current inventory of cryptographic dependencies, a credible migration plan, and a tested ability to update algorithms rapidly tell outsiders something operationally meaningful: this institution may still be attacked, but it will be harder to surprise, harder to paralyse, and harder to trap inside stale assumptions.

This is why signalling readiness rather than secrets can be so powerful. It shifts the basis of deterrence away from unverifiable boasts and towards observable discipline. An adversary trying to decide whether a target is worth broad tampering, long-term harvest, or coercive exploitation cares not only about what the target can currently withstand, but about how quickly the target can adapt when the environment changes. The abstraction of trust becomes visible in specific behaviours: public commitments to rapid algorithm updates, published deprecation schedules, vendor requirements for cryptographic agility, rehearsed incident governance, transparent statements about migration phases, and evidence that legacy exposure is being actively reduced rather than lovingly archived for future regret. The implication is straightforward. Deterrence can rest on resilience because resilience changes the expected payoff of attack.

A useful example lies in public commitments to rapid algorithm updates. Such commitments do not need to expose the details of every dependency graph or the quirks of every internal system. They do something subtler and often more valuable. They tell observers that the institution has already accepted cryptographic change as a routine operational burden rather than a one-off existential drama. The named concept here is adaptive credibility. Explain it, and the effect becomes clearer. An organisation that can update algorithms quickly, retire weak modes cleanly, and communicate that process calmly is signalling that it will not remain stuck inside the adversary's preferred timing. That matters because so much cryptographic advantage depends on catching a target flat-footed between old assumptions and new realities. If the target can move, the window narrows.

A second named, checkable example can be drawn from the broader ecosystem response to algorithm and certificate transitions on the web. The most credible actors in such transitions are rarely those that claim secret superiority. They are the ones that publish support timelines, test mixed-mode deployment, communicate client impact clearly, and demonstrate that incompatible paths will not be tolerated forever. The public record around browser and infrastructure changes has repeatedly shown that visible migration discipline shapes trust more effectively than chest-thumping about unbreakable security. The implication is not that all public road maps are sincere. Far from it. It is that when commitments are paired with actual updates, measured deprecation, and visible support for transition, they become signals others can use.

That point matters because signalling is not only for adversaries. It is also for allies, customers, suppliers, and internal decision-makers. A partner deciding whether to trust a vendor, a regulator deciding whether to accept assurances, or a procurement officer deciding which supplier has taken post-quantum preparation seriously all need something more substantial than private confidence. They need evidence that readiness lives in process. The named concept is outward legibility. Explain it, and one sees why some degree of defensive disclosure can strengthen trust without exposing vulnerabilities. An institution can reveal that it has mapped dependencies, required upgrade paths from suppliers, or rehearsed rollback and recovery without publishing the exact weak points an adversary would most like to know. The signal lies in discipline, not in the floor plan.

Still, this balance is not simple. There is always a risk that signalling readiness drifts into theatre. A glossy migration strategy with no tested implementation path, a public statement about agility unsupported by procurement reform, or a promise of fast algorithm updates resting on a fleet of unpatchable appliances is not a signal of strength. It is a performance of confidence staged on rotten floorboards. The named concept is declaratory fragility. Explain it, and the strategic danger becomes obvious. Overstated readiness can backfire by teaching adversaries that the institution mistakes policy language for operational capability. It can also damage trust internally, because engineers and operators know when the poster on the wall has outrun the condition of the building. Once credibility cracks, future signalling grows much harder.

That is why inventories matter so much. An inventory is not merely a management convenience. It is one of the few forms of defensive posture that can quietly prove seriousness. A board may never see every item. An adversary will certainly not be handed the whole list. Yet the existence of an accurate, current inventory of cryptographic dependencies changes what the institution can truthfully signal. It can say, without bluffing, that it knows where algorithm changes would matter, where vendor dependencies sit, where long-lived secrets reside, and where migration would require staged accommodation. The drill matters more than the slogan because the drill reveals whether the slogan can survive contact with reality.

Migration plans perform a similar function when they are real. A real migration plan does not promise invulnerability or total foresight. It shows sequencing, ownership, decision routes, fallback boundaries, testing expectations, and criteria for retiring old assumptions. The visible behaviour attached to this is familiar to anyone who has seen serious operational planning: named owners, supplier dependencies made explicit, client impact considered, rehearsed communication paths, and clear conditions under which transitional modes end rather than becoming permanent by emotional attachment. The implication is that a migration plan can signal deterrent value not because it frightens an adversary with mystery, but because it reduces the adversary's expectation that delay, incompatibility, or harvested future advantage will remain easy to exploit.

There is a credible limitation here, and it deserves candour. Readiness signalling cannot deter everything. It may not dissuade quiet collection, patient metadata analysis, insider cultivation, or actors willing to accept high operational costs for a narrow but significant win. It can also be misread. An adversary may interpret public discussion of migration as evidence of fear rather than maturity, or as an invitation to probe before changes complete. A partner may hear "we are preparing" and infer "we are currently exposed". Signalling, like all communication under competition, risks interpretation drift. It would be foolish to claim that better public posture automatically yields strategic restraint by others.

Yet this limitation sharpens the argument rather than weakening it. Because signalling has limits, the most useful signals are those that reduce room for dangerous misreading by being specific about process rather than grandiose about threat. A mature institution does not say, "We have solved the quantum problem." It says, in effect, that it has identified critical dependencies, prioritised long-horizon secrets, required supplier support for upgradeable cryptography, tested change pathways, and committed to rapid retirement of weak assumptions when standards and deployment conditions require it. That is less dramatic. It is also harder to dismiss. The signal is not that the institution cannot be touched. It is that touching it will not leave it static.

This is where resilience becomes a deterrent language in its own right. Resilience does not promise prevention of all harm. It signals that harm will not buy as much as the adversary hopes. A target that can rotate keys quickly, reissue certificates, update algorithms, narrow blast radius, communicate clearly, and keep public confidence during transition is telling a hostile observer something important: the costs of attack may remain, but the strategic gains will degrade faster than expected. The named concept here is payoff denial. Explain it, and the point becomes practical. Many hostile acts in cryptographic competition seek not only access but durable leverage - time to read, time to coerce, time to embarrass, time to trap a victim in outdated assumptions. Resilience shortens that time. That is a real deterrent effect, even when secrecy about offensive capability remains necessary.

The public commitment to rapid algorithm updates is especially valuable because it converts a technical competency into a visible institutional habit. It tells suppliers that excuses will expire. It tells internal teams that migration is not optional theatre. It tells customers that cryptographic maintenance is part of ordinary stewardship, not an emergency ritual performed only after headlines. And it tells adversaries that any advantage rooted in algorithmic stasis may be temporary. The signal does not need to include a secret map of the estate. It needs to include enough evidence that the institution has learned how to move.

This is also why governance can be revealed more safely than secrets. An institution can disclose that it conducts regular cryptographic inventories without listing every asset. It can state that it has segmented long-lived archives by sensitivity horizon without publishing where all the richest data sits. It can say that it demands algorithm agility from vendors without naming every fragile product line. Good signalling is neither silence nor confession. It is disciplined partial visibility. The adversary learns that the target is organised. It does not receive an annotated blueprint.

The drill returns here because it corrects one last illusion. People often think credibility comes from the impressive speech, the strategic doctrine, the phrase so sternly uttered that the room momentarily smells of polished wood and defensive resolve. In cryptographic competition, credibility more often comes from the thing everyone would rather skip: the rehearsal, the inventory review, the supplier test, the migration exercise, the update that lands on time, the weak mode that actually gets retired. Those are not glamorous acts. They are the acts from which believable signals are made.

The hard question, then, is not whether an institution can claim to be prepared. Most can. The harder question is whether it can reveal just enough of its readiness - its maps, its plans, its proven habit of change - to convince others that resilience is real, while withholding just enough operational detail that the signal strengthens trust without becoming a gift-wrapped field guide to its own unfinished edges.

## Escalation risks and misperception

In May 2017, when WannaCry spread across networks in the United Kingdom and beyond, the immediate public story seemed straightforward enough: hospitals disrupted, systems frozen, a hostile digital event with geopolitical overtones. Yet even in that case, where later attribution judgments became more confident in public reporting, the strategic temptation appeared almost at once. People wanted the incident to explain more than it really could. Was this proof of a sweeping hostile capability? A warning shot? A form of coercion? An intelligence operation gone loud? A precedent for future conflict? The breach became a mirror into which observers poured far more certainty than the evidence could safely hold.

That impulse is dangerous because cryptographic incidents rarely arrive with clean labels attached. A broken certificate chain, a compromised update path, a leaked archive, a successful intrusion into an identity tier, or a failure during migration may each look, in the first furious hours, like proof of something grand and coherent. Often they are not. They may reflect opportunism rather than doctrine, brittle design rather than exceptional adversary skill, or a contingent weakness rather than a durable strategic breakthrough. The problem is not merely that observers lack patience. It is that political systems, media systems, and bureaucratic systems all reward confident narrative faster than they reward disciplined ambiguity.

The cracked lens distorts fast.

That quiet motif suits the subject because misperception in cryptographic affairs often begins not with outright falsehood, but with partial truth viewed under pressure. Show the scene and the logic becomes plain. A major breach occurs against a sensitive target. The named concept is strategic overreading. Explain it, and the implication follows. Because cryptographic incidents involve secrecy, technical obscurity, and high symbolic stakes, observers quickly infer broad capability from narrow access, long-term intent from short-term opportunity, and centralised strategy from what may have been a localised exploit path. The consequence is not only analytical error. It is escalation risk. Institutions may answer the breach they imagine rather than the one they can actually substantiate.

Attribution uncertainty sits at the centre of this problem. Attribution is not a magical yes-or-no switch that flips cleanly from mystery to certainty. It is a layered judgment built from technical artefacts, operational behaviour, intelligence context, motive assessment, prior patterns, and sometimes classified sources that cannot be shown publicly in full. In cryptographic incidents, that uncertainty becomes especially awkward because the technical facts available early may reveal method without revealing sponsor, or may reveal compromise without revealing purpose. The abstraction of blame becomes visible in real institutional behaviour: diplomats draft statements before forensics stabilise, executives brief boards on likely actors before incident responders have mapped the full kill chain, journalists ask whether the breach proves a nation's new technical supremacy, and markets or allies react to implication as though it were already adjudicated fact. The implication is severe. Early confidence can harden into strategic posture long before the evidence is mature enough to deserve it.

A useful example lies in the 2014 Sony Pictures breach in California. Public discussion quickly moved beyond the immediate facts of stolen and destructive data into the language of geopolitical retaliation, coercion, and state behaviour. Some of those discussions reflected serious evidence. Many also reflected the irresistible pressure to make the incident stand for something larger, faster than the available proof could comfortably bear. The named concept here is narrative inflation. Explain it, and the broader lesson sharpens. A single breach, especially one that becomes culturally visible, is often treated as proof of a whole adversarial doctrine or capability set. Yet a breach can succeed through one badly governed path, one insider weakness, one reused administrative credential, or one fragile vendor relationship. The implication is that strategic interpretation must stay proportionate to the actual route of compromise, not to the political appetite for meaning.

This matters greatly in cryptographic contexts because people often infer capability from outcome with absurd haste. If an encrypted or security-sensitive system is compromised, the lazy conclusion is that the adversary has "broken the encryption". Most of the time the reality is stranger and less flattering. The route may run through endpoints, identity infrastructure, logging blind spots, supply chains, or support channels. A compromise of a cryptographically protected environment does not by itself prove a breakthrough against the underlying cryptography. The named concept is capability substitution blindness. Explain it, and the strategic implication becomes clear. When observers fail to distinguish between breaking the cipher and bypassing it through surrounding systems, they overestimate some threats, underestimate others, and can provoke policy responses aimed at the wrong layer entirely.

A second useful example lies in software supply-chain incidents such as the SolarWinds compromise disclosed in December 2020. The operation was undeniably serious. Yet even there, the temptation to infer a singular strategic lesson was strong. Some observers read it as proof that every trusted software channel had become illegitimate. Others treated it as evidence of uniquely advanced national mastery over all defensive systems. Both interpretations reached too quickly. The named concept is route conflation. Explain it, and one sees the real lesson. A trusted update pathway was successfully contested. That fact says much about supply-chain trust, vendor concentration, and the value of routine access. It does not automatically license sweeping conclusions about all products, all vendors, or an adversary's ability to compromise any target it wishes. The implication is that breach narratives grow most dangerous when they erase the difference between a path that existed and a power that is assumed to be universal.

This is where escalation risk enters with a peculiar mix of speed and vagueness. Political leaders, agencies, and organisations under pressure rarely escalate only with missiles or sanctions. They escalate rhetorically, diplomatically, economically, and institutionally. They may alter alliance assumptions, change procurement exclusions, issue public accusations, expand covert response authorities, or frame the incident as part of a broader hostile campaign before the evidence has settled. Sometimes such steps are justified. Sometimes they rest on an inflated reading of a breach that was real but narrower than the response implies. The cracked lens turns an operational fact into a strategic certainty, and institutions begin acting inside the story they have told themselves.

A credible limitation should be stated clearly. Caution about misperception does not mean paralysis, nor does it require institutions to mumble helplessly while evidence matures forever like a fine cheese in a classified cellar. Strategic actors often must respond before certainty is complete. Waiting for perfect proof can itself create vulnerability, encourage repetition, or communicate weakness. The serious point is narrower. Early response should be structured around the degree of confidence actually available, not around the theatrical certainty that political environments tend to reward. Ambiguity is uncomfortable, but false precision is more dangerous.

That limitation strengthens the central argument rather than weakening it. Because action often cannot wait, institutions need habits that separate operational containment from strategic interpretation. A mature response asks different questions in parallel. What happened technically? What is the current blast radius? Which trust pathways were used? What is the confidence level around attribution? What alternative explanations remain plausible? Which public claims can be made now without cornering the institution into later embarrassment or escalation? These are not academic niceties. They are safeguards against allowing one breach narrative to become strategic dogma before the facts have earned that honour.

This is also why internal communication matters so much. Boards, ministers, commanders, and senior executives often want a simple answer at exactly the moment the simple answer is most likely to mislead. If the technical team says only "we do not yet know", leadership may fill the gap with imagination or borrowed rhetoric. If the technical team overstates certainty to sound useful, it may create political momentum around conclusions later evidence will complicate. The named concept here is confidence calibration. Explain it, and the practical takeaway becomes plain. Institutions need a disciplined language for saying what they know, what they suspect, what they are ruling out, and what sort of response is justified at each level of confidence. Without that discipline, escalation risk begins inside the victim's own briefing room before it appears anywhere else.

A further complication is that adversaries may count on this overreading. A noisy breach can be useful not only for the data taken or systems disrupted, but for the confusion and misalignment it induces in the target. If a victim infers vast hidden capability from one contingent success, mistrusts the wrong suppliers, overhauls the wrong systems, or lashes out at the wrong actor, the breach has achieved a second-order gain. The implication is not that every incident is a cunning chess move in a grand adversarial opera. The world is usually much messier than that, blessedly or otherwise. It is that misperception itself is part of the strategic terrain. Institutions that cannot separate breach narratives from strategic reality make themselves easier to steer.

This is why careful response depends on preserving a distinction between event, pathway, and meaning. The event is what happened. The pathway is how it happened. The meaning is what one is tempted to conclude about intent, capability, and future conflict. Those three are routinely collapsed in public argument because collapse is faster and more satisfying than disciplined separation. Yet disciplined separation is precisely what keeps a damaged institution from turning one cracked pane into proof that the whole building is under invisible occupation. The visible signs of such discipline are unglamorous: layered attribution statements, public language that avoids grand extrapolation, rapid containment without maximalist interpretation, and private decision-making that tests hypotheses against alternative routes rather than rewarding the most geopolitically satisfying story.

The cracked lens returns here because it expresses the deepest caution of the subject. A cracked lens still shows the world. It simply invites distortion at the edges, and under stress those edges can become the whole frame. Cryptographic incidents are like that. They reveal something real, often something important, and yet they also seduce observers into seeing too much too quickly. The mature institution does not deny the incident, soften the harm, or hide behind jargon. It refuses the intoxication of premature grand theory.

The difficult question, then, is not whether a breach matters. It plainly does. The harder question is whether the institution responding to it can tell the difference between a compromised pathway and a demonstrated grand capability, between a plausible attribution and a politically convenient certainty, and between the need to act promptly and the temptation to let one vivid incident pull a wider conflict into motion on the strength of a story the evidence has not yet finished telling.

# Chapter 13

# Verification, Transparency, and Trust

If the code is open, the audit independent, the device certified, and the supplier reputable, what exactly has been proved? The question sounds almost impolite, which is why it is worth asking. Modern security culture often reaches for trust markers with the relief of a tired official reaching for a stamp. Open source. Third-party review. Certified hardware. International standard. Each marker does useful work. None ends the argument. Trust survives on evidence, but evidence never arrives in a pure state, untouched by institutions, incentives, and the strange human habit of wanting a seal more than an explanation.

That tension gives this part of the subject its bite. Verification is necessary because cryptography asks people to rely on systems they cannot inspect fully with unaided judgment. Transparency is necessary because secret assurance is little better than a velvet curtain over a locked cabinet. And yet neither verification nor transparency is self-interpreting. Open review can increase confidence and still leave deployment weak. Certification can create order and still leave room for theatre. Hardware can anchor trust and still inherit the opacities of fabrication, firmware, and supply. Shared standards can stabilise cooperation across borders and still create dependence on institutions others do not fully trust. The glass is clear. The room behind it is not.

The seal on the box helps.

It helps because people need signals. They need some way to distinguish sober engineering from wishful salesmanship, careful governance from decorative compliance, serious review from a well-dressed mutual admiration society. But the seal on the box also tempts them to stop looking. That is the central trade-off here. Every trust mechanism designed to reduce uncertainty can become a substitute for judgment if handled lazily enough. Open code can be treated as proof that no hidden weakness matters. Independent labs can be treated as neutral oracles rather than institutions with their own incentives and blind spots. Hardware roots of trust can be treated as sacred objects rather than long-lived components passing through opaque industrial chains. International interoperability can be treated as a moral good rather than as a bargain in which capability, dependence, and political asymmetry all take their seats at the table.

The stakes are therefore higher than procedural tidiness. If trust markers are overread, institutions grow complacent in exactly the places where scrutiny is most needed. If they are underread, coordination collapses into suspicion and every cross-border system starts to look like a disguised concession to somebody else's influence. Security practice then begins to oscillate between naive faith and corrosive doubt, neither of which can sustain serious cooperation. The question is not whether transparency and assurance matter. They plainly do. The question is how much they can honestly bear before they turn from tools of judgment into excuses not to exercise it.

This matters especially in cryptographic affairs because the underlying objects are so often socially invisible. Most users cannot inspect implementations. Most executives cannot parse protocol choices. Most states cannot fabricate every component they rely upon. Trust therefore has to be mediated through institutions: review communities, procurement rules, certification regimes, vendors, academic reputations, audit markets, and diplomatic arrangements. Once that is admitted, credibility stops looking like a purely technical property. It becomes something produced through people, money, governance, and contest. One lab's badge, one standards body's blessing, one supplier's market standing, one government's quiet preference: each may alter the climate of trust without changing a line of code. That makes verification a political economy as much as a technical exercise.

The route forward follows that institutional reality. It begins with openness, because open review remains one of the few disciplined ways to widen scrutiny and reduce the chance that cryptographic decisions rest on private authority alone. It then turns to the harder question of independent assurance, where legitimacy is built through audits, labs, and expert communities that are themselves embedded in funding structures and professional incentives. From there it moves down into hardware and supply chains, where the fantasy of a clean root of trust collides with long manufacturing paths, firmware updates, and components whose life exceeds the memory of the teams that first approved them. It ends by widening the frame to trust across borders, where cooperation requires shared standards but never escapes the fact that shared standards can also distribute strategic dependence unevenly.

The seal on the box returns because it is the right emblem of the whole problem. A box with no seal invites obvious suspicion. A box with a seal invites an equally obvious question: who printed it, who checked what went inside, who watched the supply chain after it left the factory, and who benefits if everyone agrees to stop asking after that point? The same question trails behind every phrase that sounds reassuring on first contact. Open. Certified. Reviewed. Trusted. Each word reduces uncertainty a little. Each word also creates a new site at which uncertainty can hide behind institutional ritual.

This is where the chapter's deeper continuity with the rest of the book becomes visible. Strong cryptography is never only about the elegance of its mathematics. It is about the credibility of the systems, organisations, and relationships through which that mathematics becomes usable. A verified algorithm inside an opaque deployment is not enough. A transparent codebase inside a distorted governance structure is not enough. A secure chip in a poorly understood supply chain is not enough. A shared standard between unequal partners is not enough. The world stubbornly refuses to offer a single final certificate of innocence. It offers layers of assurance, each of which must be interpreted in the light of the others.

The hard question, then, is not whether verification and transparency are good. They are indispensable. The harder question is whether the institution relying on them can tell the difference between evidence that deserves confidence and evidence that merely looks official enough to relieve it of the burden of thinking - and whether that difference still holds when trust has to cross vendors, hardware chains, audit markets, and national borders without shattering into either blind faith or permanent suspicion.

## Open review and its limits

In April 2014, when Codenomicon in Helsinki and Google engineer Neel Mehta disclosed the Heartbleed vulnerability in OpenSSL, the shock was not merely technical. OpenSSL was not a hidden black box owned by a single firm and guarded behind contractual curtains. Its code was open, widely used, and available for inspection. Yet a flaw with serious consequences had lived there in full daylight. Administrators around the world rushed to patch servers, rotate keys, and answer a quietly humiliating question: if the code was open, why had so much trust rested on so little scrutiny?

That question still bites because it punctures a lazy article of faith. Openness helps. It helps for reasons that matter deeply to cryptography. Public review broadens the set of people who can test assumptions, challenge design choices, inspect implementations, and compare claims against reality rather than against vendor theatre. But openness is not magic dust. Code can be visible and underexamined. Algorithms can be public and still poorly implemented. Governance can be transparent in form and distorted in practice. The lights were on. Hardly anyone looked.

This is the first distinction that serious discussion requires. Open review improves confidence because it enlarges the possibility of criticism. The named concept is inspectability. Explain it, and the strategic value becomes plain. A cryptographic algorithm or implementation that outsiders can study is less dependent on mere institutional prestige. Researchers can test it, competitors can challenge it, implementers can compare notes, and mistakes are less likely to remain protected solely by organisational secrecy. The implication is real and powerful. Openness makes bluffing harder. It does not make error impossible.

A useful historical counterpoint lies in the Advanced Encryption Standard competition run by the National Institute of Standards and Technology in Gaithersburg, Maryland, beginning in 1997 and culminating in the selection of Rijndael in 2000. The process mattered not only because it produced a widely trusted cipher, but because it did so through unusually public evaluation. Candidate algorithms were submitted, debated, analysed, attacked, defended, and measured in a forum where outsiders could participate. The named concept here is public contestability. Explain it, and one sees why openness can strengthen trust without requiring anyone to pretend that consensus is infallible. Confidence in AES grew not because a single authority demanded reverence, but because the process allowed scrutiny to become part of the standard itself. The implication extends beyond that case. When algorithms are selected in open competition, trust is anchored less in institutional mystique and more in observed resilience under criticism.

That is the best case for openness, and it is a serious one. Cryptography makes unusually strong claims about what adversaries should not be able to do. Those claims deserve unusually strong scrutiny. Public review lets academic researchers, independent practitioners, rival firms, and sceptical engineers test whether the object in question deserves the confidence attached to it. It also helps distribute trust internationally. A cipher or protocol subjected to open analysis is easier to adopt across borders because it need not be accepted on the authority of one vendor, one ministry, or one corporate sales team. The abstraction of legitimacy becomes visible in repeated behaviour: published analysis, reproducible test vectors, public standards discussions, reference implementations, and criticism that can be answered in the open rather than buried in private correspondence. The implication is that transparency can make cryptographic trust more portable.

Yet the Heartbleed case demonstrates the limit with almost comic cruelty. OpenSSL's source was available. That availability did not ensure that enough skilled people, with enough time, incentives, and institutional support, would examine the right parts carefully enough. Open code is a possibility structure, not an inspection guarantee. The named concept is review scarcity. Explain it, and the romantic story about openness weakens into something more honest. Visibility only helps if capable reviewers are present, motivated, and attentive. The implication is not anti-open-source. It is anti-fairy-tale. Code can be open and still depend on a tiny pool of under-resourced maintainers and irregular outside scrutiny. In such conditions, openness may reveal the truth only after failure rather than before it.

This brings us to a broader institutional point. People often treat transparency as though it were a substitute for governance, when in reality it works best as an aid to governance. An open repository does not decide maintenance priorities. A public standard does not fund review. A visible codebase does not guarantee reproducible builds, secure deployment, or disciplined patching. Show the scene and the problem becomes immediate. An organisation adopts an open cryptographic library because openness is taken as a sign of trustworthiness. The named concept is transparency substitution. Explain it, and the implication follows. Once adoption occurs, the institution may relax too quickly, assuming the wider community is somehow carrying the burden of vigilance on its behalf. That assumption can be disastrously lazy. Public code is not a maintenance contract with the universe.

A second useful example comes from the Signal protocol and its public documentation, open implementations, and extensive outside scrutiny over time. The protocol earned confidence in part because it was exposed to real criticism by serious people rather than sold as a mystical appliance. That openness improved the quality of the conversation around it and helped many outsiders evaluate the design on something firmer than branding. Yet even here the lesson is not "open equals safe". The named concept is deployment divergence. Explain it, and the limitation appears. A strong, openly reviewed protocol can still be embedded in products with different user interfaces, backup choices, device security assumptions, and governance arrangements. The implication is crucial. Open review can tell you a great deal about an algorithm or protocol. It tells you much less, by itself, about how safely a real organisation will deploy, update, configure, and govern it.

That gap between open design and lived deployment is where much misplaced trust accumulates. Open code does not force a vendor to ship reproducible binaries. It does not prevent insecure defaults. It does not ensure that update channels are well governed, that old clients are retired cleanly, that key management is sensible, or that telemetry and recovery features do not quietly reshape the threat model. The lights may be on in the engine room while the bridge remains badly run. The implication is that institutions must stop speaking as though openness by itself settles the argument. It settles one part of the argument: the part about whether inspection is possible. Security still depends on whether the organisation surrounding the code deserves confidence.

This is also why honest governance matters so much. Transparency can be manipulated. A firm or institution can publish code while obscuring build processes, delaying fixes, fragmenting responsibility, or using openness as a reputational halo around weak internal discipline. The named concept is performative transparency. Explain it, and the strategic danger becomes visible. An actor may harvest the moral prestige of openness without accepting the operational burdens that make openness valuable. The implication is not cynical nihilism. It is methodological caution. Review the governance around the code, not just the code. Ask who maintains it, who pays for it, how fixes are handled, whether users can verify what they are running, and whether claims of openness extend beyond the repository to the actual chain from source to deployed system.

A credible limitation should be stated plainly. Open review is not always sufficient for every context, and in some cases it can create its own distortions. Public code can attract uneven attention, with fashionable projects receiving abundance while obscure but critical components languish. Open processes can reward performance over depth, or signal over substance, if institutions mistake public argument for competent assurance. There are also settings, especially around sensitive hardware or specialised operational environments, where full transparency is constrained by other realities. It would be childish to insist that a single model of openness solves all assurance problems. The world is too awkward for such neat moral geometry.

Still, that limitation strengthens the main argument rather than weakening it. Precisely because openness is not a cure, it must be treated as a tool. A tool improves what capable hands and serious institutions are prepared to do with it. It widens scrutiny. It disciplines claims. It lowers the barrier to criticism. It can create legitimacy across borders and communities that would otherwise distrust one another's internal assurances. None of that is trivial. The error lies in stopping there. Institutions need review capacity, maintenance funding, reproducible practices, secure deployment discipline, and governance structures that convert inspectability into actual confidence. Otherwise openness risks becoming a pious slogan attached to brittle systems.

This is where the broader institutional lens returns with force. Trust in cryptography is never only trust in mathematics. It is trust in the arrangements through which mathematics becomes software, software becomes product, product becomes infrastructure, and infrastructure becomes ordinary dependence. Open review can illuminate those arrangements at some levels. It cannot sanctify them wholesale. A balance sheet of confidence must therefore ask several questions at once. Was the algorithm openly tested? Was the implementation publicly inspected? Are the maintainers adequately resourced? Can the deployed artefact be checked against the reviewed source? Are updates governed honestly? Are defaults sane? Is the surrounding organisation candid about its limits? These are not ornaments around the real issue. They *are* the real issue once cryptography leaves the whiteboard.

The lights return here because they express the whole dilemma in one plain image. Darkness protects error badly. That is the best argument for openness. But a lit room still needs people who know where to look, institutions willing to pay them, and habits of judgment strong enough to distinguish visibility from security. A well-lit empty room does not inspect itself.

The unresolved question, then, is not whether open review matters. It matters enormously. The harder question is whether the institution relying on openness can resist turning it into a comforting myth - a way of confusing the availability of scrutiny with the existence of scrutiny, and the publication of code with the much stranger and more demanding task of governing what that code becomes once real organisations begin to trust their secrets to it.

## Independent assurance and contested legitimacy

In August 2013, after documents disclosed by Edward Snowden intensified public scrutiny of surveillance and trust in digital infrastructure, one phrase began to sound at once more important and more slippery than before: *certified secure*. Products, services, and devices carried certifications, passed audits, and referenced laboratory reviews, yet public confidence did not settle obediently around the paperwork. In Washington, Brussels, London, and far beyond, the same credential could be read in two incompatible ways. For some, it was evidence of disciplined evaluation. For others, it was proof only that a system had satisfied a narrow procedure inside an institutional environment they no longer trusted.

The badge looked official.

That was the problem. Independent assurance exists because institutions need ways to trust what they cannot inspect directly. A minister cannot personally review a cryptographic module. A hospital procurement team cannot reproduce a semiconductor supply chain. A company buying secure communications equipment cannot rebuild the whole product from first principles merely to decide whether the claims sound honest. Audits, laboratories, academic review communities, and certification bodies emerge to mediate that problem. They do useful work. They also inherit the motives, reputations, funding pressures, and political atmospheres of the world that created them. Assurance is never only technical. It is social proof arranged under institutional conditions.

That is the first point to state plainly. Independent assurance does not merely discover legitimacy. It helps produce it. Show the scene and the logic becomes obvious. A vendor wants customers to trust a product whose internal workings most of them cannot evaluate. The named concept is delegated credibility. Explain it, and the implication follows. The vendor turns to an auditor, a recognised lab, a standards regime, a respected academic process, or a certification framework because trust can travel more easily when another institution appears to stand behind the claim. The strategic point is not that this is dishonest. It is that the "independence" doing the reputational work must itself be assessed. Once trust is delegated, the delegate becomes part of the security object.

Academic review communities provide the most intellectually admired version of this process. Their power comes from contestability. Researchers publish attacks, critique designs, test assumptions, and force claims into public argument. That argument rarely yields total unanimity, but it often raises the standard of what can be asserted without embarrassment. The abstraction of confidence becomes visible in ordinary scholarly behaviour: conference submissions, cryptanalysis papers, reference implementations, public debates over proofs and threat models, and the slow accumulation of community judgment. The implication is real and substantial. A design exposed to serious academic scrutiny is less dependent on the prestige of a vendor or state alone.

A useful example lies in the public competitions and review processes surrounding modern cryptographic standards, including those run by the National Institute of Standards and Technology in Gaithersburg, Maryland. Their value has never rested solely on who finally wins. It has rested on the fact that outsiders can challenge, measure, and attack the candidates in public. The named concept here is procedural legitimacy. Explain it, and the lesson becomes sharper. An algorithm chosen after open review can carry a different sort of trust from one selected behind closed doors, because the route to acceptance has itself become part of the evidence. Yet even here the limit appears. Academic review can increase confidence in the underlying design while saying much less about how commercial products will implement, govern, patch, or support it in practice.

Audits and formal assessments promise something different. They do not ask only whether an idea is elegant or whether a proof is persuasive. They ask whether a product, process, or organisation conforms to a defined standard. This is attractive because it converts sprawling technical uncertainty into something legible to buyers and regulators. A product has passed the evaluation. A module has the certificate. A service has undergone the audit. The badge on the box begins to speak. The named concept is compliance legibility. Explain it, and one sees why such regimes are so useful. They let markets coordinate. They let procurement teams write requirements. They let governments compare offerings. They let institutions operate without pretending that everyone involved is a cryptographer with spare weekends and a soldering station.

Yet this same strength creates the central difficulty. Formal assurance regimes rarely certify reality in the broad sense users imagine. They certify that a thing met a defined scope under defined conditions using defined methods at a particular point in time. Those boundaries matter enormously.

A product may be "certified secure" with respect to one configuration, one threat model, one evaluation depth, or one component boundary while remaining weak elsewhere. The named concept is scope compression. Explain it, and the strategic implication becomes unavoidable. When people hear the certificate and imagine total trustworthiness, while the regime intended only a narrower claim, legitimacy becomes contested not because nobody checked anything, but because the social meaning of the badge outruns the technical meaning of the assessment.

This is why disagreement over the phrase "certified secure" is so revealing. One party often means that an artefact has passed a recognised evaluation framework. Another hears a promise that the artefact is generally safe to depend upon. Both may be speaking in good faith. They are not speaking about the same thing. The visible behaviour attached to this mismatch is familiar: procurement teams rely on the certificate as a filtering device, security engineers warn that the evaluation scope was narrow, vendors highlight the approval in marketing, critics point to vulnerabilities discovered later and treat the whole assurance regime as theatre. The implication is not that certification is worthless. It is that its legitimacy is always socially negotiated and therefore politically vulnerable.

Funding complicates this further. Laboratories must be paid. Audits cost money. Academic communities are sustained by grants, employer time, conference structures, prestige systems, and sometimes commercial sponsorship. None of this automatically corrupts judgment. It would be childish to suggest that anyone receiving funding loses the capacity for honest review, as though poverty were the only secure foundation for integrity. But incentives shape attention. They shape which products are assessed, which claims are prioritised, how quickly concerns are published, and how comfortable institutions feel challenging the entities that indirectly sustain them. The named concept here is incentive shading. Explain it, and the harder institutional question appears. Independence is not simply a legal status or a line in a report. It is a practical condition that depends on whether a reviewer can afford to reach inconvenient conclusions and have them still count.

A second useful example lies in the world of commercial penetration testing and security audits. A company hires an external firm, receives a report, and then advertises that it has been independently assessed. Sometimes that assessment is serious, unsettling, and genuinely useful. Sometimes it is carefully scoped, tightly timed, and framed in ways that satisfy governance rituals while leaving deeper structural questions politely untouched. The named concept is client-shaped assurance. Explain it, and the strategic point grows clearer. Because many assurance relationships are commissioned by the party seeking legitimacy, the resulting work can drift towards what is administratively useful, commercially tolerable, or contractually bounded rather than towards what would most disturb the comforting story. The implication is not cynicism for its own sake. It is a demand to inspect the conditions under which independence is performed.

Still, a limitation deserves open acknowledgment. Independent assurance, though imperfect, is often far better than the alternatives. Without external audits, labs, and review communities, trust would collapse back into raw vendor assertion, institutional secrecy, or geopolitical preference disguised as technical judgment. Assurance regimes often catch real flaws, establish common baselines, and make irresponsible claims harder to sustain. Many reviewers are serious people doing careful work under constraints they did not create. It would be foolish to sneer at these institutions merely because they are not oracles. The world is too complex to run on private certainty alone.

Yet that concession sharpens the main argument rather than softening it. Because independent assurance matters so much, its legitimacy becomes worth contesting. States may question review bodies tied to rival jurisdictions. Firms may challenge academic critics as biased while celebrating friendly labs as neutral. Publics may distrust certificates after a highly visible failure. Security communities may split over whether a scheme was truly evaluated, merely rubber-stamped, or assessed against the wrong assumptions. Credibility is therefore not a calm reservoir into which evidence is poured until trust emerges automatically. It is a political and social achievement, built through repeated demonstration, interpretive discipline, and the willingness of institutions to expose their assurance mechanisms to scrutiny as well.

This is where the book's broader institutional lens comes into focus. A cryptographic system does not become trustworthy only because its mathematics are elegant, its code is open, or its lab report is stamped. It becomes trustworthy when the ecosystem around those things earns confidence: when the review community is serious, the lab process is legible, the scope of certification is honestly communicated, the funding arrangements do not too obviously distort judgment, and the users of the assurance understand what has and has not been established. The badge on the box helps, but only if the people reading it know how to read without hallucinating guarantees the badge was never designed to provide.

That literacy matters across borders as well. One country's accredited lab may not satisfy another's strategic anxieties. One region's certification regime may look rigorous to its participants and compromised to outsiders who distrust the surrounding institutions. This is not simply parochial stubbornness. It reflects a deeper truth: independent assurance relies on shared confidence in the institutions declaring independence. Where that shared confidence weakens, legitimacy fragments. The same certificate that opens one market may provoke suspicion in another. The implication is that assurance is part of the diplomatic and political structure of technology, not an apolitical layer floating above it.

The badge returns here because it is the right symbol for the whole problem. A badge is useful because it compresses judgment into a portable sign. A badge is dangerous because it compresses judgment into a portable sign. Once the sign begins to travel farther than the reasoning behind it, people start trusting or distrusting the symbol for reasons the underlying evaluators may never have intended. Some will believe too much. Others will reject too much. Serious institutions have to live in the narrow space between those errors.

The unresolved question, then, is not whether independent assurance can create legitimacy. It plainly can. The harder question is whether the institutions relying on that legitimacy can keep asking who paid for the review, what exactly was tested, what remained outside scope, which community conferred the reputation, and whether "independent" still means anything robust once the badge starts doing political work far beyond the modest technical claim it was first meant to certify.

## Trust in hardware and supply chains

In October 2018, a Bloomberg Businessweek report ignited one of the fiercest public disputes in recent technology security memory by alleging that tiny hardware implants had been placed on server motherboards linked to Supermicro. The report described a supply-chain compromise of extraordinary strategic consequence. The denials were equally forceful. Apple, Amazon, and Supermicro rejected the claims. For many readers, the most unsettling lesson was not whether the specific allegation would ever be settled to everyone's satisfaction. It was that the story felt plausible enough to terrify serious people. Hardware had long been treated as the place where trust became concrete. Suddenly it also looked like the place where uncertainty became hardest to disprove.

That discomfort has not gone away.

Hardware roots of trust are attractive because they promise a kind of solidity software never quite achieves. A key in a hardware security module feels more real than a key in a process. A secure element soldered into a device feels less slippery than code running on a general-purpose machine. Firmware verification at boot feels like a firmer beginning than anything that starts later in the stack. These intuitions are not foolish. They reflect real advantages. Dedicated hardware can reduce attack surfaces, isolate secrets, and make certain forms of tampering harder or at least more expensive. Yet the same move that makes trust more tangible also makes it more dependent on long industrial chains, opaque fabrication processes, proprietary tooling, update mechanisms, logistics networks, and components designed to outlive the teams that first approved them. The chip sits still. The ecosystem around it does not.

The sealed crate looks reassuring.

That image suits the subject because hardware trust often arrives as a promise already packaged. A device, module, or secure element reaches the buyer as a finished object carrying claims about authenticity, attestation, resistance, and secure storage. Show the scene and the logic becomes plain. An institution wants stronger assurance for keys, boot processes, identity credentials, or embedded cryptographic operations. The named concept is material anchoring. Explain it, and the appeal becomes clear. By moving trust into specialised hardware, the institution hopes to reduce dependence on the messy mutability of software and administration alone. The implication is real: some attacks become harder, some secrets become better shielded, and some control paths become more disciplined. The trouble begins when the object is treated as self-justifying rather than as one node in a sprawling chain of dependence.

That chain begins long before deployment. Fabrication is opaque by nature to almost everyone who depends on it. Design may occur in one jurisdiction, fabrication in another, packaging elsewhere, firmware integration somewhere else again, and final assembly under yet another set of commercial and political constraints. Even a highly capable customer rarely observes more than fragments of this process directly. The abstraction of assurance becomes visible in ordinary facts of procurement: the buyer knows the model, the certification, the vendor road map, perhaps the foundry reputation, but not every hand, tool, subcontractor, or modification stage through which the device has passed. The named concept here is production opacity. Explain it, and the strategic point sharpens. Hardware trust is never only trust in the device. It is trust in the system that made the device and in the buyer's ability to understand where visibility stops.

This is why hardware roots of trust are both attractive and vulnerable. They concentrate sensitive functions - key storage, boot validation, attestation, identity anchoring - in places where compromise can be consequential and difficult to observe. The more a system depends on one chip, module, or firmware chain to establish legitimacy for everything above it, the more precious that component becomes. That does not mean hardware roots are a mistake. It means they turn trust into a choke point. The implication is strategic rather than rhetorical. A compromised root can invalidate confidence far beyond its physical size because so many other systems inherit their claims from it.

A useful example lies in the security architecture of trusted platform modules and secure enclaves more broadly. These technologies have done serious work in improving device identity, protecting keys, and supporting measured boot and attestation. They are not ornamental. Yet their value depends on a wider ecology: firmware integrity, update discipline, manufacturing confidence, integration quality, and the operational honesty of the surrounding platform. The named concept is inherited assurance. Explain it, and the core limitation appears. A trusted hardware component may perform its narrow function exactly as intended while the system around it undermines the trust it was supposed to anchor. The implication is not anti-hardware. It is anti-fetish. A root of trust cannot redeem negligent governance, brittle updates, or poorly understood supply dependencies simply by being made of silicon.

Firmware updates expose this with almost embarrassing clarity. Institutions often reach for hardware to escape the mutability of software, only to discover that modern hardware remains inseparable from firmware lifecycles. The device is not frozen. It is updateable, and updateability is both a gift and a risk. Show the scene and the tension becomes immediate. A security module or embedded controller requires a firmware patch to address a flaw, enable a new mode, or maintain compatibility. The named concept is mutable hardware trust. Explain it, and the comforting fantasy dissolves. The component once treated as a stable anchor now depends on a signed update process, vendor maintenance discipline, deployment tooling, rollback safety, and all the familiar politics of patch management. The implication is large. Hardware assurance cannot be separated cleanly from software assurance because firmware bridges the two whether institutions like it or not.

A second useful example comes from constrained and long-lived environments - industrial controls, medical devices, transport systems, remote sensors, military platforms, and other systems whose service lives stretch far beyond the product cycles of consumer technology. These are precisely the contexts in which hardware roots of trust often appear most attractive. They offer apparent solidity in environments where updates are hard, connectivity is intermittent, and operational failure can have physical consequences. Yet those same features produce the harshest assurance problems. The named concept is longevity friction. Explain it, and one sees why the issue links so strongly to legacy. A component approved under one set of assumptions may remain in service while algorithms age, suppliers merge or disappear, firmware support grows thin, and the surrounding ecosystem evolves beyond what the device was ever designed to handle. The implication is that long service life makes hardware assurance an ongoing governance burden, not a one-time procurement achievement.

This is where supply chains cease to be a background topic and become part of the trust object itself. A serious institution cannot ask only whether the device is secure. It must ask where the device came from, who updated it, which dependencies it carries, how replacement is governed, how attestation claims are verified, which manufacturing or packaging stages remain opaque, and what contractual leverage exists if something goes wrong. The abstraction of supply chain becomes visible in painstakingly mundane questions: who signs firmware, how keys are provisioned, which subcontractors touch the hardware, how provenance is tracked, which testing artefacts are available, what happens when a vendor ends support, and whether alternative suppliers exist or the institution has quietly married itself to a single upstream dependency for the sake of convenience. The implication is plain. Hardware trust is procurement policy in a lab coat.

Still, a limitation deserves candour. It would be silly to conclude from all this that hardware roots of trust are mostly illusion or that software-only trust is somehow cleaner. Pure software trust has its own fragilities, and in many cases dedicated hardware does raise the bar meaningfully. A well-designed hardware security module, secure element, or measured-boot chain can reduce exposure that would otherwise be intolerable. Many institutions would be worse off without them. The point is not to sneer at hardware because it fails to provide metaphysical certainty. Nothing provides metaphysical certainty outside theology, and even there the reviews are mixed.

That concession strengthens the real argument rather than weakening it. Because hardware roots can be genuinely useful, institutions must learn to assess them without mythology. They should treat hardware assurance as an ecosystem problem, meaning that the security claim travels through fabrication, firmware, operational support, update channels, lifecycle management, retirement plans, and cross-border supply dependencies. A device is not "trusted" once and for all because it passed through an evaluation lab or arrived shrink-wrapped from a respected vendor. It is trusted conditionally, under arrangements that must continue making sense as the environment changes. The named concept is conditional material trust. Explain it, and the reader sees why assurance has to be revisited over time rather than inherited like a family silver set no one dares inspect too closely.

This also clarifies why earlier discussions of constrained environments and legacy systems matter so much here. The more difficult a component is to replace, the more politically and operationally expensive it becomes to question its trust assumptions. That is how weak roots survive. A secure module installed in a transport system, medical platform, or remote field device may remain trusted not because anyone actively re-evaluated it, but because the cost of disturbing it grew larger than the institutional appetite for discomfort. The sealed crate stays in service because opening it now would disrupt operations, budgets, certifications, or contractual relationships. The implication is that hardware trust degrades not only through technical compromise but through administrative inertia.

The social side of this should not be overlooked. Trust in hardware often draws strength from the human psychology of objects. People feel reassured by things that seem physically bounded, tamper-resistant, and difficult to imitate. A chip looks like a fact. A sealed module looks like discipline made visible. A secure boot indicator at startup looks like a clean beginning. These feelings are not absurd. They are simply incomplete. Hardware can anchor confidence precisely because it feels less abstract than software, and that feeling can seduce institutions into underexamining the systems of production, maintenance, and replacement on which the object actually depends. The crate looks secure because it is closed. That does not tell you who packed it.

The sealed crate returns here because it captures the strategic problem in one image. A sealed crate is useful when it protects something sensitive in transit. It is dangerous when everyone starts trusting the seal without asking who printed it, who handled the crate before delivery, what happens when the contents need servicing, and whether the warehouse that stores it has quietly changed owners twice since the first inventory. Hardware roots of trust are much the same. They are valuable, but their value lies inside a wider chain whose weakest part may not be visible from the polished surface of the component itself.

The unresolved question, then, is not whether hardware can support trust. It can. The harder question is whether the institution depending on that hardware can treat trust as something distributed across fabrication, firmware, updates, vendors, contracts, and long service life - rather than as a magical property conferred forever by a component whose physical presence feels reassuring enough to stop the harder inquiry just when it ought to begin.

## Building trust across borders

In December 2015, after the Paris Agreement was adopted in Le Bourget, outside Paris, diplomats, ministries, scientists, and businesses around the world faced a practical truth that extended far beyond climate policy: modern cooperation depends on shared digital trust among parties that do not share identical assumptions, institutions, or strategic interests. Agreements travel as documents, data, and authenticated exchanges. Their working life depends on systems that must be secure enough to rely upon and interoperable enough to function across borders. The scent of wet winter air in a conference city may feel very far from cryptography. It is not. Every multinational arrangement eventually collides with the problem of how strangers decide what counts as trustworthy communication.

That collision is now a structural feature of international life. Trade, intelligence sharing, finance, logistics, cloud services, health research, transport coordination, and diplomatic exchange all depend on cryptographic systems that must operate across legal, technical, and political boundaries. Yet the parties involved do not enter with identical beliefs about vendors, standards bodies, hardware origins, review communities, or the strategic behaviour of other states. One side may trust a protocol suite because it emerged from an open process it helped shape. Another may see the same suite as a dependency on institutions whose incentives it does not fully share. The wire carries traffic. It also carries politics.

The bridge must hold.

That plain image clarifies the problem better than grand speeches about digital partnership. A bridge is useful only if both sides trust it enough to cross, and that trust depends on more than the abstract strength of the materials. Show the scene and the issue becomes concrete. Two governments, firms, or allied institutions need to exchange sensitive data, coordinate operations, or run shared systems. The named concept is trusted interoperability. Explain it, and the strategic implication follows. Interoperability is not merely the technical ability to connect. It is the willingness to depend on that connection under conditions where failure, manipulation, or hidden leverage would matter politically. The implication is severe. A system can be interoperable in protocol terms and still fail as a basis for genuine trust if one side believes the standards, suppliers, or assurance processes surrounding it are tilted elsewhere.

This is why shared standards are both indispensable and troublesome. They enable cooperation by reducing friction. If parties use common protocols, certificate regimes, update practices, and algorithm suites, they can exchange information and build services without renegotiating the basic rules every time. The abstraction of efficiency becomes visible in ordinary institutional behaviour: procurement becomes easier, suppliers can serve multiple jurisdictions, alliance partners can coordinate rapidly, researchers can share data with fewer bespoke interfaces, and global firms can maintain common security architectures across regions. The implication is obvious and important. Without shared standards, cross-border cooperation becomes slower, more expensive, and more brittle.

Yet the same shared standards can create strategic dependence. A standard is never only a neutral technical language floating above power. It is embedded in ecosystems of vendors, certification bodies, review communities, update mechanisms, and dominant platforms. If one country, alliance of firms, or cluster of institutions shapes those systems more heavily than others, then adopting the shared standard may also mean accepting an unequal distribution of influence. The named concept here is asymmetrical interoperability. Explain it, and the tension sharpens. The less influential party may gain the practical benefits of compatibility while growing dependent on external assurance, external suppliers, or external road maps it cannot meaningfully control. The implication is that cooperation through shared cryptography can simultaneously deepen trust and redistribute power.

A useful example lies in the broad international adoption of standards associated with the public web, secure transport, and global certificate ecosystems. These standards enabled extraordinary levels of cross-border trade and communication. A payment made in one country, a browser session initiated in another, and a cloud transaction processed in a third could all rely on broadly recognised trust structures. That was not a trivial achievement. It remains one of the most important forms of practical international coordination ever built. The named concept is global trust scaffolding. Explain it, and one sees why shared standards matter so much. They reduce the need for every participant to reinvent secure exchange from scratch. The implication, however, is double-edged. Where the scaffolding is maintained disproportionately by institutions, vendors, or governance processes concentrated in a few jurisdictions, others may wonder whether the trust they are being asked to place is fully mutual or merely operationally convenient.

A second useful example lies in multinational supply chains for digital infrastructure, where organisations from different jurisdictions procure common cloud services, telecom equipment, security tools, and hardware components. Even when the same cryptographic protocols are used, trust can diverge sharply over whose hardware is acceptable, whose firmware update path is credible, whose certification lab carries weight, and whose legal environment is seen as compatible with operational dependence. The named concept is layered trust divergence. Explain it, and the strategic point becomes clearer. Parties may agree on the mathematics and still disagree on the institutions carrying it. One side's trusted platform may be another side's strategic liability. The implication is that cross-border cooperation cannot be stabilised by technical alignment alone. It also needs arrangements for interpreting assurance, handling disputes, and limiting single points of strategic dependence.

This is where the idea of trusted interoperability becomes more useful than the softer and vaguer language of shared digital values. Trusted interoperability asks a more disciplined set of questions. Can the systems connect securely? Can the parties verify the relevant claims about identity, integrity, and update behaviour? Are dependencies diversified enough that one side cannot quietly dominate the other's room for manoeuvre? Are assurance processes intelligible and credible across political boundaries? Are failure and migration procedures clear enough that cooperation can survive when assumptions change? These questions matter because they shift attention from declarations of alignment to the practical mechanics of dependable coordination. The bridge must hold not only under fair weather, but under strain.

Still, a credible limitation deserves emphasis. No cross-border cryptographic arrangement can eliminate all asymmetry, all suspicion, or all strategic dependence. A world of perfectly reciprocal technical trust does not exist outside the daydreams of people who have spent too long in conference centres with excellent coffee and terrible incentives. Stronger states, larger firms, richer markets, and more influential standards communities will continue to shape the environment disproportionately. Smaller participants will continue to weigh the cost of exclusion against the cost of dependence. It would be childish to pretend that a well-designed protocol can neutralise geopolitical reality.

Yet that limitation strengthens the main argument rather than weakening it. Because power asymmetries are real, trusted interoperability must be judged by how well it manages them rather than by whether it abolishes them. A serious framework asks at least four things. Does the shared system permit meaningful scrutiny by all parties who depend on it? Can critical components be updated or replaced without unilateral coercive leverage by one side? Are assurance and certification practices intelligible across jurisdictions, or are they merely local badges expecting global deference? And are the operational benefits of interoperability large enough that the remaining dependence is understood, bounded, and politically tolerable? The implication is that trust across borders is not a feeling. It is a negotiated settlement between convenience, scrutiny, and exposure.

This also explains why diversity and portability matter so much. A cross-border arrangement becomes less brittle when no single vendor, certificate regime, hardware lineage, or update channel silently controls the whole architecture. The abstraction of resilience becomes visible in institutional design choices: support for multiple suppliers, clear migration paths, mutual review mechanisms, technical standards that do not lock participants into one political centre of gravity, and procurement rules that preserve some bargaining power even inside a shared system. The implication is not that diversity is always efficient. It often is not. It is that trusted interoperability requires enough optionality that cooperation does not collapse into dependency disguised as harmony.

The social dimension is just as important. Trust across borders is sustained not only by protocols, but by repeated demonstrations of restraint, competence, and procedural fairness. When one party responds to a vulnerability openly, migrates standards responsibly, shares technical reasoning honestly, or refrains from exploiting its privileged infrastructural position in moments of stress, it strengthens the practical meaning of trust. When it hides critical weaknesses, politicises standards opportunistically, or uses supply dependence as leverage, it weakens that meaning even if the protocol stack itself remains intact. The implication is that cross-border cryptographic trust is always partly reputational. Technical systems remember politics because the humans governing them do.

This is why international cooperation in cryptography often looks less like a clean consensus and more like disciplined coexistence. Parties do not need identical beliefs about everything to build working trust. They need enough overlap in standards, assurance, migration discipline, and mutual expectations that cooperation remains safer than fragmentation. That threshold can be high in intelligence or defence settings and lower in commercial exchange, but the underlying logic is the same. The bridge is crossed not because nobody worries about who poured the concrete, but because the structure has been tested enough, inspected enough, and diversified enough that crossing remains a rational act rather than a sentimental one.

The bridge returns here because it expresses the whole challenge in one ordinary image. A bridge can connect economies, alliances, and institutions that would otherwise remain isolated. It can also become a chokepoint, a dependency, or a strategic liability if one side controls the repairs, the tolls, the inspection regime, and the emergency closures. Shared cryptographic standards do much the same. They enable movement. They also allocate leverage. Serious trust begins when both facts are admitted at once.

The unresolved question, then, is not whether international cooperation requires shared cryptographic standards. It plainly does. The harder question is whether those sharing the standards can also share enough scrutiny, migration capacity, and institutional confidence that interoperability becomes something more durable than convenience - without asking the weaker party to accept a bridge it can use every day but never quite trust not to become someone else's instrument when the weather turns.

# Chapter 14

# Institutional Readiness and Future Scenarios

What does it mean to be ready for a cryptographic future that cannot be dated cleanly, cannot be measured with false confidence, and may arrive through several different routes at once? The question frustrates people who like dashboards with neat colours, thresholds that look scientific, and timetables that behave themselves. Yet the frustration is useful. It forces a choice between theatre and judgment. An institution can pretend that readiness is a score waiting to be discovered, or it can accept that readiness is a practical condition made visible through habits, capabilities, and the quality of response under strain.

That distinction matters because uncertainty has a habit of inviting decorative precision. Boards ask for maturity ratings. Ministries want comparative rankings. Vendors offer maps with suspiciously tidy milestones. Consultants, bless their laminated souls, love a matrix. The trouble is not that measurement is wrong. The trouble is that bad measurement can anaesthetise thought. A number that looks crisp can conceal a weak inventory, a brittle upgrade path, or a crisis procedure that has never met a real crisis. Institutions often become most vulnerable when they confuse being legible to themselves with being ready for the world.

The drill on the shelf counts.

That modest image captures the chapter's mood. Readiness is less like a certificate on the wall and more like a tool kept in working order: unglamorous, testable, occasionally neglected, and suddenly decisive when the house starts making unpleasant noises. A tool can be inspected sensibly. It can also be admired uselessly. The same is true of institutional preparedness. What matters is not whether an organisation can recite its intentions fluently, but whether it can identify its cryptographic dependencies, change key material without chaos, move suppliers when needed, communicate under pressure, and keep decisions coherent when technical ambiguity collides with political urgency. The difference between those two states is the difference between confidence and costume.

This is why the final movement of the book cannot rest on predictions. Predictions tempt us to ask the wrong question. They encourage fascination with the date of breakthrough, the moment of crisis, the exact year in which some decisive transition supposedly becomes unavoidable. That curiosity is understandable. It is also strategically secondary. Institutions are rarely defeated by failing to guess the future with adequate theatrical flourish. They are defeated by having built systems, incentives, and routines too rigid to absorb whichever future actually turns up. Readiness, properly understood, is therefore the capacity to remain governable when certainty refuses to cooperate.

The stakes are high because cryptographic change is never merely technical housekeeping. It reaches into alliances, procurement, archives, critical infrastructure, vendor power, public trust, and the awkward moral weather of institutions that must decide before evidence fully settles. An organisation that measures readiness badly may underprepare for a sharp implementation shock, overspend on a fashionable but poorly integrated response, or discover too late that its strongest rhetoric was hiding weak internal machinery. A state that mistakes one scenario for the scenario may build policy around a timetable and then meet a pathway. A company that treats future-proofing as branding may find that customers and regulators become much less enchanted once the first real test arrives.

That is why false precision is not merely a technical error; it is a governance hazard. It flatters leaders with apparent control while draining attention from the more useful questions. Do we know where cryptography actually lives in the estate? Can we change it without tearing the organisation sideways? Are the roles around keys, vendors, and incident decisions clear? Can our systems survive a fast-moving standards shift, a sudden implementation flaw, or a long period of uneven change in which old and new assumptions must coexist? These questions are harder to compress into a score, which is one reason they are worth asking. They direct effort towards what can be improved rather than towards what can be displayed.

The route ahead follows that discipline. It begins by treating readiness as a set of capabilities that can be examined without pretending they sum neatly into a prophecy: the completeness of inventories, the quality of upgrade pathways, the seriousness of key governance, and the steadiness of crisis procedures. It then widens into several plausible futures, not to crown one as destiny, but to stress different parts of the institutional body and reveal where flexibility is real or merely advertised. The order matters. Capability comes before scenario because without a clear view of present condition, every future exercise becomes a parlour game for anxious professionals with very earnest slide decks.

A weather map is more useful than a prophecy. It shows pressure systems, likely fronts, and dangerous combinations without claiming to know the exact shape of every cloud a week from Thursday. The same should be true here. Uneven technical progress, abrupt implementation failures, long migrations through hybrid arrangements, alliance friction, vendor bottlenecks, and confidence shocks can all produce futures that differ in detail while testing similar institutional muscles. Some futures reward inventory discipline. Some punish weak supplier leverage. Some expose poor communication. Some reveal that the organisation's real weakness was not its chosen algorithm at all, but the absence of a calm procedure for changing one.

That is the final lesson the book needs to make plain. The aim is not to leave the reader clutching a timetable like a railway passenger in a country where the trains are philosophical and the stations occasionally move. The aim is to leave behind a better standard of judgment. Institutions should be asked whether they can adapt, not whether they can perform certainty. They should be measured by the quality of their questions, the honesty of their maps, the discipline of their update paths, and the seriousness with which they prepare for futures that will not flatter their plans simply because those plans were expensive to print.

The difficult question, then, is not which future will arrive first. The harder question is whether the institution facing that future can tell the difference between readiness that looks tidy on paper and readiness that can survive ambiguity, absorb surprise, and keep trust coherent when the next cryptographic decade refuses to unfold in the politely linear manner so many official road maps still pretend to expect.

## Measuring readiness without false precision

In August 2024, when the National Institute of Standards and Technology published its first final post-quantum cryptography standards in Gaithersburg, Maryland, many organisations responded with a familiar managerial reflex. They wanted a score. How ready are we: red, amber, or green? What percentage complete are we? Which maturity level have we achieved? These questions sound sensible because numbers feel like discipline. Yet in cryptographic transition they often do the opposite. They compress uncertainty into shapes that flatter decision-makers while hiding the exact places where an institution is most brittle.

The danger begins there. A readiness score can look rigorous while disguising ignorance about where cryptography actually lives, who controls the keys, which vendors can change course, or what happens when a system must migrate under pressure rather than during a polite planning cycle. The problem is not measurement itself. Institutions need ways to judge condition, allocate effort, and expose weakness. The problem is false precision: the habit of expressing uncertain organisational capacity as though it were a settled quantity, complete with decimals, colours, and the bureaucratic fragrance of command over reality.

The map beats the number.

That is the guiding principle here because readiness is not a hidden figure waiting to be extracted from the estate by a sufficiently determined spreadsheet. It is a set of capabilities, unevenly distributed across systems, teams, suppliers, and procedures. Show the scene and the point sharpens. A board asks whether the organisation is prepared for cryptographic change. The named concept is capability-based assessment. Explain it, and the implication follows. The honest answer is not a single score. It is a structured view of whether the institution can locate its dependencies, alter them safely, govern the keys that matter, and act coherently when assumptions fail faster than expected. The implication is not modesty for its own sake. It is that useful clarity comes from asking better questions, not from pretending that one answer can summarise the whole field.

Inventory completeness is the first of those questions because an institution cannot be ready to change what it cannot identify. This sounds obvious, which is one reason people underinvest in it. Inventories seem clerical, and clerical work rarely gets invited to strategy dinners. Yet cryptographic exposure is often scattered across archives, mobile devices, cloud services, vendor appliances, identity systems, signing processes, industrial controls, backup tooling, and embedded third-party products that no one initially remembers to count. The named concept here is visibility depth. Explain it, and the strategic implication becomes plain. An inventory is not merely a list of assets. It is evidence that the organisation knows where encryption, signatures, certificates, trust stores, and key dependencies actually reside. Without that knowledge, any readiness claim is a performance staged on a darkened set.

A useful example lies in the Heartbleed crisis of April 2014. Many organisations did not fail because they were incapable of understanding the underlying vulnerability. They failed because they did not know quickly enough where vulnerable OpenSSL components were present across their estates, especially inside appliances, inherited products, and software stacks whose internals had long been hidden behind vendor branding. The named concept is dependency blindness. Explain it, and one sees why inventory completeness matters more than strategic rhetoric. An institution that cannot identify where a critical cryptographic dependency sits is not unready in some abstract sense. It is concretely unable to prioritise, patch, rotate, communicate, or reassure with authority. The implication is that a good readiness assessment asks not "Do we use modern cryptography?" but "Can we name where, how, and through whom?"

Upgrade pathways come next because visibility without movement is merely better-documented helplessness. Knowing where cryptography sits is useful. Knowing whether it can be changed without breaking the business is what turns inventory into readiness. Show the scene and the distinction matters at once. Two systems rely on ageing cryptographic assumptions. One has modular interfaces, supported vendors, tested rollback, and current client compatibility. The other depends on firmware in a field device, a locked appliance, or an outsourced service with vague future plans. The named concept is migratability. Explain it, and the implication follows. The organisation's real condition is not captured by the fact that both systems are exposed to the same broad transition pressure. It is captured by how differently they can move. A capability-based readiness assessment therefore asks where change is possible, where it is costly, where it is blocked, and who controls the route out.

A second named, checkable example lies in the trust-path and client compatibility problems exposed by the expiry of the DST Root CA X3 certificate in 2021. The strategic lesson of that episode was not merely that cryptographic change can break old clients. It was that the difficulty of change lies in the estate, not only in the standard. Some organisations and platforms could adapt with relative order. Others discovered that older endpoints, neglected dependencies, and weak transition planning made even a well-signalled trust shift operationally messy. The named concept is endpoint drag. Explain it, and the point becomes harder to ignore. Readiness is inseparable from the ability to move dependent systems together, or at least to understand where they will not move together and why.

Key governance is the next capability because most cryptographic promises are defeated less by flawed algorithms than by weak control over the secrets that make them operational. An institution may proudly announce strong encryption while still allowing key generation, storage, recovery, rotation, and emergency access to drift across teams with incompatible assumptions and unclear authority. The abstraction of trust becomes visible in very ordinary decisions: who can issue certificates, who can authorise key recovery, who can revoke credentials quickly, where backups of sensitive keys exist, how cryptographic roles are separated, and whether the organisation can prove these arrangements under pressure rather than merely describing them in policy documents. The implication is severe. If an organisation cannot govern its keys clearly, its readiness is weaker than any algorithm choice might suggest.

This is where many scorecards become almost comically misleading. They reward policy existence rather than operational credibility. A line item asks whether a key management process exists, and the answer is yes, because somewhere a document exists in a folder that no one has opened since a committee discovered adjectives. A capability-based approach asks sterner questions. Has the process been exercised? Does the organisation know which keys are most sensitive, which are most exposed, and which can be rotated without collateral confusion? Are responsibility lines clear enough that a crisis would produce decisions rather than a polite stampede of emails? The named concept is exercised control. Explain it, and the difference between ceremonial governance and real readiness becomes impossible to miss.

Crisis procedures form the final major capability because readiness is tested most brutally under ambiguity, not during calm reviews. An institution may manage everyday cryptographic operations tolerably and still collapse into drift when a sudden implementation flaw, compromised vendor pathway, or urgent migration requirement appears. Show the scene and the measure becomes concrete. A critical dependency is found vulnerable, or a major standard shift now affects a politically exposed service. The named concept is decision coherence. Explain it, and the strategic implication follows. Readiness depends on whether the organisation knows who decides, what gets isolated, how communications are staged, which systems receive immediate priority, what authorities can force vendor action, and how public claims are kept aligned with technical fact. A score rarely tells you this. A rehearsal, a tabletop exercise, or a documented incident history often does.

Still, a fair limitation must be admitted. Capability-based assessment is less tidy than the dashboard culture many organisations prefer. It produces uneven pictures, incomplete confidence, and awkward answers such as "we know this area well, that one poorly, and two critical supplier dependencies remain only partly understood." Such answers can frustrate leaders who want comparability, targets, and progress percentages neat enough to fit inside quarterly reporting. The messiness is real. It may even feel administratively irritating, which is usually a sign that the assessment has begun touching the truth.

That limitation strengthens the argument rather than weakening it. Because certainty is unavailable, the goal of measurement should be actionable clarity rather than prediction. A good assessment does not tell an institution exactly when trouble will arrive or which future scenario will dominate. It tells the institution where it can move, where it cannot, where trust is concentrated, where suppliers govern timing, where keys are well managed, where crisis authority is vague, and where blind spots remain unacceptable. The named concept here is decision utility. Explain it, and the purpose of readiness measurement becomes much clearer. The measure is good not when it looks scientific, but when it helps the organisation choose what to fix next without lying to itself about how much is already under control.

This is also why better questions matter more than prettier metrics. Instead of asking, "Are we post-quantum ready?" ask, "Which systems cannot change cryptography without service redesign?" Instead of, "Do we have key management?" ask, "Which keys would hurt most if mishandled, and who can actually change their state?" Instead of, "Are crisis procedures in place?" ask, "When a cryptographic dependency fails, who can compel operational action across business, vendor, legal, and technical boundaries within the same day?" These questions are not more sophisticated because they sound harsher. They are more useful because they tie abstraction to visible behaviour.

The map returns here because it remains the right corrective to false precision. A map can be incomplete and still useful if it shows where the bridges are weak, where the roads end, and where the terrain is unknown. A fake number can be complete and still useless if it persuades everyone that the countryside has been mastered when no one has walked half of it. Institutions measuring cryptographic readiness should prefer the embarrassment of a candid map to the comfort of a fraudulent score.

The hard question, then, is not how to assign a readiness percentage that will soothe executives, auditors, or ministers for one more reporting cycle. The harder question is whether the organisation can produce an assessment honest enough to show where cryptography is understood, where it is trapped, where its keys are truly governed, and where its crisis response would either hold or unravel - because only that kind of measurement is precise in the way that matters.

## Scenarios for the next cryptographic decade

In August 2024, when the National Institute of Standards and Technology published its first final post-quantum cryptography standards in Gaithersburg, Maryland, many people asked a question that sounds practical and usually misleads: when will the real disruption arrive? The hope behind that question is understandable. A date feels manageable. A timetable can be budgeted, delegated, and rehearsed in a style that makes executives, ministries, and procurement offices feel briefly civilised. But cryptographic change is not a train schedule. It is more like weather moving through infrastructure, alliances, and inherited mistakes at different speeds. Some places flood quickly. Others crack slowly. Some look calm until the floor gives way.

That is why the next cryptographic decade should be approached through scenarios rather than prophecies. A scenario is not a prediction in costume. It is a disciplined way of asking what different futures would pressure, expose, and reward inside an institution. It shifts attention from guessing the exact year of decisive change to understanding which forms of readiness matter under more than one future. The barometer matters first.

A scenario becomes useful when it does four things at once. It names a plausible pattern of change, identifies the institutional weak points that pattern would strike, distinguishes between technical shock and organisational shock, and forces a choice about what would have to be true for the institution to act well under those conditions. The named concept is stress patterning. Explain it, and the strategic implication follows. Institutions are rarely defeated by the future they explicitly imagined in crisp detail. They are defeated by the pressure they failed to rehearse because it did not fit their preferred story about how change ought to unfold. The implication is that scenario work is not a parlour game for strategic aesthetes. It is a way of revealing which capabilities remain useful when the future refuses to behave politely.

One plausible future is uneven quantum progress. In this scenario, advances occur, but not in the clean, cinematic form that excites the public imagination. Capability emerges irregularly across research teams, states, and firms. Some claims are overstated, some are real but narrow, and some matter less as direct cryptanalytic breakthroughs than as signals that force earlier defensive decisions. The named concept here is asymmetrical timing. Explain it, and the institutional consequence becomes clear. The pressure falls not only on algorithms, but on judgment. Leaders must decide how much to invest before certainty arrives. Alliances must decide how much of their mutual trust can rest on common pacing. Vendors may exploit uncertainty by promising everything and scheduling nothing. The implication is that the most stressed capability in this future is not technical brilliance alone. It is threshold discipline: the ability to act on partial evidence without either panicking into waste or freezing into comfort.

A second plausible future is the sudden implementation crisis. This is often more likely, and usually more institutionally revealing, than the dramatic breakthrough story people cannot stop narrating to one another. In this scenario, the disruptive event is not that quantum capability instantly overturns the cryptographic order. It is that a new standard, hybrid transition, firmware pathway, certificate structure, or widely used implementation behaves badly at scale. An update collides with old clients. A trusted library exposes an unexpected weakness. A migration disables verification in edge cases. A vendor path that was supposed to carry the transition becomes the site of confusion or compromise. The named concept is transition rupture. Explain it, and one sees why institutions so often misread their own condition. They imagine themselves preparing for a future adversary and instead discover that their present architecture cannot absorb a change they publicly claimed to welcome. The implication is stark. This scenario stresses test environments, vendor leverage, operational communication, rollback discipline, and the honesty of inventories far more than it stresses abstract algorithm choice.

A useful historical guide to this kind of scenario lies in events like Heartbleed in 2014 or the trust-path disruptions surrounding certificate changes in 2021. Neither event was a post-quantum crisis, yet both exposed the same underlying truth: cryptographic order often breaks at the level of dependency, deployment, and estate awareness rather than at the level of elegant mathematics. Those episodes matter because they teach institutions what a real shock often looks like. It looks like a rushed inventory. It looks like uncertain client impact. It looks like engineers discovering that "we support the new thing" and "we can move the whole estate safely" are not remotely the same sentence. The implication is that scenario planning for the next decade should not fixate only on revolutionary science. It should take ordinary implementation chaos with unnerving seriousness.

A third plausible future is the gradual standard transition. This is the future that sounds boring and therefore deserves special respect, because boring futures often do the most cumulative institutional damage. In this scenario, post-quantum migration proceeds through long coexistence: hybrid modes, staggered vendor support, mixed client populations, procurement clauses that slowly bite, policy frameworks that mature unevenly, and systems that remain half in one era and half in another for longer than anyone publicly wanted to admit. The named concept is chronic coexistence. Explain it, and the stress pattern changes again. This future pressures patience, budgeting discipline, contract management, cross-border interoperability, and the institutional ability to retire old assumptions rather than preserving them forever out of nostalgia, fear, or operational fatigue. The implication is that some organisations fail not because they missed a breakthrough, but because they slowly turned transition into an inherited condition with no clean end.

This gradual scenario is especially demanding for alliances and multinational dependencies. Shared standards enable cooperation, but uneven adoption creates friction. One partner moves early and expects others to keep pace. Another relies on hardware or suppliers that cannot adapt quickly. A third accepts the new standard formally while continuing to run critical legacy pathways in practice. The visible signs of strain are ordinary enough: delayed procurement, ambiguous support statements, partial interoperability, and quiet exceptions for politically sensitive systems. Yet the strategic consequence can be large. Trust frays not because anyone has defected dramatically, but because the rhythm of adaptation has ceased to be shared. The barometer shifts again. In this future, the institution that matters most is often not the fastest mover, but the actor best able to keep coordination credible while the estate remains uneven.

Still, a limitation belongs here. Scenarios can become their own species of vanity. Institutions sometimes fall in love with them because they provide a respectable way to imagine the future without committing to the hard work of changing the present. A glossy scenario exercise can flatter everyone in the room while leaving the weak inventory untouched, the vendor clauses vague, the key governance untested, and the crisis procedures decorative. The named concept is speculative substitution. Explain it, and the caution becomes necessary. Scenario planning is not preparation. It is useful only when it exposes decisions that must be made under more than one plausible future. Otherwise it becomes an expensive séance for organisations trying to contact the ghost of strategic seriousness.

That limitation strengthens the real argument rather than weakening it. Because scenarios can drift into theatre, they should be judged by the questions they force. Under uneven progress, what evidence threshold would justify accelerated migration for long-lived secrets? Under sudden implementation crisis, which systems can be isolated or rolled back without operational collapse? Under gradual transition, which dependencies are most likely to become permanent legacy under the pretence of temporary accommodation? These questions matter because they tie future imagination back to present capability. A scenario earns its keep when it changes procurement language, testing practice, supplier oversight, or crisis authority before the future arrives.

This is the real toolkit the reader should leave with. Not a timetable. Not a favourite prophecy. A set of habits for thinking. Ask which future stresses inventories most harshly. Ask which one exposes weak key governance. Ask where vendor dependence becomes strategic dependence. Ask whether the institution can communicate calmly under technical ambiguity. Ask what forms of trust survive if standards shift unevenly across partners. Ask which capabilities remain useful in all three futures: visibility, migratability, disciplined key control, rehearsed crisis response, and honest communication. Those are not exciting answers in the way headlines prefer. They are durable answers, which is a better thing to be.

The barometer returns here because it expresses the chapter's final discipline. A barometer does not tell you exactly when the first drop will strike a particular window. It tells you how pressure is moving and what sort of weather the house should be ready to endure. The next cryptographic decade deserves the same kind of reading. Institutions should stop asking for a calendar that will save them from judgment and start asking whether their roofs, drains, maps, and repair crews are good enough for several kinds of storm at once.

The unresolved question, then, is not whether one of these futures will prove correct in every detail. None will. The harder question is whether the institution facing the next decade can use them to discover what it would rather not know about itself now: which assumptions are brittle, which alliances depend on shared pace more than shared principle, and whether its confidence rests on a forecast or on a capacity to adapt when the weather breaks in the least convenient direction.

# About the Author

Kenan Durveil writes about the intersection of cryptography, institutional behaviour, and the geopolitics of technology. His work is guided by a simple conviction: security failures are rarely caused by a single flawed equation, and more often by the way organisations distribute responsibility, defer uncomfortable decisions, and inherit systems they no longer fully understand. He is interested in the places where abstract guarantees meet real-world constraints such as procurement cycles, legacy infrastructure, and the need to explain technical risk to non-technical leaders without resorting to either panic or false reassurance.

Durveil approaches encryption as a civic and strategic subject as much as an engineering one. He is attentive to how standards, certification, and platform concentration shape who gets to define "secure enough", and to how intelligence incentives can quietly influence public choices about trust. A recurring thread in his perspective is the long European memory of contested communications, from wartime codebreaking to the bureaucratic infrastructures that followed, and how those histories continue to inform today's debates about secrecy, legitimacy, and verification.

Quantum Deterrence reflects his commitment to clarity: making advanced ideas readable without flattening them, and treating readers as capable of grappling with uncertainty. The result is a rigorously framed, publicly intelligible account of why stronger computation changes not only what can be decrypted, but what institutions must become in order to remain trustworthy.